Sales Taxation

Sales Taxation

State and Local Structure
and Administration

John F. Due and John L. Mikesell

The Johns Hopkins University Press
Baltimore and London

*To Dixwell L. Pierce, secretary of the California
State Board of Equalization, 1926-63, who
contributed more than any other person to the
development of effective state sales tax
administration.*

The Johns Hopkins University Press, Baltimore, Maryland 21218
The Johns Hopkins Press Ltd., London

Library of Congress Cataloging in Publication Data

Due, John Fitzgerald.
  Sales taxation.

  Bibliography: p. 335
  Includes index.
  1. Sales tax—United States—States. 2. Tax
administration and procedure—United States—States.
I. Mikesell, John L. II. Title.
HJ5715.U6D77 1982   350.72′47   82-13968
ISBN 0-8018-2842-2

Contents

Tables

Figures

Preface and Acknowledgments

This volume is designed to provide a detailed survey and analysis of the structure and operation of the state and local sales taxes. Basically it is an updated revision of *State Sales Tax Administration,* published in 1963, and *State and Local Sales Taxation,* 1971. Both of these volumes were published by Public Administration Service, which has now discontinued publishing operations. The book is not intended to provide an economic analysis of sales taxation, the appropriate role of sales taxes in the state-local structures, shifting and distributional aspects of sales taxes, or revenue elasticity. These have been dealt with in depth in other sources.

The study is based primarily on interviews that we conducted with state revenue department officials in 1979 and 1980. All states were visited except one, Wyoming, from which the information was obtained by letter and telephone. The interviews and the writing were shared equally between the coauthors. The attempt has been made to bring the material up to date so far as possible. Inevitably some of the material will become dated rather quickly, but the general patterns do not change greatly over the years. Since virtually all of the information has been obtained from interviews, acts, regulations, and similar material, the sources of particular statements are typically not identified.

We are greatly indebted to the revenue officials of the various states who gave their time for the interviews and read and provided corrections for several of the chapters. We are also indebted to Public Administration Service for releasing its rights to the study.

Appreciation is expressed to Mrs. Suzanne Leever, of the University of Illinois and Mrs. Karen Evans, of Indiana University, who typed substantial portions of the material as well as provided other assistance; to the College of Commerce of the University of Illinois, for travel funds; and to the Indiana Department of Revenue, for use of its research library.

Preface and Acknowledgments

1. Development, Forms, and Yields of State Sales Taxes

The retail sales tax is the most significant source of state tax revenue today.[1] It yields more revenue than any other tax in thirty-one of the fifty states and in twenty-three of the thirty-seven states that impose both a general sales tax and a broad individual income tax. As of July 1, 1982, the tax was in operation in forty-five states. In the 1981 fiscal year, it yielded a total of $46.1 billion, which constituted 19% of general revenue in the states using the tax and 32% of total state tax revenue. For comparison, in fiscal year 1970, it yielded $14.1 billion, or 19%, of the general revenue in the states using the tax and 30% of total state tax revenue.[2] The trend toward higher rates continues, but coverage has narrowed with exemptions for both producers and consumers. As explained in chapter 10, municipal sales taxes have spread rapidly in states permitting them.

DEVELOPMENT OF SALES TAXES

The development of retail sales taxation in the United States was a grass-roots phenomenon. It was influenced very little by experience with sales taxation in other countries and represented the first significant use of sales taxes at the retail level in the world. Forerunners were in the form of business occupation taxes based on sales, purchases, or receipts in several states, such as Pennsylvania, Virginia, and Delaware, during the nineteenth century. These taxes, in turn, had replaced flat sum occupation taxes and were designed as a more effective method than the property tax to reach merchants' stocks. Rates were fractional and yield was low.

[1]This study is directed to a review of the structure and operation of the retail sales taxes. The development of the taxes will be noted only briefly since it has been covered in a number of sources. Questions of shifting and incidence, the distribution of burden by income class, and the role of the tax in the tax structure are not covered, since they have been reviewed extensively in general studies, journal articles, and reports of state tax study commissions. Also excluded from coverage are state excises and business occupation taxes on gross receipts. Nonretail elements in predominantly retail sales tax structures are noted briefly. Also, except for major cases involving the use tax, relatively little attention is given to the legal aspects of the tax, discussed extensively in other sources.

[2]U.S., Bureau of the Census, *Quarterly Summary of State and Local Tax Revenue,* Oct. 1981; U.S., Bureau of the Census, *State Government Tax Collections in 1970;* U.S., Bureau of the Census, *State Government Finances in 1970.*

In 1921, West Virginia levied a tax at higher rates on a wide variety of business and obtained considerable revenue. This tax was, and still is, however, regarded essentially as a business occupation levy, not a tax to be shifted directly to the purchaser.[3] It applied to all levels of business and differed fundamentally from the present retail sales tax. A similar tax was imposed by Mississippi in 1930. The difficulty with these taxes was that, because of their multiple-stage feature, they were tolerable only as long as the rates were very low, and thus the revenue yield was not substantial.

Prewar Levies

Table 1.1 summarizes the introduction of the state sales taxes. In 1932, Mississippi converted its levy to a retail sales tax by eliminating most of the multiple applications and raising the rate from a fractional figure to 2%.[4] With this change, the modern state retail sales tax came into being. Through concentration on the retail level, the states could raise the rate sufficiently to make the tax a major source of revenue. The tax proved more productive than anticipated, and its success was not lost on other states. Later in 1932, Pennsylvania introduced the tax (effective in 1933) but allowed it to expire the following year. During the next six years, 1933–38 inclusive, twenty-six states (and Hawaii) imposed the tax, although five allowed it to expire after one or two years (Idaho, Kentucky, Maryland, New Jersey, and New York).

The reasons for the introduction of these taxes varied somewhat among the states but fell into a major pattern. The depression reduced revenues from other taxes at the same time that relief needs were increasing, and participation in many federal programs of the period necessitated additional state expenditures. Concurrently, the serious financial difficulties of the local governments, greatly aggravated by the depression, resulted in a tendency both to increase state grants to the local governments, particularly for education, and to reduce state reliance on the property tax. Most states had few major sources that could yield additional revenues. Their income taxes, particularly, reflected the decline in personal incomes. The sales tax, with its low rate, large yield, and relatively painless collection, was especially attractive.

Postwar Taxes

After the Louisiana tax became effective in 1938, no other state levied the tax until 1947, although Louisiana reinstated in 1942 the tax repealed in 1940. The prosperity and the shortages of manpower and material resulting from the war

---

[3]Sales taxes are distinguished from business occupation taxes by legislative intent. Sales taxes are expected, implicitly or explicitly, to be passed forward to the purchaser. Business occupation taxes are regarded as levies on the business, per se, without this expectation. The difference is in legislative intent, not in legal liability or actual shifting.

[4]Summarized in the pamphlet by V.B. Wheeless, *The Sales and Use Tax*.

TABLE 1.1 Year of Introduction of State Retail Sales Taxes to July 1982

		Taxes That Were Allowed to Expire		
Taxes That Became Permanent			Year of	Year of
Year[a]	State	State	Expiration	Reinstatement
Prewar				
1932	Mississippi	Pennsylvania	1933	1953
1933	Arizona, California, Illinois, Michigan, North Carolina, Oklahoma, South Dakota, Utah, West Virginia	New York	1934	1965
1934	Iowa, Missouri, New Mexico	Kentucky	1936	1960
		New Jersey	1935	1966
1935	Arkansas, Colorado, Hawaii,[b] North Dakota, Ohio, Washington, Wyoming	Idaho	1936	1965
		Maryland	1936	1947
1937	Alabama, Kansas			
1938	Louisiana[c] (repealed 1940; reinstated 1942)			
Postwar				
1947	Connecticut, Maryland, Rhode Island, Tennessee			
1949	Florida (and District of Columbia)			
1951	Georgia, Maine, South Carolina			
1953	Pennsylvania			
1955	Nevada		1955	1956
1956	Pennsylvania			
1960	Kentucky			
1961	Texas			
1962	Wisconsin			
1963	Indiana			
1965	Idaho, New York			
1966	Massachusetts, New Jersey, Virginia			
1967	Minnesota, Nebraska			
1969	Vermont			

[a] Years are those in which taxes became effective.
[b] Hawaii did not become a state until 1959.
[c] Imposed first on selected luxury goods in 1936.

relieved the financial pressure on the states and gave rise to budget surpluses. None of the existing sales taxes was repealed.

A slow trend toward renewed adoption of sales taxes began with the introduction of the tax in Tennessee in 1947. By 1963, ten additional states had imposed the tax and three had reimposed it, bringing the total to thirty-seven. In 1965 and 1966, New York, New Jersey, and Idaho reimposed the tax after a long lapse, and by 1969 five additional states had introduced it, bringing the total to forty-five. No tax that has remained in force for at least two years has ever been eliminated (except for the temporary repeal of the Louisiana tax in

1940), and none of the postwar taxes, passed since 1947, has been repealed. The Pennsylvania 1953 tax expired in 1955 but was reinstated in 1956.

Considerations responsible for the postwar taxes differ somewhat from those that led to their introduction during the 1930s. The primary reason was a tendency for revenues from other state taxes to lag behind the increased demands for state expenditures, particularly for education. Apart from the levies used to finance highways, the states have relatively limited potential tax sources that they are willing to use other than the sales tax. States will not use high income taxes, partly because of fear of driving people and business outside the state and partly because of popular resistance in the face of high federal income taxes. The property tax has become almost entirely a local government revenue source. Apart from the sales tax, the only other alternatives are special business levies of various types, taxes on liquor and cigarettes, severance taxes in a few states, and some minor levies. During the fifties and sixties, the states having sales taxes were faring relatively well. Those without were having increasing difficulty, and inevitably turned to the tax. The seventies was a period of strong state fiscal conditions, federal fiscal assistance to the states, and popular opposition to tax increases. Some sales tax states have added individual income taxes, but there have been no new sales taxes since 1969 (Vermont). With decline in business activity and reduced federal spending in the early eighties, however, the financial position of many states has weakened, and pressure for sales tax revenue is increasing again.

States Not Using Sales Tax

Only five states do not use the sales tax as of 1982, and in one of these, Alaska, extensive use is made at the local level, with rates comparable to state sales taxes in other states.

Four of these states have populations of less than a million, and the five have approximately 2.4% of the total population of the country. Thus, 97.6% of the population and, roughly, of sales are covered by the tax. Oregon has considered the tax many times. Its legislature has enacted the tax on several occasions, but each time the voters have rejected it at the polls. Without the referendum requirement, Oregon would have had the tax long ago. The state has one of the highest income taxes in the country and relatively heavy property taxes (about twice as heavy as those of neighboring Washington). Sooner or later the voters must face up to the alternatives of serious curtailment of service or sharp increases in other taxes, but so far the longstanding bias against the tax has remained strong. Montana has likewise considered the tax, most recently in 1981, and at times has appeared close to enactment. New Hampshire voters have a strong bias against taxes of any kind. The state has one of the lowest per capita state expenditures in the country. Alaska, as noted, uses the sales tax at the local level and now has large oil revenues. Delaware recently experienced some fiscal difficulty, but there was no enthusiasm for a sales tax. Within a few

TABLE 1.2   States Not Using Sales Taxes, January 1982

State	Population (1980)
Alaska	400,481
Delaware	595,225
Montana	786,690
New Hampshire	920,610
Oregon	2,632,663
Total	5,335,669

years, Oregon and Montana at least may add the tax. Adoption by the other three is more difficult to predict.

Conflicting Pressures

Sales taxes were usually introduced consequent to recommendations of the state administration based on the need for additional revenue. Support typically came from business groups (except retail associations), which feared the alternative of income taxation; from farm and other property-owning groups, which sought property tax reduction; and from educational associations, which sought additional funds for schools. Two groups typically led the opposition: retailers, who feared the costs of compliance and the resistance of customers, with possible loss of business; and labor unions, which frequently opposed the taxes on the grounds of regressiveness. In some states, particularly during the depression, union opposition was lessened by recognition of the urgent need for additional revenue to meet payrolls and provide needed services.

FORMS OF SALES TAX

Following the publication of the Haig-Shoup study in 1934,[5] the tendency was to classify state sales taxes into four groups: retail sales, general sales, gross receipts, and gross income. This classification was of little use and was actually misleading, because it concentrated attention on rather minor differences among the levies and diverted attention away from their basic similarity. The taxes can be classified, however, by whether they are confined entirely to retail sales or include some nonretail elements.

Only one of the sales taxes, that of Hawaii, departs from the basic single-stage retail nature of the tax. The Hawaii levy applies to all sales at all levels of production and distribution (although most sales for resale are taxed at a much lower rate) and thus has some features of a multiple-stage, or cascade type, tax recently abandoned in Western Europe and Latin America.

[5]R.M. Haig and C. Shoup, *The Sales Tax in the American States.*

Two other taxes have limited nonretail elements but without the cascade features. Mississippi applies a low rate (0.5%) of tax on the last wholesale transaction—the purchase by the retailer—in addition to the retail tax. Louisiana (and Mississippi on a few commodities) applies the basic retail rate to the last wholesale transaction and then gives the retail establishment credit for tax paid on its purchases against tax due on its sales, thereby introducing a limited value-added tax feature into the system. Arizona includes within its sales tax a severance tax on mining and logging and a low rate tax on a few wholesale transactions.

Otherwise, the taxes differ basically only in the extent of coverage of services, with difference in degree rather than kind. At one extreme, Nevada and California tax no services. At the other, New Mexico taxes all services, including professional, with few exceptions. Most states include a few services, and several states added a number of services in the 1960s. The taxes also differ in their coverage of food and various producers goods, as discussed in subsequent chapters. Essentially, however, with the exceptions already noted, they are all retail sales taxes with minor modifications, except in Hawaii, and even in that state the retail portion is the most important part of the tax.

Two states, Washington and West Virginia, accompany their retail sales taxes by gross receipts taxes on all types of business, at rates relatively low compared to the sales tax rates. Indiana still applies such a levy to nonretail businesses as an alternative to the net income tax (firms pay the higher of a tax on gross or adjusted gross income), as a carry-over from the old gross income tax. The gross income tax is currently being phased out over fifteen years. Substantial attention has been directed in all three states toward eliminating these business taxes, but because these levies are not regarded as sales taxes but essentially as occupational taxes, they will not be covered in this study.

RELATIVE YIELD

Table 1.3 indicates sales tax yield by state for fiscal year 1981. Figures published by the Bureau of the Census are not entirely satisfactory measures of sales tax revenue and must be adjusted.

1. Receipts from the Washington and West Virginia business occupation taxes and the Indiana gross income tax are included in census figures. These taxes are similar to business levies as distinguished from general sales taxes, and so are deducted for the present study.
2. Some other taxes include essentially nonsales tax elements. The Arizona tax includes a severance tax on mineral and lumber production. This tax revenue is deducted, as in other states such a levy is imposed as a separate tax.

TABLE 1.3   State Retail Sales and Use Tax Yields by State, Fiscal Year 1981

State	Total State Tax Revenue ($000)	Reported General Sales Tax Revenue ($000)	Adjustments ($000)	Adjusted Sales Tax Revenue ($000)	Adjusted Sales Tax Revenue as % of State Tax Revenue
Alabama	2,026,038	583,817	+33,758[a]	617,575	30.5
Arizona	1,699,093	773,425	−52,044[b]	721,381	42.5
Arkansas	1,189,014	399,193	0	399,193	33.6
California	20,499,483	7,262,596	0	7,262,596	35.4
Colorado	1,431,940	529,880	0	529,880	37.0
Connecticut	2,061,426	916,668	0	916,668	44.5
Florida	5,328,941	2,542,895	0	2,542,895	47.7
Georgia	3,022,810	1,013,705	0	1,013,705	33.5
Hawaii	1,088,320	548,914	−4,200[c]	544,714	50.1
Idaho	535,935	144,993	0	144,993	27.1
Illinois	7,309,981	2,333,028	+30,765[d]	2,363,793	32.3
Indiana	2,805,353	1,361,250	−366,288[e]	994,962	35.5
Iowa	1,847,645	517,273	0	517,273	28.0
Kansas	1,393,827	449,213	0	449,213	32.2
Kentucky	2,276,492	630,472	+91,329[f]	721,801	31.7
Louisiana	2,799,148	856,438	+13,391[d]	869,829	31.1
Maine	680,120	235,678	0	235,678	34.7
Maryland	2,956,092	753,673	+133,051[f]	886,724	30.0
Massachusetts	4,394,397	875,543	+22,094[d]	897,637	20.4
Michigan	6,168,153	1,799,027	0	1,799,027	29.2
Minnesota	3,385,170	686,988	+87,683[f]	774,671	22.9
Mississippi	1,416,229	725,631	0	725,631	51.2
Missouri	2,143,392	787,185	0	787,185	36.7
Nebraska	802,344	281,856	0	281,856	35.1
Nevada	514,425	202,863	0	202,863	39.4
New Jersey	4,976,630	1,201,214	0	1,201,214	24.1
New Mexico	1,202,376	489,367	+18,111[f]	507,487	42.2
New York	14,354,380	2,960,800	0	2,960,800	20.6
North Carolina	3,429,229	738,877	0	738,877	21.6
North Dakota	451,959	129,509	0	129,509	28.7
Ohio	5,242,309	1,642,439	0	1,642,439	31.3
Oklahoma	2,252,113	386,796	+58,862[f]	445,658	19.8
Pennsylvania	7,597,328	2,086,166	0	2,086,166	27.5
Rhode Island	607,925	178,074	0	178,074	29.3
South Carolina	1,825,149	616,081	0	616,081	33.8
South Dakota	296,372	158,024	+11,641[f]	169,665	57.2
Tennessee	1,956,674	1,044,155	0	1,044,155	53.4
Texas	7,886,915	2,879,721	+546,299[d,f]	3,426,020	43.4
Utah	853,878	354,215	0	354,215	41.5
Vermont	294,717	44,760	+27,995[d,f]	72,755	24.7
Virginia	3,042,255	645,203	+74,742[f]	719,945	23.7
Washington	3,127,727	1,716,918	−442,806[e]	1,274,112	40.7
West Virginia	1,265,487	623,793	+48,111[f] −465,500[e]	223,197	17.6

TABLE 1.3 *(continued)*

State	Total State Tax Revenue *($000)*	Reported General Sales Tax Revenue *($000)*	Adjustments *($000)*	Adjusted Sales Tax Revenue *($000)*	Adjusted Sales Tax Revenue as % of State Tax Revenue
Wisconsin	3,614,000	901,495	0	901,495	24.9
Wyoming	469,316	196,336	0	196,336	41.8
Total[g]	144,522,507	46,206,149	−133,206	46,074,143	31.9
District of Columbia	1,064,434	243,867	+15,253[d,f]	259,120	24.3

Source: U.S., Bureau of the Census, *Quarterly Summary of State and Local Tax Revenue,* Oct. 1981, and other information provided by the Bureau of the Census and various states. All figures are preliminary figures for 1981.

[a] Taxes on rentals, lodging, and contractors.
[b] Revenue from mining, oil and gas production.
[c] Tax on sugar processing, pineapple canning, and insurance solicitors.
[d] Taxes on hotels, motels, room occupancy, meals where separate.
[e] Gross income or business occupation taxes.
[f] Separate taxes on sales of motor vehicles, boats, aircraft, mobile homes, rentals of motor vehicles.
[g] Totals for the states using sales taxes.

The wholesale elements in the taxes of Hawaii, Louisiana, and Mississippi, however, are not excluded, since they are part of the basic sales tax structure. Admittedly, however, some elements of the tax in Hawaii and the low rate wholesale tax in Mississippi could be regarded as business, rather than sales, tax. The table does exclude the tax on sugar processing and pineapple canning in Hawaii.

3. Certain categories subject to the sales tax in most states are exempted from the tax but subjected to equivalent special levies, largely for administrative reasons, in other states. These categories include:

   a. Motor vehicles, boats, etc.—in Kentucky, Maryland, Minnesota, New Mexico, Oklahoma, South Dakota, Texas, Vermont, Virginia, West Virginia, and the District of Columbia. These states use special levies collected in conjunction with registration. Amounts are added to sales tax revenue.

   b. Hotels and meals. Separate taxes are imposed on hotel and motel service and/or meals in Alabama, Illinois, Louisiana, Massachusetts, Texas, Vermont, and the District of Columbia. These taxes are added to the totals.

Logically, adjustment should be made for the fees several states charge the local governments for collecting local sales taxes, but the small amounts do not warrant making the adjustment.

Adjustments are not made for admissions taxes separately imposed in several states or for public utility taxes. Public utility services are subject to sales taxes in a number of states. In others, they are subject to separate levies; in still others, they are subject to both. Those special levies that are essentially substitutes for sales tax application cannot be delineated and therefore are omitted. The effect, however, is to understate somewhat the sales tax yields in those states in which, at least in part, the utility taxes are levied in lieu of sales taxes.

Total Yield

The relative importance of the sales tax revenues in the various state tax structures is also indicated in table 1.3. Twelve states—Arizona, Connecticut, Florida, Hawaii, Mississippi, New Mexico, South Dakota, Tennessee, Texas, Utah, Washington, and Wyoming—gain over 40% of their revenues from the sales tax. Seven of these states have no general individual income tax. Hawaii, New Mexico, and South Dakota have broadly based sales taxes. The average for all states is 31.9% and twenty-five of the states fall within the 24% to 36% range. Only West Virginia, a state with both business and occupation taxes and income taxes, and Oklahoma obtain less than 20% from the tax.

Per Capita Yield

Table 1.4 indicates the per capita yields of the retail sales tax in 1980, first, in totals yielded and second, adjusting for the differences in tax rate, per 1% of the tax rate. The average per capita tax in the states using the tax is $209. By far the heaviest burden of the tax per capita is in Hawaii, at $564. New Mexico and Wyoming are the only other states (plus the District of Columbia) in which the tax exceeds $350. The tax is lowest in West Virginia, at $114. Per 1% of tax, Hawaii is the highest, at $141, Massachusetts and Rhode Island, the lowest, at $31. The median is $51. The nine top states are west of the Mississippi; excluding the District of Columbia, the thirteen top states are west of the Mississippi.

Variation among states and regions in yield per 1% of tax can be explained by several primary factors:
1. Food exemption. Twenty-six states with broad food exemption show an average of $50.13 per capita, compared to the overall figure of $56.42. The ten food exemption states above the overall average (Arizona, California, Colorado, Florida, Iowa, Louisiana, Nevada, North Dakota, Texas, and Washington) tend to be tourist destinations or have otherwise broad bases.
2. Other elements in coverage. The high figure of Hawaii reflects the very broad coverage of the tax. Arizona, New Mexico, Nevada, Washington, and Wyoming, the next highest group, all have broad-based taxes, whereas Massachusetts, New Jersey, Pennsylvania, and Rhode Island, the four lowest, have substantial exemptions.

TABLE 1.4 State Sales Tax Revenue per Capita and as Percentage of Personal Income, 1981

State	Adjusted Sales Tax Revenue ($000)	Per Capita Sales Tax Revenue ($)	Effective Tax Rate Fiscal 1981 (%)	Per Capita Sales Tax Revenue Per 1% of Tax Rate ($)	Sales Tax Revenue as % of Personal Income	Sales Tax Revenue as % of Personal Income Per 1% of Tax Rate
Alabama	617,575	158.75	4.00	39.69	2.13	0.53
Arizona	721,381	265.41	4.00	66.35	3.07	0.77
Arkansas	399,193	124.80	3.00	41.60	2.43	0.81
California	7,262,596	306.84	4.75	64.60	2.84	0.59
Colorado	529,880	183.41	3.00	61.14	1.85	0.62
Connecticut	916,668	294.93	7.50	39.32	2.59	0.35
Florida	2,542,895	261.07	4.00	65.27	2.92	0.73
Georgia	1,013,705	185.52	3.00	61.84	2.34	0.78
Hawaii	544,714	564.47	4.00	141.12	5.81	1.45
Idaho	144,993	153.59	3.00	51.20	1.89	0.63
Illinois	2,363,793	207.02	3.60[a]	57.51	1.95	0.54
Indiana	994,962	181.23	4.00	45.31	2.03	0.51
Iowa	517,273	177.57	3.00	59.19	1.94	0.65
Kansas	449,213	190.10	3.00	63.37	1.91	0.64
Kentucky	721,801	197.16	5.00	39.43	2.57	0.51
Louisiana	869,829	206.91	3.00	68.97	2.50	0.83
Maine	235,678	209.49	5.00	41.90	2.71	0.54
Maryland	886,724	210.32	5.00	42.06	2.05	0.41
Massachusetts	897,637	156.46	5.00	31.29	1.57	0.31
Michigan	1,799,027	194.32	4.00	48.58	1.98	0.50
Minnesota	774,671	190.01	4.00	47.50	2.00	0.50
Mississippi	725,631	287.83	5.00	57.57	4.44	0.89
Missouri	787,185	160.09	3.125	53.36	1.81	0.60
Nebraska	281,856	179.53	3.00	57.45	2.02	0.65
Nevada	202,863	253.90	3.5	72.54	2.42	0.69

New Jersey	1,201,214	5.00	163.12	32.62	1.52	0.30
New Mexico	507,487	3.75	390.38	104.10	4.92	1.31
New York	2,960,800	4.00	168.64	42.16	1.67	0.42
North Carolina	738,877	3.00	125.79	41.93	1.61	0.54
North Dakota	129,509	3.00	198.33	66.11	2.32	0.77
Ohio	1,642,439	4.50[b]	152.12	33.80	1.62	0.36
Oklahoma	445,658	2.00	147.32	73.66	1.64	0.82
Pennsylvania	2,086,166	6.00	175.80	29.30	1.90	0.32
Rhode Island	178,074	6.00	188.04	31.34	2.04	0.34
South Carolina	616,081	4.00	197.53	49.38	2.67	0.67
South Dakota	169,665	4.75[c]	245.89	51.77	3.31	0.70
Tennessee	1,044,155	4.50	227.44	50.54	2.95	0.66
Texas	3,426,020	4.00	240.79	60.20	2.54	0.64
Utah	354,215	4.00	242.45	60.61	3.24	0.81
Vermont	72,755	3.00	142.38	47.46	1.81	0.60
Virginia	719,945	3.00	134.22	44.74	1.43	0.48
Washington	1,274,112	4.50	308.50	68.56	2.99	0.66
West Virginia	223,197	2.50[d]	114.46	45.78	1.48	0.59
Wisconsin	901,495	4.00	191.60	47.90	2.08	0.52
Wyoming	196,336	3.00	416.85	138.95	3.92	1.31
Total	46,074,143		208.92		2.21	
District of Columbia	259,120	5.65[e]	406.14	71.88	3.43	0.61

Source: Same as table 1.3.

[a] Basic rate 4%, tax on food 2%.
[b] Tax rate 4% before Jan. 1, 1981, 5% thereafter.
[c] Tax rate on food 4%, general rate 5%.
[d] Tax rate on food 1%, general rate 3%.
[e] Rate raised from 5% to 6% Aug. 1, 1980.

3. "Exporting" of tax. States with large tourist travel show higher figures than would otherwise be expected. Nevada and Florida are the most obvious, but Hawaii and California are influenced by this factor to some extent. As much as 25% of Nevada's revenue apparently comes from tourists. In reverse, New Jersey undoubtedly suffers from extensive shopping by its residents in New York and Pennsylvania.

4. Per capita income. For the ten states with the lowest per capita income, the average yield per capita per 1% of tax rate was $47.65, somewhat below the average. When the tax is expressed as a percentage of total personal income, per 1% of tax rate (table 1.4), this factor is eliminated, and the figures of the low-income states are comparable to the average (0.66 vs. 0.64). Percentage of income spent on taxable goods therefore appears to be roughly the same in the low income states as the higher income states. The former can squeeze out the same percentage of income in sales tax, even though absolute incomes are lower. Only three of the ten low per capita income states (Maine, Vermont, and West Virginia) exempt food; only two of the ten high per capita income states (Illinois and Wyoming) do not fully exempt food.

Yield per 1% of tax expressed as a percentage of personal income averages 0.4% in the food-exempting states and 0.81% in the food-taxing states. Several food-exempting states have other exemptions, so not all the difference can be attributed to food. Hawaii shows by far the highest figure, 1.45%. New Jersey, the lowest, 0.30%. These figures show that with a broadly based tax and with food taxable, about 80% of the consumer's income dollar is spent on taxable goods. If 20% of the tax is assumed to rest initially on producers goods in these states, 64% of consumer income is directly reached by the tax.

Yield is also affected by the degree of enforcement but probably not to a measurable extent.[6]

Yield by Type of Vendor

The states do not require vendors to list receipts by type of commodity and could not without necessitating a tremendous change in retail record-keeping. The typical retail store has no record of sales by type of commodity and cannot easily keep one. Since vendors are classified by type, states can and do prepare figures of collections by type of vendor. Completely comparable data among

---

[6]Some efforts have been made to measure the overall degree of effectiveness. C.V. Oster, *State Retail Sales Taxation* (Columbus: Ohio State University, 1957), pp. 150–56, compared taxable sales with retail sales estimated by *Sales Management* magazine, but the concept of a retail sale for tax purposes is very different from that used in *Sales Management*, and the results are therefore of doubtful value. J.F. Due, "Evaluation of the Effectiveness of State Sales Tax Administration," extends the effort by considering both the relationship between Department of Commerce sales data and sales reported on tax returns in categories where the magnitude would be about the same and the findings from sales tax audits. That evidence indicates no mass evasion, although substantial total revenue remains uncollected.

states, however, are unavailable, since classifications and groupings of class used in reporting differ. In many states, restaurants are grouped in the food category, but in others they are kept separate. Liquor may be grouped with food or kept separate. The scope of the taxes varies, of course, thus creating further complications in comparing percentage yields. Moreover, some states break the classifications down to a greater extent than others.

Despite these qualifications, figures on yield by type of vendor give some picture of the relative importance of major categories, as shown in table 1.5. The food category alone, excluding restaurants, yields about 20% of the revenue, but at least five percentage points of this figure consist of nonfood sales by grocery stores (note the food store yields in states exempting food). In most states that exempt food, the combined figure for the food and restaurant categories runs between 8% and 12%. High percentage states are those in which liquor is taxed and restaurant meals are important. Because of variations in other aspects of the tax and the economies of the states, no exact figures of loss of income from food exemption is possible, but a reasonable estimate is 15%.

The automotive group is a second major category. The average yield figure is slightly under 20% in the states that include automobiles in the sales tax and under 10% in the states that do not.

A third major category is general merchandise—department, variety, and general stores, mail order houses, and drug and various specialty stores not included in other groups. The average yield is 16%, but the range is substantial, mainly due to differences in classification.

The building materials group ranges from 4% to 20% (except New York, at 1.8%), with a typical figure around 9% to 11%; furniture and appliances, typically 3.5% to 8%; apparel, typically 3% to 5%. In the states that tax public utilities, the yield averages around 9%. Service establishments typically yield from 4% to 6%.

Accurate figures are unavailable on sales by manufacturers and wholesalers. The range is very wide, from 2% to 39% (Minnesota). The figure includes both purchases and sales by manufacturers, not all of which are producer goods; some purchases of producers goods appear in other categories.

NUMBER OF SALES TAX ACCOUNTS

The operation of a retail sales tax is based on the registration of firms that sell at retail and the establishment of an account for each registered vendor. Registration serves to control the dissemination of information, the filing of returns and making of payments, and audit. (Registration procedures will be reviewed in chapter 5.) Basic data on numbers of registered vendors are presented in table 1.6. In-state registered consumers are persons or firms not selling at retail but regularly making purchases from out-of-state vendors subject to use tax, primarily contractors, banks, and manufacturers.

TABLE 1.5 Relative Yield by Type of Vendor, States for which Information Is Available, 1980

State	Food	Restaurant and Liquor	Automotive	General Merchandise and Specialty Stores	Building Materials, Construction
California (1979)[a,b]	5.7	9.5	21.8	16.8	4.7
Colorado[b]	9.7	8.9	12.4	8.4	7.3
Florida[b]	—	15.7[c]	18.0	14.7	9.7
Georgia	22.3	—	13.6	14.6	6.9
Idaho (1978)	16.5	6.7	16.5	—	9.9
Illinois	14.6	8.2	22.8	10.2	9.3
Iowa[b]	4.3	7.5	6.5	17.7	7.6
Kentucky[b]	18.0	—	9.5	20.0	7.6
Louisiana (1979)[a,b]	5.1	5.7	20.9	14.4	18.3
Maryland[b]	—	21.2[c]	6.6	21.3	18.1
Michigan (1979)[a,b]	7.1	8.7	26.1	18.6	8.5
Minnesota (1978)[b]	2.2	8.3	4.3	7.5	12.0
Mississippi	24.9[c]	—	21.1	12.9[e]	20.5
New York (1979)[a,b]	5.0	7.9	13.6	11.5	1.8
North Carolina	31.0	—	14.7	19.5	10.9
Ohio (1978)[a,b]	7.2	10.7	26.7	22.0	13.0
Oklahoma	22.1	—	8.0	19.2	10.2
Pennsylvania (1979)[a,b]	2.8	11.4	22.7	16.4	8.4
South Carolina	18.1	7.0	8.6	8.5	8.5
Tennessee (1979)	23.7	—	19.2	16.9	10.1

Source: Bureau of the Census, *State Government Tax Collections in 1980.*

[a] *Source:* State revenue department data.
[b] Food exemption state.

For several reasons, exact comparability among states is difficult to attain. First, some states maintain no continuing tabulation on the numbers of accounts, and therefore figures available at any time are only estimates. Even more commonly, no breakdown is available of the number of accounts between in-state vendors and out-of-state vendors registered to collect and remit use tax. Some states do not register consumers for use-tax purposes. Out-of-state figures sometimes include firms in the state subject to sales tax but with out-of-state mailing addresses. They should be included in the tabulation of in-state vendors subject to sales tax.

Second, some states (for example, Maine, Ohio, South Dakota and Tennessee) require separate registration for each store location, and the totals therefore include each location. Other states, such as Georgia, Illinois, Kentucky, and New Mexico, require and report one registration for each multiple unit system. Many states allow the firms to register either way and thus report totals that reflect some firms by location, some by consolidation; a few states report both. In Colorado, for example, 8,371 locations represent 1,834 parent

Furniture and Appliance	Lodging	Services	Public Utilities	Manufacturing and Wholesale	Apparel	Other
3.3	—	3.6	—	—	3.4	31.3
3.9	2.3	5.2	8.4	15.5	3.6	14.2
5.5	—	—	—	4.4	3.1	28.9
5.0	—	6.8	14.9	7.7	2.6	5.6
3.5	—	6.4	2.1	8.7	2.3	27.4
3.2	—	—	—	12.0	3.9	15.9
3.9	—	9.9	12.3	17.9d	3.1	9.3
8.2	—	4.9	10.1	11.9	3.9	5.8
5.6	1.1	5.0	0.9	10.5	3.8	8.6
9.1	—	—	6.0	—	5.6	12.1
4.7	0.5	2.8	7.5	2.2	4.4	9.0
3.3	—	5.6	9.1	39.3	0.3	8.1
3.3	—	4.7	5.4	0.8d	—	6.4
3.4	1.9	7.0	14.4	16.7	5.2	11.8
4.9	—	—	—	—	3.6	15.4
8.2	—	—	—	—	5.0	7.3
5.9	—	4.1	9.7	—	3.4	17.4
5.2	—	8.4	6.3	15.6	—	2.6
4.7	—	6.3	9.9	4.6	3.0	20.7
4.8	—	5.6	7.3	5.9	2.3	4.2

c Food and beverage stores.

d Wholesale only.

e General merchandise and apparel.

firms included in the totals. That state system expects returns at each level. Such variations complicate comparisons of registered accounts across states.

Third, some states (for example, New Jersey) require all manufacturers to register to buy materials tax free. Many states do not, as long as the manufacturers are not selling at retail. The result is that states requiring all manufacturers to register have a large number of inactive accounts. States also differ in the extent to which they exclude other inactive accounts from their lists or retain them, designated as inactive or not. Where available, the figure of active accounts is used in the table. Several states have available figures for both the total number of registrants and the number of active accounts receiving returns. Differences are substantial, as shown in table 1.7.

When the sales taxes are first introduced, registration is usually required of all firms selling tangible personal property. Ultimately, in some states, firms making no retail sales are removed from the rolls and allowed to buy materials tax free under certificate without registration. The result is that the number of registrants commonly falls after the first few years of operation of the tax.

TABLE 1.6 Sales Tax Registrants by State, 1981

| State | Registrants | | In-State Registered Consumers | Total Active Registrants | Active Registrants per 10,000 Population[a] |
	In-State Vendors	Out-of-State Vendors			
Alabama	49,222	5,032	5,369	59,623[b]	158
Arizona				75,000	306
Arkansas				56,561	259
California				629,533	277
Colorado	88,717	2,313	23,800	114,830	414
Connecticut				100,000	321
Florida				295,254	333
Georgia				106,000[b]	207
Hawaii				69,000	754
Idaho				31,000	343
Illinois				172,942	154
Indiana				135,000	250
Iowa				99,945	344
Kansas	66,844	6,389	2,340	75,573	319
Kentucky	72,373		4,447	76,820[b]	218
Louisiana				78,000	194
Maine				29,000	264
Maryland				91,802	221
Massachusetts				129,650	225
Michigan				138,005	150
Minnesota				105,000	259
Mississippi				73,554	303
Missouri				100,020	206
Nebraska	55,419	4,485	1,145	61,049	388
Nevada				20,500	292
New Jersey				177,235	242
New Mexico				85,651	690
New York				450,358	255
North Carolina				119,249[b]	213
North Dakota				26,000[c]	396
Ohio	201,485	5,668	11,899	229,496	214
Oklahoma			6,000	56,000	194
Pennsylvania	215,998	9,493	3,548	229,039	195
Rhode Island				23,000	248
South Carolina	61,775	10,029		71,804	245
South Dakota				33,500[c]	486
Tennessee				103,729[c]	236
Texas				289,913	217
Utah				39,233	287
Vermont				18,120	368
Virginia				80,000	154
Washington[d]				157,000[d]	400
West Virginia	37,005	2,500		39,505	210
Wisconsin				108,000	229
Wyoming				37,970	844

TABLE 1.6 (*continued*)

State	Registrants		In-State Registered Consumers	Total Active Registrants	Active Registrants per 10,000 Population[a]
	In-State Vendors	Out-of-State Vendors			
District of Columbia				33,000[b]	503
Total				5,308,291	247

[a] 1979 population estimate.
[b] One registration for multiunit system.
[c] Separate registration of each store in multiunit system.
[d] Includes business and occupation tax.

The overall national average is 305 registered vendors per 10,000 population (276, excluding Hawaii, New Mexico, and Washington). Twenty-one of the states fall in the range of 190 to 260. Four states—Alabama, Illinois, Michigan, and Virginia—have fewer than 160. The last three cases can perhaps be explained by the heavy concentration of retailing in suburban shopping centers with high volume per store. Explanations for Alabama are less obvious. Of the states with high figures above 300, nine are rural states without large metropolitan areas: Idaho, Kansas, Maine, Mississippi, Nebraska, North Dakota, South Dakota, Vermont, and Wyoming. Obviously, a relatively small population spread over a wide area increases the number of vendors per 10,000 population. Colorado, Connecticut, and Florida have unusually high figures, for which there is no obvious explanation.

The states with relatively broad coverage of services, Arizona and Iowa, have figures substantially higher, relative to population, than the rest. New Mexico and Hawaii, which tax all services, and in the latter, all nonretail businesses as well, have much higher figures.

TABLE 1.7 Percentage of Inactive Accounts in Several States

State	Total File	Currently Active Accounts	Inactive Accounts as % of Total Accounts
Colorado	194,602	114,830	41
Maine	39,597	29,000	26
Maryland	176,618	91,802	48
Michigan	206,565	138,005	33
New Jersey	263,059	177,235	33
New York	754,429	450,358	40
Pennsylvania	321,797	229,039	29

In summary:
1. A typical state, having limited coverage of services, screening lists of registrants to eliminate inactive accounts, and registering each multiple unit system as a single account, will have somewhat fewer than 250, and perhaps as
   few as 200, vendors per 10,000 population.
2. Registration of all manufacturers and inclusion of the inactive accounts in
   the total will raise the figure by 15% to 20%.
3. Registration of each store in a multiple unit system increases the number of
   registrants from 10% to 15%.
4. Sparsely settled states with small metropolitan area populations will have a
   substantially larger number of vendors relative to population, 50% or more
   in the extreme cases.
5. Addition of commercial (but not professional) services will increase the
   number of registrants by about half. The figure in Iowa went from 52,000 to
   79,000 when the tax was extended to services. If professional services are included, as in New Mexico, the number of registrants is more or less double
   the figure with only commodities taxed. If all businesses at all stages and all
   services are taxed, the figure may be as much as three times as great, as
   shown by the figures for Hawaii.

Annual Turnover of Accounts

A surprisingly high percentage of vendor accounts "turn over" every year, in
the sense of old permits being canceled and new ones issued. Changes arise
from three principal sources: the establishment of new businesses and the liq-
uidation of old; the sale of a business; and the change to, or from, the corporate
form of organization. Mere change in address is not included in the totals except in a few states, in which these changes cannot be isolated from the others.
The overall percentage that new permits issued annually constitutes of total
number of permits outstanding is eighteen (the same as in 1971). The percentage canceled is nearly as great, since the total number changes slowly. States
for which data are available can be grouped into three classes (table 1.8). A few
states have been eliminated because the data are clearly not comparable or are
not available.

Some of the differences obviously reflect variations in reporting and, in the
base, the number of vendors reported, as previously discussed. Clearly, however, the relatively stable states of New England, the mid-Atlantic area, and
parts of the Midwest have less turnover than do the rapidly changing and growing states in the far West and parts of the South.

Most states report no significant change from year to year in the totals. From
a short-run standpoint, the number of registered vendors is not significantly increasing in most areas, despite increases in population and total retail sales.
Although many new stores are opening each year, about an equal number are
closing. Average sales per store are, of course, constantly increasing.

TABLE 1.8 New Permits as Percentage of Total Accounts (annual turnover)

State	%
Low Turnover	
Mississippi	2.0–3.0
Oklahoma	7.9
Vermont	9.9
Rhode Island	10.0
North Dakota	10.6
Louisiana	10.9
New Jersey	11.3
Pennsylvania	12.5
Connecticut	13.0
Iowa	13.3
Typical Turnover	
Maine	15.2
Minnesota	15.0–16.0
Wisconsin	15.7
Kansas	15.9
West Virginia	16.1 (all taxes)
Michigan	16.5 (all taxes)
Maryland	17.2
Kentucky	17.6
Virginia	18.0
New York	18.7
Indiana	18.9
Idaho	20.0
High Turnover	
South Carolina	22.1
Arkansas	22.5
Tennessee	22.9
North Carolina	24.2
Florida	24.4
Washington	25.9
Texas	26.9
Ohio	28.5
Arizona	31.6
Nevada	46.8

Table 1.9 indicates the change, for a group of thirty states, between 1969/70 and 1979/80. Over the decade there is more evidence of change, although the figures for the two years are not entirely comparable. The overall average increase for the group of states was 36%.[7] Increases over 50% were reported by eight states: Colorado, Utah, New Mexico, Connecticut, Maryland, California, Nevada, and Vermont. Most other high increases were reported by rapidly expanding western states with high population growth. Two states showed declines, though this change may reflect in part pruning of registration rolls to eliminate inactive accounts.

[7] A 3% annual growth rate compounds to a 34% increase over a ten-year period.

TABLE 1.9 Changes in Number of Active Registrants, 1969–70 to 1979–81

State	Registrants, 1969–70	Registrants, 1979–81	% of Change
Colorado	42,000	114,830	173
New Mexico	36,000	85,651	137
Utah	19,000	39,233	107
Connecticut	51,000	100,000	96
Maryland	50,000	91,802	84
California	385,919	629,533	63
Nevada	13,000	20,500	58
Vermont	11,841	18,120	53
Kansas	53,000	75,573	43
Florida	208,748	295,254	41
Georgia	75,000	106,000	41
Arizona	53,500	75,000	40
Idaho	22,379	31,000	39
Hawaii	50,000	69,000	38
Tennessee	75,000	103,729	38
South Carolina	53,532	71,804	34
Maine	30,000	39,597	32
North Dakota	19,732	26,000	32
Alabama	45,789	59,623	30
Louisiana	60,000	78,000	30
Texas	225,000	289,913	29
Mississippi	57,496	73,554	28
Rhode Island	18,000	23,000	29
West Virginia	31,200	39,505	27
North Carolina	95,461	119,249	25
Washington	125,364	157,000	25
Wisconsin	87,050	108,000	24
Arkansas	47,000	56,561	20
Nebraska	52,036	61,049	17
Minnesota	90,180	105,000	16
Kentucky	66,705	76,820	15
Oklahoma	49,199	56,000	14
Virginia	73,432	80,000	9
Ohio	211,000	229,496	8
Michigan	127,500	138,005	8
Massachusetts	120,000	129,650	8
Iowa	93,019	99,945	7
Pennsylvania	214,538	229,039	7
New York	430,000	450,358	5
Indiana	135,000	135,000	0
Illinois	177,539	172,942	−2
New Jersey	198,709	177,235	−11

California data are available in sufficient detail to ascertain the primary sources of change. Greatest relative growth was in permits held by nonretail outlets, by specialty stores, and by household furnishing and appliance stores. General merchandise store permits increased only slightly. The automotive group declined, because of almost 30% fewer service station permits and some fewer new automobile dealers. The average taxable transactions per permit rose by roughly 90% over the period.

In general, therefore, given typical population growth, coverage of the tax, and policies on inactive accounts, the number of accounts is likely to increase by no more than 1% a year. Without population growth, the number is almost certain to decline. Basically, this reflects a trend toward larger and larger retail establishments.

Returns by General Vendor Class

Although most states publish data of collections by type of vendor, only a few publish the number of outlets by type of vendor. Such information, where available, stresses a major neglected aspect of the taxes: a large portion of the total number of vendors is not retail stores in any usual sense. Figures for California, which does not tax services, for Iowa, which taxes commercial services, for Minnesota, and for Washington, which includes all forms of business in its business and occupation tax, give some indication of the importance of non-retail activities (see table 1.10). Retail stores therefore constitute less than half the registered firms in California, even though services are not taxed; there are

TABLE 1.10 Outlets by Major Vendor Class, Four States, 1978

Vendor	Iowa[a]	Washington[b]	Minnesota	California
Retail stores	46,727	38,818	42,558	206,951
Contractors	c	19,078	3,368	21,201
Service establishments and financial institutions	24,238	50,951	21,313	72,003
Manufacturers	c	6,983	6,026	
Wholesalers	8,672	11,367	8,181	
Governments	c	184	1,045	332,443
Public utilities and transport	2,205	4,961	1,442	
Hotels, motels		1,336	3,181	
Miscellaneous	11,432	3,775	12,757	
Total	93,274	137,453	99,871	611,397

Source: Annual reports of the state tax administration agencies.

[a] September 1980.
[b] Business and occupation tax.
[c] Included in other categories. Figures are based on returns for particular periods and therefore do not equal the number of registered vendors.

about one-third as many service establishments as there are retail stores. In Iowa, with many services taxed, retail stores constitute about half the registrants; service establishments, about one-fourth. In Washington, retail stores constitute about 28% of all registered businesses; service establishments, about 37% — all of which are required to register. There are nearly half as many manufacturers and wholesalers as retail stores.

2. Sales Tax Structures, Measures of Tax Liability, and Rates

Most states modeled their sales taxes after the taxes of other states. There are, nevertheless, significant differences in structure. Legal liability varies, as do provisions on shifting, rates, coverage of nonretail sales, exemptions, and treatment of services. This chapter reviews the general structure of sales taxes, measures of tax liability, tax rates, and nonretail elements in the taxes. Chapters 3 and 4 cover other aspects of structure.

STANDARDS FOR EVALUATING SALES TAX STRUCTURES

To evaluate various features of sales taxation, standards must be established based on consensus in contemporary society. The following standards appear to be widely accepted:

1. The sales tax is designed to be a uniform tax on consumer expenditures, except where there is specific justification for exception. Its structure, therefore, should (a) facilitate shifting the tax to the ultimate consumer, (b) apply to all consumption expenditures at a uniform rate, except in those circumstances in which deviation from this rule has specific justification, and (c) apply to the amounts actually paid by final consumers.[1]

2. The tax structure should be designed to minimize regressivity in the

---

[1] The rule that sales taxes should be uniform on all consumption expenditures has been questioned in recent years by the theory of optimal taxation, on the grounds of economic effects. The demand for some commodities is more elastic than the demand for others; to the extent that tax rates are higher on inelastic demand commodities and lower on elastic demand commodities, alteration of economic activity as a result of the tax will be minimized. Taxes should be heavy on commodities complementary to leisure and low on those complementary to work in order to avoid effects of substitution of leisure for work. There are two problems, however, in implementing such a system. First, elasticity of demand for various goods is not known with any high degree of accuracy, especially when all or most prices are changing. Second, this rule would conflict with usual standards of equity, since the demand for basic necessities is probably more inelastic than the demand for luxuries. Most of this work was stimulated by the papers of P.A. Diamond and J. Mirrlees, "Optimal Taxation and Public Production I: Production Efficiency; and II: Tax Rules," *American Economic Review* 61 (1971): 8–27, 261–78. For an easier treatment of the problem, see A. Sandmo, "Optimal Taxation—An Introduction to the Literature," *Journal of Public Economics* 6 (1976): 37–54.

distribution of tax burden in order to conform as closely as possible with accepted standards of equity.

3. The tax structure should not create competitive disturbances among various types of distribution channel, method of doing business, form of business organization, and the like; otherwise, economic efficiency will be lost.

4. The tax structure should facilitate administration and vendor compliance.

VENDOR, CONSUMER, AND HYBRID TAXES

Customarily, various state sales taxes were classified into two neat packages: privilege taxes on the vendor and consumer taxes on the sale. Each has certain characteristics relating to shifting, compensation to vendors, requirements for separate quotation, and other features. Actually, careful examination of the taxes suggests that this classification is less than useful and is in fact misleading. A more satisfactory classification involves three groups. Even this approach, however, has substantial nonuniformity of various features within each class. The most significant feature of the taxes is the uniformity with which they operate despite some differences in structure.

Vendor Taxes

Taxes in thirteen states are, at least by law, basically vendor levies. They are imposed on the legal basis of the "privilege" of engaging in business as a retailer or of the closely related concept of the "privilege" of selling at retail. This vendor-tax group consists of Arizona, California, Connecticut, Hawaii, Kentucky, Michigan, Nevada, New Mexico, North Dakota, South Carolina, South Dakota, Tennessee, and Wisconsin.

None of these states requires shifting of the tax to the consumer. California, Connecticut, Nevada, and Tennessee require shifting "insofar as possible," a phrase having little significance except to make clear the legislative intent. Kentucky, Michigan, North Dakota, South Carolina, South Dakota, and Wisconsin indicate that the tax "may" be shifted. Absorption is unlawful in Connecticut and North Dakota. Vendors in Michigan have a right to reimbursement but are not required to shift or quote separately. The laws in Arizona, Hawaii, and New Mexico, providing the most strictly "vendor" taxes of all, do not mention shifting.

Consumer Taxes

In seventeen states the sales tax is basically a consumer levy, imposed upon the retail *sale*.[2] In all these states, the measure of tax liability is the selling

[2]Idaho, Iowa, Louisiana, Maryland, Mississippi, Missouri, Nebraska, New York, North Carolina, Ohio, Pennsylvania, Rhode Island, Utah, Vermont, Washington, West Virginia, and Wyoming.

price, whereas in the vendor privilege states, the measure is either gross receipts or gross proceeds. All consumer sales tax states require the vendor to collect the tax from the consumer and remit it to the state, and to keep the tax separate from the price. All such states prohibit retailers from advertising that they are absorbing the tax. All prescribe the brackets for collection, whereas some of the vendor states do not.

Hybrid Taxes

In fifteen states, plus the District of Columbia, the sales taxes contain both vendor and consumer features.[3] The courts determine the precise legal status and most are held to be vendor taxes. Taxes are imposed on the vendor for the privilege of carrying on business or selling at retail, but the laws contain mandatory shifting provisions. In other words, the tax is legally imposed upon the vendor, but he is required to collect it from the consumer.

Relative Merits of the Three Types

Long experience has shown that any of the three types of sales tax will operate satisfactorily, but some advantages occur from placing the full legal liability on the vendor. Responsibility for payment is clear cut and undivided. The significance for tax liability of use to be made of the product and intent of purchase is reduced. Much greater freedom exists in the choice of tax treatment of sales to the federal government, to state and local governments, and to institutions or organizations that may be exempted by state constitutional provision. There is much less danger that troublesome exemptions by class of buyer will be placed in the law. Some consumer law states have found it difficult to collect the tax in the event of bankruptcy of a vendor. Priority of tax claims is frequently lower in such instances than with a vendor tax. Oklahoma shifted away from the consumer tax primarily for this reason. There is also less danger that vendors will be required to account for the exact amount of tax collected and pay this sum to the state. This annoying requirement, which accomplishes little and creates substantial expense for the vendor, is discussed later.

[3] Alabama, Arkansas, Colorado, Florida, Georgia, Illinois, Indiana, Kansas, Maine, Massachusetts, Minnesota, New Jersey, Oklahoma, Texas, and Virginia. The Illinois sales tax system is unique, with vendor and consumer types of sales tax united in a single tax structure. The older part, the retailers' occupation tax, is imposed on vendors for the privilege of engaging in the business of selling tangible personal property at retail. The law makes no mention of shifting. Prior to 1955, this law was the classic example of a strictly vendor-type levy. When the use tax was imposed, it was, for reasons relating to the state constitution, imposed upon the use of tangible property bought at retail, whether bought inside the state or outside. The use tax is a consumer levy; collection by the vendor from the customer is required where possible. To prevent double taxation, the vendor is allowed to credit the use tax collected from the customer against the retailers' occupation tax liability; the vendor does not pay both taxes to the state.

SHIFTING, SEPARATE QUOTATION, AND ADVERTISING

Since the philosophy of sales taxation is that the burden should rest on the consumer, inclusion of the following provisions in the sales tax act may be justified:

1. The tax must be collected from the consumer whenever feasible. This rule makes clear the intent of the legislature without impairing the legal liability of the vendor.
2. The tax must be quoted separately from the selling price.
3. Advertising that the tax is being absorbed is prohibited.

Strictly consumer tax states and all of the hybrid states have mandatory shifting provisions. Only Arizona, Hawaii, and New Mexico, strictly vendor states, make no reference to shifting. Other vendor tax states indicate that the vendor may shift, or is expected to shift, as far as possible.

Some laws and regulations are obscure on requiring separate quotation of the tax from the price. In general, however, almost all the consumer and hybrid taxes require separate quotation (though Iowa will accept a "tax included" statement). Several vendor tax states, including Arizona, Hawaii, Michigan, New Mexico, South Dakota, Tennessee, and Wisconsin, do not require separate quotation, though Arizona and New Mexico give strong incentive by disallowing deduction of the tax element in calculating tax unless it is quoted separately.

General observation suggests that separate quotation is almost as universal in the states that do not require it as in those that do. For example, prior to the 1955 enactment of the use tax in Illinois, there was little tendency to include the tax in the price, even though the law did not mention shifting or quotation. The 1955 change, which made separate quotation mandatory, had very little effect on practice. In earlier years, this situation had not been true in Hawaii, where many merchants included the tax in the price. The trend, however, has been toward separate quotation, which is now almost universal.

All states, except the strictly vendor tax state of Arizona, prohibit retailers from advertising that they will absorb the tax or refund it after it is paid.

Provisions relating to mandatory shifting, separate quotation, and advertising were introduced into the laws primarily because the retail merchant groups sought them, and the states were anxious to obtain the cooperation of the retailers. Retailers wanted the states to make it clear to the public that they were required to collect the tax from the consumer to avoid any charge of being responsible for a price increase. They also believed that the separate quotation rule would increase the likelihood of uniform shifting of the tax, since all retailers would be required to treat the tax in like fashion. Departure from established price lines (prices for women's clothing ending in 95¢) could be avoided; so would the need for repricing all goods. For the retailer, adding tax to the entire bill at the cash register is much simpler than adding tax to each price separately. Legislators also recognized that separate quotation provisions would discourage retailers from raising prices by amounts in excess of the tax.

No law can actually compel shifting of a tax, since retailers are free to reduce the price net of the tax and show the tax separately, thus complying with the act and yet, in fact, absorbing the tax. Provisions in the act for shifting, however, are significant in promoting uniformity of treatment of the tax by competing retailers. If the law provides for shifting, retailers feel more confident that their competitors will shift and, in turn, will be more inclined to do so themselves. A provision prohibiting the advertising of tax absorption makes it difficult for a firm that does absorb the tax to take advantage of it by increasing sales.

Significance of specific provisions can easily be exaggerated. Shifting occurs in much the same fashion in states without legal provisions, since the merchants' associations encourage the voluntary adoption of this policy. The only difference between the two sets of states is one of degree in some lines of retailing. If the states prohibited separate quotation (as is the rule in some European countries), shifting would be more difficult.

BRACKETS

All but three states, the strictly vendor states of Arizona, Hawaii, and New Mexico, establish the brackets for collection.[4] (Of the forty-two that establish brackets, twenty-four designate them in the act and eighteen in administrative documents.)[5] In the three states not prescribing brackets, merchants' associations have established "suggested brackets."

The established brackets vary substantially among states with the same tax rate. The initial figures vary: with 25¢ in the state with 2%; from 10¢ in North Carolina to 25¢ in Wyoming, with a 3% rate; from 10¢ (Florida) to 16¢ Indiana and New York) with a 4% rate, and 6¢ (West Virginia) to 20¢ (Maryland) for a 5% rate; and from 9¢ (Rhode Island) to 13¢ (District of Columbia) for a 6% rate.

The bracket structures are indicated in table 2.1. Brackets for state rates

---

[4]In the early 1930s, a number of states used mill tokens to facilitate collection of the exact amount of tax. One mill was due on each 5¢-purchase under the 2% tax rate then common. The tokens were a great nuisance to vendors, consumers, and revenue departments and gradually fell into disuse. World War II, with its shortage of materials to make tokens, brought the practice almost to an end. Some were used in Missouri in isolated instances until the late 1950s, but the legislature eliminated the system in 1961. Not till the mid-sixties was the provision for tokens eliminated from the Oklahoma Act.

[5]Statute: Alabama, California, Connecticut, Florida, Idaho, Indiana, Maine, Maryland, Massachusetts, Michigan, Missouri, New Jersey, North Carolina, North Dakota, Ohio, Oklahoma, Pennsylvania, Rhode Island, South Carolina, South Dakota, Texas, Vermont, Virginia, and West Virginia.

TABLE 2.1 Bracket Systems for Sales Tax Collections, February 1981

	Tax (in ¢)							Rule on Higher Figures
	1	2	3	4	5	6	7	
2% Rate								
Major Fraction (Oklahoma)[a]	0.25-0.74	0.75-1.24	1.25-1.74					
3% Rate								
Major Fraction (Colorado, Nebraska)[a]	0.17-0.49	0.50-0.83	0.84-1.16					
Arkansas	0.15-0.44	0.45-0.74	0.75-1.14					same brackets
Georgia[a]	0.11-0.35	0.36-0.66	0.67-1.00					same brackets
Idaho	0.16-0.42	0.43-0.72	0.73-0.99					same brackets
Iowa	0.15-0.44	0.45-0.74	0.75-1.14					same brackets to $5.74, then major fraction
Kansas[a]	0.15-0.39	0.40-0.69	0.70-1.14	1.15-1.44	1.45-1.83			same brackets to $29.84, then major fraction
Louisiana[a]	0.13-0.42	0.43-0.82	0.83-1.00					same brackets
North Carolina[a]	0.10-0.35	0.36-0.70	0.71-1.16					major fraction
North Dakota[a]	0.16-0.33	0.34-0.67	0.68-1.00					same brackets
Vermont	0.14-0.33	0.34-0.66	0.67-1.00					same brackets
Wyoming	0.25-0.49	0.50-0.83	0.84-1.16	1.17-1.49	1.50-1.83	1.84-2.16		major fraction
3.12% Rate								
Missouri[a]	0.15-0.47	0.48-0.79	0.80-1.11					1¢ for each 32¢
3.5% Rate								
New Mexico: no brackets								
4% Rate								
Major Fraction (South Dakota,[a] Texas,[a] Wisconsin)	0.13-0.37	0.38-0.62	0.63-0.87	0.88-1.12				
Alabama[a]	0.11-0.30	0.31-0.54	0.55-0.73	0.74-0.99				
Arizona: no brackets								same brackets
Florida	0.10-0.25	0.26-0.50	0.51-0.75	0.75-1.00				same brackets
Hawaii: no brackets								
Indiana	0.16-0.37	0.38-0.62	0.63-0.87	0.88-1.12	1.13-1.37			major fraction

							Notes
Michigan	0.13–0.31	0.32–0.54	0.55–0.81	0.82–1.08	1.09–1.35	1.36–1.62	1¢ for each 25¢
New York[a]	0.16–0.47	0.48–0.80	0.81–0.99					major fraction
Ohio[a]	0.16–0.31	0.32–0.51	0.52–0.71	0.72–1.00				same brackets, except extra 1¢ for 8–31¢ over even $
South Carolina	0.11–0.25	0.26–0.50	0.51–0.75	0.76–1.00				major fraction
Utah[a]	0.13–0.34	0.35–0.59	0.60–0.87	0.88–1.12	1.13–1.37			same brackets to $2.12, then major fraction
Virginia[b]	0.15–0.34	0.35–0.59	0.60–0.84	0.85–1.14	1.15–1.34			same brackets to $5.00, then major fraction
4.5% Rate							
Major Fraction (Washington[a])	0.12–0.33	0.34–0.55	0.56–0.77	0.78–0.99	1.00–1.22	1.23–1.44	1.45–1.66	major fraction
Tennessee[a]	0.11–0.32	0.33–0.54	0.55–0.76	0.77–0.99	1.00–1.21			
4.75% Rate							
California[a]	0.11–0.29	0.30–0.50	0.51–0.72	0.73–0.94				major fraction
5% Rate							
Major Fraction (Massachusetts, Minnesota)	0.10–0.29	0.30–0.49	0.50–0.69	0.70–0.89	0.90–1.09			
Illinois[b]	0.13–0.25	0.26–0.46	0.47–0.67	0.68–0.88	0.89–1.09	1.10–1.29	1.30–1.49	same brackets
Kentucky	0.11–0.25	0.25–0.46	0.47–0.67	0.68–0.88	0.89–1.09			major fraction
Maine	0.11–0.20	0.21–0.40	0.41–0.60	0.61–0.80	0.81–0.99			same brackets
Maryland	0.20	0.21–0.40	0.41–0.60	0.61–0.80	0.81–1.00			same brackets
Mississippi	0.12–0.26	0.27–0.47	0.48–0.68	0.69–0.88	0.89–1.09	1.10–1.29		brackets continue
New Jersey	0.11–0.25	0.26–0.46	0.47–0.67	0.68–0.88	0.89–1.00			same brackets
West Virginia	0.06–0.20	0.21–0.40	0.41–0.60	0.61–0.80	0.81–1.00	1.01–1.20		same brackets
5.75% Rate							
Nevada	0.09–0.26	0.27–0.43	0.44–0.60	0.61–0.78	0.79–0.95	0.96–1.13		major fraction
6% Rate							
Major Fraction (Rhode Island)	0.09–0.24	0.25–0.41	0.42–0.58	0.59–0.74	0.75–0.91	0.92–1.08		major fraction
District of Columbia	0.13–0.17	0.18–0.35	0.36–0.53	0.54–0.71	0.72–0.89	0.90–1.12		6¢ for each $ plus brackets
Pennsylvania	0.11–0.17	0.18–0.34	0.35–0.50	0.51–0.67	0.68–0.84	0.85–1.10		same brackets
7.5% Rate							
Major Fraction (Connecticut)	0.07–0.19	0.20–0.33	0.34–0.46	0.47–0.59	0.60–0.73	0.74–0.86		major fraction

[a] Local tax included here.
[b] Additional brackets given for state plus local combinations.

only are presented, unless there is a single predominant state-local combined rate. In that case, only the combined rate appears. The first line under each percentage rate in the table gives the figures for the major fraction rule.

Major Fraction Rule. Twelve states (Colorado, Connecticut, Massachusetts, Minnesota, Nebraska, Nevada, Oklahoma, Rhode Island, South Dakota, Texas, Wisconsin, and Washington) follow the major fraction rule throughout. Three more states (Indiana, Missouri, and Wyoming) follow that rule except for the first bracket. Any fraction less than one-half cent is disregarded, and any fraction of one-half or more is treated as another cent. This approach should, on the average, provide the retailer with no "breakage" at all; collections should equal the amount owed the state. Only if the retailer has a concentration of sales below the first bracket or a concentration just below a bracket figure will the retailer take in less than the amount owed the state. This approach, of course, minimizes the burden on the consumer.

Another group of eleven states uses the major fraction rule for larger purchases but provides somewhat more liberal treatment for the retailer on smaller ones. The breaking points are set below the major fraction figures. The breakage serves to compensate the retailer for the inability to collect on the very small purchases and helps to compensate for expenses in collecting the tax (unless the retailer is required to pay it to the state), yet it ensures that on the larger purchases the consumer does not pay more on the average than the figure indicated by the tax rate. Most states in this group shift to the major fraction rule at the sales figure directly above $1, but some do not, extending the initial bracket structure, or a modification of it, up to a higher figure.[6]

Brackets Favoring the Retailer throughout. The remaining states and the District of Columbia set up brackets for the under-$1 range yielding greater collections than the major fraction rule and thus more favorable to the retailer, unless breakage must be paid to the state. These states provide for the use of this same bracket system for the portion of larger sales in excess of an even dollar. This system does little for large transactions retailers, except to provide a small breakage. If used instead of vendor compensation, this bracket system is not necessarily objectionable. Most gain goes to the small-transactions retailer, who incurs the greatest expense in handling the tax. In the states requiring vendors to pay breakage, this rule in no way aids vendors but merely ensures greater tax collection than does the major fraction rule. Some states intend this and automatically audit any vendor not reporting more than the tax rate times taxable sales.

[6]California, Kentucky, North Carolina, New York, Rhode Island, and South Carolina shift around $1.00. Iowa, Kansas, Utah, Virginia, and Wyoming shift at purchase levels ranging from $2.12 (Utah) to $29.84 (Kansas).

Tax on Small Sales

In most states, vendors owe tax on sales under the first bracket figure, even though they cannot collect tax from their customers. No hardship results for the typical firm because of breakage on sales just over the breaking point. Several states, however, have provided exemptions of small sales. Vendors can exclude receipts from sales under these specified figures provided they have adequate records:

25¢: Wyoming (subject to 1% rate only, if records segregated)
19¢: Maryland
16¢: Ohio
15¢: Idaho
     Indiana (formula if not separated)
13¢: Vermont
12¢: Texas (if half of sales below that figure)
11¢: Pennsylvania
10¢: Maine (if primarily engaged in those sales)
     Florida
 7¢: Connecticut (half of such sales deductible)
 6¢: West Virginia

Rhode Island excludes 60% of sales below the first bracket. Several other states have special rules for vending machine operators, as subsequently noted.

The problem of small sales has become progressively less serious as the tax rates have gone up and the price level has risen. With 1933 prices and a 2% tax rate, many vendors would have substantial sales under the first bracket figure (typically 25¢). With a 5% tax rate and 1982 prices, few firms have any substantial concentration of sales under 11¢, the usual bracket line.

EXCESS COLLECTIONS OR BREAKAGE

Vendors are vitally interested in the definition of the exact amount of tax owed. There are two principal alternatives. First, the vendor owes an amount equal to the tax rate times the figure of taxable sales, regardless of how much is collected from the customer (calculated amount). Second, the vendor owes the exact amount collected or the figure of the tax rate times taxable sales, whichever is greater.

In twenty-eight states, plus the District of Columbia, the vendor owes an amount equal to the tax rate times the figure of taxable sales, regardless of the actual amounts collected from the customers.[7]

[7]Alabama, Arkansas, California (except when more is collected than the bracket system provides for), Connecticut, Hawaii, Idaho, Illinois, Indiana, Iowa, Kansas, Kentucky, Louisiana, Maine, Massachusetts, Minnesota, Missouri, Nebraska, Nevada, New Mexico, New York, North Dakota, South Carolina, South Dakota, Texas, Vermont, Virginia, Washington, and Wisconsin.

Seven states nominally require payment of any amount collected from the customers in excess of tax rate times taxable sales, but they make little serious effort to collect any excess, beyond ensuring that all amounts showing up as sales tax in the firm's tax accounts are paid. These states are Arizona, Colorado, Oklahoma, Michigan, Rhode Island, Utah, and Wyoming.

Varying, but serious, efforts to assure that the firm pays all that it collects are made by Florida, Georgia, Maryland, Mississippi, New Jersey, North Carolina, Ohio, Pennsylvania, Tennessee, and West Virginia. The tax due cannot be less than the figure of the tax rate times the taxable sales, regardless of the amount taken in. In Maryland and Pennsylvania, the tax return form has no line for calculated tax, but merely for total tax collected.[8]

The requirement that vendors keep an exact record of tax collected and remit this amount to the state is one of the most objectionable rules developed in sales taxation in the United States. (In Canada, the requirement resulted from constitutional problems.) To the extent that firms actually follow this requirement, they are involved in unnecessary bookkeeping. With a reasonable bracket schedule, the typical firm will collect so little above the tax rate figure that the requirement is unnecessary. In reality, the requirement is an attempt to introduce a costly refinement into the tax structure in hope of preventing "profiteering" from the tax, an occurrence that is in fact largely nonexistent. Many firms, especially smaller ones, do not take the requirement seriously and report no excess collections. Any attempt to enforce the rule precisely will divert substantial audit time from much more productive pursuits.

Distinct from this rule is one that requires the vendors to remit to the state any amount collected in tax above that required by law, other than amounts resulting from the prescribed bracket system. Such a rule, though seldom used, is needed to protect against a few firms that deliberately seek to make the consumer pay more than required, as, for example, on contract work.

USE OF FORMULA TO EXCLUDE SALES TAX FROM TAXABLE SALES

In general, the states that do not require payment of excess collections permit the firms to remove the tax from the figure of taxable sales by formula before ascertaining tax. For example, a firm recording price including tax would divide the figure of taxable sales by 103 (with a 3% tax rate) to eliminate the tax element. Exceptions, at least in theory, are Arizona and New Mexico, where the tax element must be recorded separately or be included in the base subject to tax. States that require payment of excess collections must require recording of tax separately from the price, though some

[8]Nevada administrators report that vendors sometimes pay actual collections, with resulting confusion in the return processing system.

permit the use of formulas based upon experience. Thus, if a store typically has a ratio of tax to taxable sales of 3.4%, it may, with approval, ascertain tax each month based on the 3.4 figure, instead of the basic tax rate of 3%.

In reporting excess collections, rule and practice are not identical. Without question, some firms in every state exclude the tax element by formula and then apply the tax rate to ascertain tax liability, instead of keeping a separate record of tax. Prevention of this practice is extremely difficult and objectionable. On the other hand, many firms, primarily larger ones, prefer to keep a separate record of tax collected for their own internal accounting and control. Tax is rung separately on the cash register and totaled separately or computer calculated by modern checkout scanning systems. When invoices are written, tax is listed. Sums of tax collected are credited to a tax account, and amounts paid in tax each month are charged against the account. This technique provides greater assurance that clerks are applying tax correctly and avoids including the tax sums in figures of gross sales. Most small firms, however, keep no such tax records, even if the law requires it.

Hawaii alone applies the tax to total receipts including reimbursement for tax, whether or not the tax is recorded separately. This rule interferes with precise shifting of the tax.

MEASURES OF TAX LIABILITY

Sales taxes differ in the precise definition of the measure of taxable sales.

Cash Basis versus Sales (Accrual) Basis

A question of major importance for vendors is whether liability for tax on credit sales is incurred in the period in which the sale is made or in the period in which collection is obtained. In other words, does the tax apply on a cash or sales (accrual) basis? Closely related to the question of cash versus sales is the question of whether deduction of bad debts is permitted when the sales basis is employed. With the cash basis, of course, the question does not arise.

The actual practice of the states in this matter is not easy to ascertain. Frequently, the question is not mentioned in the acts or even in the rulings and regulations. Even when it is mentioned, practice does not always agree with the wording of the published material. Twenty-seven of the forty-five sales tax states and the District of Columbia require the sales (accrual) basis as standard procedure for determining tax liability.[9] Four states have exceptions: Arkansas and Maine permit vendors to request a cash basis, South

---

[9]Arkansas, California, Connecticut, Florida, Idaho, Iowa, Louisiana, Maine, Massachusetts, Michigan, Nevada, New Jersey, New York, North Dakota, Ohio, Oklahoma, Pennsylvania, Rhode Island, South Carolina, South Dakota, Tennessee, Utah, Vermont, Virginia, Washington, West Virginia, and Wisconsin.

Carolina permits vendors to apply for a cash basis on installment sales, and Vermont vendors making over 80% of sales on installment are placed on the cash basis. Eight of this group, plus the District of Columbia, permit no deduction of bad debts: Arkansas, Connecticut, Massachusetts, Nevada, Pennsylvania, South Carolina, Washington, and West Virginia. Washington will allow a deduction after 1983. Of these, Pennsylvania allows deduction when goods are repossessed; West Virginia allows the deduction for repossessed goods only if a refund of tax is made to the purchaser.

The other states, in practice, permit use of either basis, often determined by the federal basis used. Three states (Alabama, Connecticut, and Illinois) indicate the cash or receipts basis as the standard. Most states encourage use of the sales basis, and many states will not allow a firm to change its basis without specific approval.

All states in this group permit deduction of bad debts if the sales basis is used. Otherwise, they would discriminate against the sales basis and encourage firms to use the cash basis. Normally, bad debts can be deducted only if written off for income tax purposes.

Relative Merits of the Two Approaches. Which approach is preferable? In general, the sales basis is more satisfactory than the cash basis for most types of vendor. Recognition of this fact has led states that initially used a straight cash payments basis to shift to widespread use of the sales basis. The sales approach conforms more satisfactorily with typical retail bookkeeping systems and is almost imperative for stores selling both exempt and taxable items. Mississippi, for instance, requires the sales basis for firms selling items at mixed (retail, wholesale) rates. If such items are charged in one month and partial payment is made in another, no basis exists for allocating the payments to the taxable and exempt items except some purely arbitrary one. Typical retail records will give a much more accurate figure of taxable sales during the period than of cash receipts from taxable sales. Likewise, applying tax to the entire amount of the transaction at the time the sale is made is much more satisfactory than applying it to subsequent cash payments. With many types of open credit accounts, the customer is not directly billed the amount to be paid but simply sends in a payment for the month. With formal conditional or installment sales contracts, technical problems are less serious. Even so, application of the tax to the entire sale is much simpler. The sales basis likewise ensures that the state receives its tax money during the period in which the consumer acquires the goods.

When a tax goes into effect or when a firm's credit sales are increasing rapidly, the vendor is required under the sales basis to pay a sum not yet received, thereby losing some working capital. The justification sometimes given is that the vendor should always make the customer pay tax at time of purchase, regardless of when the goods are paid for. West Virginia actually has such a provision in its act; the tax must be paid within thirty days of sale.

This approach is unworkable on the usual charge account or credit card type of transaction, however, and most firms do not find it feasible even on installment sales. Rather than collect the tax as an addition to the down payment, they much prefer to include the tax in the overall price on which monthly payments are figured. Actually, this problem is not serious. As soon as the tax gets into operation and a firm's credit sales are more or less uniform from month to month, payments made to the state each month are almost the same under one approach as under the other. The tax is merely being paid on a different set of transactions. Working capital requirements are somewhat greater.

Despite the merits of the sales approach, one difficulty prevents its universal application regardless of the requirements of the act, that is, the failure of some small retail shops to keep a record of sales. They keep records only of cash taken in. Some can be induced or pressured to keep records of sales, but others cannot. Fortunately, many of these firms have no credit sales or exempt sales.

In summary, the most satisfactory rule is one that requires use of the sales basis, except upon specific authorization of the revenue department to use the cash basis. This authorization will be granted only in exceptional cases in which the vendor's accounting is entirely on a cash basis, and its use will not significantly affect payment of correct amounts of tax. Most retailers will use the sales basis if they are given an option. States that allow either approach generally find that few firms using the cash basis should not use it. Earlier attempts to require the cash basis were clearly mistaken.

Deduction for Bad Debts and Returned and Repossessed Goods

As indicated earlier, eight states and the District of Columbia permit no deductions of bad debts. If free choice between sales and cash bases is given, allowance for bad debts must be granted, or firms will be encouraged to use the less satisfactory cash payments basis. If the sales basis is required except in a few isolated instances, the state has choice on the issue. There are two positions. One is that the state is entitled to its tax money even if the customer does not pay the vendor. If the vendor is willing to extend credit on the tax money, he thus indicates willingness to absorb the loss if payment is not made. The other position is that the sales tax is intended to rest upon consumers, and making retailers pay the tax when consumers fail to pay is unfair since collecting the tax at the time the sale is made is not feasible. The choice is not clear-cut between the two alternatives. The main advantage of deductibility is to avoid a major complaint of retailers and increase their willingness to cooperate in the operation of the sales tax. It also avoids any danger of discrimination in those instances in which particular firms, by authorization or unofficially, use the cash approach.

One question on bad debts concerns returned goods and repossessions.

Credit for tax is universally permitted when goods are returned, and refund, including the amount of tax, is given to the customer. Essentially, the sale is considered to have been cancelled. Some states set a time limit, for example, ninety days, beyond which credit is not allowed. On repossessed goods, the rules are less liberal. In most states that allow bad debt deductions, repossessions are treated essentially as bad debts, and credit is allowed for tax on the unpaid balance. In the other states, some deny adjustment on repossessions; others permit it. The repossessed articles are almost universally taxable when resold.

Trade-in Allowances

A major issue in the definition of the measure of the sales tax relates to trade-in allowances. Should the sales tax apply to the full price including the trade-in allowance? Should deduction of the trade-in allowance be permitted and the tax applied to the cash difference? Here the pattern is clear-cut: thirty states tax the difference (one more than in 1971 and fifteen more than in 1959);[10] fifteen states and the District of Columbia tax the full price.

Both groups, however, have exceptions. Seven states (Colorado, Minnesota, Nebraska, New Jersey, New York, North Dakota and Vermont) allow the deduction only if the goods were taken in for resale. Eleven (Florida, Illinois, Indiana, Kentucky, Louisiana, Mississippi, New Jersey, New Mexico, New York, South Carolina, and Tennessee) limit the deduction to allowances for "like goods." Mississippi limits the deduction privilege to sales tax, thus discriminating against interstate commerce. New Mexico does not permit deduction of mobile home trades. Kentucky has a separate motor vehicle tax levied on retail price (allowing no trade-in deduction); for trucks over 10,000 pounds, the base is 90% of retail price. Iowa limits the deduction to goods normally sold by the retailer, intended to be resold at retail and subject to tax on resale.

There are also exceptions in the states not allowing general deductions. Alabama and Massachusetts allow for trade-in allowance on motor vehicles, trailers, farm tractors, boats, and vehicle parts. Connecticut allows for trade-ins of vehicles, snowmobiles, vessels, and farm tractors. Maine taxes the difference after trades of like property for motor vehicles, tractors, boats, aircraft, and self-propelled timber-harvesting vehicles. Rhode Island deducts trades of new or used passenger cars. Finally, South Dakota deducts farm machinery trades (motor vehicles are not subject to the regular sales tax law).

The policy of taxation of the full price is clearly contrary to the position that sales taxes are levies on consumer spending. If a person buys a new car

---

[10]Arizona, Colorado, Florida, Georgia, Hawaii, Idaho, Illinois, Indiana, Iowa, Kansas, Kentucky, Louisiana, Minnesota, Mississippi, Missouri, Nebraska, New Jersey, New Mexico, New York, North Dakota, Pennsylvania, South Carolina, Tennessee, Texas, Utah, Vermont, Virginia, West Virginia, Wisconsin, and Wyoming tax the difference.

this year for a gross price of $8,500 and is allowed $1,500 on his old car, his expenditure on cars for the period is $7,000, not $8,500. In essence, he has used only $7,000 of the value of the original car and should not be taxed again on the remaining portion. Apart from the principle involved, the prime objection to taxation of the gross price is the constant complaint it engenders on the part of individual customers and retail stores. It is unfortunate to have a feature in a sales tax that gives rise to endless complaints that are well justified. The only argument for taxing the gross price is to maximize revenue for the state at a given rate, but this purpose is inadequate justification.

The policy in some states of allowing deduction of trade-in allowances only on motor vehicles involves gross discrimination. Reduction of the effective tax on motor vehicles compared to other goods increases the relative regressiveness of the tax. This policy is a political concession to the motor vehicle dealers, who are particularly concerned about the trade-in question because of the relatively large amounts involved.

Administratively, either rule on trade-in allowance works satisfactorily. If the gross price is taxable, there is some tendency to reduce both gross price and trade-in allowance in a transaction, leaving the dealer in the same position but reducing the tax. With taxation of cash difference, no similar adjustment is possible. Only falsification of the records to overstate the trade-in allowance will reduce the tax.

North Carolina and Arkansas exempt the traded-in article from tax when it is sold, a rule designed to reduce double taxation. Unfortunately, this rule does so in the wrong way and does not accomplish the desired result. Sales taxes are designed to rest on consumers, and there is no logic to exclusion of a used article from tax merely because it is a trade-in, particularly when other used articles are taxable, as is generally the case. Exemption of the trade-in attaches the tax to the object involved, whereas it must logically be considered in relation to consumer expenditures on taxed items. The goal in the treatment of trade-ins is not to free the subsequent purchaser from the tax but to avoid taxing the purchaser of the new items on a sum in excess of his actual expenditure on the commodity. Furthermore, the rule that trade-in articles are not taxed when sold creates difficulties for the vendor and complicates audit.

Deduction of Discounts

Cash, trade, and other discounts taken at the time of sale are deductible, since the intent is to tax the actual selling price. Discounts taken at a later date, such as for paying in a shorter period of time, are often not deductible. Trading stamps, however, are not regarded as discounts and their value is not deductible.

Tax status of goods obtained through the redemption of trading stamps is troublesome, and most states do not specify their treatment in their regulations and instructions. The most common rule is to regard the redemption with stamps as a type of purchase, and thus the customer is, quite justifiably, required to pay tax at the time he acquires the merchandise. The alternative is to treat the trading stamp company as the consumer of the items given in redemption, but this practice is discriminatory against the vendors of similar articles.

Treatment of coupons differs from state to state, although there is a pattern based on whether the coupon is issued by the vendor or by the product manufacturer. The tax typically applies to undiscounted price if the coupon is issued by the manufacturer because the vendor receives the coupon value from that source. Receipts from the sale thus come partly from the purchaser and partly from the manufacturer. Store coupons are treated simply as price reductions, so the tax applies to the net of coupon price.

Sales through Vending Machines

Sales of goods through vending machines pose another troublesome problem. With larger items, prices may be adjusted to take care of tax, or the size may be reduced—pieces of pie in an automat, for example. But with ten-cent sales, once numerous, the problem is difficult. Most states require full payment of tax even though the vendor cannot collect from the customer, a rule that has been subject to extensive complaint by the vending machine operators and their associations. Because of these difficulties, some adjustments have been made.

In twelve states, as noted earlier, relief is obtained because sales under a specified figure are not taxable, and the vendor is not required to remit tax if a record is kept of these sales. Alabama and South Dakota apply a lower rate (3%) to all vending machine sales. The District of Columbia taxes vending machine sales of food or drink at a lower (2%) rate. Washington taxes vending machine operators on 60% of gross receipts on sales below the first bracket, including food products. Several states, including Utah, Vermont, Louisiana, and the District of Columbia, exempt coin-operated laundries. Several states exempt vending machine sales below a certain figure: 30¢ in Colorado; 16¢ in Texas; 15¢ in Idaho, Nebraska, and North Dakota; 10¢ in Florida (25¢ for candy), Massachusetts, New Jersey, New York, South Carolina, and Virginia; and 1¢ in Connecticut, Illinois, Kentucky, and North Carolina. Maine exempts items of 15¢ or less if 50% of gross receipts are from vending machines. Others have more complex rules. Arkansas and California regard vendors of items sold for 15¢ or less as consumers, and payment is made on their purchases. Otherwise, California treats one-third of the gross receipts of food vendors as taxable. In similar fashion, Louisiana and Virginia tax vending machine items at their cost to the vendor, as does New Jersey for items priced at more than 10¢. Idaho exempts vending machine items sold for 15¢ or less; items priced between 16¢ and $1.01

are taxed at 11.7% of their purchase price to the vendor. Tennessee provides vending machine operators the option of paying $2.00 plus $1.00 per machine and 1.5% of gross receipts (2.5% for tobacco). Utah exempts vended items below $1.00 if the operator reports 120% of cost of items as goods consumed.

The solution to this problem is not easy. Complete exemption of vending machine sales is contrary to the intent of the general consumer levies and allows outright tax avoidance. Adjustments should not be permitted to interfere with the basic structure of the tax or to open avenues of escape that will lead to demands for others. These vendors must find means of making quality or quantity adjustments to escape the burden of the tax. Inflation has lessened the problem, since there are fewer items marketed at 10¢ or less.

In states with mandatory shifting provisions, special provisions must be made for the machine operators. Virginia and Washington specify, for instance, that vending machine items are presumed to sell on a tax-included basis. Usually, a sign on the machine that the price includes tax of a certain amount is regarded as adequate.

Other Tax Elements in Prices

Taxable price includes federal taxes except when imposed on the retailer and separately stated. A primary example is the telephone tax. State excises are often excludable if quoted separately.

This issue is not very significant. There is no inherent objection to the application of the tax to a price that includes another tax. Virtually any price includes some tax elements (for example, property taxes on articles used to produce the item). On the other hand, deduction does no particular harm except to complicate, in some instances, the application of tax by clerks.

The sales tax itself is universally excluded from the figure of taxable sales (except in Hawaii) to facilitate exact shifting.

Payment in Kind

Laws usually require that tax be paid on the total price including any amount paid for with goods, unless the trade-in rule is applicable.

STATE SALES TAX RATES

As of January 1982, the median state sales tax rate was 4%, with thirteen states using it, sixteen states (and the District of Columbia) above and sixteen states below. The distribution of rates is shown for 1982, 1981, 1971, and 1962 in table 2.2. Twenty-seven states have the same rate as they applied in 1971 and two (North Dakota and New Mexico) have lower rates in 1982 than in 1971, a reflection of the generally strong state finances of the decade.

TABLE 2.2 State Sales Tax Rates, 1962, 1971, 1981, and 1982

	No. of States			
Rate	1962	1971	Jan. 1981	Jan. 1982
2	11[a]	2	1	1
2.5	2	1	0	0
3, 3.125, 3.25	17	20[b]	16[c]	14[c]
3.5, 3.75	3	0	1[d]	1
4	3	14[a]	13	13
4.5, 4.75	0	1	3	2
5	0	6	8	9
5.5, 5.75	0	0	0	2[f]
6	0	1	2[a]	2[a]
6.5	0	0	0	0
7	0	0	0	0
7.5	0	0	1	1

[a] Plus District of Columbia (basic rate).
[b] One state at 3.750.
[c] One state at 3.125.
[d] One state at 3.750.
[e] One state at 4.750.
[f] One state at 5.750.

(Rates given are state rates alone. As explained in chapter 10, local sales taxes are universal or almost so in several states and used in part in others.)

Table 2.3 gives information on rates for selected years prior to 1950 and for each year since. In 1938, six states had 3% rates and sixteen, 2% rates. The median rate went to 3% in 1959, where it stayed until 1969. Although the median has increased little since 1971 (when it was between 3% and 4%), the number of states with rates of 5% or more has risen from seven to thirteen (plus the District of Columbia), and those with rates of 3% or less has fallen from twenty-two to fourteen. Only one state (Oklahoma) retains a 2% rate, and city taxes are widespread there.

TAX RATE DIFFERENTIATION

A basic characteristic of United States sales taxation has been the tendency to use a single uniform rate on all taxable transactions. In several instances, however, lower rates are provided in addition to those applied on sales under specified figures, a reduction that affects only the vendor, not the customer.

Principal categories include:

1. *Motor vehicles:* Currently, six states provide lower rates on motor vehicles than on other transactions: Alabama (1.5% vs. 4%); Mississippi (3% vs. 5%); New Mexico (2% vs. 3.5%, via a separate titling tax); North Caro-

lina (2%, with a maximum tax of $120, vs. 3%; the rule also applies to aircraft, boats, locomotives, and railroad cars); South Dakota (3% vs. 4% in a separate tax); and Virginia (2% in a separate tax vs. 3%; the rule applies to aircraft and watercraft as well). This differential, pushed by the motor vehicle dealers, is one of the most unwarranted features of state sales taxes. By usual standards, the tax on motor vehicles could well be higher than that on other goods if any differentiation were made at all. To tax motor vehicles less heavily than basic food and clothing is the height of absurdity by any usual standards of equity. The revenue loss is substantial because of the large volume of motor vehicle sales. One state taxes motor vehicle sales at a higher rate: Vermont (4%, or $300, whichever is smaller, vs. 3%).

2. *Food and drugs:* Illinois taxes food, drugs, and medical appliances at a reduced rate (2% in 1982) during a possible phase-in period toward full exemption. West Virginia taxed food at reduced rates during a phase-in period from 1979 to mid-1981, when full exemption became effective. South Dakota taxes food at a 3% rate (vs. 4%), using the Food Stamp definition of food. This reduction is equivalent to partial exemption and must be evaluated on the same basis as food exemption, discussed in chapter 3.

3. *Certain producers goods:* Several states provide lower rates on goods used for production purposes. Industrial machinery is taxed at lower rates in several states: Alabama (1.5% vs. 4%); Mississippi (1% vs. 5%); and North Carolina (1% vs. 3%, with a maximum on any one item of $80). Lower rates apply to industrial fuel in Mississippi, North Carolina, and Tennessee (1.5% vs. 4.5%; fuel used directly in production is fully exempt). Tennessee taxes water sold to manufacturers at 1%. Farm equipment receives a lower rate in Mississippi (1% for tractors, 3% for other implements, vs. 5%); North Carolina; Florida (self-propelled or power drawn only, 3% vs. 4%); Minnesota (3% vs. 5%); North Dakota (2% vs. 3%, farm machinery and irrigation equipment); and South Dakota (3% vs. 4%, farm machinery, irrigation equipment, and agricultural aircraft). New York applied a temporary tax (September 1, 1980–February 28, 1981) on parts, tools, and supplies directly and predominantly in production (2%). Tennessee is phasing out the tax on farm and industrial machinery; until 1983 there will be various lower rates on these goods. Finally, all sales of horses and mules are taxed at 1% in North Carolina. These represent compromises between the argument to tax such equipment fully and the argument that it should be completely exempt and can be evaluated on the same basis as exemption. Taxing it partially is neither more difficult nor easier than exempting it.

There are a few other miscellaneous deviations. Tennessee and Utah apply lower rates to fuels for domestic use (1.5% and 1%, respectively). Connec-

TABLE 2.3 State Sales Tax Rates, 1934, 1938, and 1950–82 (January, except as otherwise indicated)

State	1934	1938	1950	1951	1952	1953	1954	1955
Alabama	—	2	2	2	3	3	3	3
Arizona	1.5	2	2	2	2	2	2	2
Arkansas	—	2	2	2	2	2	2	2
California	2.5	3	3	3	3	3	3	3
Colorado	—	2	2	2	2	2	2	2
Connecticut	—	—	2	2	2	3	3	3
Florida	—	—	3	3	3	3	3	3
Georgia	—	—	—	—	3	3	3	3
Hawaii	—	2.5	2.5	2.5	2.5	2.5	2.5	2.5
Idaho	—	—	—	—	—	—	—	—
Illinois	2	3	2	2	2	2	2	2
Indiana	—	—	—	—	—	—	—	—
Iowa	—	2	2	0	2	2	2	2
Kansas	—	2	2	2	2	2	2	2
Kentucky	—	—	—	—	—	—	—	—
Louisiana	—	2	2	2	2	2	2	2
Maine	—	—	—	—	2	2	2	2
Maryland	—	—	2	2	2	2	2	2
Massachusetts	—	—	—	—	—	—	—	—
Michigan	3	3	3	3	3	3	3	3
Minnesota	—	—	—	—	—	—	—	—
Mississippi	2	2	2	2	2	2	2	2
Missouri	—	2	2	2	2	2	2	2
Nebraska	—	—	—	—	—	—	—	—
Nevada	—	—	—	—	—	—	—	2
New Jersey	—	—	—	—	—	—	—	—
New Mexico	—	2	2	2	2	2	2	2
New York	—	—	—	—	—	—	—	—
North Carolina	3	3	3	3	3	3	3	3
North Dakota	—	2	2	2	2	2	2	2
Ohio	—	3	3	3	3	3	3	3
Oklahoma	1	2	2	2	2	2	2	2
Pennsylvania	—	—	—	—	—	—	1	1
Rhode Island	—	—	1	1	2	2	2	2
South Carolina	—	—	—	3	3	3	3	3
South Dakota	1	3	3	3	2	2	2	2
Tennessee	—	—	2	2	2	2	2	3
Texas	—	—	—	—	—	—	—	—
Utah	2	2	2	2	2	2	2	2
Vermont	—	—	—	—	—	—	—	—
Virginia	—	—	—	—	—	—	—	—
Washington	—	2	3	3	3	3	3	3.3
West Virginia	2	2	2	2	2	2	2	2
Wisconsin	—	—	—	—	—	—	—	—
Wyoming	—	2	2	2	2	2	2	2
District of Columbia	—	—	—	—	—	—	2	2

1956	1957	1958	1959	1960	1961	1962	1963	1964	1965
3	3	3	3	3	3	3	3	4	4
2	2	2	2	3	3	3	3	3	3
2	3	3	3	3	3	3	3	3	3
3	3	3	3	3	3	3	3	3	3
2	2	2	2	2	2	2	2	2	2
3.5	3	3	3	3	3	3.5	3.5	3.5	3.5
3	3	3	3	3	3	3	3	3	3
3	3	3	3	3	3	3	3	3	3
2.5	2.5	3.5	3.5	3.5	3.5	3.5			
—	—	—	—	—	—	—			
2.5	2.5	2.5	2.5	3	3	3.5	3.5	3.5	3.5
—	—	—	—	—	—	—	—	2	2
2.5	2.5	2	2	2	2	2	2	2	2
2	2	2	2.5	2.5	2.5	2.5	2.5	2.5	2.5
—	—	—	—	—	3	3	3	3	3
2	2	2	2	2	2	2	2	2	2
2	2	2	2	2	2	2	2	4	4
2	2	2	3	3	3	3	3	3	3
—	—	—	—	—	—	—	—	—	—
3	3	3	3	3	4	4	4	4	4
—									
3	3	3	3	3	3	3	3	3	3.5
2	2	2	2	2	2	2	2	3	3
—	—	—	—	—	—	—	—	—	—
2	2	2	2	2	2	2	2	2	2
—	—	—	—	—	—	—	—	—	—
2	2	2	2	2	2	2	2	3	3
—	—	—	—	—	—	—	—	—	—
3	3	3	3	3	3	3	3	3	3
2	2	2	2	2	2	2	2	2.25	2.25
3	3	3	3	3	3	3	3	3	3
2	2	2	2	2	2	2	2	2	2
1	3	3	3	4	4	4	4	5	5
2	2	3	3	3	3	3	3	3	3.5
3	3	3	3	3	3	3	3	3	3
2	2	2	2	2	2	2	2	2	2
3	3	3	3	3	3	3	3	3	3
—	—	—	—	—	—	2	2	2	2
2	2	2	2	2	2	2.5	2.5	3	3
—	—	—	—	—	—	—	—	—	—
—	—	—	—	—	—	—	—	—	—
3.3	3.3	3.3	3.3	4	4	4	4	4	4
2	2	2	2	2	2	3	3	3	3
—	—	—	—	—	—	—	3	3	3
2	2	2	2	2	2	3	3	3	3
2	2	2	2	2	2	2	3	3	3

TABLE 2.3 (*continued*)

State	1966	1967	1968	1969	1970	1971	1972	1973
Alabama	4	4	4	4	4	4	4	4
Arizona	3	3	3	3	3	3	3	3
Arkansas	3	3	3	3	3	3	3	3
California	3	3	4	4	4	4	3.75	4.75
Colorado	3	3	3	3	3	3	3	3
Connecticut	3.5	3.5	3.5	3.5	5	5	6.5	7
Florida	3	3	3	4	4	4	4	4
Georgia	3	3	3	3	3	3	3	3
Hawaii	4	4	4	4	4	4	4	4
Idaho	3	3	3	3	3	3	3	3
Illinois	3.5	3.5	4.25	4.25	4	4	4	4
Indiana	2	2	2	2	2	2	2	2
Iowa	2	2	3	3	3	3	3	3
Kansas	3	3	3	3	3	3	3	3
Kentucky	3	3	3	5	5	5	5	5
Louisiana	2	2	2	2	2	3	3	3
Maine	4	4	4.5	4.5	5	5	5	5
Maryland	3	3	3	3	4	4	4	4
Massachusetts	—	3	3	3	3	3	3	3
Michigan	4	4	4	4	4	4	4	4
Minnesota	—	—	3	3	3	3	4	4
Mississippi	3.5	3.5	3.5	5	5	5	5	5
Missouri	3	3	3	3	3	3	3	3
Nebraska	—	—	2.5	2	2	2.5	2.5	2.5
Nevada	2	2	3[d]	3	3	3	3	3
New Jersey	—	3	3	3	3	5	5	5
New Mexico	3	3	3	3	4	4	4	4
New York	2	2	2	2	2	3	4	4
North Carolina	3	3	3	3	3	3	3	3
North Dakota	2.25	2.25	3	3	4	4	4	4
Ohio	3	3	4	4	4	4	4	4
Oklahoma	2	2	2	2	2	2	2	2
Pennsylvania	5	5	6	6	6	6	6	6
Rhode Island	4	4	5	5	5	5	5	5
South Carolina	3	3	3	3	4	4	4	4
South Dakota	3	3	3	3	4	4	4	4
Tennessee	3	3	3	3	3	3	3.5	3.5
Texas	2	2	2	3	3.25	3.25	4	4
Utah	3	3	3	3	4	4	4	4
Vermont	—	—	—	—	3	3	3	3
Virginia	—	2	2	3	3	3	3	3
Washington	4.2	4.2	4.5	4.5	4.5	4.5	4.5	4.5
West Virginia	3	3	3	3	3	3	3	3
Wisconsin	3	3	3	3	4	4	4	4
Wyoming	2.5	2.5	3	3	3	3	3	3
District of Columbia	3	3	4	4	4	4	4	5

All rates shown are the basic figure when states use multiple rates.
—indicates tax not in operation.

[a] Increased to 5% May 1, 1982.
[b] Increased to 3.5% from May 1, 1982, to December 31, 1982.

1974	1975	1976	1977	1978	Jan. 1979	July 1979	Jan. 1980	Jan. 1981	Jan. 1982
4	4	4	4	4	4	4	4	4	4
3	4	4	4	4	4	4	4	4	4
3	3	3	3	3	3	3	3	3	3
3.75	4.75	4.75	4.75	4.75	4.75	4.75	4.75	4.75	4.75
3	3	3	3	3	3	3	3	3	3
6.5	6	7	7	7	7	7	7	7.5	7.5
4	4	4	4	4	4	4	4	4	4[a]
3	3	3	3	3	3	3	3	3	3
4	4	4	4	4	4	4	4	4	4
3	3	3	3	3	3	3	3	3	3
4	4	4	4	4	4	4	4	4	4
4	4	4	4	4	4	4	4	4	4
3	3	3	3	3	3	3	3	3	3
3	3	3	3	3	3	3	3	3	3
5	5	5	5	5	5	5	5	5	5
3	3	3	3	3	3	3	3	3	3
5	5	5	5	5	5	5	5	5	5
4	4	4	4	5	5	5	5	5	5
3	3	5	5	5	5	5	5	5	5
4	4	4	4	4	4	4	4	4	4
4	4	4	4	4	4	4	4	4	5
5	5	5	5	5	5	5	5	5	5
3	3	3	3	3.125	3.125	3.125	3.125	3.125	3.125
2.5	2.5	2.5	3[c]	3	3	3	3	3	3[b]
3	3	3	3	3	3	3	3	3	5.75[d]
5	5	5	5	5	5	5	5	5	5
4	4	4	4	4	3.75	3.75	3.75	3.75	3.5
4	4	4	4	4	4	4	4	4	4
3	3	3	3	3	3	3	3	3	3
4	4	4	3	3	3	3	3	3	3
4	4	4	4	4	4	4	4	5	5
2	2	2	2	2	2	2	2	2	2
6	6	6	6	6	6	6	6	6	6
5	5	5	6	6	6	6	6	6	6
4	4	4	4	4	4	4	4	4	4
4	4	4	4	4	4	4	4	5	4
3.5	3.5	3.5	4.5	4.5	4.5	4.5	4.5	4.5	4.5
4	4	4	4	4	4	4	4	4	4
4	4	4	4	4	4	4	4	4	4
3	3	3	3	3	3	3	3	3	3[e]
3	3	3	3	3	3	3	3	3	3
4.5	4.5	4.5	4.6	4.6	4.6	4.5	4.5	4.5	5.5[f]
3	3	3	3	3	3	3	3	3	5
4	4	4	4	4	4	4	4	4	4[g]
3	3	3	3	3	3	3	3	3	3
5	5	5	5	5	5	5	5	6	6

[c] Increased to 3.5% from July 1, 1977, to January 1, 1978.

[d] Includes 1% state-wide rate for county school support. Effective May 1, 1981, combined rate increased to 5.75% (2% state, 1.5% school support, and 2.25% county, all mandatory).

[e] Increased to 4% from July 1, 1982, to July 1, 1987.

[f] Scheduled for reduction to 4.5%, June 30, 1983.

[g] Increased to 5% May 1, 1982.

ticut taxes specified services at 3.5% (vs. 7.5%). Hotels and meals are taxed at 5% instead of 3% in Vermont. Maryland taxes passenger car rentals at 8% (vs. 5%). West Virginia and Mississippi tax mobile homes purchased as a principal residence at 3%. In the District of Columbia, hotels are taxed at 10% and meals at 8%, against the regular 6% rate; motor vehicle parking (12%) and renting (8%) also bear higher rates. Mississippi uses a 1% rate on fuel for vehicles, and Illinois schedules a gradual taxing of gasohol (exempt through mid-1982, 1% from then to mid-1983, and increasing to 4% by mid-1985). The state of Washington has a special tax of 15% (plus a unit tax) on spirits and strong beer. Rates on certain utility services differ from the sales tax rates in some states, where separate rates are employed.

Rate differentiation in a retail sales tax causes exactly the same problems as exemptions. Vendors must differentiate among the products in the various categories and keep appropriate records. Audit is made much more difficult, and the way is paved for evasion. The problem is least serious with specialized establishments, such as hotels, or with industrial machinery not sold to individuals. It is most difficult with goods regularly sold by stores also selling other goods to the public. If several rates are introduced, as sometimes proposed, and applied to a variety of types of goods, the tasks of both vendors and auditors would become almost hopeless. There is little justification for doing so in a tax structure in which effective progression can be established through income taxes. Differential rates create a new form of inequality, namely discrimination among families on the basis of their preferences for different goods. Small degrees of differentiation as, for example, 2% on food and 3% on other goods, is of very doubtful desirability. Administrative disadvantages outweigh any possible equity gain. The most objectionable differentiation of all is the lower rate provided motor vehicles in several states. This rate violates all usual standards of equity.

The peculiar feature of the North Carolina law setting a maximum tax on particular items is very troublesome, because of the problem of defining what constitutes a single item and because of its obvious violation of the most elementary standards of equity.

NONRETAIL ELEMENTS IN SALES TAXES

Most sales taxes are purely retail taxes, no taxes being applied to any nonretail sales. Arizona, Hawaii, Louisiana, and Mississippi include certain nonretail transactions in their sales tax structures.[11] Two other states, Washington and West Virginia, employ separate gross receipts business taxes in addition to their sales taxes, as does Indiana with the dying remnant of the gross income tax.

[11]New Mexico formerly included some nonretail sales, which have now been excluded from the tax.

Arizona.   The Arizona tax has a relatively broad coverage of public utilities, including transportation, and applies to mining, oil and gas production, lumbering, and contracting. Its nonretail coverage, other than the severance tax portion on mines and lumbering, is limited to a 0.25% tax on meat packing and on wholesale sales of livestock feed, in lieu of a retail tax on this product.

Mississippi.   In Mississippi, a 0.125% tax is applied to all wholesale sales made for resale at retail, that is, the last wholesale transaction. Although this provision yields little revenue (about $10 million per year), its primary purpose is to get wholesalers to keep better records to facilitate audit of retail purchases. On the whole, the tax is probably more trouble than it is worth, though relatively harmless, since it does not cumulate in the fashion of the Hawaii tax noted later. In addition, a 5% tax is applied to sales to retailers by wholesale suppliers of beer, whiskey, motor fuel, soft drinks, and soft drink syrup. The retailer is subject to tax on his sales at the regular rate but is allowed to deduct the tax he has paid on his purchases. This rule was introduced in the fields of retailing where losses through evasion were heavy to ensure that at least the retailer's purchase price would be reached. It involves limited use of the value-added principle and is not inequitable or discriminatory. Most states, however, regard this system as unnecessary, believing that they can effectively enforce tax against the retailers in these fields.[12]

Louisiana.   Whereas the Mississippi tax makes limited use of the value-added principle, the Louisiana tax has extended the principle to cover all fields of business at the wholesale-retail level. All sales to retailers are subject to the basic state sales tax rate of 3%. Retailers, in turn, receive credit for tax paid to their suppliers on their purchases and are thus taxed only on their margins (value added). The state revenue administration is convinced that the change has improved administration and raised revenues. In 1965, the first full year the system was in operation, revenue increased 14% over the previous year, whereas the annual increase in revenue had been about 6% for the preceding five years. Some firms reported as deductions because of tax they had paid more than they had been reporting as tax due on sales.[13]

This system is not discriminatory against any firm and is not objectionable from the standpoint of the sales tax. The basic question is whether collection at the wholesale level is necessary. Could the same results be attained by more intensive audit of retailers, with check on wholesalers' records when necessary? The Louisiana administration is convinced that the system is more effective. Most states, however, do not believe that it is necessary.

---

[12]New Jersey employed similar wholesaler collection for alcoholic beverages until deregulation of liquor prices in 1979 destroyed the general price basis used for application of the tax.

[13]A.J. Mouton, "Collection by the Wholesaler of the Retail Sales Tax," in *Proceedings of the National Tax Association for 1965,* pp. 286–89.

Hawaii. The retail sales tax in Hawaii is a portion of the state's so-called general excise tax, a very broad tax covering all sales by processors, manufac-, turers, wholesalers, and service establishments as well as sales by retailers. There are two basic rates: a 4% tax on retail sales; all services, including professional; all rentals; and a 0.5% tax on all nonretail sales of goods.[14] The tax therefore takes on the form of a complete turnover tax on the old German *Umsatzsteuer* pattern, but the adverse consequences are mitigated by the rate being only 0.5% on nonretail transactions. Even with the low rate, however, the tax inevitably favors the integrated firm over the nonintegrated and encourages integration. Complaints against it constitute a major obstacle to increased revenue from the nonretail portion of the tax. The state also uses a general corporate income tax. In fiscal year 1979, the yield from the various parts of the tax was as follows:

Activity	Thousands of $
Retailing	208,498
Services	53,127
Contracting	46,319
Rentals	63,938
Sugar processing	1,282
Pineapple canning	733
Producing	802
Manufacturing	2,554
Wholesaling[a]	11,865
Use	7,802
Insurance commissions	543
All others	32,796
Total	430,259

[a]Includes certain retail sales, such as livestock feed, classified for tax purposes as wholesale sales.

SEPARATE GROSS RECEIPTS LEVIES

Washington and West Virginia impose general gross receipts taxes on most forms of business as general business levies, in Washington in lieu of corporate income or other forms of general business tax.[15] Detailed examination of these levies is beyond the scope of this study, but the rates are noted here. The operation of the taxes is coordinated with that of the sales tax, with a single return employed and a joint audit.

[14]The rate on insurance solicitors is 0.15%.
[15]Municipalities in both states levy business and occupation taxes as well, locally administered in both instances.

Washington. A basic rate of 0.44% is applied to extracting, most manufacturing and wholesaling, printing, cold storage, broadcasting, government contracting, road construction, and retailing. Other rates are as follows:

Activity	%
Flour milling, seafood processing	0.125
Processing dried peas	0.25
Processing meat	0.33
Manufacturing aluminum	0.40
Fruit and vegetable processing	0.30
Wholesaling grain, etc.	0.01
Wholesaling cigarettes	0.176
Service activities	1.00
Travel agent commissions	0.25
Manufacturing nuclear fuel assemblies	0.25
Timber harvesters	0.29
Real estate brokers	1.00

The large number of rates is a source of major complications in operation, and there is no logical basis for distinctions.[16]

West Virginia. The state gross receipts tax rates were in 1982 as follows: severance, 2.2% to 8.63% on the extraction of minerals, oil, and timber; manufacturers, 0.88%; wholesalers, 0.27%; retailers, 0.55%; public utilities, 2.46% to 4.4%; contracting, 2.2%; amusement businesses, 0.71%; and services, rentals, and other business, 1.15%.

Note that these taxes apply to retailers as well as to other types of business. The taxes are not quoted separately, however, but are regarded as a part of overhead. The Washington law specifically states that such taxes shall constitute a part of the operating overhead of the businesses.

Indiana. Indiana retains the remnants of its old gross income tax. Business firms are required to pay a 2% corporate income tax or the gross income tax, whichever is higher. In 1981, the rate on wholesaling, advertising, hotels or motels, and dry cleaning or laundering was 0.03% and on other activities, 1.35%. A phase-out of the gross tax began in 1977; both rates decline by 0.005% each year. The tax will be eliminated by that process in 2007, unless the phase-out rate changes. Except in bad economic periods, importance of the gross income tax declines each year. Because of the multiple application of the tax without credit, the tax is objectionable because it encourages integration of business and tends to discriminate against the smaller, nonintegrated business.[17]

---

[16]An additional litter control tax of 0.015% is placed on certain retail, wholesale, and manufacturing activities.

[17]Low-rate gross receipts taxes have recently been repealed in Alaska (1979) and New Jersey (1977).

3. Exclusions and Exemptions from Sales Taxes

No state sales tax applies to all sales of all tangible personal property. Two major types of sale are not subject to tax, either as a result of the definition of taxable sales or by specific exemption in the act. The first category, which will be called *exclusions*, consists of specified classes of goods purchased for business rather than personal use. The second consists of specific *exemptions* of consumption goods. The two categories, of course, overlap somewhat.

EXCLUSIONS OF PRODUCERS GOODS—NONAGRICULTURAL

In principle, sales taxes are designed to be levies on consumer expenditures. If goods used in production are taxed as well as the final products, an element of multiple taxation of the same consumer expenditures is introduced. There are several specific objections:
1. The tax will not constitute a uniform percentage of consumer expenditures, since some goods require more taxable producers goods than others, per dollar of sales. The consequence of the multiple taxation is discrimination against certain families because of their relative preferences for various goods. Some consumer "excess burden" occurs as persons shift from high-tax goods to low-tax goods. Commodities that the legislature seeks to exempt will carry some tax burden.
2. The tax will affect the choice among various methods of production, since the tax liability will not be uniform with all methods, thus causing loss of efficiency in production processes. Replacement of old equipment will be delayed.
3. Firms will be given incentive to produce for their own use goods that are subject to tax, since they can reduce tax liability by so doing. They will pay tax only on materials.
4. Firms in the state will be placed at a competitive disadvantage in competing with firms in states not taxing producers goods and in selling in world markets. The trend toward value-added sales taxation in Europe is a result largely of efforts to exclude producers goods from tax to hold down export prices.

To fully implement this objective, the sales tax would be confined to purchases for personal consumption only, and purchases for business (including agriculture) would be excluded from the tax. No state has ever attempted to implement the objective completely, however, although the West Virginia sales tax (as distinguished from its business tax) approximates it. In practice, sales taxes have been established in such a way as to exclude—in all cases and usually by definition of taxable sales—sales for direct resale, and sales of materials that become physical ingredients of goods produced for sale by the purchasers. Some states have stopped at this point. Others have excluded certain other major categories of producers goods from tax. Technically, these additional exclusions take the legal form of exemption, but they differ from the usual exemptions in intent.

Sales for Resale

The basic taxing clauses of the various acts (except in Hawaii) apply to "sales for use or consumption and not for resale." Thus, any purchase made for resale is automatically excluded from the coverage of the tax, without specific exemption. Under early interpretations, a purchase of a material or part acquired to be incorporated physically into property being produced for resale was held to be a purchase for resale and therefore automatically free of tax. Some later state acts specifically exempted such materials and parts to avoid any possible doubt. Therefore, either by interpretation or specific provision, physical ingredients or parts are exempt from the retail sales taxes. The primary exceptions to this rule are in Hawaii, in which sales for resale, including sales of materials, are taxed but at a rate of 0.5% instead of the basic 4.0% figure, and in Mississippi, in which sales to a licensed retailer for resale are taxed at the 0.125% wholesale rate.

Resale certificates. To facilitate control of the exemption of physical ingredients and parts, forty-one states and the District of Columbia require the purchaser to execute a resale certificate to indicate that he is making the purchase for resale (figure 3.1). Kentucky, Missouri, Tennessee, and other states print and distribute the form. Most other states prescribe the form. Arizona and Washington are exceptions; Washington suggests the form and identifies required information. In some states, such as South Carolina, the certificate may take the form of a rubber stamp on invoices. Ordinarily, a retailer executes only one blanket certificate for the supplier indicating the nature of the commodities to be purchased tax free for resale. (The vendor keeps the certificate on file and, so long as it is in effect, the retailer can purchase, tax free, items of the classes indicated without executing a separate certificate for each transaction.) In most states, certificates are valid for an indefinite period. When a firm makes a purchase for resale from other than a usual supplier, it executes a certificate for that specific transaction. In vir-

Form ST-5
(Rev. 5-80)
RV01003-02

MINNESOTA DEPARTMENT OF REVENUE
SALES AND USE TAX DIVISION

RESALE EXEMPTION CERTIFICATE

I, the undersigned purchaser, hereby certify that I am engaged in the business of selling, leasing or rentir

_____
(List items sold, leased or rented)

_____

and that the tangible personal property described below, which I shall purchase, lease or rent fro

_____
Name of Seller

_____
Address

will be resold, leased or rented by me; however, if any such property is used for any purpose other than retentio
demonstration or display while holding it for sale, lease or rental in the regular course of business, I understand th
I am required to report and pay the tax on the purchase price of such property.

Detailed description of property to be purchased for resale: _____

_____

_____

_____

Check applicable box: ☐ Single purchase certificate   ☐ Blanket certificate

If blanket certificate is checked, this certificate continues in force until cancelled by the purchaser. If the purchas
uses this property for other than exempt purposes, and fails to file a sales or use tax return declaring the taxab
use of such property, with the intent to evade the tax, the purchaser will be subject to the full penalty of the lav

_____   _____
Purchaser's Business Name   Signature of Authorized Purchaser

_____   _____
Address   Title

_____   _____
City   State   Zip Code   Date

┌─────────────────────────────────────┐
│ Purchaser's Sales and Use Tax   │
│   Account Number   │   If no number,
│   │   state reason _____
└─────────────────────────────────────┘

NOTE: Sellers must keep this certificate as a part of their records.
Incomplete certificates cannot be accepted in good faith.

FIGURE 3.1   RESALE CERTIFICATE, MINNESOTA

tually all cases, the certificate must contain the registration number of the purchaser for audit control. One basic rule is widely followed: purchases can be made tax free for resale only by a registered vendor. The only exceptions are purchases of certain materials or containers by farmers and, in some states, by nonregistered manufacturers and purchases in the state by out-of-state vendors for resale outside the state. A supplier without a valid resale certificate in his possession is liable for tax on the transaction. Every sale is assumed to be a retail sale unless there is evidence to the contrary.

When a blanket certificate is in effect, the retailer may make all purchases of goods of a type regularly handled tax free under certificate, even if some particular items are to be used for the store's own purpose and are thus taxable. The store must, of course, report and pay tax on these items. The retailer cannot legally buy tax free under certificate items other than those handled for resale. Four states (Colorado, Michigan, Mississippi, and Oklahoma) require no certificate but do require that the supplier have evidence that the sale was for resale and thus a file of purchaser registration numbers or indication of numbers on the invoices.

The states do not usually require that each invoice bear the purchaser's registration number or a statement that the purchase is made for resale. The states that attempt to enforce such a rule find it difficult.

Resale certificates are unnecessary for successful operation of a sales tax, but they offer certain merits for very little additional effort. They provide a more systematic file of evidence of sales for resale and lessen the tendency for businesses to buy items tax free from other than their regular suppliers when they are going to use them for taxable purposes. A grocer planning to buy a TV set will be less likely to do so tax free if he has to sign a specific certificate for a TV supplier than if all he has to do is to mention his sales tax registration number. Some evasion will occur in either case, but certificates should reduce it. All states introducing the tax in the last thirty years have included this requirement.

Responsibility when certificate is issued.   In the absence of a certificate, the vendor (supplier) is liable for tax. Suppose, however, that a certificate has validly been executed by a registered firm and the item has been used for a taxable purpose and not reported by the purchaser. In general, in all states, if the item is of a type regularly handled by the purchaser for resale, the buyer is solely responsible for payment of the tax. The supplier is not expected to distinguish between the light bulbs bought by a hardware store for use in the store and those bought for resale. When the goods are not normally handled by the purchaser, practice varies substantially in regard to liability, and precise characterization is difficult. Discussion of the problem with officials of the states suggests the following approaches:

1. Arkansas, Arizona, Hawaii, Michigan, Mississippi, Oklahoma, and South Dakota hold the vendor (supplier) exclusively responsible. The ven-

dor remains responsible in South Carolina, but a certificate shifts the burden of proof away from the vendor.

2. Twenty-seven states and the District of Columbia follow a "good faith" (or "reasonable care") rule. If the vendor took the certificate *in good faith*, and it appeared reasonable that the purchase was made for resale, the vendor is free of liability, and the tax is collected from the buyer. In practice, the buyer is assessed in most cases. Pennsylvania specifies three items for a good-faith test: the business of the purchaser, the item purchased, and the exemptive basis claimed.

3. Ten states go still further in emphasizing the liability of the buyer: Alabama, Colorado, Florida, Indiana, Iowa, New York, North Dakota (the vendor is freed by law), Ohio, Utah, and Wyoming (although the state can go after either party). The vendor firm is virtually freed of responsibility if it has a certificate from the buyer, except in the most extreme cases.

The trend has been definitely toward placing primary or exclusive liability on the buyer, partly as a result of complaints and federal review of taxation of interstate transactions. In general, the suppliers cannot be expected to police the use of resale certificates. Firms make occasional sales of goods they do not normally handle, and they should be able to purchase these goods tax free. If certificates are wrongfully used, the purchaser, not the vendor, seeks to violate the law.

Containers

A special problem is created by containers, wrapping paper, and similar items. The treatment, however, is surprisingly uniform in conformity with the following rules:

1. Purchase by a retailer of nonreturnable containers, which go to a subsequent customer with the merchandise and are not returned, is regarded as a purchase for resale and is tax free under resale certificate. The container is considered to be sold with the commodity and thus to form an ingredient part of it. Containers include, among others items, tin cans and non-returnable bottles, wrapping paper, bags, and cord for tying packages.

   Administration of the exemption of containers is complicated for farmers. They frequently buy sacks, boxes, and baskets for handling their produce, but the farmers are not registered for sales tax. The items are normally exempt, but the vendor is required to show evidence the sale was made for farm use. In some states, a special certificate is required of the farmer.

2. When containers are not sold with the merchandise and are returned to the firm owning them, their purchase by the retailer is taxable. Thus, soft drink bottles are taxable when purchased by the bottling plant. Although

some are not actually returned, they are insignificant for tax liability. Deposits required of customers are not subject to tax—a rule that store clerks are very careless in applying. A simpler method is to tax the deposit and give a refund of the tax along with the refund on the containers.

Containers that are used in the rendering of services (such as bags in which cleaning and pressing firms place suits) are taxable except in those states that tax the services. Maine, however, exempts reusable containers and containers that go with an item on which a service has been performed; Iowa taxes purchase of some containers used in rendering a taxed service.

Consumables

Two-thirds of the sales tax states extend the exemption of materials to include some or all items that are directly used in the production but do not actually become physical ingredients of the product produced (e.g., processing chemicals, catalysts). The exact coverage of this exemption varies. The states may be categorized as follows:

1. Fully taxing these items are seventeen states and the District of Columbia: Arizona, Arkansas (unless item becomes recognizable component), California, Florida, Hawaii, Illinois, Louisiana, Missouri (except anodes with life less than one year), Nebraska, Nevada, New Mexico, New York (unless used as a bath), North Dakota, South Dakota, Utah, Washington (some catalysts are exempt), Wyoming (unless used to destruction).
2. North Carolina taxes them at a lower rate.
3. Limited exemptions apply in Alabama, Colorado, and Kansas.
4. Wider or general exemptions appear in twenty-four states: Connecticut, Georgia, Idaho, Indiana (direct consumption in direct production only), Iowa, Kentucky, Maine, Maryland, Massachusetts, Michigan, Minnesota, Mississippi, New Jersey, Ohio, Oklahoma, Pennsylvania (direct use only), Rhode Island, South Carolina, Tennessee, Texas, Vermont (catalysts), Virginia, West Virginia, and Wisconsin (manufacturing only).

Industrial Fuel

Most of the states providing wide exemption for consumables also exempt industrial fuel. Exceptions include Georgia, Maine, Vermont, and Wisconsin. Wisconsin does exempt fuel converted to electric energy, gas, or steam by utilities and tax paid on fuel and electricity consumed in manufacturing against corporate franchise/income taxes. Several of those that do exempt fuel limit the exemption to fuel used in production, processing, or manufacturing: Indiana, Iowa, Maryland, Minnesota, Ohio, Pennsylvania, and Rhode Island. Mississippi, North Carolina, and Tennessee tax fuel used for manufacturing at a lower rate. Kentucky exempts fuel only for firms in which fuel cost represents more than 3 percent of total production cost. Among the states taxing consumables, some exempt industrial fuels at least in part: Alabama (kilns only), California (if delivered in mains), Colorado, Florida (except hotels and restaurants), Louisiana, Nebraska, New York, Utah, Wyoming, and the District of Columbia. Otherwise, the treatment is the same.

When industrial fuel is exempt as part of a general fuel exemption, no particular administrative problems are created. When only industrial fuel is exempt, as is common, somewhat arbitrary allocations are necessary between costs of fuel used directly for manufacturing and costs of fuel used for office heating and other nonmanufacturing purposes. (Nebraska and Wyoming require separate metering). The task is not insuperable, since the number of firms involved usually is not great.

When industrial (but not other) fuel and consumables are exempt, their purchase usually can be made tax free only through the use of certificates.

Electric Power Used in Industry

The treatment of electric power is identical with that of fuel—including the direct use in production or manufacturing requirements—with few exceptions. North Carolina exempts electric power for industrial use instead of applying a lower rate. Nevada taxes fuel but not electricity. California exempts electricity but taxes fuels except natural gas, propane, or other gases delivered through pipes. Alabama, Hawaii, Washington, and a few other states exempt electricity but tax it under separate public utility taxes. Florida exempts fuel but taxes electricity. Missouri, which taxes fuel, exempts electric power if the cost of the power exceeds 10% of the manufacturing cost, which it seldom does. Arkansas, while generally taxing industrial electricity, exempts it when used for aluminum manufacturing. Maine taxes electricity except when separately metered to an electrolytic process. In most states except those taxing no utilities, electricity for other business purposes is taxed.

Industrial Machinery

Virtually all earlier state sales taxes were applied to industrial machinery, the sale being taxable as a final sale, even though the machinery was used to produce taxable goods. The noticeable trend, however, has been to exempt such machinery. As of 1982, the situation is as follows:

Fully taxable (twelve): California, Hawaii, Iowa, Kansas, Minnesota (except tools with less than one year of useful life exempt), Nevada, North Dakota, South Dakota, Texas (except equipment and machinery with a useful life when new of six months or less), Utah, Washington, and Wyoming, plus the District of Columbia.

Subject to lower rate (five): Alabama (1.5%), Mississippi (1% on invoice amounts over $500), North Carolina (1% and $80 maximum per article), and Tennessee (rate declining to exemption in July 1983). Illinois currently is applying a lower rate (2%), with planned phase-out to full exemption.

Exemption for new and expanded industry only (eight): Arkansas, Florida, Georgia, Kentucky, Louisiana (may contract with new manufacturing establishments for exemptions up to ten years), Missouri, Nebraska, and New Mexico (by refund). Louisiana also exempts certian energy-conserving property purchases.

Fully exempt (twenty): Arizona, Colorado ($1,000 minimum, $500,000 maximum), Connecticut (machinery only), Idaho, Indiana, Maine, Maryland, Massachusetts, Michigan, New Jersey, New York, Ohio, Oklahoma, Pennsylvania, Rhode Island, South Carolina, Vermont, Virginia, West Virginia, and Wisconsin.

Geographic concentration in the groups is substantial. For example, all the fully taxable states are west of the Mississippi River. (The District fully taxes, but lacks manufacturing.) Most lower rate states and the "new and expanding" rule states are in the South. The full exemption states, though scattered through all regions, are concentrated in the industrial area from the Midwest to the East Coast. Most states (except Michigan and Ohio) that introduced the tax before 1945 did not provide the exemption. Most states that introduced the tax since 1945 have included it, and several states (eight since 1971) have added the exemption in recent years. The exemption of machinery for only new and expanded industry is, of course, designed to aid industrial development with minimum loss of revenue. It is basically inequitable, however, as among competing firms, and difficult to administer. Arbitrary rules are required to delimit expanded output. For example, in Florida, output must increase by at least 10% if the exemption is to apply.

General exemption of industrial machinery obviously has merit, under the principle that producers goods should not be subject to tax. Taxation of such equipment places a tax penalty on investment. If some states exempt it, industrial development in the states that do not may be restricted, though no concrete evidence is available.

On the other hand, exemption reduces revenue and lessens the degree to which a state can "export" tax to residents of other states. Exemption also creates some administrative problems, the greatest of which centers around the interpretation of "direct use in manufacturing," the usual phrase. A line must be drawn at both the beginning and the end of the industrial process. Usually, equipment employed in handling raw materials is not covered, nor distribution activities after processing is complete. Thus, a fork truck purchased to move raw materials in a warehouse is taxable, one used to move the material in actual production is exempt, and one used in a warehouse for storing finished product is taxable. A number of interpretative rulings must be issued, but experience of the states over the last twenty years in this field suggests that the problems can be solved. Administration of the tax is not seriously impaired by the exemption. The number of manufacturers is relatively small, and interpretations are frequently worked out in cooperation with industry groups. Dividing lines are somewhat arbitrary, but they are workable. On the whole, exemption clearly appears to be warranted. A certificate is often required, as shown in figure 3.2.

Air and water pollution control equipment merits separate discussion because some states treat this equipment differently from other types. Among the states that fully tax industrial machinery, Hawaii (air only), exempts such equipment. Nebraska and Utah tax, but the amount paid is refundable. The states applying a lower rate to machinery follow that practice for pollution control equipment as well, except in the case of Alabama, where the equipment is fully exempt. All the states extending an exemption to new and expanding industry exempt pollution control equipment; Arkansas limits the exemption to equipment that the firm has been required to purchase. There is much less uniformity of treatment among the states exempting industrial machinery. Six of these states do not exempt air and water pollution control equipment: Arizona, Colorado, Massachusetts, New Jersey, Oklahoma, and Vermont. Kentucky, Maine, Michigan, Ohio, Rhode Island, South Carolina, Texas, and Virginia have special certification requirements for exemption; Indiana exempts only equipment that has been required and only part of the purchase price is exempt (total exemption was phased in for 1982). The other seven states exempting industrial machinery follow that standard for pollution control equipment. The causes for the difference in exemption usually hinge on revenue impact and dispute over whether the equipment is in the direct flow of production. Treatment of chemicals used in the pollution control equipment typically follows that pattern for the equipment itself, except in Minnesota which exempts the chemicals but not the equipment, and Idaho, Illinois, Kentucky, Maryland, New York, and South Carolina, which tax the chemicals but not the equipment. Because control requirements differ dramatically among industries, exemption decisions have greater consequences for certain firms than overall revenue impacts might suggest. Because these expenditures are a real cost of production, the standard of the sales tax as a consumption levy strengthens the case for their exemption.

Other Producers Goods Exclusions outside of Agriculture

Relatively few states have extended their exclusions of producers goods beyond the categories indicated, apart from items used in agriculture, discussed in the next section. Major exceptions are noted here.

Transportation.   Railroads are subject to tax on their purchases in all states except Indiana, Pennsylvania, and Texas (which exempt all purchases for public transportation), Arizona, Minnesota, Ohio, Virginia (only property in common carrier service), and West Virginia, though they receive a reduced rate on ties, rails, and the like in some states (1% in Mississippi, and one-half the regular rate in South Dakota). In fact, however, they are not taxed on their rolling stock in any state because of interstate commerce considerations. Rolling stock is immediately placed in interstate commerce, and the states cannot collect either sales or use tax on it. The exception in some states is purchase by purely local or industrial railroads unable to take advantage of this escape hatch (2% on locomotive and cars in North Carolina).

The same considerations apply to commercial aircraft, which is, so far as can be discovered, not actually taxed by any state. Private planes are typically subject to tax, and some states successfully tax fuel for commercial air lines. Motor transport vehicles are typically taxed (except in Indiana), other than those used by interstate carriers. There is no constitutional barrier to taxation of these trucks by the state of registration (as there is with railway equipment), but in fact most states do not attempt to tax them. Colorado is one of the few states to tax them. Why the other states have not pursued their taxation is not clear.

Logically, all goods for performing freight transport by any mode should be excluded from tax as a producers good, as in Indiana. Some complaint, however, can be raised about providing complete exemption for transport, whereas other industries are taxed on various goods they acquire. Passenger transport equipment could logically be taxed if the service itself is untaxed, though a case can be made for exclusion on the grounds of the need for maintaining an efficient public transport system to lessen traffic congestion and air pollution.

Equipment used in retailing. Ohio and West Virginia extend their exclusion of industrial equipment to cover equipment used directly in retailing (but in Ohio not that used in wholesaling, a rule that makes no sense whatever, except to reflect the greater political strength of retailers than wholesale firms). No objection can be raised to the exemption except the administrative nuisance, but uniform treatment should be given wholesalers.

General exclusion. West Virginia is the only state to exclude from tax virtually all producers goods in manufacturing, retailing, and agriculture. The only major exception in this field is of motor vehicles. The exclusion has been in effect since the earliest days of the tax. It was suspended during 1969/70, but became effective again in 1970 with no great effort to eliminate it permanently. Although administration may not be perfect, the state revenue department does not regard the exclusion rule as unworkable. Experience tends to contradict the usually accepted principle that exclusion of all goods used in further production would destroy the effectiveness of operation of the sales tax.

ST-104
Rev. 06-79

IDAHO STATE TAX COMMISSION

SALES TAX EXEMPTION CERTIFICATE

Seller's Name

Address

THIS FORM IS TO BE COMPLETED AND FURNISHED BY THE BUYER TO THE SELLER OF TAX EXEMPT ARTICLES, AS PROVIDED BY IDAHO CODE 63-3622. INSTRUCTIONS ARE ON THE BACK OF THIS FORM. Instead of completing this form the Buyer who purchases tax exempt articles may certify on the face of the sales invoice to one of the four categories listed below. This certification may be in the form of the Seller's rubber-stamped wording which is signed by the Buyer.

PRODUCTION EXEMPTION

1. I certify the property which has been purchased will be used for the following purpose: *(Check the appropriate box)*

☐ Raw materials or catalysts used in the production of tangible personal property by mining, manufacturing, processing, fabricating or for farming.

☐ The equipment or machinery listed below, to be directly and primarily used in the production of tangible personal property for resale, is exempt from sales or use tax. Describe the machinery or equipment and its use below.

_____

_____

_____

_____

OUT-OF-STATE REALTY

2. I am an Idaho resident contractor, this material will be used by me exclusively in the performance of a contract with _____ for improvement of real estate located at _____ .
This is real property located in another State and I will not be subject to a like tax in that State.

MOTOR VEHICLE TAKEN OUTSIDE STATE

3. The vehicle which has been purchased will be taken by me directly to _____ ,
   (State)

   will be immediately titled and licensed in _____
   (State)

   and will not be used by me in Idaho more than 25% of the vehicle's mileage in any calendar year.

OTHER QUALIFYING EXEMPTIONS

4. Check the following institution or materials which qualify under I.C. Section 63-3622.

   a. Qualifying Institutions:
      ☐ Hospital
      ☐ Educational Institution
      ☐ Canal Company
      ☐ Red Cross
      ☐ Federal Land Bank
      ☐ State Credit Union
      ☐ Federal Credit Union
      ☐ Government Instrumentality
      ☐ Forest Protective Association
      ☐ Certain Qualifying Newspapers

   b. Qualifying Materials:
      ☐ Broadcasting Firm
      ☐ Motor Fuels
      ☐ Pollution Control Equipment
      ☐ Matter Used to Produce Heat by Burning
      ☐ Irrigation Equipment and Supplies Used for Agriculture Production Purposes
      ☐ Occasional Sales Defined in I.C. Section 63-3612A
         (Copy of Affidavit executed by seller must be attached)

I CERTIFY THAT ALL STATEMENTS HEREIN MADE OR INDICATED BY ME ARE TRUE AND CORRECT.

Name of Purchaser (Print) _____

Nature of Purchaser's Business (if applicable) _____
(Farming, Mining, Manufacturing, Processing, etc.)

Address _____

| SIGN HERE ▲ | Signature of Purchaser | Date |

— Seller Must Retain This Form —

FIGURE 3.2   EXEMPTION CERTIFICATE FOR INDUSTRY, AGRICULTURE, AND OTHER EXEMPTIONS, IDAHO

EXCLUSION OF GOODS FOR USE IN AGRICULTURE

In practice, variation is considerable in the treatment of goods purchased for use in agriculture. Idaho, Indiana (direct use), Massachusetts, Michigan, Minnesota, New Jersey, New York, Ohio, Pennsylvania (direct use), Virginia, and West Virginia have broad exemptions that exclude virtually all purchases for farm use except motor vehicles and improvements to real property. Other states restrict the exclusion narrowly. Oklahoma for a time provided none at all.

Feed, Seed, Fertilizer

These items are in part or entirely exempt in all states except Hawaii (in which sales of livestock feed are taxed at a low rate). The exact treatment varies, however:

1. *Farm use:* By far the most common rule excludes from tax sales of livestock feed, seed, and fertilizer to persons engaged in production of farm products for sale.[1] A few of these states seek to narrow the coverage to actual commercial farming, as distinguished from persons incidentally producing and selling farm products. Maine interprets the definition broadly to exclude all vegetable seeds. Many of these states, for example, Idaho, Georgia, Kansas, Kentucky, New Jersey, New York, and Utah require the farmer to provide an exemption certificate to the supplier (figure 3.2). Others, such as Washington, do not. Washington does require that farmers sign a resale certificate. No state requires registration of farmers. Farmers regularly making retail sales would register and collect, however.
2. *Goods used for production of food:* California, Nevada, and Rhode Island follow a different approach. Items purchased for the production of food for human consumption, whether or not by a farmer, are exempt. This rule was an outgrowth of California's exemption of food and was taken over by other states. Thus, an individual can buy vegetable seed, feed for a pet hen, or fertilizer for a vegetable garden tax free, but flower seed or fertilizer for lawn or flower beds is taxable. Nevada restricts the fertilizer exemption to sale for commercial production of food.
3. *Variations on one or more items:* Several states provide, often for no sound reason, different treatment for one of the three items:
   a. Colorado: all feed and seed exempt; fertilizer exempt for farm use only.
   b. Connecticut: all seed and fertilizer exempt; feed exempt on "food for human consumption" basis.
   c. Tennessee: all feed exempt; farm use rule on seed and fertilizer.
   d. South Dakota: farm use for feed; seed exempt when sold in excess of 25 pounds; fertilizer exempt when sold in excess of 500 pounds. This

[1]Plants and trees receive similar treatment as seeds in most, but not all, states. Nonfruit trees and flower plants are almost always taxed.

device, which is unusual, is designed to simplify delineation of sales to commercial farmers from others. Further, fertilizer and commercial feed must be registered with and approved by the state department of agriculture.

4. *Broad exemptions:* Alabama, Mississippi, North Carolina, and Vermont exempt all or virtually all sales of feed, seed, and fertilizer. In North Carolina, the fertilizer exemption is confined to commercial fertilizer, but in fact includes virtually all. Mississippi continues the 0.125% rate on wholesale sales of those items.

5. *Restrictive exemptions:* In two states, the exemption is drastically restricted:
   a. Arizona: seed and fertilizer are fully taxable. Livestock feed is subject to a 0.375% wholesale tax in lieu of the retail tax.
   b. Hawaii: fertilizer is fully taxed; seed and livestock feed are taxed at the 0.5% rate.
   c. District of Columbia: no exemption, since it has no farming activity.

Livestock

Sale of farm livestock by individual farmers is never taxed, and, in fact, sale by commercial dealers is rarely taxed. In Wyoming, livestock is interpreted not to be tangible personal property and thus is not subject to tax at all. In most states, sale for farm use is excluded by law. Sale of pets and race horses (other than to farmers) is typically taxable. North Carolina specifically taxes horses and mules at a reduced rate (1%). Pet food, in the sense of prepared dog, cat, and similar food, is likewise taxable. Vermont repealed a pet food exemption in 1976; the state now provides a $13 credit to blind users of seeing eye dogs. Nominally in many states, food for ponies and horses is taxable, but in fact, when bought through regular feed dealers, the food is often not reached. It is impossible to distinguish at time of sale between the oats a farmer buys to feed a pet pony and those to feed hogs.

Insecticides

Most states that exempt feed, seed, and fertilizer now exempt insecticides and similar items when sold for farm use or for producing food. These items are not as yet exempt in Arizona, Arkansas, California, Colorado, Hawaii, Nevada, and Wyoming. Several of these states restrict the farm exemption in other ways as well.

Farm Equipment and Machinery

In earlier years, equipment used in agriculture was almost universally taxed. In recent years, however, the noticeable trend is toward exemption of such items. As of 1982, thirteen states tax farm equipment at regular rates; twenty-five states exempt it (though with differing coverage) and seven apply lower rates.

Exemption. The scope of the exemption varies:
1. *Narrow:* Georgia confines the exemption to machinery and equipment used directly in preparing and harvesting crops, including farm tractors. Maine exempts items above a $5,000 selling price (depreciable items below that are subject to tax refund).
2. *Relatively broad:* Indiana, Ohio, and Vermont exempt equipment and machinery used directly in agricultural production. (Indiana specifies direct use in direct production.) Kentucky, Maryland, Missouri, Oklahoma, Texas, and Wisconsin have fairly broad exemptions. Tennessee has reduced rates as the exemption is phased in. These exemptions are limited to equipment and machinery, as distinct from tools and supplies. Illinois is phasing in the exemption of items whose sales price is above $1,000, temporarily taxing at a reduced (2%) rate. Arkansas is phasing in the exemption to full status in 1984.
3. *General exemption:* Connecticut, Idaho, Massachusetts, Michigan, New Jersey, New York, Pennsylvania, Utah, Virginia, and West Virginia have very broad exemptions of most items purchased for farm use, often including hand tools but excluding motor vehicles and goods becoming a part of real property. Virginia exempts certain property affixed to realty; Pennsylvania exempts realty items as well and motor vehicles not required to be registered. Massachusetts excludes farm tractors from the exemption. In New Mexico, the rate applies to half the sales price. Louisiana imposes the tax only on the equipment sales price above $50,000 per item (1982).
4. *Reduced rate:* The following states tax farm machinery and equipment, but typically not other farm items, at reduced rates: Alabama, 1.5%; Florida, 3%; Minnesota, 4%; Mississippi, farm tractors, 1%; tractor drawn implements, 3%; North Carolina, 1% ($80 maximum tax on any one item); North Dakota, 2% on farm machinery and irrigation equipment; and South Dakota, 3%.

The Best Approach

The problem of taxation of farm purchases is one of the most troublesome to solve. Taxation of major items used in agriculture is contrary to the general philosophy of the taxes and is particularly burdensome on farmers relative to owners of other businesses. Farm produce prices are determined largely in nationwide markets and are likely to reflect the taxes only very slowly and imperfectly. Widespread sales taxes are most likely to influence prices but still not completely. Particularly discriminatory is the taxing of agricultural items that are equivalent to the materials used in manufacturing, which are never taxed. Taxation of expensive farm machinery is likewise unfortunate. Exclusion by the usual certificate techniques is impossible, however, since the farmers are not registered vendors, and auditing them is not feasible as it is with registered firms. There are large numbers of farmers, many with very small operations. Many items they purchase are also used for nonfarm purposes. Particularly troublesome is broad exemption of hand tools and supplies frequently purchased for both farm and nonfarm use from usual retailers.

The following recommendations are suggested, though they offer no perfect solutions:

1. Exempt all livestock feed, seed, plants, fruit trees, insecticides, and fertilizer purchased for farm use, that is, for the production of crops for sale, with a simple certificate filed with the supplier. Other sales of these items would be taxable, unless they were sales for resale.
2. Exempt all livestock, including poultry, regardless of the buyer or seller, except dogs, cats, horses, and other nonfood-producing animals. This exemption creates no administrative problems, because most livestock is either sold by the farmer (so tax cannot in effect be applied) or is sold for obviously tax-free uses. Exempting all of it outright is far simpler.
3. Exempt farm machinery and equipment, but not hand tools or miscellaneous supplies. This category constitutes another major element of farm costs, and administration of the exemption is not difficult if it is confined to major items of equipment. For administrative reasons, the exemption should not extend to replacement tires, batteries, and other such standard items.

This exemption is not urgently needed in states where there is little large-scale agricultural production utilizing expensive equipment, but it is desirable in those states where mechanized agriculture is a significant element in the economy.

CONSUMPTION GOODS EXEMPTIONS

A strong case can be presented against introducing exemptions of consumption goods into a sales tax, except when the specific justification is strong. First, exemptions erode the base and reduce revenue, and each exemption leads to demands for additional exemptions. Second, loss of uniformity of coverage discriminates in favor of those persons having relatively high preferences for exempt goods and leads to reallocation of resources and to consumer excess burden. That is, persons shift from taxed to untaxed goods and lose satisfaction, but the government gets no revenue. Third, in virtually all cases, compliance and administration are made more difficult because vendors must distinguish between taxable and exempt goods at the time of sale in their records. Audit is made more complicated, and chances for evasion are increased.

Although most state sales taxes are relatively broad in coverage of commodities, a number of states have introduced some exemptions, either to make the distributional pattern more acceptable, to meet certain administrative problems, or to avoid so-called double taxation.

Food Exemption

Since the earliest days, the principal complaint that has been advanced against sales taxation has centered around regressivity and the absolute burden on the lowest income groups. Two general approaches have been followed to meet this objection: the exemption of food, medicine, and, in a few states, certain other items; and the provision of a credit against income taxes representing tax paid on basic necessities. Each approach will be considered.

As of January 1982, twenty-six of the forty-five sales tax states plus the District of Columbia exempt all, or almost all, food. The twenty-six are: Arizona, California, Colorado, Connecticut, Florida, Indiana, Iowa, Kentucky, Louisiana, Maine, Maryland, Massachusetts, Michigan, Minnesota, Nevada, New Jersey, New York, North Dakota, Ohio, Pennsylvania, Rhode Island, Texas, Vermont, Washington, West Virginia, and Wisconsin. Washington repealed the exemption from May 1, 1982, except for purchases with food stamps. Several initiatives seek reinstatement of the exemption. Of the twenty-three sales tax states emerging from the pre–World War II period, only California and Ohio exempted food throughout. North Carolina did so for a time but eliminated the exemption in 1961—the only other state to exempt food and then make it taxable. Of the twenty-one early states without food exemption, only North Dakota had moved to food exemption by 1971 (and only partially); since then, six of them have exempted food. Overall, eleven states that taxed food in 1971 now exempt such purchases or tax them at reduced rates. Sales taxes levied since World War II usually have food exemption, either on establishment or added later: only five of the twenty-two tax food. Illinois taxes food at a lower rate than other goods, as part of a phased-in food exemption.

The exemption covers all goods for human consumption, except, in most states, candy and soft drinks—though they are exempt in some: Arizona (except drinks in open containers), California (candy, non-carbonated beverages), Florida (candy only), Massachusetts, Ohio, Pennsylvania (candy only), Vermont, and West Virginia (unless purchased from food service establishment or vending machine). Wisconsin has a much broader exclusion from the exemption, making such items as popcorn and soda fountain drinks taxable.

Meals. No state exempts from taxation all meals, although Connecticut and Maryland exempt meals under $1—a concession of no great importance in view of present day meal prices. Vermont and the District of Columbia place higher rates on meals (5% vs. 4%, and 8% vs. 6%).

Evaluation of food exemption.   Because such a high percentage of family expenditures in the lowest income groups is for food, food exemption without question accomplishes the objective of lessening regressivity and the absolute burden on the poor. This result has been demonstrated empirically in a number of studies and need not be reviewed here. These studies uniformly show that a sales tax with food taxed is regressive; with food exempt, it is more or less proportional to income except at the lowest income level.[2] Of perhaps even greater importance is the effect of the exemption on reducing the absolute burden on the poor. Food exemption also lessens discrimination against large families compared to smaller ones.

Food exemption, however, has a number of objectionable features:

1. *Revenue:* Food exemption causes a loss in revenue between 15% and 20% of the total. Thus, a state with a 5% rate must increase the rate by one percentage point to obtain more or less equivalent revenue.
2. *Major administrative problems:* First, questions of interpretation are numerous and some are hard to solve. Several relate to whether or not certain items are food—vitamin tablets, for example. The most serious questions, however, relate to the exclusion of candy and soft drinks and of meals from the exemption. The line between candy and cookies is not easily drawn, nor that between candy and nuts and various other confections. Soft drinks are even worse to delimit, because there is no sharp line between noncarbonated soft drinks and various fruit drinks, which merge into strictly fruit drinks. To tax only carbonated soft drinks, as some states do, is discriminatory. A few states try to draw the line relative to fruit juice content. The logic of taxing candy and soft drinks is clear, but difficulties in doing so when other food is exempt are serious.

   Quite apart from interpretative matters is that of ensuring that the tax is applied correctly at the cash register and is reported correctly. Since supermarkets and many other stores carry food and nonfood items, for clerks to ring up the two types of item properly is a source of additional time and nuisance, and mistakes are numerous, particularly with the high rate of turnover of clerks. The new scanner computer-linked checkout systems lessen the problem for stores using them. Stores are given strong incentive to overstate the percentage of sales consisting of food items. To prevent such overstatement, additional audit time is required, which would better be put to other uses.

   Even more troublesome is the delineation between food and meals, in view of modern trends toward drive-in restaurants and warm-food depart-

---

[2]For example, J.M. Schaefer, "Sales Tax Regressivity under Alternative Tax Bases and Income Concepts"; H.M. Somers, *The Sales Tax* (California Assembly Committee on Revenue and Taxation, Sacramento, 1964); R. Hansen, "An Empirical Analysis of the Retail Sales Tax with Policy Recommendations."

ments in grocery stores. Scarcely any two states follow exactly the same rule. The most common general approach is to tax all take-out food from restaurants, including drive-ins. Michigan taxes if the food is prepared for immediate consumption, as do Pennsylvania (but a court ruled exempt carry-out pizza sold from a business with no on-premises place for consumption) and Rhode Island. In these states, take-out food from a grocery store is not taxed. Rhode Island requires combination food store–eating establishments to collect tax on prepared food. Wisconsin adds to this rule the requirement that grocery stores must charge tax on *heated* food that is taken out. California exempts takeout foods unless the food is sold for consumption at facilities—tables, trays, parking area—provided by the retailer, is sold by a drive-in establishment, or is sold within a place where admission is charged. However, hot prepared food whether sold on take-out basis or not is taxed. Maine taxes if there is a place to eat prepared food.

Ohio is tangled even deeper. The food is taxable if the customer plans to eat it in the establishment or on the parking lot. If he will not sink his teeth into the hamburger until his car's rear bumper has cleared the parking lot, then he can buy tax free. Such rules (Ohio is based on a constitutional provision!) are ridiculous and cannot possibly be enforced at all accurately. Maryland had the on/off premises until 1978; the revision to the vendor facilities rule greatly simplified the operation of the tax.

When meals under a certain price are exempt, problems arise when several persons eat together. Usually, single checks are required to keep the meal tax free if the total exceeds $1, and following this rule is something of a nuisance.

Some of these problems are of the state's own making, such as the silly rule in Ohio on drive-ins, but in part they are inherent in the exemption. If only restaurant meals above a relatively high figure, such as $5, were taxable, the problem would be greatly reduced. Taxing meals assumes that all restaurant eating is luxury eating, but of course it is not. Although taxing the really luxurious variety is reasonable, states attempt much more.

3. *Discrimination in favor of families concentrating luxury spending on expensive foods:* Many foods are in no sense necessary for a minimum living standard. Many families spend substantial amounts on expensive cuts of meat, fresh fruit out of season, exotic seafoods, and other items. Exempting these purchases is unnecessary, and there is no need to exempt any food expenditures of higher income families. As noted, any deviation from uniform coverage of a tax is inherently objectionable on grounds of inequity and possible "consumer excess burden," and exemption of food is no exception to this rule.

At the same time, food exemption leaves substantial absolute burden on the lowest income groups. The sales tax with food exempt is still regressive at the very lowest levels. Restaurant meals are almost never exempt, yet many older persons must eat in restaurants for lack of cooking facilities.

Exemption of Other Necessities

Many states, in order to reduce the regressivity and the burden on the poor still more, provide other exemptions:

1. *Utility service:* As noted, in a number of states, public utility services are not taxed in part or in entirety. This rule causes no administrative problem, but it does reduce revenue and is discriminatory among consumers.

2. *Household fuel:* Recent increases in the price of fuel for household use have induced many states to exempt household fuels of various types. The concern is predominantly heating, but many different fuels are used and several are used for purposes other than domestic heat. Thus, the exemptions and their administration have become messy. Thirty-one states exempt natural gas and/or other household fuels in various combinations: Colorado, Connecticut, Florida, Idaho, Kansas, Kentucky, Louisiana (natural gas and liquid propane gas only), Maine (any fuel, first 750 kwh of electricity), Maryland, Massachusetts, Minnesota (natural gas and electric from November through April only), Mississippi (electricity, natural gas, liquid propanegas), Missouri, Nevada, New Jersey, New York, North Carolina, North Dakota (fuels other than natural gas), Ohio (fuels other than natural gas and electricity largely taxed), Oklahoma (not exempt from local sales taxes), Pennsylvania, Rhode Island, South Carolina (phasing in), Tennessee (1.5% rate), Texas (natural gas and electricity), Utah (1% rate), Vermont, Virginia, Washington (natural gas only), West Virginia, and Wisconsin (natural gas and electricity for November through April only). These exemptions can create definitional problems and, as fuels extend beyond those sold by traditional and specialized dealers, administrative troubles can arise. The other objections to specific commodity exemptions are valid as well.

3. *Drugs and medicines:* Exemption of medicines and drugs has spread rapidly in recent years. By May 1982, forty-one states plus the District of Columbia had exempted all prescription drugs and some related items.[3] Twenty-six states had that exemption a decade ago. Eight of the forty-one states (Colorado, Florida, Maryland, Minnesota, New York, Pennsylvania, Rhode Island, and Vermont) plus the District of Columbia also ex-

[3]Alabama, Arizona, Arkansas, California, Colorado, Connecticut, Florida, Idaho, Indiana, Iowa, Kansas, Kentucky, Louisiana, Maine, Maryland, Massachusetts, Michigan, Minnesota, Mississippi, Missouri, Nebraska, Nevada, New Jersey, New York, North Carolina, North Dakota, Ohio, Oklahoma, Pennsylvania, Rhode Island, South Carolina, South Dakota, Tennessee, Texas, Utah, Vermont, Virginia, Washington, West Virginia, Wisconsin, and Wyoming. Alabama extended the exemption beyond the elderly and disabled in 1981, and in the same year Oklahoma added the exemption.

empt nonprescription drugs and medicines. Many states exempt devices used to alleviate physical incapacities (wheel chairs, prosthetic devices, etc.). Colorado extends the exemption to "theraputic devices," a category difficult to define satisfactorily. Illinois taxes prescription and other drugs at a lower rate. The other three states (Georgia, Hawaii, and New Mexico) tax all drugs and medicines.

This exemption not only reduces the burden on the poor, but it also avoids a heavy burden on those who are unfortunate enough to require heavy expenditures for medicine. These costs are very unevenly distributed over various families. Control is not difficult so long as the exemption is confined to prescriptions. Extension to all drugs and medicines, however, creates the same types of problems as food exemption. There is no clear cut line between these goods and others (for example, ointments and face cream) and endless interpretative questions arise. These items are sold by a wide range of stores. States that limit the exemption to prescriptions report relatively few troubles; the others report serious difficulties in administration.

4. *Clothing:* Five states—Massachusetts, Minnesota, New Jersey, Pennsylvania and Rhode Island—all late comers to the sales tax field, exempt most clothing. Massachusetts, New Jersey, and Pennsylvania do not exempt "formal" clothing or fur coats. Pennsylvania taxes clothing for sporting activities. Rhode Island does not exempt protective clothing or that suitable only for sporting activity. Massachusetts limits the exemption to clothing selling for less than $175. Connecticut exempts children's clothing, now defined as that designed for children under ten.

The clothing exemption is clearly the most unjustified. It produces the usual undesirable consequences: discrimination in favor of persons spending large amounts on clothes; numerous interpretative, compliance, and audit problems; and reduced revenue. At the same time it makes the tax more, not less, regressive, contrary to the usual intent.[4] Experience of the Canadian provinces with the clothing exemption has been equally unsatisfactory.

5. *Miscellaneous:* Pennsylvania excludes soap and other household supplies.

Formula Reporting for Stores Selling Exempt Commodities

To lessen compliance and administrative difficulties, several states permit firms selling exempt goods to report tax based on a formula. Taxable sales are ascertained by taking a specified percentage of gross sales rather than

---

[4]J.M. Schaefer, "Clothing Exemptions and Sales Tax Regressivity," *American Economic Review,* 59 (September 1969): 596–99; D.G. Davies, "Significance of Taxation Services for the Pattern of Distribution of Tax Burden by Income Class," *Proceedings of the National Tax Association for 1969,* pp. 138–47.

recording the former separately. This percentage may be derived by experience in a test period or from the percentage of total purchases consisting of taxable goods.

California. Grocery stores are permitted to use a formula derived by ascertaining the percentage of purchases of exempt food products to total purchases for the period and applying this ratio to total sales to ascertain exempt sales of food. The presumption is that markups are the same on food and nonfood items in grocery stores. Stores that carry lines not usually handled in such stores cannot apply the formula to their entire sales but must segregate these items. Liquor and hardware must be handled separately. Reports are subject to audit and assessment of any difference in tax.

Rhode Island. Some small stores report on a formula, but the practice is discouraged. The general practice of permitting grocery stores to exclude 88% of their sales as exempt food sales—with potential assessment of additional tax on audit—has been discontinued.

Maine. A system of classified permits issued on application is utilized. A temporary permit is issued authorizing use of a specified ratio, but sales are subject to additional assessment upon audit. After careful audit is made and a ratio of taxable to total sales is established from the experience of the particular store, a permanent permit is issued. The established ratio may then be used without additional assessment based on audit so long as the general character of the firm's business does not change. The figures are reviewed at five-year intervals. Stores are now encouraged to use separate accounting, and firms, especially supermarkets, are shifting away from formulas.[5]

Pennsylvania. Firms may apply for formula reporting. An audit is made before accepting the proposed formula. Results from the formula are then accepted. At recent count, eight firms used that basis.

Wisconsin. Vendors may apply for permission to report by formula the figure related to the relative purchases of taxable and exempt goods, but few have done so.

Texas. Small retail grocers (less than $100,000 gross receipts per year) may presume that taxable receipts are 15% of total receipts. Other grocers and vendors whose taxable receipts are less than 10% of total receipts may

[5]J.T. Singer, "The Advantages of Maine's Classified Permit System," *Revenue Administration,* 1963, pp. 60-63.

apply the prior year's ratio of exempt merchandise purchased to sales during the reporting period. For the latter, actual liability would be established on audit.

North Dakota. Formula reporting is permitted informally for small stores, subject to audit and assessment of additional tax.

Maryland. Some firms (vendors at athletic events) use a formula in circumstances in which collection is difficult. The state sets the percentage. The accounts involved are few.

Iowa. Formula reporting is permitted, but few firms request it.

Ohio. Prearranged and prepaid accounts for vending machines and fast food service pay a percentage established by the department on an individual basis.

Other states. A number of states (for instance, Washington and Michigan) indicate that small firms often use formulas informally, even though their use is not sanctioned and separate reporting is required. Such reporting would be found and assessments made on audit.[6] Nevada, where food exemption is new, reports that it is considering formula reporting, and West Virginia permitted formula reporting during the transition to food exemption, subject to audit of register tapes. Modern cash registers have done much to reduce the need for formula reports.

Summary. Although exemption of medicine on prescription can be justified on the grounds of uneven distribution of medical expenses among families and creates no serious control problems, exemption of food, clothing, fuel, and nonprescription drugs seriously complicates the operation of the tax, discriminates against some persons relative to others, reduces revenue significantly, frees far too many expenditures from the tax, and does not remove all the burden from the poor. These problems have led to attempts to find an alternative.

Credit against Income Tax

The recent development in methods to lessen regressivity and burden on the poor is a system of credits against income tax liability reflecting sales tax

---

[6]Two states use formula reporting in nonfood areas: Indiana (sales under 15¢) and New Jersey (separation of services from the price on leased car contracts).

paid on minimum necessary purchases, with cash refund for those having no income tax liability. Credit may be uniform throughout or vanish at higher income levels. Several systems tailor relief by providing credit only to low income elderly or disabled. Use as of January 1982 can be summarized as follows:

Flat Credit:

Kansas: $20 per person. Recipients must have household income not more than $10,000 and be disabled or elderly—fifty-five or older. Refunds operate outside the income tax system.

Nebraska: $28 per person.

Massachusetts: $4 for taxpayer, $4 for spouse, $8 for each dependent, if income is under $5,000; no credit if above $5,000. The credit is not closely tied to the sales tax nor regarded as a substitute for food exemption. The tax also exempts food.

New Mexico: $45 per person and a medical and dental expense rebate of $7.50 per exemption or 4% of those expenses allowed on the federal income tax return.

Systems replaced by food exemptions in Colorado and Indiana were both flat credits.[7]

Graduated Credit, Declining with Income and Vanishing:

Hawaii:	Adjusted Gross Income ($)	Credit/ Exemption ($)
	0– 4,999	48
	5,000– 6,000	39
	6,000– 7,000	34
	7,000– 8,000	32
	8,000– 9,000	27
	9,000–10,000	24
	10,000–11,000	20
	11,000–12,000	17
	12,000–13,000	14
	13,000–14,000	10
	14,000–20,000	8

[7] A number of states have general income tax credits distinguishable from these sales tax credits by their lack of legislative tie to the sales tax and their relation to age, disability, etc. Examples include systems in Idaho and Minnesota.

Vermont:	Adjusted Gross Income ($)	Total Credit ($) (1 dependent)	Total Credit ($) (10 or more dependents)
	0– 999	29	121
	1,000–1,999	28	108
	2,000–2,999	27	100
	3,000–3,999	25	87
	4,000–4,999	24	80
	5,000–5,999	23	67
	6,000–6,999	21	61
	7,000–7,999	0	56
	8,000–8,999	0	43

Note: Figures lie between those given for exemptions between 1 and 10—the credit per exemption declines as the number of exemptions is greater.

South Dakota: Refund limited to persons aged sixty-five or older and disabled persons receiving Social Security.

One-Individual Household		More-Than-One-Individual Household	
Income ($)	Refund ($)	Income ($)	Refund ($)
0–2,749	110	0–5,500	220
2,750–4,625	46 plus 3.4% of difference between 4,625 and income	5,501–7,375	74 plus 7.8% of difference between 7,375 and income
over 4,625	0	over 7,375	0

Note: Those receiving refund are not eligible for refund of realty taxes on their dwelling.

Wyoming: Limited to those sixty-five or older or totally disabled with income less than $8,000. For individuals, a refund of $572 is reduced by the percentage that income exceeds $4,500 per year. For married couples with one member meeting the age or disability criteria and income less than $11,500, the refund is $657, reduced by the percentage that their income exceeds $6,750 per year.

Iowa and District of Columbia: Now repealed; the systems were graduated.

Evaluation of the Credit Systems

The general experience with the system, in the views of the tax administrators, has been satisfactory. All prefer it to food exemption.[8] Little effort is required for taxpayers to obtain the refund. A simple return is required if the

[8]W.L. Fortune, "The Indiana Sales Tax Credit," in *Revenue Administration,* 1965, pp. 20–21; Y.S. Leong and I. Rhyne, "Hawaii's Inversely Graduated Tax Credits."

person would not otherwise file a return. Computerization makes the handling of the claims for credits relatively simple, and social security numbers serve to prevent duplicate refunds.

There are, however, certain problems:

1. The graduated scale minimizes revenue loss and makes the tax more progressive but requires the selection of an income base to use and complicates the operation somewhat. The usual rule is to use adjusted gross income (AGI), plus certain income items excluded from AGI, such as welfare and social security payments, exempt bond interest, and untaxed capital gains. Disclosure laws can make verification of some modifications difficult. The flat system is simpler but causes more revenue loss.

2. The number of income tax returns increases. The estimated increase has been as follows: Indiana, 8% (old credit system); Massachusetts, 15%; Colorado, 12%; Vermont, under 10%; District of Columbia, less than 15%; Nebraska, 5%.

3. Some persons do not file to obtain the refund. Before termination of its general credit in 1973, Indiana income tax returns showed a total of 4,780,000 persons listed on all tax returns out of a population of 5.1 million, for example.

4. Some chiseling is inevitable, through giving fictitious social security numbers and through listing as dependents children who are filing their own returns and getting their own credit. The general attitude among the revenue officials, however, is that it is not serious.

5. Some interpretative questions about residence arise, particularly with service personnel, and some laws were defective in allowing inmates of prisons and other institutions to get the refund although they made no purchases.

Some opposition comes from persons who dislike the principle of cash payments to individuals. In Iowa, the system was abandoned, not because it was not working well, but because the Republican party became committed to its repeal as a matter of principle. Despite the system's superiority in almost all respects to food exemption, the latter has greater political appeal, for reasons by no means clear. When the credit system was proposed in the province of Ontario in 1969 to replace food exemption, violent protests came from many groups, some not making any sense.

On the whole, despite some defects, the system is greatly to be preferred to food exemption. The revenue loss necessary to accomplish a given equity objective is much less. Administration is much simpler than that with food exemption; discrimination against persons spending large amounts on food is avoided; and all burden can be removed from the poor. Pressure to exempt clothing and other items is reduced. The provision of both a credit and food exemption, as in Massachusetts and Vermont, makes no sense at all; it results from a political compromise.

The system in Idaho, whereby a credit is given for those persons paying income tax, but with no refund for those not having income tax liability (except for persons over sixty-five), defeats the purpose of the system and makes the tax structure more, not less, regressive.

Other Exemptions

The laws contain a few other exemptions, for several reasons largely unrelated to regressivity.

Newspapers, other periodicals, and books.   Newspapers created a special problem because they were often sold for less than the price on which a one-cent tax could be collected. Many are sold by persons who handle nothing else. Carrier subscriptions are often sold by newsboys. These sales created no problem in the few states in which the vendor owed the exact amount of tax collected or where small sales were specifically exempt. In the other states, however, the vendors owed tax that they could not collect. As a consequence, as of January 1982, thirty-eight states plus the District of Columbia exempt newspapers.[9] Some states extend this rule to magazines, either to all, as in Illinois, Maine, Massachusetts, New Jersey, New York, and Wisconsin; to those on subscription, as in Connecticut, Florida, Ohio, Virginia, Texas, and Wyoming; to those admitted as second-class mail or as controlled circulation publications, as in Michigan; to those published at specified intervals or more frequently, as in California (quarterly), Minnesota (quarterly), Nebraska (monthly), and Rhode Island (quarterly); to those regularly published for general circulation and containing matters of current events, in Pennsylvania; or to those selling below a specified price, as in Oklahoma (75¢). The difficulty of enforcing payment of tax on magazine subscriptions, book club purchases, and newspaper subscriptions from out of the state is one reason for the exemption in several states of subscriptions but not of over-the-counter sales.

Prior to 1961, Illinois, by interpretation of a retail sale, had a general exemption of books (the only state ever to have such an exemption). Several states, including Arizonia (junior college, college, university), Kentucky, Massachusetts, Minnesota, Mississippi, New Jersey, North Dakota, Pennsylvania, South Carolina, Tennessee, Vermont, and West Virginia, exempt sales of textbooks to students. Four others (Florida, Indiana, Michigan and North Carolina) exempt textbook sales for kindergarten through high school but tax other text sales. Many other states exempt them indirectly by freeing from tax all purchases by (or sales by) school boards. Some states, including

[9]Arkansas, California, Colorado, Connecticut, Florida, Illinois, Indiana, Iowa, Louisiana, Maine, Maryland, Massachusetts, Michigan, Minnesota, Mississippi, Missouri, Nebraska, New Jersey, Nevada, New Mexico, New York, North Carolina (through route carriers), North Dakota, Ohio, Oklahoma (carrier only), Pennsylvania, Rhode Island, South Carolina, South Dakota, Tennessee, Texas, Utah, Vermont, Virginia (subscription only), Washington, West Virginia (route carriers only), Wisconsin, and Wyoming.

Florida, Georgia, Maine, North Carolina, North Dakota, Rhode Island, South Carolina, and Texas, exempt bibles and, in some cases, certain other religious publications from tax, regardless of the seller or buyer.

All in all, these exemptions have very little justification. Taxing all transactions appears preferable. For paper carriers selling papers, the tax would be collected from the publisher or distributor. The question of bibles must be considered and decided in light of policy relating to support of religion.

Articles subject to excises.   The most unfortunate of all the major exemptions is that of goods subject to special excises. The purpose of the exemption has been to avoid a form of "double taxation," the taxing of one commodity by two different taxes. Actually, there is no justification for such an exemption, and there are some very good reasons for not providing it. If the excises were justifiable prior to the use of the sales tax, the relative burden on these commodites should not be reduced when the sales tax is introduced. If the combined burden is regarded as excessive, the downward adjustment should be made in the excise tax, not by exempting items from the sales tax. This kind of exemption complicates the operation of the sales tax. Vendors must ensure that the tax is not applied to the items and must therefore keep a separate record of their sales. Since records are often inaccurate, audit is complicated and made more time consuming, and the way is paved for outright evasion. Applying two taxes to the same item is far more satisfactory than exempting the item from the general levy. This argument is particularly relevant to cigarettes, which are sold by very large numbers of vendors, many with poor records, and virtually all of whom sell other goods as well. It also applies in large measure, however, to liquor and gasoline.

Gasoline and, in most, but not all, cases, other motor fuels subject to the motor fuel tax are exempt from sales tax in all but seven states.[10] Two states tax motor fuels on full pump prices: California (gasoline; diesel subtracts both excises) and Mississippi. Five states subtract motor fuel taxes before applying the sales tax: Hawaii (federal and state), Illinois (state), Indiana (federal and state), Michigan (state), and New York (state and local). In Georgia, motor fuels are exempt from the sales tax but are subject to an equivalent second motor fuel tax applied at a 3% rate to the price exclusive of excise. States are unnecessarily losing significant amounts of sales tax revenue by their exemption and are needlessly adding complexity to compliance and administration by subtracting the motor fuel tax component (other tax components of prices are not extracted, after all). The gasoline tax is earmarked for highway operation and thus resembles a toll for highway use. By usual standards, gasoline users should contribute also to general government revenues. Some states tax gasoline (mainly for farm use) on which a gas tax refund is given. Several exempt it with other farm fuel.

[10]Illinois is phasing in gasohol taxation under the sales tax.

Cigarettes are taxable in twenty-seven states and the District of Columbia, are taxable net of specific excise in six, and are exempt in twelve.[11] Administratively, as noted, this exemption is the most objectionable in this group.

The treatment of liquor is more complicated. In general, liquor, beer, and wine are subject to the sales tax. Only two states exempt all liquor: Massachusetts and Vermont. Special taxes in lieu of sales tax are used in Kansas and North Carolina. Maine and Virginia exempt liquor sales through state stores. Oklahoma exempts 3.2 beer. Washington applies a special 15% rate on liquor and New Jersey places a 6.5% rate on liquor at the wholesale level only. Kentucky exempts but applies an extra wholesale level tax.

Miscellaneous. In general, the states have refrained from exempting a large number of minor and miscellaneous items. Used goods sold by a vendor (other than traded-in items, already noted) are almost universally taxable (Arkansas exempts them if tax was paid on the initial sale). Several states exempt ice, presumably because water is not taxed. Mississippi and Wisconsin exempt coffins, and South Dakota exempts used farm machinery.

EXEMPTION BY CLASS OF VENDOR OR PURCHASER

A type of exemption of some importance is the one granted to certain classes of vendor or purchaser.

Sales to Charitable, Religious, and Educational Institutions

Five states (California, Hawaii, Louisiana, South Carolina, and Washington) provide no general exemptions to charitable, religious, and educational institutions. Louisiana exempts nonprofit retirement center purchases, California and Washington exempt American Red Cross purchases, and South Carolina exempts purchase of texts used in schools. These exemptions are far narrower than those found elsewhere.

Twenty-five states and the District of Columbia exempt purchases by all charitable, religious, and educational institutions when the items are for their own use and consumption.[12] Kentucky, Massachusetts, New Mexico,

[11]Taxed net of excise in Alabama, Georgia, Illinois, Michigan, Missouri, and New York. Fully taxed in Arizona, California, Connecticut, Florida, Hawaii, Indiana, Iowa, Kansas, Kentucky, Louisiana, Minnesota, Mississippi, Nebraska, Nevada, New Mexico, North Carolina, North Dakota, Ohio, South Carolina, Tennessee, Utah, Virginia, Washington, West Virginia, and Wisconsin.

[12]Colorado, Connecticut, Florida, Illinois, Indiana, Kentucky, Maryland, Massachusetts, Michigan, Minnesota, Missouri, Nevada, New Jersey, New Mexico, New York, North Carolina (applies the tax to the purchaser, but allows a refund of tax), Ohio, Pennsylvania, Rhode Island, Tennessee, Texas, Utah, Vermont, West Virginia, and Wisconsin.

Vermont, and West Virginia define charitable organizations by the U.S. Internal Revenue Code, section 501 (c) (3). Nonprofit hospitals are also exempt.

Fourteen states provide partial exemption, as follows:

Educational institutions and nonprofit hospitals: Georgia (private schools, university system) Idaho, Kansas, and Mississippi.

Educational institutions only: Alabama (plus some organizations by separate legislation) and Iowa.

Hospitals and religious organizations and educational institutions: Maine and Nebraska.

Nonprofit hospitals and children's homes: Arkansas.

Nonprofit hospitals and religious educational institutions: Nebraska, South Dakota, and Virginia.

Nonprofit hospitals only: Arizona and North Dakota.

Religious and charitable institutions: Wyoming (plus hospitals run by religious/charitable organizations).

Many of these states also extend exemption to specific nonprofit organizations, as illustrated by exemption of volunteer fire departments (Maine and Maryland), blood banks (Georgia and Kansas), youth organizations, like scouts and FFA (Arkansas, Mississippi, and Oklahoma), and state historical societies (Virginia).

States that provide exemptions vary in the degree of administrative control they exercise. In Florida, Massachusetts, Pennsylvania, South Dakota, Tennessee, and some other states, institutions must be certified by the state before they are eligible. In most states, any such institution may buy tax free merely by indicating its nature to the vendor or filing an exemption certificate.

North Carolina uses the refund system entirely. This approach checks evasion but necessitates substantial paper work in processing refunds.

Exemption from sales tax of purchases by institutions is a source of major nuisance and some tax evasion. Institutions frequently make purchases in small quantities from regular retailers who have no easy way of checking to ensure the items are really bought for use by the institutions. Record-keeping for retailers and auditing by the state are complicated. Outright abuse is common. These difficulties must be weighed against the desirability of encouraging the work of these organizations. Most of them perform some functions that governments would otherwise have to assume. The final decision must be based on a value judgment.

Sales to Governments

States that use one of the forms of sales tax considered by the courts to rest upon the consumer cannot for constitutional reasons tax sales to the federal government. The vendor sales tax states presumably can do so, but in recent years only Arizona (partially) and South Carolina have. New Mexico taxes services but not commodities. A few states that did tax such sales exempted them because their firms were losing sales to competing firms in other states, the primary argument against such taxation. A much greater tendency is to tax contractors on federal projects.

Eight states (Arizona, Arkansas, California, Hawaii, Louisiana, North Carolina, South Carolina, and Washington [except housing authorities]) tax sales to the state itself and to the local governments. Arizona exempts state hospitals. North Carolina allows refund of tax paid by local governments. The other states exempt sales to themselves and their municipalities, except, in some states, for proprietary activities, such as public utilities. The only reason why the states should tax themselves is to avoid the administrative problems of exemption, since they gain no net revenue. It should be noted, however, that when highway contract work is taxed, monies are shifted from the highway fund to the general fund. The question of taxing local governments, however, is somewhat different. Taxation aggravates the financial problems of municipalities, which are in general more serious than those of the states. On the other hand, blanket exemption creates problems for retailers, complicates audit and gives rise to evasion. No problem exists in exempting major contract purchases of municipalities; rather, difficulties arise concerning purchases in small quantities from retail stores.

Sales by Various Institutions

In most states, charitable, religious, and nonprofit educational institutions are not taxed on casual sales or other events, such as occasional church dinners for members only or an occasional rummage sale.[13] They are taxed, however, on sales to the public through a store or other establishment on recurrent activities in which the public is served, such as dinners served at booths at the state fair or regularly recurring dinners open to the public. Several states set specific rules for defining "casual." For example, in Indiana sales during 30 days a year or less are defined as casual; in Maine, four days a year or less; in Ohio, six days a calendar year, with no more than one a month; in Pennsylvania, three times a year or less or more than 7 days in total. These rules are reasonable in protecting private firms from competition of tax free sales, yet avoiding nuisance collection problems. There are, however, exceptions. Missouri exempts all sales, regular or not, by religious, educational, and charitable institutions. Iowa exempts the sales only if all of the proceeds are used for purposes relating to the activity, without deductions for expenses.

The rules on sales by government are somewhat different. Virtually never is a government required to collect tax on a basically governmental activity,

---

[13]Kentucky exempts the first $500 per year at fundraising events; Connecticut does not apply tax to items sold for $2 or less for school organization support; Utah exempts only if net proceeds are used for purposes relating to the activity.

whereas tax is frequently applicable (but not in all states) in such commercial activities as bookstores or cafeterias in student unions at state colleges or on the sale of electricity by municipal power plants when electricity is subject to tax. Since sales by the federal government cannot be taxed, states are barred from collecting tax from PXs and other federal vendors.[14] Virginia could not apply the tax to sales by private vendors at Washington National Airport until authorized by federal law in 1970. School lunches in public schools and meals served hospital patients are almost universally exempt.

Sales to National Banks

States were limited in their powers to tax national banks by Section 5219 of the national banking legislation.[15] As far as sales and use taxes are concerned, the courts, in a series of decisions, held that the states could apply their sales taxes to sales to national banks if the taxes were of the vendor type, but not if they were of the consumer type. Some consumer-tax states, however, did collect tax on sales to national banks, and the banks did not contest the tax. When Massachusetts and New York imposed sales taxes in 1966, both sought to apply tax to sales to national banks, even though the latter state had a strictly consumer tax and the former had a hybrid tax with some consumer-tax characteristics. The lower courts upheld the power of the states to apply the taxes, but the United States Supreme Court, in the case of the *First Agricultural National Bank of Berkshire County*[16] overruled the lower court and held the bank to be exempt. The consequence was the enactment of federal legislation in 1969 ending restrictions on the power of the states to apply any form of sales and use tax to national banks. Most states proceeded to do so in the following year. National banks are now treated the same as state banks.

Casual Sales

Sales made by persons other than regular vendors are defined as "casual," "isolated," or "occasional" sales. Laws of Colorado apply tax to all such sales, the responsibility being upon the purchaser to report tax if the vendor does not do so. Oklahoma has no casual sale exemption, expecting the seller to remit, regardless of registration, and seeks to collect from purchasers only when fixtures are sold as a part of a going business. Most states also exempt casual sales by business firms, that is, sales of equipment and other items not normally handled in the course of business. Such sales are taxed, however, in

---

[14]Advisory Commission on Intergovernmental Relations, *State Taxation of Military Income and Store Sales,* A-50. Washington, July 1976.

[15]C.F. Conlon, "Repeal of National Bank Tax Immunity," *National Tax Journal* 23 (June 1970): 223–28.

[16]392 U.S. 339, 346. (Massachusetts legally applied its tax to the purchaser.)

Georgia (if the annual figure exceeds $500), Kentucky (if the annual figure exceeds $500, except when the business is sold), Louisiana, Maryland (if the sales price exceeds $1,000), Missouri (if the annual figure exceeds $3,000), Nevada, New York, Oklahoma, Washington, Wisconsin, and the District, plus the two states taxing all casual sales.

A number of states encountered difficulty with exemption on motor vehicles. Used-car dealers would jump title from the seller to the buyer, and the sale would appear to be a casual sale. This evasion, plus the possibility of making the tax effective on sales of motor vehicles by the registration requirement, has led twenty-eight states to make all casual sales of motor vehicles taxable, even though other casual sales are exempt. These states are Alabama, California, Connecticut, Florida, Idaho, Indiana, Kansas, Louisiana, Maine, Maryland (special titling tax), Massachusetts, Michigan, Minnesota, Missouri, Nebraska, New Jersey, New York, North Dakota (special tax), Ohio, Pennsylvania, Rhode Island, Tennessee, Texas, Utah, Vermont, Virginia, Wisconsin, and Wyoming. Iowa subjects them to use tax. Most likewise extend that treatment to watercraft, aircraft, trailers, and snowmobiles.

As noted, casual sales are usually defined to be sales by persons other than those offering the goods for sale in the ordinary course of business. Some variation exists in interpreting this rule, but the general idea is relatively standard: status as a vendor depends upon regularity of sales, number of days of selling per year (3 in New York, 4 in West Virginia, 2 in Idaho), solicitation of regular business, and maintenance of a place of business.

4. Taxation of Services and Real Property Contracts

When state sales taxes were first developed, most were imposed exclusively upon the sale of tangible personal property. One reason was simplicity. Blanket application of tax to such property was possible, but services seemingly could be taxed only by singling out specific ones. The notion was widely accepted that a tax on services is a tax on labor, whereas under usual assumptions it rests on the consumer of the service. Various states also tended to copy others.

As time passed, revenue needs became more urgent, states were reluctant to raise rates, and the failure to tax services caused administrative difficulties. These developments, coupled with the equity justification for applying sales taxes to services, led toward taxing services. The transition has been slow, however, and most taxes are still confined largely to tangible property.

PUBLIC UTILITY SERVICES

There were some doubts in the early days of sales taxation about the status of public utility services under the definition of tangible personal property. After conflicting court decisions, most statutes were amended to mention such services specifically, and virtually all new statutes refer to them. A large number of states differentiate between residential and industrial use of the utility service, some exempting the former but not the latter, others doing the reverse. The situation for residential use in January 1982 was as follows:

1. *No tax on any utility service*: California, Connecticut, Idaho, Florida, Kansas, Louisiana, Maryland, Massachusetts, Nevada, New Jersey, North Carolina, Oklahoma, Pennsylvania, Texas, Vermont, Virginia, and the District of Columbia. In six additional states (Alabama, Illinois, Hawaii, Ohio, Washington, and West Virginia) all utility services are excluded from the sales tax but subject to somewhat comparable special taxes. Not all utilities are, however, covered by these taxes.

2. *Limited coverage*: Local telephone service, gas, electricity, and water: Nebraska.

Local telephone service, gas, electricity, and passenger transportation: Georgia.

Local telephone service, plus gas and electricity from May to November only: Minnesota.

Telephone, telegraph, electricity (over 750 KWH per month): Maine.

Telephone, telegraph and transportation: Missouri.

Telephone and telegraph: Kentucky, Mississippi, New York (local), Oklahoma (passenger transportation taxed if fare over one dollar), Rhode Island, and South Carolina (local, other utilities phase out).

3. *General Coverage*: All utilities, including intrastate transportation: Arizona and New Mexico.

All utilities except water and transportation: Colorado (other utilities were exempt through June 30, 1982), Michigan, (domestic gas and electricity taxed at 1%), South Dakota, Utah and Wisconsin (includes interstate telephone and telegraph).

All utilities except water: Wyoming (passenger transportation, intrastate only).

All utilities except water, transportation, and electricity: North Dakota.

All utilities except transportation: Arkansas, Indiana, Iowa, Minnesota (long distance telephone and telegraph exempt), Missouri (passenger transport taxed), and Tennessee (lower rates on electricity and gas).

The District of Columbia and a number of states that exempt residential use do apply sales tax to business and industrial use: Florida, Kentucky, Maine, Mississippi (lower rate than normal), Missouri, Pennsylvania, Rhode Island, Utah (commercial taxed, industrial exempt) and Vermont. Texas taxes commercial use and allows cities to tax residential use. As was described in chapter 3, electricity and gas used directly in manufacturing are frequently exempt, even when other uses are taxed. When transportation is taxed, for constitutional reasons tax applies only to intrastate shipments or travel.

From an administrative point of view, whether utility services are taxed or exempted makes little or no difference. Under the philosophy of making the tax base as broad as possible, the services can logically be taxed. Revenues are increased substantially, as much as 10%. Although they are basic necessities used by all income groups, including the lowest, they are no more so than many goods taxed.[1] Adjustment for this burden can be made by a credit against income tax liability, explained in chapter 3. The exclusion of electric power and gas used directly in production complicates somewhat the operation of the tax. Such exclusion, however, is clearly warranted.

Freight transportation is particularly unsuited for taxation. First, it is almost entirely a production good. Second, public transportation is subject to severe competition from private freight transportation, which cannot be taxed.

---

[1]The question is considered in detail in *Sales and Use Tax on the Consumption of Utility Services,* Report of the Assembly Committee on Revenue and Taxation, California, General Assembly, Sacramento, 1970.

Third, the inability of the states to tax interstate movements creates serious distortion and inequity. Passenger transportation is subject to competition from the private automobile. Exemption is warranted in view of the general difficulties of maintaining an adequate public transportation system and the discrimination suffered by intrastate movements, which are taxable, whereas interstate movements are not. For example, a ticket from Kansas City, Missouri, to St. Louis, Missouri, would be taxable, but one to East St. Louis, Illinois, five miles farther on, would be completely tax free.

The trend has been toward reduced coverage of utility services, particularly electricity and natural gas for residential use. There is little economic logic to support this special exemption.

RENTALS

Transient Accommodations

Only two sales tax states, California and Nevada, tax no hotel, motel, and other transient accommodations, but in both these states there are local taxes on these services. The levies are technically separate taxes with separate returns in Alabama, Illinois, Massachusetts, Texas, Utah and Vermont.

Hawaii taxes transient housing and all rentals of real property by persons engaged in the business of renting.[2] Florida taxes rent for commercial property; Indiana taxes all temporary rentals of accommodations for people (e.g., display space, banquet facilities).

Other states limit their taxes to transient accommodations, usually defined as those involving rentals for less than a certain number of days, as follows:

6 months: Florida (including apartments)

4 months: Maryland (for resorts)

90 days: Georgia, Kentucky, New Jersey, New York, North Carolina, South Carolina, Virginia, Massachusetts, Tennessee, and the District of Columbia.

60 days: Louisiana (if more than six sleeping rooms and over 50% of rooms reserved for transients)

28 or 30 days, or

1 month: Alabama, Arizona, Arkansas, Colorado (30 days), Connecticut (30 days), Idaho (30 days), Maine (28 days), Maryland (month, nonresort), Michigan (one month, technically use tax), Minnesota (30 days), Missouri (30 days), Nebraska (30 days), New Mexico (month), North Dakota, Ohio, Pennsylvania, Rhode Island, South Dakota (28 days), Texas, Utah, Vermont, Washington, and Wisconsin (month).

[2]Except low or moderate income housing projects. Arizona no longer taxes permanent residential rentals.

There has been a sharp trend toward the use of the thirty-day figure.

Some of these states (Maine is one example) permit a refund if the person stays beyond the specified days; others do not.

The use of a number of days is arbitrary and leads to refund questions. As a consequence, some states apply tax based on the type of establishment. Those offering transient accommodations are taxed on all rentals regardless of time. These states are Mississippi, Oklahoma, West Virginia (excludes hotel or motel rentals on "permanent basis"), and Wyoming. This rule is unfair to persons making permanent homes in hotel rooms and leads firms to separate their transient and permanent businesses. Some states find the establishment rule unsatisfactory and would prefer a date rule.

Most states exclude small boarding houses and tourist homes and set a minimum number of rooms that a renter must offer to be subject to the registration requirements.[3]

Taxation of hotel and motel service is entirely justifiable. Expenditures on this service tend to be progressive relative to income. Taxation also avoids the major nuisance of separating charges for room and meals in American-plan resorts, camps, and the like. It is also a way of reaching tourists. (Several states—Idaho and Indiana, for instance—authorize local hotel and motel taxes, even though they do not permit general local sales taxes.) The Hawaii practice of taxing permanent as well as transient rentals is open to serious question because of equity. Persons renting the types of accommodation subject to the sales tax are discriminated against compared to home owners or persons renting homes from other individuals. Unfortunately, these renters are likely to be in the lower income groups, and renters are already discriminated against by the income tax.

Rental of Tangible Personal Property

Most states tax rentals of taxable tangible personal property. Firms engaged in the business of renting buy the articles tax free under resale certificate and then collect tax on the rental charges. The only exceptions to the rule of buying tax free are found in Hawaii (taxed as wholesale sales) and for motor vehicles in Iowa (for lease out of state) and Maryland. Vermont limits exemption to items to be rented for the entire period the purchaser owns them. In Mississippi, rental firms pay tax on purchases but receive credit for this tax on tax due on rentals; leasing dealers pay no retail tax when inventory items are leased but are liable for tax on the gross lease. If articles are bought partly for use and partly for rental or for use and then occasionally rented, the rental is taxable even though tax is paid on the original purchase in Florida, Georgia, Kansas, Maryland, Massachusetts, Minnesota, Nebraska, Rhode Island, Washington, and Wisconsin. Most states do not tax

---

[3]In New Jersey, New York, and Texas, tax does not apply if the rental charge is $2 a day or less.

casual rentals. Rentals of vehicles and utility trailers are taxed at a higher rate in the District of Columbia (8% vs. 6%); short-term car rentals in Maryland are taxed at a higher rate (8% vs. 5%) with credit for titling tax paid under certain circumstances.

Five states (California, Michigan, Missouri, Nevada, and Rhode Island) give the lessor the choice: he may pay tax on the purchase or buy tax free and collect and pay tax on the rental charges. California does require those leasing property in a form different from its form when acquired (manufacturer-lessor) to collect the tax on rentals. Nebraska provides the option for motor vehicle rentals. Frequently, the tax-free-purchase alternative will involve less tax, but the tax-on-rental approach may facilitate collection of the tax from the customer. Colorado requires that items purchased for lease periods of three years or less be taxed on acquisition or, by application to the department, on rental. Items for longer rental periods are taxed as they are rented.

Four states tax no rentals: Alabama (but there is a separate rental or leasing tax providing wide coverage), Arkansas (so long as tax was paid on the purchase), Illinois, and Maine. The last two do tax motor vehicle rentals. South Dakota taxes all rentals of tangible personal property except personal property and motor vehicle leases for more than twenty-eight days and mobile homes. In these states and in many allowing choice, the lessor will often collect a tax from the customer on the rental though he is paying on the purchase price, a much lower amount.

Under the intent of the tax, there is justification for taxing rentals, since the amounts paid represent the consumer expenditures on the goods, and revenue will be greater with this method. The problem of casual rentals is more difficult to solve. Failure to tax them discriminates against the regular rental firms, yet taxing produces some double burden.

Rental contracts held to be in lieu of conditional sales contracts are almost universally treated as sales, and tax applies at the time of sale (Utah is an exception), or in a few states, at the time of making of payments.

OTHER SERVICES

Admissions

Twenty-seven states plus the District of Columbia tax admissions to movie theaters and other places of amusement under the sales tax.[4] Connecticut, Maryland, North Carolina, South Carolina, and Tennessee do so by separate

[4]Alabama (except membership theater), Arizona, Arkansas, Florida, Georgia, Hawaii, Idaho, Iowa, Kansas, Kentucky, Louisiana, Minnesota, Mississippi, Missouri, Nebraska, New Jersey, New Mexico, New York (except movies, theaters, participating sports), North Dakota, Oklahoma, South Dakota, Utah, Vermont, Washington, West Virginia, Wisconsin, and Wyoming. The District of Columbia exempts legitimate theater, painting exhibitions, etc. Mississippi applies a reduced rate (3%) for publicly owned facilities.

taxes. Nevada has a cabaret tax. Rhode Island applies an admission tax to racing events with pari-mutuel betting. Dues to country clubs and similar organizations are taxed under the sales tax in only a few states—Arkansas, Iowa, Kansas, Louisiana, New Mexico, New York (in excess of $10 a year), Oklahoma, Vermont, West Virginia, and Wisconsin. Washington applies its business and occupation tax to dues if significant goods or services are rendered without additional charge or if dues are graduated according to service. Colorado does not tax admissions but does extend the tax to cover charges. Admissions and club dues are particularly suitable for taxation under a sales tax, since no objection can be raised on either equity or administrative grounds. This coverage makes the tax less regressive.

BROADER APPLICATION OF THE TAX TO SERVICES

In a number of states during the 1960s, the issue of extending the sales taxes to a wide range of services was considered by the legislatures. The actual change, however, was not great. As of 1982, half of the sales tax states—twenty-two of the forty-five—have not extended the coverage of taxation of services beyond the utilities, hotel, and admissions categories. This group includes some early sales tax states, such as California, and some that have introduced the tax in recent years, such as Massachusetts and Nebraska. The states are listed in table 4.1. A second group of states, twenty in number, plus the District of Columbia, have extended the tax to some additional services. Variation, however, has been substantial. Arizona, for example, taxes only local advertising service, which most states do not, whereas Iowa includes a wide range of commercial services.[5] Only three states (Hawaii, New Mexico and South Dakota) tax virtually all services other than those rendered by employees to employers. These states tax all services except those exempted, whereas other states specify those categories to be covered.

Thus, as of 1982, repair of tangible personal property is taxed by nineteen states plus the District of Columbia, laundry and dry cleaning by twelve, and repair of real property by eight. Only four states (Hawaii, Iowa, New Mexico, and South Dakota) tax barber and beauty parlor services, and only two include professional services. South Dakota taxes services according to the federal Standard Industrial Classification (S.I.C.).

Issues in the Taxation of Services

Several primary arguments can be presented for including services within the scope of the tax. First, expenditures on services constitute consumer ex-

---

[5]The Arizona tax on local advertising is being phased out over a three-year period.

penditures, just as do purchases of goods. The difference is not significant between the two from the standpoint of satisfaction of wants. The distinction is highly artificial.

Second, greater revenue can be obtained at a given tax rate, thus avoiding the adverse consequences, such as loss of business to out-of-state firms, from higher rates. The extension of the Iowa tax in 1967, for example, to a relatively wide range of services increased the yield by about 12%. A California estimate suggests that in that state, which taxes no food or services, taxation of utilities, transient rentals, and nonprofessional services would increase the yield by 20%.[6] Evidence from New Mexico and Hawaii suggests that taxation of all services, including personal and professional, but exclusive of contracting and rentals, will add about 30% to the yield of the tax.

Third, broad taxation of services should make the tax somewhat less regressive, since expenditures on services as a whole tend to rise as incomes rise. Unfortunately, however, some of these expenditures are the ones most difficult to catch under a sales tax, particularly foreign travel, expensive education, and household personal service. Evidence suggests that inclusion of the usual types of service, such as laundry and dry cleaning, repair, and barber and beauty parlor service, though not adding greatly to the burden on the very poor, may not lessen the overall regressivity. A study by David Davies shows that taxation of all retail services would make the sales tax including food in the base slightly more progressive, whereas taxation of utility services and medical care make the tax more regressive, as does taxation of all housing services. Taxation of insurance, particularly difficult, is the most progressive of all taxes on service items. He concludes that, in general, taxing services has little impact on the distributional pattern.[7]

Fourth, inclusion of services facilitates administration of parts of the taxes. Since many firms, particularly repair shops, are already registered vendors and at present must distinguish between sales and services, taxing their entire receipts is much simpler. This situation is not true, however, of barber and beauty shops, small contractors doing repair work, and the professions. Currently, about 25% of the vendors in Iowa are service establishments. When the tax was extended to services, the number of registered in-state vendors rose from 52,000 to 84,000. The number has since fallen to 82,000 because some contractors and others have been removed from the rolls. Taxation of services would also eliminate some distortion otherwise arising. For example, repair shops are now encouraged to bill parts and labor separately to minimize tax. Failure to tax services likely creates some shifting of purchases from goods to services, with consequent excess consumer burden.

[6]R.N. Schoeplein, "Some Perspectives in the Sales Taxation of Services," in *Proceedings of the National Tax Association for 1969*, pp. 167–77.

[7]"The Significance of Taxation of Services for the Pattern of Distribution of Tax Burden by Income Class," in *Proceedings of the National Tax Association for 1969*, pp. 138–46.

TABLE 4.1 Tax Treatment of Services Other than Utilities, Admissions, and Transient Accommodations, January 1982

No Taxation of Additional Services	Limited Taxation of Services			General Taxation of Services
	Narrow	Substantial	Broad	
Alabama	Arizona[a]	Arkansas[b]	Iowa[c]	Hawaii
California	Connecticut[d]	Florida[e]	Washington[f]	New Mexico[g]
Colorado	North Carolina[h]	Kansas[i]	West Virginia[i]	South Dakota[j]
Georgia	South Carolina[h]	Louisiana[e]		
Idaho		Mississippi[k]		
Illinois[l]		New Jersey[m]		
Indiana[n]		New York[o]		
Kentucky		Ohio[p]		
Maine		Pennsylvania[e]		
Maryland[r]		Tennessee[q]		
Massachusetts		Utah[i]		
Michigan		Wisconsin[s]		
Minnesota[n]		Wyoming[t]		
Missouri		District of Columbia[u]		
Nebraska[n]				
Nevada				
North Dakota				
Oklahoma[v]				
Rhode Island[n]				
Texas				
Vermont[n]				
Virginia				

[a] Local advertising services taxed (three-year phase out).

[b] Alteration, repair, etc. of motor vehicles, aircraft, farm machinery and implements, motors, tires and batteries, boats, electrical appliances, furniture, televisions, watches, engineering instruments, medical and surgical instruments, machines, bicycles, office equipment, shoes, tin and sheet metal, and mechanical tools and shop equipment; printing.

[c] Repair of motor vehicles, garments, farm equipment and appliances, investment counseling, bank service charges, barber and beauty shops, carpentry, laundry and drycleaning, photography, equipment rentals, flying service, interior decorating, warehousing of agricultural products, printing, wrapping, packing, and packaging of merchandise other than meat and vegetables, optional service on warranty contracts.

[d] Selected business services taxed at 3.5%: computer and data processing, credit information, collection and employment agencies, marketing, private investigation, armored car, sign construction, interior design, photo finishing, telephone answering, stenographic, photocopying, certain services to realty, business analysis, and piped-in music. Also, cable television.

[e] Repair of tangible personal property. Except wearing apparel and shoes in Pennsylvania. Florida taxes cable television.

[f] Repair and installation of real and tangible property; laundry and dry cleaning; credit bureaus; abstractors; parking. Virtually all services covered by the business and occupation tax.

[g] Excludes agricultural harvesting and warehousing, nonprofit hospital services, retirement accommodations, insurance premiums.

[h] Laundry and dry cleaning.

[i] All services except personal (including barber shop and beauty shop parlors) and professional (licensed by the state). Included in the tax, for example, are bookkeeping, collection services; private detectives.

[j] Exempts health and education services.

The Approaches

There are two approaches to taxation of services: taxing all services and taxing a specified list.

General Coverage. The general approach, as in New Mexico and Hawaii, is to tax all services other than those rendered by employees to employers and other than those specifically exempted. This approach is simplest, maximizing revenue (unless too many exceptions are made) and avoiding the escape of taxable services that did not occur to the enumerators. It also avoids borderline cases. Unfortunately, serious objections can be made to the taxation of certain groups of services:

1. *Services rendered to business firms*: Many services, such as legal, accounting, advertising, architectural, and janitorial services, are rendered primarily to business firms, not to individual consumers. Taxing these services would encourage firms to provide the services with their own employees instead of obtaining them from separate firms. If a firm places a lawyer on its staff, the tax would not apply, whereas payment for the services of a law firm would be taxable. Larger firms would be in a better position to provide their own services than smaller firms, and efficient organization of business would be impaired. Taxation of freight transportation would give incentive to firms to use their own trucks instead of public carriers and would create serious interstate distortion.

    Exclusion of all services specifically rendered to business firms would avoid these problems but would create serious enforcement difficulties. No simple way exists at present for delineating the two uses of service. Taxing sales of producers goods to business firms currently has some adverse effects, but incentive is less for firms to produce the goods than to provide services.

---

[k] Repair of tangible personal property, laundry and dry cleaning. Cable television and installation of tangible personal property in Kansas. Cable television in Mississippi.

[l] Service Occupation Tax applies only to tangible personal property transferred by servicemen.

[m] Repair of real and tangible personal property.

[n] Cable television taxed. Indiana also taxes water softening and conditioning service.

[o] Maintenance, servicing, and repair of real and tangible personal property (except laundry, dry cleaning, tailoring, services contracted by private homeowner), information services, installation, printing.

[p] Repair and installation of tangible personal property; washing, waxing, polishing, and painting of motor vehicles; and industrial laundry and linen services.

[q] Repair and installation of tangible personal property, laundry and dry cleaning, parking.

[r] Laundry services rendered to commercial establishments are taxed.

[s] Repair of tangible personal property, laundry and dry cleaning, photocopying, parking, cable television, landscaping and lawn maintenance.

[t] Repair, alteration, or improvement of tangible personal property; geological services.

[u] Repair, reproduction, addressing, mailing, textile renting, parking.

[v] Printing, parking, and advertising are taxed.

2. *Professional services*: Major questions of social policy can be raised about the taxation of medical, dental, and hospital care. The objection involves value judgment, but certainly opposition is widespread to such taxation, particularly because the incidence of these costs is so unevenly distributed among various families. Legal service is rendered in large measure to business firms. For individuals, placing a tax on legal service necessary to obtain justice is usually regarded as inappropriate.

3. *Personal services*: Administrative considerations make almost impossible the taxation of personal services rendered by individuals, for example, domestic workers and baby-sitters.

Listing of specified services. Given these objections, most states have preferred to single out particular types of service. This approach offers limited revenue potential—no more than 10% additional revenue unless real property contracts are included—and involves interpretative and enforcement problems as well as some discrimination. On the whole, however, this approach appears to most states to be preferable. The primary criteria for selecting services include the following:

1. Are the services rendered primarily by commercial firms, as distinguished from the professions and from individuals not regularly engaged in business (e.g., baby-sitters)?

2. Are the services rendered primarily to individual consumers rather than for production? As noted, there are serious objections to taxing business services.

3. Is administration feasible? If most firms are already registered, administration will be simplified rather than impeded. If most are not, added returns must be handled. Some states have been unwilling to tax barber shops for this reason, though states that do so find the problem not too serious.

4. Are there significant equity objections against taxing the particular services, as compared, for example, to the taxation of food and other items already covered by the tax? Virtually all services are used to some extent by the lower income groups. Although this argument is not conclusive against taxing such services, heavy concentration of use in the lower income groups is.

5. Is the revenue worthwhile? Iowa experience suggests that some categories listed produce so little revenue that taxing them is not worthwhile.

Services for Resale and Business Use

A few issues warrant noting on taxing services. One is the question of what goods may be purchased tax free for use in producing services. If a state follows the basic sales-for-resale rule noted in the previous chapter, only those items directly conveyed to the customer with the service, such as repair parts, would be purchasable tax free. In fields in which certain expenses are highly significant, however, such as expenses of a laundry for soap and water, broadening the exemption may be strongly justified—certainly to keep the taxpaying firms mollified. When subcontracting of services is involved, the subcontract, per se, would not be taxed. For example, if an appliance is brought into a dealer for repair and the dealer sends it on to a repair shop, the charge made by the latter to the former would be tax free as a service for resale; only the charge to the customer would be taxed. This rule, unfortunately, has not been firmly established in the few states with broad coverage of services. In Hawaii, a group of specified services rendered to business firms (e.g., dental laboratory work, photo printing) are taxed at the lower (0.5%) rate. Other services rendered to businesses are taxable at the basic 4% rate, even if essentially for resale. This rule gives incentive to firms to supply the services with their own employees.[8] This situation is a source of strong complaint. New Mexico deducts "sales of services for resale" when a "Nontaxable Transaction Certificate" is given.

NONTAXABLE SERVICES RENDERED WITH SALE

Large portions of the regulations, rules, and instructions concerning state sales taxes deal with questions on services rendered with the sale of goods. On some of these, practice is substantially uniform; on others, variation is substantial. Comparing the practices of all states in detail is not worthwhile. Some reference to the troublesome questions and the typical patterns of treatment will suffice.

1. *Charges for financing, warranty service, installation, transportation, and delivery*: The basic, and almost universal, rule is: charges are included in the taxable price unless they are quoted and invoiced separately; if so, they are excluded from tax. There are exceptions; for example, all charges for warranty and installation are taxed in Pennsylvania.

   Rules on transportation and delivery are somewhat more rigid than on the others. Normally, for the charge to be excluded, not only must the charge be made separately, but delivery, in a technical sense, must be made F.O.B. store or other distribution point. A few states, including Pennsylvania, tax transportation and installation charges whether or not itemized separately.

2. *Other services*: Except for the states that specifically tax various of these services, the following rule is almost universal: charge for a service rendered separately from the sale of a good is not taxed. Unless the establishments also sell taxable goods, they are not registered as vendors. Whether or not they are registered, they are for tax purposes consumers of goods

---

[8]F.W. Bennion, "Broad Coverage of Services-Hawaii's Experience under the General Excise Tax Law," *Proceedings of the National Tax Association for 1969*.

used in rendering of services. If they are not registered, tax applies to their purchases of the goods. If they are registered vendors and also sell the same articles used for repair work, they buy all of the items tax free and account for tax themselves on items used in the repair work based on cost. Since they are consumers, they do not invoice the customer separately for the tax. Major examples include:

a. Advertising agencies: In their usual activities, they are not taxable on the services rendered to customers.

b. Barber and beauty shops: They are not taxable on their services, but they are consumers of hair tonic and other materials used in rendering of services. If such a shop also sells tangible personal property, it must be registered. This registration is something of a nuisance for all concerned since the sales are often of minor consequence. Many states therefore do not register them if the volume is small; instead, they pay tax on their purchases.

c. Bookbinderies: On used books, the entire charge is usually taxable unless materials and services are segregated. If so, only the material charge is taxable.

d. Dentists and dental laboratories: The services of dentists are free of tax, but dentists are taxable as consumers. Sales of dentures by laboratories to the dentists are normally taxable (not the charges by the dentist to the customer). A few states treat even the dental laboratories as consumers of the materials used to make dentures.

e. Garages: Garages are consumers of grease used in chassis lubrication but vendors of oil and transmission fluid.

f. Laundries and dry cleaning: They are treated as consumers except in the states where their charges are specifically taxable.

g. Linen, uniform, and diaper supply firms: Typically, the rental charge is not taxable. The activity is regarded as a service, not rental of tangible personal property. The articles are taxed when purchased by the supply firm. North Dakota, Alabama (2%), and Texas tax these services as rentals. Maryland taxes linen and uniform services as rentals. Virginia taxes linen and diaper charges as rentals.

h. Oculists, optometrists, and opticians. These fields are complicated and diverse, so the rules vary. Generally, the charge by the oculist or optometrist for eye examination is not taxable, nor is the charge for the glasses themselves if supplied with the examination. The firm is the consumer of the materials used to produce the glasses. Opticians, however, are vendors of glasses provided on prescription of oculists or others. In several states, glasses are completely exempt.

i. Pharmacies: Charges are fully taxable since pharmacists are normally treated as vendors of the medicines they compound, not as renderers of services. There are, however, exceptions. Illinois regards pharmacists as consumers of the materials used to compound the prescriptions.

j. Photographic establishments: All charges are normally taxable except a separate charge for developing negatives, which in many states is exempt.

k. Physicians: Physicians are treated as consumers.

l. Printers, photostaters, etc.: Printing is almost universally regarded as manufacturing, not as the rendering of a service. Thus, the entire charge for printing is taxable, even if the materials are supplied by the customer. A few states, however, including Indiana, Maine, and Rhode Island, do not tax printing charges if the customer supplies the material. This rule is discriminatory against the printer who also supplies the materials.

m. Professions other than those specified: They are treated as consumers of materials.

n. Taxidermists: They are normally treated as consumers of materials.

o. Undertakers: Hardly any two states follow exactly the same rules. A few, among them Kentucky, treat all undertakers as consumers rather than as vendors; thus their purchases are taxable. Most states permit either a separation of charges for services and materials or the use of a formula for the entire charge or a portion thereof (the portion not covering the basic items charged for separately), usually 50% to 60%. Tax is applied to the materials portion of the charge. Kansas has a mandatory rule applying tax to 50% of the entire charge. At the other extreme, a few states exempt the activity entirely or, as in Tennessee, the first $500 of the charge for casket and burial vault. North Carolina taxes funeral expenses over $150. Coffins are specifically exempted in a few states.

3. *Fabrication and repair of taxable tangible property*: Fabrication of new items, as distinguished from repair, is always fully taxable even when repair service is not. If a machine or blacksmith shop makes a new window box or truck body, the entire charge is taxable. The same is true of shoes made by a shoemaker or clothing made by a merchant tailor.[9] For repair service, however, several approaches are used when it is not taxable.

The most common practice is to establish two classes of repair establishments: those whose materials costs are a minor portion of the total repair charge and those whose materials costs are significant. Group one includes firms that repair tires, tubes, clothing, fishing rods, clocks, watches, and jewelry and do repainting and refinishing work. They are treated as consumers of the materials used in performing the repair work and are not registered if they carry on no other activity. Tax applies to their purchases. Group two includes firms that repair motor vehicles, major appliances, and the like. These firms are vendors and must collect and remit tax on parts and materials, the charges for which must be segre-

[9]Illinois was an exception to this rule prior to 1961.

gated. If they are not, the entire repair charge is taxable. Several states essentially make it mandatory to segregate the charges for parts and materials to protect the customer.

Several states provide for a variation from this dual classification rule by establishing formulas for calculation of tax on certain types of repair work. For example, Michigan applies tax to 35% of the charge for shoe repair.

Computer Software

Computer software consists of the instructions that cause electronic data processing machines to perform desired tasks. Those instructions are in the memory of the machine while the tasks are being performed; the instructions are stored on a machine-readable medium (disk, drum, punched card, or magnetic tape) when not in use. The instructions may be written by the owner of the machine, purchased with the machine, purchased in prepared form separate from the machine ("canned" programs), or written on contract especially for the owner. The first software source is not taxed because there is no sale or transfer of property. A number of states do, however, tax software sales, either by arguing that the sale is one of tangible personal property (the software will ordinarily be delivered in physical form), not one of a service, or by taking direct statutory action.

A recent survey shows the trend toward taxation of computer software.[10] Nineteen states (Arkansas, Connecticut, Georgia, Idaho, Kansas, Kentucky, Missouri, Nevada, New Mexico, North Carolina, Oklahoma, Pennsylvania, Rhode Island, South Carolina, South Dakota, Tennessee, Virginia, West Virginia, and Wisconsin) tax all software, usually subject to other possible exemptions because of sale to exempt entities or for exempt use. Sixteen states (Alabama, California, Colorado, Florida, Iowa, Maine, Maryland, Massachusetts, Michigan, Mississippi, New York, North Dakota, Ohio, Utah, Vermont, and Washington) plus the District of Columbia tax at least canned software. Seven (Arizona, Illinois, Louisiana, Minnesota, Nebraska, New Jersey, and Texas) generally exempt software. Indiana taxes canned programs, which are *always* transferred on tangible personal property. The taxation of software is usually based on the premise that it constitutes tangible personal property. Six states (Connecticut, Kansas, New Mexico, Oklahoma, South Dakota, and Tennessee) tax by statute and six (Colorado, Idaho, Massachusetts, Pennsylvania, Rhode Island, and South Carolina) by regulation. West Virginia taxes software as a service, depending on the purchaser for taxability. The seven states exempting software regard it as a service or as an intangible, as directed by courts in Illinois, Nebraska, and Texas. Tax-

---

[10]G. Bystrom, "Taxation of Computer Software," paper presented to 1981 Annual Meeting of National Association of Tax Administrators (NATA). Massachusetts exempts only custom software readable by humans. The compilations here extend the Bystrom survey.

ability is under litigation in several states currently taxing software without special statutory provision, and at least one state (Tennessee) applied statutory coverage of software after an unfavorable court decision on taxability.

The California law, for example, taxes any services that are part of a sale of tangible personal property (regardless of separate statement of associated services), unless the tangible personal property is incidental to the sale of a service. Thus, the state applies tax to custom programs transferred to the customer in the form of punch cards, tapes, disks, or drums, or in the form of typed or printed sheets for input to an optical character recognition system. The tax does not apply to transfer of custom programs in the form of written procedures (instructions on coding sheets). In this case, the service of writing a program is the element purchased, not the coding sheet used to transmit the instructions, an incidental element to the basic transaction. Canned programs (programs prewritten for any prospective purchaser) are taxed because the solution to the data processing problem exists and the tangible personal property containing that solution are of value in themselves.[11]

On the other hand, Texas taxes only nonoptional software included in the operational unit of the computer when purchased. Neither custom nor canned programs are taxed. Such treatment emerges from the case *First National Bank of Ft. Worth* v. *Bob Bullock,* 584 S.W. 2d 548 (Tex. Civ. App., Austin, 1979, writ ref'd): the court held that the sale of software was not taxable because the desired instructions could have been transferred in several different ways, so the transfer was that of a service, not of tangible personal property. The information transferred is much more valuable than the physical material transferred. A similar argument appears in the recent Illinois case *First National Bank of Springfield* v. *Department of Revenue* (Ill. Sup. Ct., March 31, 1981): computer programs transfer information, not tangible personal property. Not only could the desired property have been transferred by other mediums, but the tapes actually used could have been destroyed once the instructions were in the bank computer.

Similar extensions of the sales tax have, however, been upheld in Ohio (*The Cleveland Trust Co.* v. *Edgar L. Lindley*) and in South Carolina (*Citizen and Southern Systems, Inc.* v. *South Carolina Tax Commission*). In both instances, the argument hinged on a search for the true object of the transaction: Was the desired object the service of the programmer or the property produced by the service? Such logic leads to taxation of software under the existing statute, as the program reduced to tangible form was the desired product. That judicial attitude does, however, appear to be the exception.

Overall, taxability of computer software as tangible personal property can create judicial challenges. Even though canned programs differ little from

---

[11]J.D. Dotson, "Taxation of Software under the California Sales and Use Tax Law," *Revenue Administration* (1979).

videotapes, paperback books, records, and films in that they are valued for content, not physical ingredient, and can be transmitted in alternate form while retaining their basic value, the courts have not always extended equivalent treatment to software. Statutory action to include software in the tax base involves fewer judicial risks. Of course, many programs are for business use and, hence, ought not be part of a consumer sales tax.

REAL PROPERTY CONTRACTORS

Neither real property nor the labor service used to construct real property is taxable under the usual rule. Real property contracts could be made subject to the tax and have been in several states, but most states have not done so. Treatment of contractors is complicated because many do other types of work, such as fabrication or retail selling. The treatment of contractors has undergone basic change over the years, but today treatment is almost uniform, except in a few states.

The Basic Rule

In forty states, contractors—prime or subcontractors—are regarded as consumers of the materials, supplies, and equipment used in performing real property contracts, regardless of the nature of the contract. In these states, firms doing only a contract business are not registered as vendors, and pay tax on all purchases, including those of building materials. (In Indiana and Texas, they are regarded as consumers on fixed-price contracts only.) If they are registered vendors and buy goods for use in contract work tax free, they account for tax on the goods actually used in the contract work on the basis of cost, not selling price. Since they are not vendors on contract work, they do not bill the customer for tax as such, though presumably the tax will be reflected in their contract bids. The basic rule is applied regardless of the nature of the contract, whether it be cost-plus, time and materials, fixed-price, or another form, and even if the materials are billed separately to the customer, except in the two states noted.

The states have found through experience that it is better not to register general contractors as vendors, since many of them are very small and keep poor records, and the rate of turnover of firms is high. Therefore, their suppliers collect tax on sales to them, and they do not bill the tax separately to their customers, regardless of the legal nature of the contract.

There are few exceptions. The District of Columbia, Florida, Indiana, and Texas follow the rule that was common in early years of treating as vendors contractors who perform time and materials or other contracts in which they bill the materials separately. They are required to register, to collect tax, and to bill the tax separately to the customer. Other states abandoned the rule because of its discrimination against this form of contract (the tax base is higher because of markups) and because of the difficulties involved in enforcing payment from the contracting firms. It is no longer a significant type of contract, in any event.[12]

Common practice is to register as a registered consumer those contractors purchasing extensively from outside the state to facilitate enforcement of the use tax. Such firms, however, cannot buy tax free from in-state suppliers. North Dakota deviates from the usual pattern in registering all contractors as regular vendors, enabling them to buy tax free. States taxing repair of real property also register many contractors, since the same firms typically do repair work and new construction. Nevada also deviates from the usual rule in registering all air conditioning, plumbing, and electrical contractors as vendors, primarily for better control.

Taxation of Contract Price

Six states (all with broadly based sales taxes) follow an entirely different approach. All contractors are registered, buy materials tax free, and pay tax on the contract price, with some deductions permitted.

Arizona: The regular tax rate applies to the full contract price of the general contractor only. There is a 35% deduction to represent labor cost. Land value is excluded if it is part of the contract price.

Hawaii: The entire contract price, less the payments on subcontracts, is taxable; materials sold to contractors are taxed at 0.5%.

Mississippi: Contracts in excess of $10,000 are taxed on the full amount of the contract at 2.5% (one-half the regular sales rate); on those under $10,000, the contracts are not taxed, materials purchased being taxed at the regular 5.0% rate. On larger contracts, the prime contractor must pay the tax or furnish a surety bond. Upon so doing, the prime contractor receives a material purchase certificate authorizing purchase of component materials at the 0.125% tax rate. Subcontractors may use that certificate to purchase materials at that rate.

New Mexico: All prime contracts are taxed at the full rate; subcontracts are not taxed.

South Dakota: A state taxing most services, South Dakota follows an intermediate approach likely to produce pyramiding and uneconomic transactions. The contractor pays the regular tax on materials. Further, a tax at a 1.5% rate applies to the gross receipts of prime contractors and subcontractors on realty improvement contracts. The general contractor thus has an incentive to buy materials for subcontractors.

Washington: Prime contracts are fully taxed; subcontracts are tax free. The tax applies to materials bought by speculative builders.

[12]Until 1973, Indiana had exempted purchases made by speculative builders.

The question of whether real property contracts should be fully taxable is largely a matter of equity. A large portion of contract work is for housing, on which, as a matter of social policy, many states prefer not to place the full impact of the tax. The remainder of the contracts are on business property. Full taxation of the contracts increases the share of the tax on producers goods and encounters the usual objections to taxing producers goods noted in chapter 3.

Manufactured Housing

The spread of factory-built housing, including mobile homes as primary dwellings, creates an apparent imbalance in comparison with traditional housing. Although the labor service used in the construction of traditional structures is not taxable, the full purchase price of mobile homes and similar housing is taxable. In addition, resale of mobile homes can be taxable as well, whereas resale of structures always is completely outside the tax. Several states have made changes to relieve the tax from mobile homes, most since 1979. New Jersey exempts mobile homes that will be taxed as real property, and New York exempts in-state sales of manufactured housing. New Mexico, Washington, and Wyoming exempt later sales of the property, after the tax has been paid once. California, Maine, and North Dakota exempt all used mobile and modular home sales. Several states have elected to exclude specified percentages of the purchase price from taxation: California (25% of the dealer's purchase price exempt for mobile homes for residential use installed on foundations and 60% of the contractor's purchase price exempt for factory-built housing), Colorado (48% exempt), Idaho (55%), Indiana (amount not attributable to material cost, defined as 35%, exempt), Maine (amount not attributable to materials, not above 50%, exempt), and South Carolina (phasing in to 35%). There are problems in defining manufactured housing and the portion of the cost not from materials, (as in Maine), but the development of mobile homes as primary residences does suggest a case for special treatment of these purchases. Mississippi and West Virginia tax mobile home purchases at a lower rate (3%, 60% of the ordinary rate). The latter exempts fully those installed by vendor on a permanent foundation. North Dakota also taxes new mobile homes at a lower rate (2% vs. 3%). Texas excludes manufactured housing from the sales tax but applies a 6.5% tax on 65% of the sale price less shipping. Arizona taxes mobile home dealers as general contractors with the labor cost and land value adjustments previously outlined.

Contractor-Retailers (Dual Businesses)

Many contractors in the electrical, plumbing, heating, sheet metal, tile, and similar fields also operate retail stores and sell over the counter in the usual fashion. These firms must, of course, register as vendors. The usual rule is that they may then buy all of their materials—those for contract work and those to be sold over the counter—tax free. They then account for tax on the items sold at retail on the selling price in the usual fashion and on items going into their contract work at cost. Since most states are reluctant to register contractors, however, they will not require (or permit) registration of a firm that makes a retail sale only on rare occasions.

Various exceptions occur to the general practice. Whereas most states allow firms to make all purchases tax free if they have a substantial element of retail sales, Minnesota does so only if 50% or more of the firm's receipts are from retail sales, Nebraska does so only if 80% or more of receipts are retail, and Connecticut does so only if the receipts are predominantly from retail sales. The firms receive credit for tax paid on purchases against tax due on their sales. A few states, including Arizona, Illinois, New York, Pennsylvania, Vermont, Virginia, and Wisconsin, require the firms to buy tax paid those materials that are purchased specifically for contract work. Idaho allows dual firms to buy tax free only with permission of the revenue department. Kentucky limits certificate use to items for resale and inventory for resale. Wisconsin permits contractors to choose between using a resale certificate or paying the tax when the future use of such purchase is unknown. Georgia and Kansas require two registrations from dual firms as vendor and as contractor, issue two registration numbers, and require the firm to keep separate records for the two portions of its business. Vermont uses direct pay permits for dual firms and registers contractors for use tax as well.

There is no ideal method for these firms, though all systems used will work satisfactorily. Most states find, however, that getting firms to distinguish carefully between purchases for contract work and for resale is very difficult, and most do not find it worthwhile to try forcing firms to do so. States that tax all contracts at the regular rate have no problem with the dual business firms. Contractor-retailers must be registered, buy all materials tax free, and account for tax on their contract work on the total contract figure and on retail sales on the total sales figure. If the contract rate is lower than the retail rate, sales must carefully be distinguished.

Manufacturing Contractors

Certain types of contractor, particularly those in sheet metal work, fabricate such articles as furnaces, gutters, and downspouts that are then installed in real property. This work may be done in the shop or on the site. The problem, taxwise, is to obtain equity between these transactions and those in which similar articles are purchased complete from other vendors and then installed.

It has become increasingly common to apply tax only to the materials cost of such goods, whether fabricated in the shop or on the site; this avoids artificial encouragement for fabrication on the site but encourages contracting firms to produce the items themselves instead of buying them from other firms. (Oklahoma is one of the few states to follow the old rule that fabrication in the shop is fully taxable and that on the site taxable only on materials.) Alabama, Idaho, Maine, Missouri, New York, Tennessee, and Vermont seek to require payment on the full price of fabricated articles going into contract work. Economically, this solution is best, but it is difficult to enforce due to problems of delineation between fabrication and installation (which is typically not taxed). Arizona and Nevada require payment of tax on the full price of fabrication if the articles are placed in stock rather than placed directly into contract work—a rule hard to interpret in some cases. Michigan requires tax on the full price if the firm is producing similar items for sale on the market.

In general, all workable solutions to this problem result in some discrimination and distortion of economic activity. The problem is, of course, avoided completely if the entire real property contract is taxable. Similar problems arise with ready-mixed concrete and prefabricated houses. They are usually taxable in full, though this policy is somewhat discriminatory against these activities in favor of on-the-site production.

Installation Contracts

Contractors frequently install various types of tangible personal property in real property, the tangible personal property essentially retaining its identity. Examples include stoves, refrigerators, and window air conditioners. Under the regulations of most states, the contractor is the vendor of such articles. If he engages in this type of work, he must be registered as a vendor and collect and remit tax. Tax applies (except in those states that specifically tax installation charges) to the price less installation charges, if the latter are itemized separately, or to the entire charge, if no breakdown is made.

The line between these items and construction materials is drawn in various ways. In most states, the criterion is whether the item becomes legally a part of real property. This point, in turn, depends upon whether the article is permanently attached in such a way that it cannot be removed without substantial damage to the real property, though interpretations of this rule vary. For example, electric ranges and ovens are frequently built into the wall of the kitchen. In many states, they are considered a part of real property. Thus, the contractor is the consumer and the tax is much less than on an equivalent electric range set in the kitchen and does not become real property. Some states draw the line based on whether the title passes before the article becomes a part of real property.

In addition to materials and items, like stoves, that remain tangible personal property, California has designated a third category as "fixtures." This category includes lighting and plumbing fixtures, furnaces, air-conditioning and refrigeration units, elevators, awnings, venetian blinds, prefabricated cabinets, and similar items. The contractor is defined to be the vendor and must collect tax. In most states, however, fixtures are regarded as becoming a part of real property and are treated as materials, the contractors being consumers thereof.

The obvious aim in this area should be to preserve equity between contract and noncontract acquisition of appliances and similar items. This equity can be accomplished only by regarding the contractor as the vendor and applying tax to the full price (less installation charge if quoted separately).

Exempt Entity Contracts

States are divided in the manner in which they treat sales to contractors of material for use on government contracts and sales to entities whose purchases are exempt under their tax. (On these transactions, they may tax federal contractors if they wish, because the courts regard the contractor, not the federal government, as the consumer.) Twenty-four states permit no pass through of exemption to the contractor.[13] Nebraska, Iowa, and North Carolina do not exempt, but refund amounts collected to, respectively, exempt organizations and political subdivisions. Nebraska requires the exempt entity to appoint the contractor its agent for these materials. The remaining states have a pass through of organization exemption to contractors for at least some entities. Michigan limits the pass through to nonprofit hospitals and housing; Washington limits it to housing authorities and the federal government; and Maryland excludes governments from pass through. Some agencies have avoided the tax by buying the materials themselves and then contracting for the work to be done. They must actually buy the materials, however; they cannot escape tax merely by having the contractor bill the materials directly to them.

SUMMARY: EVALUATION OF THE TAXATION OF SERVICES

In outline, major considerations relating to taxation of various principal categories of services are summarized below:

1. *Utility services*: Taxation of utility services broadens the base of the tax and yields substantial revenue. Basic justification is that of making a general consumption levy as broad as possible to maximize revenue at a given rate and minimize distortion of consumer choice. Administratively,

---

[13]Alabama, Arizona, Arkansas, California, Florida (some federal exempt), Georgia, Hawaii (except federal cost plus), Idaho (except for U.S. nuclear test facility at Arco), Kentucky, Louisiana (except Toledo Bend Dam), Massachusetts, Minnesota, Mississippi, Nevada, New Mexico, North Dakota, Pennsylvania, South Carolina, South Dakota, Tennessee, Virginia, and Wisconsin. Utah and Missouri do exempt pollution control equipment contractors.

there is no gain or loss from taxation. The main objection is the burden on the poor, which can be alleviated by a credit against income tax. Gas, electricity, and water used directly in production should not be taxed because they are major elements in business cost, and freight service should not be taxed under any circumstances. There is likewise strong justification for excluding passenger transport.

2. *Rental of tangible personal property*: The case for taxing is very strong, since the consumer expenditures involved are those on the rental charges.

3. *Transient rentals*: The case for taxation is strong because of equity and revenue. Permanent rentals should not be taxed because of discrimination against tenants and in favor of home owners.

4. *Admissions and club dues*: The case is very strong because of equity.

5. *Repair of real property*: The desirability of taxing such repair is seriously doubted, unless all real property contracts are taxed, because of the difficulties in delimiting repair from new construction. Taxation of such repair encourages firms to do repair work with their own employees.

   On the other hand, a number of items that become technically real property but retain their identity (e.g., built-in stoves, furnaces) can be defined as fixtures, and their repair and cleaning made taxable by specific provision of the law. To do otherwise discriminates in favor of built-in items over competitive items that are not built in.

6. *Installation*: Charges for installing tangible personal property in real property can justifiably be made taxable, but some borderline problems are created between installation and construction work.

7. *Laundries and dry cleaning*: There is strong justification for taxation, and few administrative problems are created.

8. *Barber shops and beauty parlors*: Taxation of this service does require registration of numerous small barber shops, and some evasion may occur, but otherwise the justification is strong on the principle of providing as broad a base for the tax as possible.

9. *Bank service charges and safe deposit charges*: No objection is made to taxation of safe deposit charges. Taxation of bank service charges does favor those persons freed of service charges because their bank balances are large.

10. *Parking charges*: There is strong justification for taxing these charges—other than street parking meters.

11. *Storage*: Charges for storage, other than that of goods held for resale or as materials by business firms, can be taxed, but little revenue is involved.

12. *Pest control*: Little objection can be made to taxing this service, other than that rendered to commercial farmers for their crops.

13. *Advertising*: Experience of the states with seeking to tax advertising has not been satisfactory. Part of the trouble is the interstate aspect. To tax local advertising (e.g., radio, TV, newspaper), although national adver-

tising in magazines cannot be taxed, is seriously discriminatory. Most advertising is provided for business firms and is essentially a producers good. Charges for the service are made in numerous ways. Despite "popular" appeal of taxing something which many regard as "obnoxious," on the whole the states would apparently do well to stay out of the field.

14. *Professional services*: Serious objections are made on equity grounds against taxing medical, dental, hospital, and related services. Expenditures for these services are distributed unevenly over various families. Because of social policy, objection is strong to any action that would discourage expenditures for these services. Legal services are not usually regarded as taxable. Other professional services are provided primarily to business firms, and taxation is objectionable on the grounds previously noted.

15. *Bookkeeping, collection, janitorial, and similar services*: These services are rendered primarily to business firms, and taxation is objectionable because it will encourage firms to provide these services with their own employees instead of hiring outside firms, thus causing inefficiency and loss of specialization.

16. *Investment counseling, real estate and insurance commissions*: These services relate to investment, not consumption activities, in the usual sense, and thus are not appropriate in a consumption-related tax.

17. *Contracting*: The taxation of the full contract price has merit in avoiding a number of dividing lines between taxable and nontaxable activity. It does increase the relative burden on housing and on business investment, however, and objections can be raised in both cases.

18. *Other*: Most other specific services that could be included either have nominal revenue yield or are primarily business services.

5. Organization and Personnel for State Sales Tax Administration

GENERAL STRUCTURE FOR TAX ADMINISTRATION

State agencies for tax administration may be headed by a person or by a commission, either appointed or elected.

Appointed Commissioner or Commission. By far the most common organizational structure for revenue administration is that of a revenue or taxation department headed by a commissioner or director. The titles vary; the term *commissioner of revenue* is used in twelve states, many in the South: Alabama, Alaska, Connecticut (Revenue Services), Georgia, Indiana, Kentucky, Massachusetts, Michigan, Minnesota, New Hampshire, New Mexico (Taxation and Revenue), and Tennessee; *commissioner of taxation* (or *taxes*) or *tax commissioner* in six states: Nebraska, New York (*commissioner of taxation and finance*), Ohio, Vermont, Viginia, and West Virginia; *director of revenue* in eight states: Arizona, Delaware, Illinois, Iowa, Missouri, Montana, Oregon, and Washington; *executive director* in Colorado and Florida; *director of taxation* in New Jersey and Hawaii; *director of finances and administration* in Arkansas; *tax assessor* in Maine; *tax administrator* in Rhode Island; and *secretary of revenue* in Kansas, Louisiana, North Carolina, Pennsylvania, South Dakota, and Wisconsin. Differences in titles have little or no significance relative to functions.

Most commonly, the commissioner is appointed by the governor and serves at the governor's pleasure. Thirty-seven states now use this structure, with only minor variations. Frequently, the person appointed as commissioner has had only limited experience in the tax field; he is rarely an expert in taxation but primarily an administrator and political liaison person, brought in from outside the state government with a major task of implementing the governor's policies in tax administration. Although many commissioners are lawyers, there are exceptions. In several states (Arizona and Louisiana, in recent years; Maine, New Jersey, New Mexico, Vermont, and Virginia; and at times Minnesota, for example) the commissioners have in practice become nonpolitical appointments, regarded strictly as administrators, persons being kept in the position regardless of changes in a state administration.

When Commissioner Morrissett retired in Virginia in 1970, he had completed forty-three years of service as commissioner. Apart from these career situations, the competency of the commissioners varies widely, from political hacks who give little attention to the job to persons with expert background in taxation or administration who bring remarkable improvements over a short period of time. In at least four instances in the last two decades (Arizona, Iowa, Kentucky, and Virginia), an experienced person has been brought in from outside the state as commissioner—a rare occurrence in American state government.

In two states (Michigan and Rhode Island), the head of the revenue service is a civil service appointee and thus a career person who usually has risen through the ranks. In Michigan, the commissioner, formerly directly responsible to the governor, is now responsible to the state treasurer; in Rhode Island, revenue administration is included in the state department of administration.

Seven states retain the old appointive-commission system of organization for tax administration. They are (with numbers of members in parentheses) Idaho (four), Mississippi (three), Nevada (seven), Oklahoma (three, appointed for six-year terms), South Carolina (three), Utah (four), and Wyoming (three). There are commissions in Massachusetts and New York also, but the chairman is, in effect, the tax administrator. The usual rule is for the commission to appoint a secretary or executive director who serves as the principal adminstrator, some of whom are longtime career personnel. In Utah, the chief auditor is, in effect, the executive director. Idaho is an exception; each commissioner serves as the director of particular taxes, with no executive director. The net effect of the commission system, especially with long and staggered terms, is to insulate somewhat the operation of the administration from the control of the governor, even if the latter appoints the members of the commission.

Elected Officials. In four states, tax administration is under the jurisdiction of an elected official or officials. California has an elected board, the five-person State Board of Equalization, with the state controller an ex officio member (himself elected) and the other four elected from districts. In Maryland and Texas, tax administration is under the jurisdiction of the comptroller, an elected official. In North Dakota, the tax commissioner is elected, but persons have served for very long periods. The recent commissioner was elected to Congress in 1980.

Trends. Over several decades, the trend has been slowly toward a single commissioner appointed by the governor; Arizona, Iowa, Montana, New Hampshire, Oregon, and Washington replaced commissions by a single revenue director, and Florida transferred revenue administration from the jurisdiction of the comptroller to an appointed official. The only state to move the opposite way was Idaho, which transferred the administrative functions from a single tax collector to the state tax commission.

A strong case can be made for a system with a single official responsible for all tax administration, the person either appointed by the governor or selected on a civil service basis with competency for the position. The commission system divides responsibility and is generally unsatisfactory for any administrative activity. Election of commissioners is particularly undesirable—as is selection of any purely administrative officials. In addition, concentration of responsibility for state administration in the hands of the governor is usually essential for the best administration. In the end, however, the results depend more on the persons than the organizational structure. California, with the worst possible type of administrative structure, has one of the best, if not the best, sales tax administrations, and some states with appointive commissioners have weak administrations. Improvement in administration requires strong commitment by the governor to improve administration, appointment of an energetic and competent tax commissioner, and provision of adequate financial support by the legislature. South Dakota and, earlier, Iowa and New Mexico, are good examples of states in which governors have brought great improvements in tax administration.

Organizational Structure for Sales Tax Administration

The most significant change that has occurred in sales tax administration over the last two decades has been the shift from the type-of-tax organizational structure to the functional one, in which either there are no tax divisions at all, or if they exist, they do not have their own field forces.

Completely Functional Organization. Fifteen states have no sales tax division or unit at all; the organization is entirely functional, with the units, such as audit, handling all taxes.[1] Four additional states, while having an overall functional organization, do have separate sales tax units in subordinate divisions. Arizona, Idaho, and Utah have separate sales tax audit sections, and Maine has a sales tax unit in the tax division.

An additional thirteen states have a sales tax division, under a director, but without a field force. The functions of the division are typically interpretive, although some extend to office audit (Alabama and Kansas), a role in audit selection (Georgia and Virginia), and audit review (North Carolina). Georgia

---

[1]Dates indicate year of change to functional: Colorado, Connecticut (1979); Florida (1978); Hawaii, Illinois, Kentucky, Massachusetts, Missouri, Nebraska, New Jersey, New Mexico, New York (1972–79); Pennsylvania (1978), Rhode Island, and Wisconsin. New York does have a sales tax section in office audit, and Rhode Island an excise division with very minor functions.

and Virginia have transferred the compliance work from the sales tax unit in the last decade and Minnesota, the audit work.

Partially Functional Field Operations. Several states are using hybrid systems, at least at the moment, although some are considering further functionalization. In Oklahoma, Tennessee, and West Virginia, the sales tax divisions have their own audit staffs, the most significant arm of field operations. In Indiana, South Dakota, and Wyoming, the reverse pattern is found; the sales tax division has compliance but not audit personnel.

Nonfunctional Organization. Only four states, compared to twelve in 1970, retain the old type-of-tax organization: Maryland, Ohio (which has limited functionalization of compliance in the two major cities), North Dakota (which tried the functional organization and abandoned it), and South Carolina. In three states, however, the sales tax dominates the operation. In California, income taxes are administered by an agency distinct from the Board of Equalization; the sales tax operation is integrated with that of related taxes in the Business Tax Department, in which the sales tax is the principal element. Nevada has a functional organization, but with no income tax, and the sales tax dominates. In Washington, with no income tax, the sales tax is integrated with the closely related business and occupation tax.

The trend toward functionalization derives from several sources: the desire to lessen nuisance to business firms arising from visits by two sets of auditors; the belief that better use can be made of the time of field personnel; the recommendations of public administration consulting firms or other outside groups that have favored the functional organization; and the acceptance of the "trend." In several states, such as Wisconsin, the sales tax was introduced in a situation with an effective income tax administration and thus grafted onto it.

It is difficult to assess the net gain or loss. There are clearly some advantages of functionalization along the lines indicated. No longer, however, is any one person clearly directly responsible for the administration of the sales tax. Where a sales tax division does exist with the functional form, the director often has little power, and coordination with the functional units is not always good. The relationship seems to vary from excellent to very poor, on the basis of information gained from interviews. Several state officials expressed the view that the loss of specialized responsibility was a definite disadvantage, but in most states the functional form was operating effectively. A major part of the case for functional organization rests on the argument for integrated audit, but audit is not in fact always integrated. An incidental disadvantage of the functional form is that comparing sales tax administrative cost and adequacy of audit staffs among the states has become difficult.

CENTRALIZATION VERSUS REGIONAL CONTROL

A question of importance on administrative structure is: To what extent should operations be centralized in headquarters or decentralized through the use of regional offices and assignment of personnel to certain areas? States cannot be classified into a few clear-cut categories based on centralization.

Centralized Systems. Centralized control at one extreme is found in Rhode Island and Maryland, where virtually all operations are centralized in headquarters. There are no regional offices, and no field personnel are assigned to particular areas. Arizona has only a suboffice in Tucson. West Virginia and Wyoming have no district offices. The former assigns compliance personnel and auditors to areas, but they are supervised from headquarters. North Dakota has two offices for audit only.

Regional Offices with Centralized Control. The most common pattern involves the use of district offices, usually under the jurisdiction of a senior auditor, for supervision of enforcement and audit personnel but with basic control over most enforcement and audit in headquarters. The enforcement personnel are usually assigned to a specific county or counties or area within a city, whereas the auditors work usually over the entire district. Maryland, with a highly centralized system, does have a branch, mainly for taxpayer information, but with some audit and collection work. In Florida, North Carolina, and Texas, there are two sets of district offices—a relatively small number for audit, a larger number for enforcement. Illinois and New York have an upper layer of two regional offices, with jurisdiction over district offices. Records kept in the district offices are limited in most states to a list of vendors and current lists of delinquents, plus records of audits made, although, in many states, the district office now has computer terminals connecting them with headquarters. In almost all instances (Colorado, Maine, and Wyoming being exceptions) the offices, plus additional branches in many states, are open to the public for information. In many states, the offices handle all taxes. Data on district offices are given in table 5.1.

Of these states, Florida, North Carolina, and Virginia place relatively greater authority in the district offices for audit selection and review and enforcement initiative than do the other states and provide more information to the district offices about taxpayer accounts.

Decentralized States. Three states place primary responsibility for audit and enforcement on the district offices. In Mississippi, the district offices select accounts for audit, review the audits, and follow their own procedures, on their own initiative, on delinquents, subject to general guide rules es-

TABLE 5.1 District Offices

State	District Offices	Special Features
Alabama	9	in field division—all functions
Arizona	1	Tucson only
Arkansas	5	headed by auditor
California	17	key role in audit selection
Colorado	10	enforcement personnel only
Connecticut	5	audit personnel only
Florida	21 enforcement, 6 audit	greater role than in many states
Georgia	9	
Hawaii	4	complete decentralization; select audits, etc.
Idaho	6	compliance management
Illinois	18	2 regions; Chicago and downstate (Springfield)
Indiana	13	auditors assigned
Iowa	13	plus 7 out-of-state offices
Kansas	2	enforcement personnel only assigned
Kentucky	9	
Louisiana	8	plus 18 branches; mainly taxpayer assistance
Maine	5	for auditors only; compliance personnel assigned to counties but not to district offices; not open to public
Maryland	9	limited audit and collection work; taxpayer information
Massachusetts	10	compliance work; no control over auditors
Michigan	9	
Minnesota	6 regional	plus 8 district offices, audit and compliance personnel assigned
Mississippi	9	high degree of autonomy in audit and compliance
Missouri	5	supervise audits, compliance
Nebraska	5	auditors and compliance personnel assigned to
Nevada	3	auditors and compliance personnel assigned to
New Jersey	6	auditors and compliance personnel assigned to
New Mexico	6	auditors and compliance personnel assigned to
New York	13	plus 7 branches (three regions: upstate, downstate, and Chicago offices)
North Carolina	64	collections offices
	15	audit districts
North Dakota	2	audit personnel only
Ohio	9	
Oklahoma	7	compliance personnel only
Pennsylvania	26	all functions, all taxes
Rhode Island	0	
South Carolina	5	all functions, and accept returns
South Dakota	2	headquarters for personnel, taxpayer assistance
Tennessee	7	all taxes
Texas	56 enforcement, 22 audit	personnel assigned to
Utah	5	audit only
Vermont	3	audit only
Virginia	8	substantial autonomy to district offices; head is from audit
Washington	17	plus 58 suboffices; control from Olympia
West Virginia	0	auditors and compliance personnel to areas
Wisconsin	3	plus 33 branches, both functions field men assigned to districts
Wyoming	0	

tablished in headquarters. There are nine district offices, with field personnel assigned to particular counties.

Hawaii has the most completely decentralized system. No records of taxpayers are kept in headquarters at all; all records are kept in the district offices, of which there are four; audit selection and control of delinquency rests with the district offices, subject to general guidelines.

California has twenty-two district offices headed by a district tax administrator. The district office selects the individual accounts for audit from the print-outs of eligible firms sent from headquarters and in conformity with the policies established. Initial action on delinquents is taken in Sacramento, but final action against those not paying after notices is left largely to the district office. California cites advantages of such decentralization: (1) personnel can live at home, (2) travel time is kept to a minimum, (3) close contact can be maintained with the retailers, (4) information can be provided locally, and (5) personnel can gain a knowledge of local conditions.

On the other hand, decentralization makes attainment of uniform policies more difficult, and in smaller states it may result in ineffective use of personnel and in the inability to use data processing equipment effectively. It may invite local favoritism, if not outright dishonesty. Knowing retailers and their financial standing and being aware of the opening of new stores and the closing of old ones without question facilitate certain aspects of enforcement, but they may also result in friendship and local influence that prevent uniform treatment of all taxpayers.

The potential danger of less efficient use of the best available personnel and equipment particularly suggests that decentralization should not be carried too far, especially in audit. For most states, it would appear that decentralization should be limited to establishing district offices to which compliance personnel (as distinguished from auditors) are assigned. Notices of delinquency, bad checks, and other collection problems would be sent to the regional supervisor, who would assign the work to the appropriate persons.

There is merit in having the district offices open to the public, with personnel readily available for taxpayers who have questions, although widespread use of 800 numbers lessens the necessity for this. Ready accessibility of tax information is of utmost importance for successful operation of the tax.

A strong argument can be made for placing all audit selection, review, and control over the work of the auditors in the audit unit at headquarters and not in the regional offices, except in a few large states in which a small number of audit districts may prove desirable. Audit and delinquency control are basically very different functions. If the district supervisor has responsibility for audit, the requirements and salary for the post must be much higher than otherwise. Uniformity in audit policy is imperative. Top quality audit personnel are usually scarce and should be available for use wherever they are most needed. Under this policy, the district supervisor would have no jurisdiction over auditors, who would receive all instructions from headquarters and make all reports directly to headquarters.

HEADQUARTERS AND SUPERVISORY PERSONNEL

Sales tax personnel include several groups in addition to the field force subsequently noted.

Regional Supervisors or District Managers.   In the states with a decentralized organization, regional supervisors occupy a key position in the organization. These persons typically have had long experience with the sales tax divisions, often as auditors, some in compliance, or were hired for these positions on the basis of adequate business experience. In some states the managers have no jurisdiction over auditors.

Supervising and Review Auditors in Headquarters.   The chief of the audit unit occupies a key position in the larger states, assisting in the evaluation of prospective new employees, supervising the work of the auditors, controlling the program of audit selection, and reviewing major audits. In the smaller states the work may be performed by a senior auditor who is not designated as the chief of a separate unit.

Most states have several review auditors, senior auditors with long experience, who review all field audits. In small states the chief auditor does all review work.

Preaudit Personnel.   Personnel used for the "preaudit" of returns check arithmetic, completeness of returns, and, in some instances, deductions. In a few states, as noted, this preaudit work is merged with cursory internal audit for selection of accounts for field audit.

Internal Auditors.   A few states make a systematic office review of all returns to select those that appear to warrant field audit. In some, in-training auditors are used for this type of work, plus some senior audit personnel, and individuals who for one reason or another are not currently suitable for field work. In other states, this work is performed by senior clerical personnel, who, though they are not auditors, have learned to spot returns that are likely to be in error. There has been a tendency in the last decade toward establishing a separate office-auditor classification distinct from field auditor, with lower qualifications and lower salaries. Iowa, Kansas, New York, Oklahoma, Washington, and Wisconsin have adopted such classifications.

Technical Personnel.   In a few of the larger states, legal, programming, tabulation, statistical, and other technical personnel are assigned directly to the sales tax unit. More frequently, these persons are assigned to the entire revenue department, or even to a general administrative service unit. In most states, legal personnel assigned to the revenue department are technically on the staff of the attorney general.

Selection of Personnel

The great majority of states provide for selection of revenue personnel, except at top levels, via some type of civil service merit system. There are, however, exceptions, and the exact coverage and procedures differ.

Non–Civil Service States.   Six states (Arkansas, Mississippi, Missouri, North Dakota, South Carolina, and Texas) do not have civil service systems. In Pennsylvania and Indiana, only a portion of revenue personnel are covered by the systems. The actual situations differ among these states. All have some type of classification of personnel and selection system administered by the revenue department. In Mississippi, North Dakota, South Carolina, and Texas, there has been relative permanence of employees but no assurance of job security, and employees may be fired if the state administration changes. Some of these states have at least limited political influence in hiring of personnel. The more technical personnel, such as auditors, are more likely to be retained than other types. Missouri has been notorious for replacement of personnel on a political basis, although some have been retained. In Indiana, auditors are covered by civil service, but the remainder of the personnel are not, and with considerable turnover—although the governorship has been in Republican hands for a long period. In Pennsylvania, only audit and data processing personnel are covered, and there has been substantial turnover of other personnel.

In the last two decades, the trend has been toward greater use of merit systems. Ten of the thirty-three sales tax states in 1962 had no merit systems, formal or informal. The disadvantages of a strictly patronage system for personnel are so obvious that the states have moved away from it in the revenue area, either by law or practice, in large degree. At its worst, the patronage system involves hiring persons on the basis of political influence regardless of qualifications and discharging persons who may have become qualified simply because the party in power in the state has changed. Such a system is intolerable for as technical a function as tax administration.

Recent U.S. Supreme Court decisions have raised serious questions as to the right of a state to fire persons in nonpolicy positions simply because they belong to a particular political party; if this decision is applied to state revenue personnel, all states may be forced to use civil service systems or the equivalent.

The Civil Service, or Merit System, States.   The remainder of the states employ civil service or merit personnel systems. Typically, all except top level policy-making personnel are covered. To be hired, persons must demonstrate qualifications on the evidence of their education and employment records and/or examinations, promotions are made on an established schedule, and discharge is possible only for cause. The systems vary slightly, however, in coverage and procedures.

The typical system covers all revenue personnel except the director and the deputy or assistant director(s). In Nebraska and Virginia, only the director is not covered; in Michigan and Rhode Island, even the directors of revenue are covered. There are, however, ten states, plus the District of Columbia, in which the division heads (as well as the directors and deputies) are not subject: Connecticut, Florida, Kansas, Kentucky, Louisiana, Massachusetts, Minnesota, New Mexico, Tennessee, and Wisconsin (in part), although in practice these persons often are retained when the state administration changes. Usually the top personnel are excluded on the grounds that they are in part policy-making officials, one of whose functions is to implement the governor's policies in matters relating to administration of taxes. There is grave doubt, however, that the exemption should carry as far down as heads of divisions, essentially technical posts requiring persons with long experience in the work.

The discretion allowed the revenue department in selecting from the lists provided by the state personnel agency varies widely. In some states (e.g., Alabama and Louisiana), the department must select from the top three; in a number, from the top five;[2] and in Maine and Iowa, from the top six. In several states and the District of Columbia,[3] the department can reject all of the names, but in others (e.g., Maine and Vermont), it cannot. In a few states the revenue department has been given most of the authority for establishing examinations and lists of eligibles, recruiting, and selection, subject to the general rules of the state legislation—for example California, Nebraska, Oklahoma, and Washington. By contrast, others, such as New Jersey, find their recruiting seriously hampered by the state personnel agency. Some states (e.g., Alabama, Maine, and Nebraska), require examinations; others, such as Arizona, Nebraska, and Pennsylvania, establish qualifications on the basis of the education and training record without examination. Several states (e.g., Arkansas, California, Louisiana, North Dakota, and Texas) do substantial recruiting for auditors at the universities and colleges, as does Wisconsin, which is now limited to in-state schools only; it formerly recruited out-of-state for minority personnel.

The persons hired are given probationary status, usually for six months, and the revenue agency is free to let them go during probation if their work is unsatisfactory. Thereafter, they can be fired only for cause, with appeal to designated bodies. Promotions are usually from within, based on performance, length of service, and, often, examinations.

Obviously, the merit system has some limitations; a certain amount of dead wood accumulates that is hard to eliminate. Effective administration can minimize this problem, however, and in time the incompetents can be eased into other jobs or retired.

[2]Connecticut, Idaho, Kansas, Maryland, Oklahoma, Tennessee, Utah, Vermont, and Wisconsin, among others.
[3]Georgia, Iowa, Kansas, Nevada, and South Dakota.

FIELD FORCES

Successful sales tax operation depends to a great extent on the field forces. Their work will be described in detail in chapters 7 and 8, but at this point some preliminary comment is necessary concerning the two distinct field functions—enforcement (compliance) and audit.

The enforcement staff provides information to taxpayers and ensures that firms not filing and paying comply with the law. This involves contact with delinquents, action to enforce payment when other methods fail, collection of tax from firms that file but do not pay in full, collection on bad checks, verification to ensure that licenses are obtained, and related activities. Titles for personnel assigned to enforcement work vary.[4] The term *compliance officer* will be employed in this study. A few states make a distinction between collection personnel, who take action against hard-core delinquents, and other enforcement personnel.

The audit staff examines taxpayer returns, accounts, and records to ensure that the correct amount of tax was reported.

Single or Dual Field Forces

One decision concerning the organization of the field force is whether a single force should handle enforcement and audit work, or whether each function should have a separate force.

Single Field Force. Six states (Alabama, Hawaii, Maine, Minnesota, Ohio, and Vermont) group all field personnel (except regional supervisors) into one class, but often with segregation within the class.[5] The personnel in the junior levels, plus some senior ones who for some reason are no longer able to do field audit work, perform the enforcement functions. In Georgia, Grade I auditors do the enforcement work; there is a small, separate collection group.

In these states, all persons hired typically have the minimum background regarded as necessary for audit, even if much of the work initially is enforce-

---

[4]There are almost as many titles as states: revenue collection officer (Illinois), collection and enforcement officer (New Mexico), field collector (Arizona and Arkansas), revenue compliance officer (Washington), tax compliance agent (New York), revenue agent (Connecticut, Florida, Nebraska, and South Dakota), field agent (West Virginia), field inspector (North Dakota), field examiner (Indiana), field investigator (Pennsylvania), investigator (New Jersey), tax compliance representative (California), revenue examiner (Maryland), field representative (Kansas, Kentucky, Mississippi, Virginia, and Wyoming), field men (Missouri), revenue deputy (Louisiana), revenue representative (Iowa), enforcement officer (Colorado, Texas), tax field agent (Georgia), revenue officer (District of Columbia, Idaho, North Carolina, Rhode Island, and Tennessee), tax examainer (Massachusetts and Minnesota), tax collection representative (Michigan), revenue officer (Nevada), tax collector (South Carolina), and tax representative (Wisconsin).

[5]Both audit and compliance personnel in Massachusetts are called tax examiners, but they are assigned separately.

ment, though in practice they have less accounting background than those hired as auditors in other states for audit work. The single field force system may also minimize travel, especially in more remote areas, allow optimal overall use of time, and ensure close integration of the two types of work. If an investigation indicates need for an audit, the latter can be made by the same person. A single force suffers, however, from inevitable limitations. The time of competent auditors is too valuable to devote to enforcement, and the backgrounds required are not entirely the same.

Dual Field Force.   Other sales tax states use dual systems. The auditors, with rare exceptions, do no enforcement work whatsoever, and in most states the compliance officers perform nothing that could actually be called audit. In the past, compliance personnel did limited simple audit work, but the trend is away from this practice.

The numbers of compliance personnel and auditors are shown in tables 5.2 and 5.6.

TABLE 5.2 Numbers and Monthly Salaries of Compliance Personnel, 1970 and 1979-81 (in $)

			1979-81		
Number	*State*	*1970*	*Beginning*	*Senior*	*Supervisory*
35[a]	Alabama[a]	477-627	1,264-1,531		
17	Arizona	518-630	903-1,152	1,029-1,318	
13	Arkansas	359-680	817	1,255	
328	California	717-959	1,327-1,724	1,724-2,073	2,073-3,019
34	Colorado	—	1,277-1,712	1,408-1,888	1,630-2,185
9	Connecticut	762-1,045	1,115-1,347	1,229-1,474	1,456-1,771
48[b]	Florida	488-793	806-1,048	896-1,175	
145	Georgia	591-783	946-1,253	1,023-1,362	1,204-1,619
—	Hawaii	555-1,153	—	—	
13[c]	Idaho	610-742	1,014-1,232	1,233-1,499	
54[d]	Illinois	—	1,131-1,675	1,647-2,499	1,858-2,822
35	Indiana	400-450	716-	-900	
99[d]	Iowa	527-859	1,094-1,381	1,255-1,548	1,442-1,771
29[c]	Kansas	463-584	831-	868-1,039	948-1,186
97[d]	Kentucky	480-906	710-	782-	951-
191	Louisiana	420-1,050	734-1,222	884-1,505	1,068-2,031
6[a]	Maine	535-977	898-1,135	957-1,219	
19[e]	Maryland	604-885	912-1,272	1,121-1,584	
45[c]	Massachusetts	633-832	1,170-1,365	1,304-1,534	1,577-1,872
91	Michigan	696-964	—		
100[a]	Minnesota[a]	569-1,112	999-1,241	1,103-1,366	
32	Mississippi	560-930	810-1,245	875-1,375	100-1,590
15	Missouri	425-575	748-990		
22[d]	Nebraska	550-650	876-1,006	927-1,250	1,394-1,670
14	Nevada	733-841	1,200-	-1,653	

TABLE 5.2 *(continued)*

			1979–81		
Number	*State*	*1970*	*Beginning*	*Senior*	*Supervisory*
150[d]	New Jersey	450–916	952–1,416	1,215–1,898	1,628–2,198
60[e]	New Mexico	360–785	887–1,517	931–1,513	1,132–1,937
349[d]	New York	721–833	1,144–	1,209–1,339	1,401–2,388
228[d]	North Carolina	596–1,260	981–1,289	1,231–1,969	
1[f]	North Dakota	525–739	930–	–1,752	1,186–1,752
240[a]	Ohio	499–890	926–1,298	1,180–1,993	1,428–2,193
55[d]	Oklahoma	310–685	—	—	
278[d]	Pennsylvania	460–617	833–1,033	925–1,183	1,083–1,408
20[d]	Rhode Island	455–540	1,254–1,420	1,380–1,597	1,597–1,797
37	South Carolina	548–734	968–	–1,372	
18	South Dakota	500–600	1,062–1,592	1,154–1,744	1,365–2,093
80[c]	Tennessee	445–560	933–1,337	1,015–1,421	1,096–1,524
761	Texas	610–768	1,160–1,415	1,615–1,669	2,320–2,919
8	Utah	471–700	1,001–	1,231–	1,799–
9	Vermont[g]	548–734	740–1,048	878–1,086	988–1,206
33[a]	Virginia	560–732	1,116–1,523	1,219–1,666	1,457–1,990
65	Washington	580–1,041	1,095–1,401	1,269–1,794	1,547–2,185
35	West Virginia	485–570	689–1,116	792–1,293	
100[d]	Wisconsin	692–917	1,062–1,365	1,305–1,801	1,535–2,150
14	Wyoming	571–762	1,226–	–1,902	
65	District of Columbia	546–992	983–	–2,342	2,158–3,950

[a] One type of field personnel only.
[b] Plus 62 in office.
[c] Adjusted for time devoted to sales tax.
[d] Total, not allocable by type of tax.
[e] Mostly telephone work.
[f] Plus 6 telephone personnel.
[g] Compliance personnel.

Qualifications for Compliance Personnel

There has been substantial shift in emphasis over the last two decades in the background of persons hired for compliance work. In the past, the usual requirements, if any, for appointment were high school graduation and some experience, typically in retailing. The persons hired were often older, some of whom had lost jobs in retailing or given up their own small stores. This tradition still exists in some states (as, for example, Missouri), but the trend has been toward requiring or preferring college education and/or a relatively high level of experience, particularly in collections work.

States Emphasizing College Degrees. At least six states require college degrees, usually in business administration, with some work in accountancy—

Kentucky, Nebraska, New Jersey, Rhode Island, South Carolina, and South Dakota. Strong preference for a degree is expressed in North Dakota and Wisconsin.

The majority of states require either a college degree (business administration preferred) or several years experience, preferably in investigation or collections work.[6] A number of the persons hired do have college degrees—about half of the new employees in Illinois, for example. These states tend to get two groups—younger persons directly out of college and older ones with substantial business experience.

Other States. A second group requires experience, typically without college work, some requiring background in accounting.[7] Indiana stresses "self-starter" personal characteristics.

Salary Ranges. Table 5.2 shows salary ranges for compliance personnel, for 1970 and 1979-81. The beginning salary, in most states, is between $700 and $1,100 a month. At the senior levels salaries range over a much wider span, but half are between $1,100 and $1,400. These are not high-paying jobs to attract and retain university graduates. Rough comparison with the 1970 figures shows that with some exceptions the pay has not kept up with inflation; the cost of living index roughly doubled between 1970 and 1980. It is not possible to make a more precise comparison without detailed data of numbers of persons at various salary grades.

Qualifications for Auditors

Primary qualifications for auditors are shown in table 5.3.

The states fall into two major groups on qualifications for auditors:

Twenty-two of the sales tax states, almost half, require a college or university degree, some requiring a degree in accountancy, others a specified minimum amount of work in accountancy, ranging from twelve hours (Illinois, South Carolina) to twenty-four in a number of states. Most of these states seek young college graduates and report that they are able to get them—California, Colorado, Hawaii, Illinois, Kansas, Kentucky, Mississippi, Nebraska, Rhode Island, South Dakota, Texas, Washington, and Wisconsin. The aim is to hire young persons with accounting training who will make a career of the state service.

The second major group, eighteen states plus the District of Columbia, requires either a college degree with a certain number of hours of accountancy

[6]California, Connecticut, Florida, Georgia, Illinois, Iowa, Louisiana, North Carolina, Ohio, Tennessee, Utah, Washington, West Virginia, and Wisconsin.

[7]Colorado, Idaho, Indiana, Maine, Maryland, Michigan, Mississippi, Nevada, New Mexico, and Pennsylvania.

TABLE 5.3 Qualifications for Auditors, 1979–80

State	Qualifications
Alabama	degree[a] or exp.
Arizona	degree and 6 mo. exp., or 12 hrs. accy. and 1 yr. exp.
Arkansas	degree with 24 hrs. accy.
California	degree in accy. or equivalent
Colorado	degree with 18 hrs. accy. plus 6 in related areas
Connecticut	degree in accy. or degree and 1 yr. exp., or 5 yrs. exp.
Florida	degree with 15 hrs. accy.; can substitute exp.
Georgia	degree in accy. or equivalent
Hawaii	degree in accy.
Idaho	accy. background, from college or exp.; exam required
Illinois	degree with 12 hrs. accy.
Indiana	college level knowledge of accy.
Iowa	degree or exp. but must have 12 hrs. accy.
Kansas	degree with accy.
Kentucky	degree in accy. or degree in B.A. with 20 hrs. accy.
Louisiana	degree with 24 hrs. accy.
Maine	degree with some accy., or exp.
Maryland	some accy., from college or exp.
Massachusetts	degree with accy.
Michigan	degree in accy. or bus. adm.
Minnesota	3 to 9 hrs. accy. training
Mississippi	degree in accy., plus exam
Missouri	degree with 12 hrs. accy.; will accept exp.
Nebraska	degree with 24 hrs. accy.
Nevada	degree and/or exp.
New Jersey	degree with 18 hrs. accy. plus 1 yr. exp.; can subs. exp. or courses for degree
New Mexico	degree or exp. with 15 hrs. accy.
New York	degree with 24 hrs. accy.
North Carolina	degree in accy. or bus. adm. with 12 hrs. accy. or exp.
North Dakota	degree with accy. or exp.
Ohio	accy. from courses or exp.
Oklahoma	degree with 6 hrs. accy. or exp.
Pennsylvania	one yr. exp. plus 6 hrs. accy. beyond high school
Rhode Island	degree in accy.
South Carolina	degree in bus. adm. with 12 hrs. accy.
South Dakota	degree in accy.
Tennessee	degree in accy. or degree with 36 hrs. accy.
Texas	degree with 24 hrs. accy. or 3 yrs. college with 24 hrs. accy. plus 2 yrs. exp.
Utah	degree plus exam; can subs. exp.; must have 30 hrs. accy.
Vermont	A: degree plus 2 yrs. exp. work exp. can be subs. for degree B: degree in accy. or bus. adm. plus 3 yrs. exp.
Virginia	degree plus 2 yrs. exp., or more exp.
Washington	degree in accy. or bus. adm.
West Virginia	degree in accy.
Wisconsin	degree in accy.
Wyoming	degree or 3 yrs. exp.
District of Columbia	24 hrs. accy.

[a] Degree refers to college or university degree.

or accounting experience, as specified. Some members of this group, such as the District of Columbia, Maine, and Massachusetts, much prefer college graduates and are able to get them; others are unable to recruit many and primarily get persons with business experience—Minnesota and Nevada, for example. New Mexico, which did require a college degree, has moved away from this rule. On the whole, however, there has been a trend toward greater stress on college work.

The final group requires both college and experience, making it impossible, usually, to recruit new college graduates, as many states prefer to do. This group includes Arizona, New Jersey and Utah (which will permit substitution of experience for college), Vermont, and Virginia. Several states, as for example, Illinois and Michigan, do not require an examination if the requirements are met; others, such as Idaho, Mississippi, and Wisconsin, do.

Salaries of Auditors

Table 5.4 shows salary ranges of sales tax auditors in 1970, table 5.5, the ranges in 1981.

Exact comparison among states is impossible. Some states can hire above the beginning grade, whereas others cannot. The progress upward varies among states. For the beginning grade, almost half the states pay initial salaries between $950 and $1,150 per month; only nine are below this, and fifteen above.

At the top salary of the senior levels, there is a greater range, from $1,300 to $2,800; the distribution is as follows:

Salary	No. of States
Under $1,350	1
$1,350–1,550	4
$1,550–1,750	6
$1,750–1,950	10
$1,950–2,150	12
$2,150–2,350	3
$2,350–2,800	7
Over $2,600	2
1970:	
Under $750	5
$750–950	11
$950–1,150	16
$1,150–1,350	8

TABLE 5.4 Monthly Salary Levels, Sales Tax Auditors, 1970 (in $)

State	Trainee	Beginning	Experienced	Senior	Supervisory
Alabama		627–806	686–865	746–927	
Arizona		636–774	746–929	808–1,006	1,090
Arkansas		523–736	583–861	583–861	686–1,015
California		710–821	863–1,100	1,048–1,337	1,155–1,882
Colorado		693			928
Connecticut	679–748	762–947	945–1,152	1,052–1,270	1,150–1,423
Florida		581–793	615–814	685–945	
Georgia		649–859	713–943	783–1,036	
Hawaii		643–996	744–1,153	801–1,336	949–1,624
Idaho		610		742	
Illinois		625–685	710–795	805–1,110	985–1,048
Indiana		420–525	480–600	600–720	660–1,110
Iowa		673–902	779–1,044	902–1,209	1,044–1,469
Kansas		574		714	
Kentucky		583–821	643–906	782–1,100	951–1,213
Louisiana		660–960	720–1,020	840–1,246	930–1,320
Maine		535–771	585–771	641–847	737–977
Maryland		604–794	635–873	731–961	805–1,057
Massachusetts		529	615–780	663–1,120	
Michigan		828–1,070	901–1,171	988–1,288	
Minnesota		611–771	951–998	844–1,112	792–1,129
Mississippi		625–865	690–930	755–1,075	
Missouri		450		750	
Nebraska		575	592	825	950
Nevada		734	841	841	1,111
New Jersey		583			1,000
New Mexico	660–900	720–980	860–1,160	860–1,160	
New York	682–775	721–833		865–1,048	1,127–1,661
North Carolina		652–820	859–1,090	942–1,119	1,039–1,321
North Dakota		525		737	
Ohio		747–983	846–1,118	960–1,118	1,092–1,464
Oklahoma		520–685	650–810	725–950	
Pennsylvania		560–751	648–869	869–923	1,006–1,347
Rhode Island		630–754	695–832	962–1,150	
South Carolina		618–790	682–915	789–1,060	850–1,150
South Dakota		600	—	700	
Tennessee	500–620	650–790	755–900	825–980	
Texas		719		936	1,000–1,179
Utah		560	618	682	1,350
Vermont		745–1,014	795–1,090	899–1,221	
Virginia		700		911	
Washington		640–778	778–991	900–1,148	764–1,000
West Virginia		600	915	915	

California and Michigan (plus the District of Columbia) are the best paying states, Missouri the lowest. The median figure is between $1,950 and $2,050; the median in 1970 was between $950 and $1,050. Thus, on the whole, the salary schedules have just kept pace with the price level and thus have fallen relative to many salaries.

The states, generally, in the last few years have been able to fill their auditor positions; exceptions are New Jersey and Arizona. A number of states indicate, however, that they cannot get enough top quality persons. The best accountancy graduates go into public accounting or business accounting positions, while the next group, with some exceptions, select state revenue departments. The main limitation is that of salaries, which are typically below starting salaries for other accountancy positions. The 1981 average starting salary for graduates in accounting was $1,481.[8] Clearly, the initial salaries paid by most of the states are not high enough to be competitive with private business. A number of the state tax administrators indicate that the salaries for auditors are far too low—for example, California (despite its relatively good salaries), Hawaii, Maine, Massachusetts, Nebraska, North Dakota, Vermont, and Virginia. In a number of states, work in state tax audit does not qualify for experience requirements for the CPA (for example, Kansas, Nevada, and North Dakota)—thus discouraging persons from entering state service. In other states (e.g., California, Idaho, Iowa, Mississippi, Nebraska, New York, and Wisconsin), the experience does qualify and in some of these states most of the senior auditors are CPAs.

Relative Adequacy of Audit Staffs

The shift toward functional organization and integrated audit staffs has made the comparison of and determination of the relative adequacy of the audit staffs between 1970 and 1981 difficult. Some of the apparent increases in numbers reflect merely that, in 1970, only the number of sales tax auditors was listed, whereas, in 1981, only the total figure of all auditors was available. For twenty-nine states, however, either the sales tax audit staff is separate or a reasonable estimate can be made of total audit time going into sales tax audit, on the basis of figures applied by the states; the number of sales tax auditors is estimated on this basis.

Although it is difficult to define the optimal number, and the optimal figure undoubtedly varies among states according to the complexity of audit, studies in various states suggest that one auditor per 1,000 accounts may be regarded as a reasonable figure. Ten states meet this requirement: California, Illinois, Rhode Island, Tennessee, Texas, Utah, Vermont, Washington, West Virginia, and Wisconsin. Five additional ones are close—under 1,250: Connecticut, Iowa, Nevada, Oklahoma, and Virginia. At the other extreme, the number of accounts per auditor exceeds 2,500 in Kansas, Minnesota,

8College Placement Council, *CPC Salary Survey*, July 1980.

TABLE 5.5 Monthly Salary Levels, Sales Tax Auditors, 1981 (in $)

State	Trainee	Experienced			Senior	Supervising	Management
		Beginning	Lower	Upper			
Alabama		1,264-1,531	1,388-	-1,726	1,471-1,870	1,791-3,309	
Arizona		1,101-1,450	1,289-1,693			1,506-2,047	
Arkansas	817-1,255	927-1,426	1,077-1,655			1,237-1,898	1,390-2,143
California		1,327-1,578	1,724-2,173	2,073-2,621	2,278-2,879	2,278-3,167	2,748-3,481
Colorado		1,103-1,478	1,277-1,712	1,478-1,982	1,798-2,409	2,081-2,991	2,294-3,073
Connecticut	1,106-1,482	1,115-1,347	1,355-1,613	1,528-1,850	1,342-1,805	1,603-1,947	
Florida		945-1,242	1,058-1,402	1,187-1,583	1,688-2,291		
Georgia		1,307-1,761	1,421-1,922	1,547-2,099	1,221-1,806	1,547-2,099	2,392-3,259
Hawaii		1,104-1,508	1,128-	-1,649		1,380-2,086	
Idaho		1,065-1,652	1,295-1,913	1,428-2,109	1,650-2,441		
Illinois	1,060-1,365	1,131-1,675	1,254-	-1,882	1,390-2,024		
Indiana		1,207-1,541	1,365-1,740	1,541-1,974		2,067-2,763	
Iowa		1,250-1,543	1,473-	-1,830	1,615-2,018	1,740-2,224	2,231-3,150
Kansas		994-1,252	1,141-1,432				
Kentucky		951-	1,048-	1,155-1,405	1,048-1,976	1,274-2,399	
Louisiana		1,068-1,579	1,200-1,885	1,346-2,031	1,493-2,164	1,650-2,480	1,955-2,757
Maine		957-1,219	1,030-1,319	1,212-1,597		1,395-1,825	
Maryland		912-1,272	1,121-1,584	1,299-1,706	1,399-1,838	1,507-1,980	1,749-2,298
Massachusetts		1,045-	1,303-1,532		1,433-1,701		
Michigan		1,452-1,922	1,651-2,234	1,943-2,669	2,082-2,871		

Minnesota		1,227–1,644	1,366–1,841	1,470–1,985	1,470–2,350	1,583–2,140	
Mississippi	1,000–1,590	1,100–1,755	1,210–1,935	1,330–2,135		1,060–1,371	
Missouri		875–1,234	926–1,130	991–1,229			
Nebraska		1,250–	1,344–	1,445–	1,553–		
Nevada		1,148–1,577	1,314–1,813		1,375–1,898	1,670–	1,795–2,075
New Jersey	999–1,049	1,158–1,562	1,339–1,808	1,550–2,093		1,709–2,308	
New Mexico		1,078–1,845	1,189–2,034	1,310–2,243		1,517–2,597	1,757–3,006
New York	1,253	1,401–1,667	1,567–1,857		2,037–2,388	2,518–2,931	3,396–
North Carolina	1,131–1,623	1,551–2,261	1,701–	–2,403		1,869–2,735	
North Dakota		930–1,372	1,024–1,513			1,372–2,028	1,726–2,416
Ohio		926–1,298	1,080–1,428	1,180–1,726	1,428–1,993	1,428–2,193	
Oklahoma		977–1,514	1,112–1,773	1,275–2,048		1,651–2,139	
Pennsylvania		952–1,218	1,167–1,447	1,273–1,651	1,447–1,880	1,879–2,137	
Rhode Island		1,424–1,667			1,667–1,891		
South Carolina		968–1,372	1,273–1,888	1,324–1,877	1,490–2,133		
South Dakota		1,061–1,591	1,154–	–1,743	1,254–1,916	1,364–2,092	
Tennessee		947–1,096	1,056–1,421	1,230–1,632		1,375–1,796	
Texas		1,239–1,415	1,415–1,615	1,615–1,905	1,905–2,171	2,171–2,733	2,320–2,919
Utah	1,001–1,461	1,106–1,616	1,231–1,799	1,390–2,029		1,543–2,251	1,716–2,773
Vermont		988–1,040	1,121–	–1,315	1,201–1,728	1,274–1,800	
Virginia	1,179–1,504	1,472–1,805	1,333–1,820	1,457–1,990	1,885–2,412	1,593–2,426	
Washington		1,043–1,692		1,707–2,185	1,372–2,242	2,080–2,663	2,296–2,939
West Virginia			1,142–1,858	1,251–2,041	1,655–2,300		
Wisconsin		1,406–1,928	1,526–2,121	1,655–2,300		2,144–2,980	
Wyoming		1,256			1,980		
District of Columbia		983–1,250	1,500–		–2,803	3,167–4,167	

TABLE 5.6 Sales Tax Audit Staffs Relative to Number of Registered Vendors, 1981

State	Reported No. of Active Accounts		Reported No. of Auditors Total[a]		Figure of Auditors Adjusted for Allocation of Time		No. of Accounts per Auditor	
	1970	1981	1970	1981[b]	1970	1981	1970	1981
Alabama	45,789	58,265	100	91	—	—	458	—
Arizona	53,500	75,000	30	41	30	41	1,783	1,829
Arkansas	47,000	56,561	20	113	20	—	2,350	—
California	385,919	629,533	743	838	700	727	551	866
Colorado	42,000	91,200	28	90	—	—	2,100	—
Connecticut	51,000	100,000	45	80	45	70[c]	1,135	1,429
Florida	208,748	295,254	100	293	100	—	2,087	—
Georgia	75,000	106,000	85	95	85	72	882	1,472
Hawaii	50,000	69,000	45	47	42	42	1,250	1,643
Idaho	22,379	31,000	11	18	11	18	2,034	1,722
Illinois	177,539	172,942	234	352	187	276	949	626
Indiana	135,000	137,723	208	288	100	—	1,350	—
Iowa	93,019	99,945	68	110	68	88	1,368	1,136
Kansas	53,000	75,493	20	13	18	13	2,944	5,807
Kentucky	66,705	76,820	50	110	25	—	2,667	—
Louisiana	60,000	78,000	60	108	30	—	2,000	—
Maine	30,000	39,597	28	45	28	25	1,072	1,584
Maryland	50,000	91,802	85	90	85	90	589	1,020
Massachusetts	120,000	129,656	45	83	45	83	2,667	1,562
Michigan	127,500	138,000	331	261	100	—	1,275[a]	—

Minnesota	90,180	105,000	125	100	63	40	722	2,625
Mississippi	57,496	73,554	65	92	55	80	1,044	919
Missouri	78,526	100,020	80	95	80	—	981	—
Nebraska	55,285	56,000	12	50	12	—	4,601	—
Nevada	13,000	20,500	22	18	22	18	591	1,139
New Jersey	198,709	177,235	40	124	40	—	4,967	—
New Mexico	36,000	85,651	50	46	45	38	800	1,862
New York	430,000	450,358		1,200	600c	—	716	—
North Carolina	97,202	122,281	115	149	86	—	1,110	—
North Dakota	19,732	26,000	10	15	10	15	1,973	1,733
Ohio	211,000	229,496	309	240	175	240	1,206	956
Oklahoma	49,199	56,000	36	49	36	49	1,366	1,143
Pennsylvania	214,538	229,039	164	142	164	—	1,308	—
Rhode Island	18,000	23,000	37	50	35	37	514	622
South Carolina	53,532	71,804	48	52	48	52	1,115	1,381
South Dakota	21,000	29,756	8	27	8	17	2,625	1,750
Tennessee	75,000	95,141	80	79	80	98	937	971
Texas	225,000	289,880	123	429	123	400	1,830	676
Utah	19,000	33,000	34	35	25	35	760	943
Vermont	11,841	20,880	12	25	9	20	1,316	1,044
Virginia	73,423	80,000	74	104	74	80c	992	1,000
Washington	62,000	157,000	114	129	75	100c	826	1,570
West Virginia	31,200	39,505	32	40	27	40	1,155	988
Wisconsin	87,050	108,000	217	144	33	60c	2,638	1,800
Wyoming	15,000	28,073	2	14	2	10	7,500	2,807
District of Columbia	13,700	33,000	12	54	9	18	1,529	1,833
Total	3,085,809	5,277,172			3,935	2,928	1,047	1,066

a Number of field auditors, including supervisory staff.
b Total for sales tax when sales tax audit force is separate; overall total when not.
c Estimate.

Nebraska, and Wyoming. The remainder of the states have figures between 1,250 and 2,500.

For the states for which figures are available, Idaho, Nebraska, South Dakota, Texas, Vermont, and Wyoming have made the greatest percentage increases in audit staffs since 1970, although some are still inadequate. By contrast, Kansas and Minnesota appeared to have experienced significant reductions in the size of the audit staffs.

Revenue officials of fifteen of the states were asked whether they believed their audit staffs to be adequate. Eleven of these indicated that the numbers were inadequate—for example, in both Minnesota and Wyoming the number should be two to three times the present figure. Others indicating the need for an increase were Arizona, Idaho, Massachusetts, Mississippi, Nevada, North Dakota, South Dakota, and West Virginia. Rhode Island, which has good audit coverage, expressed the view that the numbers were adequate, and Vermont and Kansas, that the staffs were approximately adequate. Only New Mexico indicated that the number for sales tax was excessive and that some auditors would be shifted to other taxes. The source of the inadequate numbers is primarily state budget officers and the state legislatures, which will not provide an adequate number of positions.

Although the states are, for the most part, able to fill their positions, some have substantial turnover of audit personnel; persons are trained and then are lured away by higher salaries elsewhere. Among others, California, Illinois, Iowa, Maine, Massachusetts, Missouri, Virginia, South Dakota, and Wisconsin complain of turnover, particularly of the most qualified personnel.

One of the most significant changes that has occurred in audit staffs is the increase in the number of women. Whereas women auditors were virtually unknown in 1960 and very limited in numbers in 1970, they are now found in most states. In a sample of nineteen states in which the question was specifically asked, all of these states have women on the audit staff or have had them recently. In Nevada, for example, three of eighteen field auditors are women. Despite the long reluctance to hire women, the administrators in all of these states reported that the women performed very well. A number of states also have women compliance personnel. At the time the interviews were conducted, two states—Louisiana and Vermont—had women directors of revenue, Tennessee had in 1981, and other states had them at times. A similar development has occurred in the hiring of blacks, long employed in some of the northern states, but resisted in many southern states no more than a decade ago. Now even Mississippi, for example, has black auditors. Unfortunately, the number of blacks graduating with degrees in accountancy is very small.

An Examiner Class

Five states have established a third class of personnel, frequently called tax examiners, primarily for office audit and in some instances audit review, with qualifications less substantial than those of the auditors (see table 5.7).

TABLE 5.7 Staffs of Tax Examiners or Equivalent Positions

State	Number	Title	Primary Function	Salary Range ($)	Qualifications
Illinois	—	tax examiner	income tax	1,011–1,248	some accy.
Iowa	8	examiner	audit review	1,141–1,427	degree or exp.
Kentucky	53	tax examiner	office audit	782–1,946	degree or exp.[a]
Missouri	31	audit analyst	office audit	678–1,332	some bookkeeping
New York	60	tax technician	office audit	870–2,540	12 hrs. accy.[b]
Texas	256	accounts examiner	review returns	1,160–1,905	degree or exp.
Vermont	10	tax examiner	office audit	825–1,400	degree or exp.
Washington	35	excise tax examiner	office audit	1,017–2,240	degree or exp.
Wisconsin	30	tax examiner	office audit	1,008–1,349	move up from clerical after study and exam

[a] Degree in B.A.; other degree and 6 mos. exp., or move from clerical after exp.
[b] and 2 yrs. college; by promotion, 1 yr. exp., 12 hrs. accy.

In almost all instances, a high percentage of these persons are women, moving up from clerical positions in some states, such as Wisconsin. The general aim of this system is to save the time of field auditors from this type of work, using less well trained and less expensive personnel for the purpose.

Training Programs

On the whole, for both compliance personnel and auditors, formal training programs are very limited. The typical pattern for auditors is to give the newly hired persons a one- to three-week indoctrination program at headquarters, with limited instruction in tax law, department organization procedures, and policies, and then send them to the assigned district office for on-the-job training under the district supervisor or a senior auditor. At the end of the probation period, typically six months, but in some states a year, the decision is made whether or not to retain the person. The program for compliance personnel is similar but simpler. A few states send the persons almost directly to on-the-job training and then bring them into headquarters for some formal training. In Indiana formal training alternates with continued on-the-job training.

At the other extreme, California has a lengthy formal training program, given in Sacramento and in the major district offices, with classroom instruction in the tax structures, tax auditing, and department procedures. Arizona has a four-month training program, the persons spending half the time during this period in the training sessions, the other half on the job. The Texas system is similar, covering one year. Connecticut and Florida have formal training programs, that of the former six months in length. New Mexico provides formal training one day a week for twelve weeks and the other days are spent on the job. New York alternates on-the-job and formal training over a two-year period. Illinois provides four weeks of classroom training before on-the-job work. Wisconsin gives four weeks of formal training, and then one year at desk audit before assignment to the field. South Dakota plans a three-month formal training program.

Training does not appear to be taken too seriously in many states. States hiring only one or a few auditors at any time cannot provide formal classroom training. Some of the larger states, however, might be advised to give more careful attention to formal training.

In order to supplement the training of new compliance persons and auditors, a number of states provide periodic seminars, usually one or two days, for their field personnel to aid in updating information and bringing greater uniformity in practice. Others encourage employees with a limited background in accounting to take correspondence or extension courses.

6. Registration of State Sales Tax Vendors and Processing of Sales Tax Returns

Successful operation of a sales tax requires the establishment of suitable operating procedures for the handling of tax returns and money received and for the ascertainment of delinquents—firms not filing and paying on time. Such procedures, in turn, necessitate a system of registration of all vendors. These operating procedures vary somewhat among the states. Optimal methods depend upon the numbers of returns and other considerations.

REGISTRATION OF VENDORS

All sales tax states have some system for registration of vendors. Vendors file an application for registration with the tax administration. From this application, a certificate is issued that authorizes the vendor to make sales at retail. This authorization is known as a *license* in thirteen states: Alabama, Arizona, Colorado, Hawaii, Maryland, Michigan, Missouri, Ohio, Pennsylvania, South Carolina, South Dakota, Utah, and Wyoming. The term *registration certificate* is used in seventeen states and the District of Columbia: Connecticut, Florida, Georgia, Illinois, Kansas, Louisiana, Maine, Massachusetts, Mississippi, New Jersey, New Mexico, New York (certificate of authority), North Carolina, Tennessee, Vermont, Virginia, and Washington. The *permit* designation is employed in Arkansas, California, Idaho, Iowa, Kentucky, Minnesota, Nebraska, Nevada, North Dakota, Oklahoma, Rhode Island, Texas, and Wisconsin. The term used in West Virginia is *business franchise registration certificate* (covering all related taxes); in Indiana, *registered retail merchant certificate*. The term *registration certificate* has increased in relative usage since 1960.

Several states, such as Georgia, Nebraska, South Dakota, Tennessee, and Virginia, require separate registration for each store location. More commonly, however, only one registration is required, with a listing of various locations. Even the states, except Tennessee, requiring separate registration for each location permit consolidated returns, usually with a breakdown of data by location. Other states permit registration either on a consolidated or individual store basis.

Several states, including Hawaii, Idaho, Illinois, Indiana, Kentucky, Louisiana, Michigan, Minnesota, Missouri, New Mexico, New York, Pennsylvania, Vermont, and Washington, use a single registration for both sales and use tax, that is, out-of-state, vendors. More commonly, out-of-state use tax vendors, firms located out of state but making sales in the state, are separately registered. No fee is charged even if a charge is required for sales tax registration. Many states also provide a separate type of registration for registered consumers, that is, in-state firms not making sales at retail and therefore not obligated to register as vendors but regularly making purchases from out of state on which use tax is not collected by the suppliers. Primarily these firms are contractors, some types of manufacturing and repair firm, professionals, and the like. These firms are not entitled to make purchases free of tax under quotation of registration number, but they are sent return forms regularly for payment of use tax. Registration of such purchasers has substantial merit and involves little work. Inevitably, the reminder to pay tax on goods bought tax free increases revenue.

Mississippi requires both sales and use tax registration of all firms that make taxable sales and incur use tax on purchases. Florida requires both sales tax registration and application for permission to import from out of state and pay use tax.

A few states require registration of tax-exempt institutions to enable them to buy tax free: Colorado, Florida, Kentucky, Maine, Maryland, Minnesota, Nebraska, New Jersey, North Dakota, Pennsylvania, Rhode Island, Tennessee, Utah, and Vermont. Those meeting the requirements are issued a special number to quote their suppliers, in conjunction in some states with issuance of an exemption certificate.

A major question relates to the need for registering those manufacturers and wholesalers who do not make retail sales. Many manufacturers and wholesalers make some incidental retail sales to employees or operate coffee shops, but many do not. Initially, virtually all states required registration, and many still do to exercise better control over purchases for resale and purchases of materials and to collect use taxes that are due. Exemption of purchases is conditional upon quotation of a vendor account number. Careful attention to this question in a number of states, however, including North Carolina, Ohio, Pennsylvania, and South Carolina, and in the province of Ontario, has led to the conclusion that such registration is unnecessary. The firms are authorized to buy tax free for resale or for use as materials by the execution of an exemption certification, without a registration number. The other jurisdictions, however, fear that eliminating the registration requirement weakens control. One compromise solution is to give all manufacturers and wholesalers a registration number for exempt purchases but to classify them as inactive if they do not make retail sales, and therefore not send them returns.

Unlike most European and developing economies, none of the states exempt small retailers. Such exemption is regarded as unnecessary and discriminatory, as well as costing revenue. The question does arise, however, concerning house-to-house sellers of cosmetics, kitchenware, Girl Scout cookies, and Christmas cards. The last two groups of sellers are usually small children. Although the law usually provides no exemption, by administrative action the itinerant sellers, particularly children, are not registered. Instead, tax is collected if possible from the supplying firm on the retail price. This procedure is feasible when the supplier is an in-state firm (since the itinerants are not registered they cannot buy tax free) or with large national organizations that are willing to cooperate with the states, as many are. With other out-of-state suppliers it is not feasible to enforce the tax, however, and many states make no serious effort to do so.

Several states are moving toward single registration for a number of state taxes—Kentucky, Maryland, Michigan, Mississippi, Nebraska (income, sales use, contractor, wholesaler), and New Mexico.

Application Forms

All states provide forms for vendors to use to apply for registration, as illustrated in figures 6.1 and 6.2. The basic information required is more or less uniform, but some states require information on the financial situation of the firm, primarily for the bond requirement. There is an increasing tendency to require the employer social security number. Applications are mailed to revenue headquarters, with a fee, if required, except in a few states in which they are submitted to district offices.

Fees

Six states require an annual reissue of licenses. The chief advantage of this system is the annual purging of the lists of inactive vendors. On the other hand, this practice causes considerable nuisance for vendor and state, and inevitably some firms are delinquent in filing, though the amount due is small. The fee is $1.00 in Michigan, $2.50 ($8.00 for chain stores), in Colorado, $2.50 in Hawaii, and $15.00 per store location in West Virginia. In these states, a notice to renew the license is mailed near the end of the year. In South Carolina, the annual charge, which is essentially a chain store tax, is $5.00 for a single store, rising by increments of $5.00 for each additional store. Arizona requires renewal every five years, with a $1.00 fee.

In thirty-eight states, the registration is permanent so long as no change occurs in the ownership of the business. No fee is required in twenty-four of these states and the District of Columbia. Fees are as follows: $1 in Connecticut, Iowa, Minnesota, Nebraska (each store), and Ohio; $2 in Wisconsin and

ST-1 (REV. 7-79)

APPLICATION FOR CERTIFICATE OF REGISTRATION

STATE OF GEORGIA

Department of Revenue
Sales and Use Tax Division
303A1 Trinity—Washington Bldg.
Atlanta, Georgia 30334

Coded		
	Key Punched	
	Cert. Mailed	

EVERY QUESTION MUST BE ANSWERED IN FULL   (Please print or type)

1. BUSINESS TRADE NAME _____

Area Code and Telephone No. _____   County in Georgia where Business located _____

2. MAIL RETURNS TO: _____
(Street & Number, P. O. Box or RFD No.)   (City)   (State)   (Zip Code)

3. LOCATION OF BUSINESS _____
(Street Address, Hwy., Route)   (City)   (State)   (Zip Code)

4. Is this business located within the incorporated limits of above city or town?   Yes [   ]   No [   ]

5. When did or will you start business for which THIS application is made? _____
(If out of state applicant, give date of first activity in Georgia.)   (Month)   (Day)   (Year)

6. If a seasonal business, state months business will be open. _____

7. Type of   [   ] Individual   [   ] Corporation _____
   Ownership   [   ] Partnership   Corporate Name
               [   ] Other (Explain) _____
               (Date Inc.)   (State)   (County)

8. Name of owner(s) or
   Corporate Officers: _____
   Title   Residence Address   Social Security No. (See Line 8 of instructions)

   _____
   _____
   _____

9. If you have a Federal Employer's Identification number (E. I. Number) enter here. _____

10. Nature of Business. (If combination of two or more, list percentages of sales).

Retail [ ] _____ %   Services [ ] _____ %   Manufacturing [ ] _____ %   Mining [ ] _____ %

Wholesale [ ] _____ %   Construction [ ] _____ %   Processing [ ] _____ %

11. What kind of business will you operate? _____

12. If your State sales and use tax liability each month will be less than **$100.00 and you want to report and remit sales and use tax on a quarterly basis, check this box** [ ].

13. If this business operates in a Leased Department, does the Lessor report the sales tax for you? Yes [ ] No [ ]. If "yes", enter here the Lessor's name, address and Georgia Certificate of Registration: _____

14. Will you sell: (1) Alcoholic Beverages? Yes [ ] No [ ] (2) Gasoline and/or other Motor Fuel? Yes [ ] No [ ]

15. Address at which records will be kept and telephone _____

16. List the trade name, address and sales tax certificate number of all other businesses owned and/or operated by you and/or previously owned and/or operated by you in Georgia. (If additional space is needed, attach separate sheet.)
_____

17. The method of reporting will be (Cash-Accrual) _____ Basis.

18. If a former owner operated this business, fill in pertinent data below:

Former owner's name _____

Trade Name _____

Address _____
             City   State

Certificate of Registration Number _____ Effective date of change _____

19. If this business is a successor to the business shown on line 17 above, then state the amount paid former owner for inventory, equipment, building and/or other assets $ _____

This application has been examined by me and to the best of my knowledge is true and correct.

Date Signed _____

_____
Agent, Dept. of Revenue

_____
SIGNATURE   TITLE

(See reverse side of the original of this Application for instructions for completing. See reverse side of the copy of this Application for general information.)
(Must be signed by owner, partners or authorized officer of corporation.)

FIGURE 6.1   APPLICATION FOR RETAILER'S SALES AND USE TAX PERMIT, GEORGIA

NEVADA DEPARTMENT OF TAXATION

REVENUE DIVISION

CARSON CITY, NEVADA 89710

COMBINED APPLICATION FOR SELLER'S PERMIT AND REGISTRATION UNDER NRS 372, 374 AND 377

☐ NEW

☐ REVISED

☐ REINSTATED

DO NOT WRITE IN THIS COLUMN

DEPARTMENT OF TAXATION USE

ACCOUNT NUMBER ☐

PRINT OR TYPE - NO CARBON PAPER REQUIRED

Name of
Organization
(DBA) _____

Phone
Area
Code _____

Phone
Number _____

Full Legal Name
of Corporation _____

Owner's or
Corporate
Officer's
Names

(owner or)
(president) _____

(owner or)
(vice-president) _____

(owner or)
(secretary) _____

(owner or)
(treasurer) _____

Describe specifically and as briefly
as possible the nature of your business
(Attach additional sheets if necessary) _____

Will sell alcoholic beverages—Yes ☐ No ☐
Will sell cigarettes---------Yes ☐ No ☐

Date your
business
started
in Nevada Month _____ Day _____ Year _____

Federal Tax
Identification
Number 1

OR if none,
Social Security
Number 2

Type of
organization
(check one)   ☐1 INDIVIDUAL   ☐2 PARTNERSHIP   ☐3 CORPORATION   ☐4 OTHER (Explain)

INCLUDE ALL APPLICABLE ADDRESSES BELOW

A Business
mailing
address street _____ City _____ State _____ Zip Code _____

B Primary
business
location street _____ City _____ State _____ Zip Code _____

C Corporate
address street _____ City _____ State _____ Zip Code _____

Format ☐

State code ☐

Area code ☐

City code ☐

NBC ☐

NBC - Sub ☐

D Location of business records street _____ City _____ State _____ Zip Code _____

BRANCHES IN NEVADA USING THE SAME FIRM NAME MUST BE LISTED BELOW. ATTACH ADDITIONAL SHEETS IF NECESSARY.

E Business location street _____ City _____ State _____ Zip Code _____

F E E   There is a $3.00 fee for every business location in a 3 1/2 percent county and a $2.00 fee in a 3 percent county.

Total business locations _____ Fees required $ _____

Estimated monthly gross receipts $ _____

Estimated monthly taxable receipts $ _____

Reporting * (see security below) cycle (check one) 1 _____ monthly 2 _____ quarterly

S E C U R I T Y   With this application, security is required equal to three times your monthly tax liability for monthly accounts; and six times your monthly tax liability for quarterly accounts. No permit will be issued unless sufficient security accompanies application.

Security required $ _____

Have you ever been issued a Nevada sales or use tax permit? _____ yes _____ no   If yes, indicate account number and name.

Account number _____   Firm name _____

Was this business taken over from a former owner or operator? _____ yes _____ no

CERTIFICATE: The above statements are hereby certified to be correct to the best knowledge and belief of the undersigned who is authorized to sign this application.

If yes, did you acquire all or only part of the sellers business activity? _____ all _____ part

SIGNED _____

TITLE _____

Former account number _____

DATE _____

Former owner _____

APPLICATION TAKEN BY _____

Former firm name _____

DEPARTMENT OF TAXATION OFFICE _____

Return original to Nevada Department of Taxation. Retain duplicate for your records.
DOT ST 1

FIGURE 6.2   APPLICATION FOR PERMIT TO MAKE SALES AT RETAIL, NEVADA

S.I.C. code _____

Dist. _____
Sub-Dist. _____

Aud-Dist. _____
Fees required _____

Fees received _____

Type security _____

Security amount _____

Security date _____

Security device number _____

7133

Wyoming; $3 in Nevada; $5 in Maryland (each store), North Carolina, Rhode Island, and Virginia; $10 (each store) in Massachusetts; $25 (each store) in Indiana; and $25 in Washington, with subsequent refund against tax. The Washington rule is designed to discourage persons from registering who are not legally entitled to do so.

There are two schools of thought on the question of a fee. One believes business firms should pay an amount sufficient to cover the costs of handling the registration. The other argues that registration is of primary importance to the state and the vendor should not be charged. No answer to this question is obvious.

Check to Ensure Registration of Vendors

When the sales taxes were first introduced, most states made a systematic inquiry to ensure that all firms were registered. This inquiry involved checking yellow pages in telephone directories and lists of holders of store licenses, registrants under other taxes, and the like. Application forms were mailed to all such firms. In part it involved a door-to-door check by compliance personnel, who visited each place of business, partly to ensure that the vendor was registered, partly to provide information.

The states soon discovered, however, that failure to register by regular businesses was very uncommon. The primary force that ensures that firms do register is their inability to buy tax free under a registration number unless they comply. Most suppliers insist on obtaining the registration number because they otherwise become liable for the tax. Most states regard the problem as negligible and make no deliberate effort to check.[1] Some do have the compliance personnel watch for unregistered firms, but without any systematic program.[2] Of these, Washington encounters difficulty with firms liable for the business and occupation tax rather than sales tax, Vermont, with contractors and bars. Massachusetts has problems with restaurants. Maryland and North Dakota indicate that audit turns up a few firms. The final group indicates some problems: Hawaii, Idaho (about one a month), Indiana (with flea markets), Kansas (with out-of-state firms), Maine (with restaurants), Maryland (with part-time establishments), Minnesota (with flea markets), Mississippi, Missouri, Nevada, New Jersey (with flea markets), and New York (with shows, flea markets).

On the whole, therefore, evasion through failure to register is a negligible problem. With an effective program of audit of wholesalers, a retailer could escape detection for any period of time only if he bought solely from out of state or from farmers or other nonregistered suppliers. Except in unusual cir-

---

[1] For example, Colorado, Kentucky, Michigan, Minnesota, Nebraska, Pennsylvania, South Dakota, and Virginia.

[2] Alabama, Connecticut, Iowa, Louisiana, Nevada, Oklahoma, Tennessee, Texas, Vermont, Wisconsin, and Washington.

cumstances, such as drastic change in a tax or reorganization of administration, door-to-door checks are not worthwhile.

Excessive Registration

Most states have some problem with registration by firms that are not required to register. Particular difficulty occurred when the tax was first introduced. In an effort to ensure that all firms that should be registered in fact did so, the states were inclined to cast their nets too wide and register groups that should not have been. Some firms, being in doubt, registered when they did not need to.

The continuing problem is much less serious, but many of the states report some excessive registration.[3] In part, this condition results from misinformation, but some registration is deliberate—the desire to buy "at wholesale." Many suppliers accept possession of a vendor's permit as evidence that a firm is a retailer, not an individual consumer, and so will sell at a discount. The principal categories involved are farmers, small repair shops, contractors, antique dealers, hobbyists, and, in states where the tax is collected by the motor vehicle department, used-car dealers.

Registration of these persons results in some loss in tax revenue since they can buy tax free, though rarely does this advantage appear to be the motive. It also results in much pseudo-delinquency. Since these firms owe little or no tax and file no tax returns, they are listed as delinquents, but when they are tracked down they owe little or nothing. If they do file, the number of returns is increased with little revenue gained.

Closely related to the problem of excessive registration is that of failure to weed out the active tax roll. Most states today seek to remove the accounts of the vendors going out of business or becoming inactive, but not all are entirely careful to do so, especially with the inactives. The result is substantial deadwood, unnecessary costs of processing returns, and an excessive number of reported delinquencies, with costs incurred to track down firms that have quit business or are not making taxable sales.

Discovery that a firm has quit business may occur when the firm notifies the revenue department. Many however, do not do so. The next step is the post office return of the forms when they are mailed out first class and cannot be delivered; the following step is the failure to file returns; with proper enquiry, by phone, letter, or visit by a compliance officer, the fact that the firm is out of business is finally ascertained. This system should work with a high degree of precision, and in some states it does—but for reasons not entirely clear, in a number it does not. Massachusetts, for example, by 1978 had extensive deadwood in the active accounts.

[3]The exceptions are Alabama, Arkansas, Indiana, Louisiana, Maryland, and Rhode Island. Arizona, Iowa, Minnesota, Mississippi, and Nevada report few instances. Most of the other states report some problems.

There is also the problem of firms that continue to file returns but owe no tax, period after period, and probably should not be registered; there is the danger that they will continue to buy tax free. As a result, several states have established purge cycles; in one- to three-year intervals, all zero-return accounts are reviewed and those not liable for registration are removed from the active files. Pennsylvania, for example, found 21,000 accounts in 1979 that had owed no tax for three years, and a substantial percentage of these were removed from the tax rolls. Minnesota, by contrast, does not review firms continuing to file zero returns indefinitely.

Many states transfer the accounts removed from the active list to an inactive file, retained for several years, in case questions should arise about past liability if the firm returns to selling at retail.

Screening of Applications for Permits

All applications are checked as received for completeness of information, and, in most states, to see if back taxes are owed from previous registration. This is not always easy to determine, as different names may be used. More careful screening has become increasingly limited. Mississippi, North Dakota, South Dakota, and Texas all require a check by compliance personnel, partly for informational purposes, partly to see if the firm should be registered. Missouri, Nevada, and Wisconsin typically make a careful check to see if security bond is required, and, if so, how much. Florida and Tennessee check by phone.

Account Numbers

At present, most states issue special account numbers for sales tax. The most common pattern is a number made up of a two-or three-digit county identification number and a five- or six-digit account number sequential by county, or, in California and Colorado, by district. Some states use numbers sequentially statewide. City coding is used in some. In Washington, the number is also used for the business and occupation tax; the Nebraska and New Mexico numbers are used for most state taxes. Several states—Massachusetts, Michigan, New Jersey, New York, Tennessee, Texas, and West Virginia—use the federal income tax employer withholding or social security number for the sales tax number so far as possible, and the District of Columbia is moving to the federal number.

The obvious merit in using a single number for all taxes, preferably the federal number, is convenience and cross audit among taxes. Using the number, however, is not as simple as may appear. The most suitable number is, of course, the employer withholding number, but many vendors do not have one. The social security numbers, in turn, are issued to individuals, not businesses, per se, and the various persons involved in the ownership of a business will each have a number. The problem is not insurmountable, and the use of a single master file number obviously represents an ultimate goal. At the present, however, many states regard the change as not feasible or advantageous, partly because there is little cross audit. Some states reissue lapsed account numbers after several years; others do not.

Business Classification

Only two states, Alabama and Massachusetts, have not classified businesses by type in recent years. Utah had not done so until June 1981. Most states regard classification as essential for distributing information on certain types of business; for selection of accounts for audit; for analysis of delinquency and other aspects of operation of the tax; and for publication of statistics, as frequently sought by various organizations. Serious difficulties occur in establishing a satisfactory classification, primarily because many firms carry on more than one type of business. An attempt is made to code based on the principal activity, but it is by no means entirely satisfactory. The net result is to lessen, but not completely to destroy, the usefulness of the classification.

Twenty-four states use the S.I.C., most, the four-digit classification, others, three.[4] Missouri, New Jersey, and South Carolina, and Texas use a slightly modified S.I.C. Most states do not find the S.I.C. entirely satisfactory and modify it to fit the circumstances of particular firms. The other states use their own classifications.[5] In general, these classifications are simpler than S.I.C., and some regard them as adequate; others would prefer shifting to the federal. The more detailed the classification, the more meaningful the results.

One of the most serious limitations to the system in most states is the failure to alter the classification of businesses as the activity changes. Frequently, the change does not appear in any report received from the firm. The only effective way to update the classification is to use, at five- or ten-year intervals, a special questionnaire sent with the return forms, designed to provide current information. Follow-up is rare, however, except when a state revamps its classification system. In many states, coding is very poor, impairing usefulness, particularly for Electronic Data Processing (EDP) selection of accounts for audit based on norms.

---

[4]The first two digits indicate the major type of business; the third and fourth give further details. For example, 56 designates the apparel and accessories category of retail trade; 561, men's and boys' clothing and furnishing stores; 5612, clothing stores in this category; and 5613, furnishing stores in the category.

[5]Georgia, North Carolina, and Tennessee use a common classification. Indiana, Kansas, Kentucky, Louisiana, Maine, Oklahoma, Rhode Island, Virginia, and West Virginia use their own systems.

SALES TAX RETURN FORMS

Of key importance in sales tax operations are the tax return forms.

Card versus Paper Returns. A decade ago, the states fell into two sharply delineated groups so far as tax return forms were concerned: the IBM-type card and the paper returns. The cards were prepunched to facilitate processing and sorting when they were returned. Modern computers, however, with entry through video (CRT) keyboard or similar input unit, coupled with the increasing tendency to batch file and microfilm early in the process, have lessened the advantages of the card returns. Only nine states still use IBM-type returns—Idaho, Iowa, (for quarterly filers), Kansas, Maine, Massachusetts, North Dakota, Pennsylvania, Virginia, and Wisconsin.[6] Five other states use small, stiff paper or ordinary paper returns: Arkansas, Minnesota, New Jersey, Rhode Island (figure 6.3), and West Virginia. Mississippi uses a slightly larger card, and Indiana, a slightly larger paper form. The primary advantage of these small returns, especially if on stiff paper, is greater ease in handling. On the other hand, there is less space for detailed information. The remainder of the states use standard size paper returns (figure 6.4). A few states, such as Hawaii, use slightly smaller sizes. All provide a duplicate copy for the taxpayer files. Some are produced in a form such that the duplicates are fastened to the original copies as they come off the computer printer, with carbon insert, and are mailed to the taxpayer. In Iowa for monthly deposits there are three parts.

Basic Information. With minor exceptions, certain information is required on all of the returns: gross sales, total deductions, net taxable sales, tax due, and penalty and interest due, if any. The requirement of figures of total sales is subjected to some complaint, primarily from those firms that have large nontaxable sales (usually sales for resale) relative to their retail sales. Not infrequently, they simply omit the figure of total sales or manufacture one of the figures. They may keep records of taxable sales and total sales and merely derive the figure of exempt sales by subtracting one from the other. This procedure does not necessarily result in underpayment of tax.

Many states provide a separate line for tax due on taxable purchases, and lines for other adjustments. Where firms are required to remit excess collections, a separate line is provided.

The returns, however, differ significantly in the requirements for listing of deductions and reporting local sales tax due. Some of the card-type return states do not require a listing of exempt sales by category (e.g., food); the

---

[6]Pennsylvania and Wisconsin still prepunch. The District of Columbia also uses an IBM-type return.

others require this listing. Spaces for the listings are provided on the back of the form in all of these instances (see figure 6.3). Nine of the thirty-one paper-type return states likewise do not require a breakdown of exempt sales. These are Florida, Indiana, Maryland, Nevada, New York, Ohio, Texas, Utah, and Vermont. The aim is to keep the returns as simple as possible, with the belief that listing of such transactions accomplishes nothing in the absence of audit and an auditor can check the figures from the firm's records.

The remainder of the states require listing of exempt sales and other deductions by category. In about half, the spaces are provided on the front of the return (see figure 6.4), on the others, on the back. Most states provide separate lines for each nontaxable category; a few merely provide blank spaces. The great merit of this listing requirement is to call the firm's attention to the nontaxable categories and to provide a basis for audit selection. As with income tax deductions, returns showing disproportionate exempt sales of certain types are good candidates for audit. Selection on this basis may be done manually, or, if the information is introduced into the computer memory, by the computer, using established norms. Many states, however, lack computer capacity to enter each type of deduction.

Those states with state-collected local sales taxes follow different paths for the reporting of these taxes on the return forms. The most common pattern is to require listing of the local sales taxes on the back of the return (with a total line on the front). This form is used in Alabama, Arizona, Georgia, Illinois (an additional sheet if more than one location), New York, South Dakota, Tennessee, and Washington. A few states—Missouri, Nevada (figure 6.5) Oklahoma, and Texas (four locations only)—provide spaces on the front of the return for local taxes by local jurisdiction. Colorado, New Mexico, North Carolina, Texas (for more than four locations), Utah, and Virginia require separate sheets for the local taxes, at least if the vendor is subject to more than one local tax.

Special Return Forms

The majority of states uses only one return form, covering sales and use tax liability. There are, however, a number of exceptions:

1. *Separate consumer use return form:* Several states—Kansas, Kentucky, Minnesota, Nevada, Rhode Island, and South Carolina—provide a separate form for consumer use tax payments, which are payments by individuals and nonregistered firms. Figure 6.6 is an example.

2. *Separate consumer use and vendor use tax return:* A number of states have separate forms for both consumer use and out-of-state vendors registered to sell in the state: Alabama (plus a separate form for taxable rentals), Arkansas, Colorado, Iowa, Michigan (plus a separate form for entertain-

STATE OF RHODE ISLAND

DIVISION OF TAXATION   289 PROMENADE ST., PROV. R. I. 02908

SALES & USE TAX RETURN   Permit No.

1. Fill out both sides completely.
2. RETURN THIS FORM WITH YOUR CHECK OR MONEY ORDER.
3. See separate sheet for detail instructions.

FEDERAL IDENTIFICATION NO.

I hereby certify that this return to the best of my knowledge
and belief is a true, correct and complete return.

Name of Firm	Date

Signature of Owner, Partner, or Authorized Agent	Title

T-204 This Form to be Filed by Sellers of Tangible Personal Property.

Return for MONTH of	19
A. Gross sales (item 6 on reverse).	
B. Less total deductions (item 7 total).	
C. Net Taxable Sales	
D. Amount of tax @ 6% $ LESS credit for sales tax paid in other states $	.
	.
TAX DUE $	.
E. Interest @ 2/3 of 1% per mo. or fraction thereof of Item D from due date.	
F. Penalty 10% of Item D if not paid when due.	
G. Total amount due— (total of items D, E & F)	

SCHEDULE A

1a. Gross sales.

1b. Unreported collections on sales prior to 6-1-77.

2. Room occupancy sales.

3. Cost of Personal Property purchased on resale certificate but used by you.

4. USE TAX: Cost of personal property purchased outside of state but used by you.

5. Other additions (Describe).

6. Total sales
(Total of preceding items) to ITEM A other side.

Any change in organization or ownership of business REQUIRES a new permit.

If business has been sold or closed, answer the following:

	ON WHAT DATE?	IS THIS YOUR FINAL RETURN?
☐ SOLD ☐ CL		☐ YES ☐ NO

If sold give name of buyer

SCHEDULE B
LEGAL DEDUCTIONS—SALES.

7. LEGAL DEDUCTIONS

a. Food for human consumption (grocery stores) DO NOT DEDUCT "take-out" orders sold by a restaurant, drive-in or other eating place.

b. For resale

c. Interstate

d. To governments & exempt institutions

e. Exempt Publications

f. Gasoline and other exempt fuels

g. Cigarettes

h. Prescription and patent medicines

i. Clothing and footwear

j. Sales of motor vehicles

k. Other (Explain)

TOTAL DEDUCTIONS
(to item B other side)

FIGURE 6.3 CARD-TYPE RETURN, RHODE ISLAND, FRONT AND BACK

SOUTH DAKOTA
Department of Revenue
State and City Sales and Use Tax Return

MAIL TO: DEPARTMENT OF REVENUE, SALES TAX DIVISION, PIERRE, S. DAK. 57501
PHONE: 605-773-5141

MAKE REMITTANCE PAYABLE TO STATE TREASURER.

IF NO TAXES DUE, RETURN MUST BE MAILED WITH PROPER NOTATION.

FOR THE PERIOD	RETURN DUE	BUS. CODE	FILE CODE	ISSUE DATE	LICENSE NUMBER	DO NOT USE THIS SPACE
						PERIOD

1. **GROSS** (INCLUDE CASH, CHARGE, TRADE, EXCHANGES, AND SERVICES) .... $

2. USE TAXABLE (ITEMS TAKEN FROM STOCK OR PURCHASED FOR OWN USE WITHOUT PAYING TAX) ....

3. TOTAL GROSS (ADD LINES 1 AND 2) ....

4. DEDUCTIONS

   A. SALES TO OTHER RETAILERS FOR RESALE .... A $

   B. MERCHANDISE DELIVERED OUTSIDE OF STATE .... B

   C. U. S. GOVERNMENT, SOUTH DAKOTA COUNTIES, CITIES SCHOOLS AND HOSPITALS C

   D. PRESCRIPTION DRUGS AND ARTICLES .... D

   E. RETURNED MERCHANDISE .... E

   F. MOTOR VEHICLE SALES - NEW AND USED .... F

   G. MOTOR FUEL FOR HIGHWAY AND AGRICULTURE USE: LP GAS FOR AGRICULTURAL USE ONLY .... G

SALES TAX LICENSES
CANCELLATION

1. Date business was discontinued or transferred_____

2. Name and address of new owner

H. CIGARETTES, NEWSPAPERS

I. LIVESTOCK, FEED, FERTILIZER, SEED, PESTICIDES, INSECTICIDES, FUMIGANTS, HERBICIDES FOR AGRICULTURAL USE.

J. TOTAL PRIME AND SUBCONTRACTOR RECEIPTS RESULTING FROM REALTY IMPROVEMENT CONTRACTS WITHIN SOUTH DAKOTA BID AFTER JUNE 1, 1979 AND REPORTED ON CONTRACTOR'S EXCISE TAX RETURN.

K. OTHER (EXPLAIN)

RETURN THIS COPY

H		
I		
J		
K		

5. RECEIPTS FROM SALES OF FARM MACHINERY, IRRIGATION EQUIPMENT AND VENDING MACHINES ON OR AFTER MAY 1, 1980 (SUBJECT TO 4% TAX) — X.04 $

6. RECEIPTS FROM SALES OF FARM MACHINERY, IRRIGATION EQUIPMENT AND VENDING MACHINES PRIOR TO MAY 1, 1980 (SUBJECT TO 3% TAX) — X.03

7. FOOD — AS DEFINED BY FOOD STAMP ACT (SUBJECT TO 4% TAX) — X.04 $

8. ALL OTHER ITEMS NOT LISTED ABOVE TAXABLE AT 4% PRIOR TO MAY 1, 1980. — X.04

9. TOTAL DEDUCTIONS AND EXEMPTIONS (ADD LINES 4 (A-K), 5, 6, 7, 8).

10. NET AMOUNT SUBJECT TO 5% STATE TAX (SUBTRACT LINE 9 FROM LINE 3) — X.05 $

11. TOTAL CITY AND TRIBAL TAX DUE —— (Total From Page 2)

12.

13.

14. PLUS INTEREST — SEE INSTRUCTIONS

15. TOTAL DUE _____ $

I DECLARE UNDER THE PENALTIES OF PERJURY THAT THIS RETURN HAS BEEN EXAMINED BY ME AND TO THE BEST OF MY KNOWLEDGE AND BELIEF IS A TRUE, CORRECT AND COMPLETE RETURN.

_____ _____ _____
DATE   SIGNATURE OF LICENSEE   SIGNATURE OF PREPARER

FIGURE 6.4 STATE AND CITY SALES AND USE TAX RETURN, SOUTH DAKOTA

STATE OF NEVADA   ORIGINAL
NEVADA DEPARTMENT OF TAXATION REVENUE DIVISION

YOUR DISTRICT NUMBER IS:
YOUR ACCOUNT NUMBER IS:

COMBINED SALES, LOCAL SCHOOL SUPPORT, USE AND COUNTY OPTION TAX RETURN

FOR DEPARTMENT USE ONLY

MAIL TO:

NEVADA DEPARTMENT OF TAXATION
1100 E. WILLIAM ST.
CARSON CITY, NEVADA 89710

☐ CHECK IF YOU ARE OUT OF BUSINESS
AND THIS IS YOUR FINAL RETURN.

SUCCESSOR _____

THIS RETURN IS DUE ON OR BEFORE

FOR   ENDING

▶

IF THE NAME OR ADDRESS AS SHOWN IS INCORRECT, OR IF THE
OWNERSHIP OR BUSINESS LOCATION HAS CHANGED, OR IF YOU
ARE NO LONGER IN BUSINESS, NOTIFY THE NEVADA DEPARTMENT
OF TAXATION IMMEDIATELY.

READ INSTRUCTIONS ON REVERSE SIDE BEFORE PREPARING THIS RETURN.

SCHEDULE 1	COLUMN A 2% SALES-USE TAX	COLUMN B 1% SCHOOL TAX
1. TOTAL SALES (SEE INSTRUCTIONS)		
2. TOTAL AMOUNT SUBJECT TO USE TAX (SEE INSTRUCTIONS)		
3. TOTAL TAXABLE AMOUNT (LINE 1 PLUS LINE 2)		
4. TOTAL EXEMPTIONS (SEE INSTRUCTIONS)		
5. TOTAL TAXABLE SALES (LINE 3 LESS LINE 4)		
6. ENTER COMPUTED TAXES (SEE INSTRUCTIONS)		
7. ENTER COMPUTED COLLECTION ALLOWANCES (SEE INSTRUCTIONS)		
8. TOTAL CALCULATED TAXES (LINE 6 LESS LINE 7)	+	= 9.

SCHEDULE 2
1/2% COUNTY TAX

THIS SCHEDULE TO BE COMPLETED ONLY BY THOSE TAXPAYERS MAKING SALES OR REPORTING USE TAX IN ANY COUNTY HAVING THE COUNTY-CITY-RELIEF-TAX.

TOTAL TAX FROM SCHEDULE 1 (LINE 8, COLS. A & B SEE INSTRUCTIONS) ADD TO LINE 13 ENTER TOTAL TAX DUE ON LINE 14

COUNTY-CITY-RELIEF-TAX ENTER AMOUNTS IN COUNTY OF ORIGIN	TOTAL SALES	AMOUNT SUBJECT TO USE TAX	EXEMPTIONS	TAXABLE AMOUNT
C1 CHURCHILL				
C2 CLARK				
C3 DOUGLAS				
04 ELKO				
C7 HUMBOLDT				
C9 LINCOLN				
10 LYON				
11 MINERAL				
12 NYE				
13 CARSON CITY				
14 PERSHING				
15 STOREY				
16 WASHOE				

10. TOTAL TAXABLE AMOUNT OF SCHEDULE 2.

11. ENTER COMPUTED TAX (½ % OR .005 OF LINE 10, SEE INSTRUCTIONS)

12. ENTER COLLECTION ALLOWANCE (½ % OR .005 OF LINE 11, SEE INSTR.)

13. **TOTAL TAX FROM SCHEDULE 2 (SEE INSTRUCTIONS)**

14. **TOTAL TAXES (LINE 9 PLUS LINE 13)**

15. TOTAL PENALTIES (TEN PERCENT OF LINE 14, SEE INSTRUCTIONS)

16. TOTAL INTEREST (½ % OR .005 OF LINE 14, SEE INSTRUCTIONS)

17. PLUS DEBITS FROM PRIOR PERIODS (SEE INSTRUCTIONS)

18. LESS CREDITS FROM PRIOR PERIODS (SEE INSTRUCTIONS)

19. **TOTAL TAXES DUE AND PAYABLE (SEE INSTRUCTIONS)**

13.
14.
15.
16.
17.
18.
19.

I HEREBY CERTIFY THAT THIS RETURN INCLUDING ANY ACCOMPANYING SCHEDULES AND STATEMENTS HAS BEEN EXAMINED BY ME AND TO THE BEST OF MY KNOWLEDGE AND BELIEF IS A TRUE, CORRECT AND COMPLETE RETURN.

_____
SIGNATURE OF TAXPAYER OR AUTHORIZED AGENT

_____ _____
TITLE   PHONE NUMBER (WITH AREA CODE)

_____ _____
FEDERAL TAX IDENT. NO.   DATE

DOT-ST-18 (REV. 3/77)

FOR DEPARTMENT USE ONLY

SUT	LSST	CCRT

FIGURE 6.5 COMBINED SALES, LOCAL SCHOOL SUPPORT, USE AND COUNTY OPTION TAX RETURN, NEVADA

Form ST-7A (Rev. 7-76)

COMMONWEALTH OF VIRGINIA
DEPARTMENT OF TAXATION

CONSUMER'S USE TAX RETURN

FOR THE PERIOD OF: _____ YEAR: _____

CITY OR COUNTY OF USE OR CONSUMPTION: _____

NAME AND ADDRESS OF USER OR CONSUMER:

A. ITEM	B. STATE	C. LOCAL
1. Total cost price (From reverse side).............	$	$
2. Use Tax (State:3% Item 1, Col. B; Local:1% Item 1, Col. C)...		
3. Penalty for late filing and payment (See Items 3 and 5 of instructions)...............		
4. Interest for late filing and payment (See Items 4 and 5 of instructions)...............		
5. Total tax, penalty and interest (Sum of Items 2, 3, and 4)...............	$	$
6. Combined State and local tax, penalty and interest due and payable (Item 5, Col. B, plus Item 5, Col. C)...............	$	

I declare that this return (including any accompanying schedules and statements) has been examined by me and to the best of my knowledge and belief is a true, correct and complete return.

SIGNATURE: _____ DATE: _____

KEEP THIS COPY

FIGURE 6.6 CONSUMER USE TAX RETURN, VIRGINIA

ers, etc.), North Carolina, Ohio (plus several other forms: car distributors, direct-pay-permit holders, advance payments), Oklahoma, Virginia (figure 6.6), and West Virginia. This approach allows simpler forms and special processing of the out-of-state vendors.
3. *Other:* Connecticut and Illinois require separate returns for hotels and motels (technically separate taxes), Indiana, for sellers of gasoline, South Dakota, for contractors, and Vermont, for lodging and meals (separate taxes). New York has separate forms for lodging and utilities, Rhode Island, for motor vehicles. Iowa uses a single form for sales and hotel/motel taxes.

In Mississippi, the sales and use taxes are distinct levies, and registered vendors (having any use tax liability) must file two sets of returns.

Combined Returns for Sales Taxes and Other Levies

Only a few states have sought to integrate the processing of other taxes with the sales tax and provide returns covering more than one type. In Arizona and Hawaii, the retail sales tax is an element in a gross receipts tax structure involving other elements as well, and these are included on the returns. Three states go beyond this. Michigan uses a single return covering sales and use tax, the single business tax (a value-added-type general business occupation levy), and withholding of income tax. New Mexico includes withholding for income tax; Washington, the business and occupation tax (figure 6.7). These are all levies with periodic payments at the same intervals as those of the sales tax; single returns cannot be used for levies collected on different time intervals.

Return Intervals

Forty states now use varying return intervals based on the amount of tax paid, whereas only four (compared to twelve in 1970) use a single monthly or quarterly interval. The picture has become highly complex:
Monthly returns (with exceptions):
Alabama (quarterly for use tax)
Virginia
By contrast, in 1962, seventeen out of thirty-two sales tax states used the monthly interval, in 1970, six of forty-five.
Quarterly returns only (with exceptions):
New Jersey (with monthly remittances by larger firms)
North Dakota
Utah is predominately a quarter state, as are California, Missouri, Pennsylvania, and Vermont.

COMBINED EXCISE TAX RETURN

STATE OF WASHINGTON
DEPARTMENT OF REVENUE   AX-02
EXCISE TAX DIVISION
OFFICE OPERATIONS
OLYMPIA, WASHINGTON 98504

SHOW CHANGES IN ADDRESS OR OWNERSHIP ON LINES BELOW AND
DATE OF CHANGE:

_____

_____

_____

DATE _____ / _____ / _____

PERIOD _____   YEAR _____

NAME _____

FIRM NAME _____

STREET ADDRESS _____

CITY, STATE, ZIP _____

REG.
NO. _____

STATE BUSINESS AND OCCUPATION TAX

LINE	Column 1 TAX CLASSIFICATION	CODE	Column 2 GROSS AMOUNT	Column 3 DEDUCTIONS Totals from Page 2	Column 4 TAXABLE AMOUNT	Column 5 RATE	Column 6 TAX DUE	Do Not Write In This Column
1	EXTRACTING, EXTRACTING FOR HIRE	16				.0044		
2	TRAVEL AGENT COMMISSIONS	30				.0025		
3	MFG WHEAT INTO FLOUR, RAW SEAFOOD PRODUCTS, SOYBEAN PROCESSORS	22				.00125		
4	NUCLEAR FUEL ASSEMBLY MFG, SPLITTING OR PROCESSING DRIED PEAS	28				.0025		
5	SLAUGHTER BREAKING PROCESS, PERISH MEAT-WHLSE INTL CHARTER FREIGHT BROKERS AND STEVEDORING	18				.0033		
6	MANUFACTURING ALUMINUM	27				.004		
7	MANUFACTURING FRESH FRUIT AND VEGETABLES	21				.003		
8	PROCESSING FOR HIRE PRINTING AND PUBLISHING	10				.0044		
9	MANUFACTURING—OTHER	07				.0044		
10	WHOLESALING WHEAT, OATS, CORN, BARLEY, DRY PEAS	15				.0001		
11	WHOLESALING—CIGARETTES FROM MFR'S STOCK IN STATE	23				.00176		
12	INTERNAL DISTRIBUTION—2 OR MORE OUTLETS—NO SALES	06				.0044		
13	WHOLESALING—OTHER	03				.0044		

14	COLD STORAGE WAREHOUSING, RADIO AND TV BROADCASTING	17	.0044
15	PUBLIC ROAD CONSTRUCTION GOVERNMENT CONTRACTING	11	.0044
16	SERVICE AND OTHER ACTIVITIES	04	.01
17	RETAILING	02	.0044

STATE SALES TAX, USE TAX AND TOBACCO TAX

18	RETAIL SALES TAX	01	.045
19	USE TAX	05	Value of articles used by taxpayer as a consumer on which no Washington Sales Tax has been paid — .045
20	TOBACCO PRODUCTS	20	.45

STATE PUBLIC UTILITY TAX

21	RAILROAD, EXPRESS, CAR COMPANY	24	.036
22	WATER DISTRIBUTION, POWER	09	.036
23	TELEPHONE, TELEGRAPH	25	.036
24	GAS DISTRIBUTION	26	.03
25	MOTOR TRANSPORTATION	08	.018
26	URBAN TRANSPORTATION VESSELS UNDER 65 FEET	12	.006
27	OTHER PUBLIC SERVICE BUSINESS	13	.018

31	TOTAL LOCAL SALES TAX From Page 2	45
32	TOTAL LOCAL USE TAX From Page 2	46

33	TOTAL TAX DUE	50
34	PENALTY	55
35	INVENTORY TAX CREDIT ONLY	57
36	TOTAL PAYMENT ENCLOSED	65

ADD PENALTY IF LATE
5% 1st Mo.
10% 2nd Mo.
20% 3rd Mo.
(MINIMUM 2.00)

TRANSIENT RENTAL INCOME - ENTER LOCATION CODE AND INCOME ONLY [47]

LINE	4 DIGIT LOCATION CODE	INCOME	4 DIGIT LOCATION CODE	INCOME
28				
29				
30				

SIGNATURE _____ • DATE _____

PHONE _____

AVOID PENALTIES

FORM REV 40 2406 (7-79)

RETURNS DUE 15TH OF MONTH, DELINQUENT IF NOT FILED BY END OF MONTH FOLLOWING TAXABLE PERIOD. TAXPAYER MUST FILE RETURN EVEN IF NO TAX IS DUE.

PAGE 1

FIGURE 6.7 STATE COMBINED RETURN, WASHINGTON

Monthly and quarterly returns:[7]
  Arkansas (almost all monthly)
  Connecticut (plus a few annual)
  Florida
  Georgia
  Hawaii
  Idaho (plus a few seasonal semiannual)
  Louisiana
  Mississippi (wholesale tax, semiannual)
  North Carolina
  Oklahoma
  Rhode Island
  South Carolina
  Tennessee
  West Virginia
  Wyoming
Monthly, quarterly, and annual returns:
  Arizona (monthly dominant)
  California (quarterly dominant)
  Colorado
  Indiana
  Kansas
  Kentucky
  Massachusetts[8] (meals semiannual)
  Michigan
  Minnesota
  Missouri
  Nebraska
  Nevada
  New York (primarily quarterly)
  Pennsylvania
  Texas
  Vermont
  Washington
  Wisconsin
  District of Columbia
Monthly, quarterly, semiannual, and annual returns:
  Maine
  Maryland
  South Dakota (quarterly dominant)
Monthly and annual returns:
  Illinois

[7]With exceptions.
[8]Plus weekly deposit for larger firms.

Quarterly and annual returns:
  Iowa (with monthly payment)
  Utah
Monthly and semiannual returns:
  Ohio
  New Mexico

Table 6.1 indicates the dividing lines used between the various intervals, and Table 6.2, the number of returns, where available, in each category. These figures for the most part include only in-state sales tax vendors and therefore do not show all registered firms.

The range for placing firms on a quarterly interval extends from $5 per month tax in Arkansas to $100.00 per month in New York. Using figures under $50 leaves most firms in the monthly category. A $300 figure places a large portion of the firms in the quarterly category.

Relative Merits

The monthly basis was originally defended on the grounds of the lessened delinquency, since firms would be unable to build large liabilities that they could not meet. It smooths out peak work loads and obtains the money more quickly for the states. The quarterly system lessens the work load by two-thirds but also decreases the regularity of the flow. The primary reason, however, that most states were unwilling to change to a quarterly interval basis was the time lag in getting the revenue. The lag is not a continuing problem if receipts are constant, but it is a serious matter when the tax is introduced or a change made to a longer interval, and when revenues are rising because of higher rates, prices, or greater sales. The monthly interval reduces the lag of revenues behind changes in economic activity and therefore has advantage from a fiscal policy standpoint. Early tabulating equipment made classification of firms and use of more than one period relatively difficult.

Trends

Thus, in the last decade, there has been relatively little change, with some net shift from the few remaining monthly and quarterly states to the use of more than one period. The primary shift occurred in the sixties, made possible by modern computers, which facilitate selection of returns for mailing and control over filing. The basic principle used by most states now is to keep the large accounts on monthly filing to ensure continuous flow of funds to the state and to use the quarterly interval, with reduced paper work, for the smaller retailers. The smallest firms are often placed on an annual return basis. They owe little tax and are most likely to appear as delinquents and fail to file a return in periods in which they have no tax liability. A few states have reduced the number of intervals; Illinois, for example, eliminated the

TABLE 6.1 Sales Tax Return Intervals, 1980–81

State	Standard Interval	Tax Liability per Month ($)				Prepay
		Monthly, over $	Quarterly, under or between ($)	Semiannual	Annual Monthly Tax under	
Alabama	mo.	(all)	use tax only	—	—	
Arizona	mo.	16.67	8.33–16.67	—	8.33	
Arkansas	mo.	5.00	5.00	—	—	
California	quar.	250	12.50–250	—	12.50	10.50
Colorado	mo.	300	15–301	—	15	
Connecticut	mo.	333	333			
Florida	mo.	33	33ᵃ	a		
Georgia	mo.	100	100	—	—	M tax over 2,500
Hawaii	mo.	38.46	38.46	—	—	
Idaho	—	150	150	few seasonal		
Illinois	mo.	20			20	M tax over 10,000
Indiana	mo.	10	.83–10	—	.83	
Iowa	quar.	—	over 10 a mo.	seasonal	10	M tax over 50 a quar.
Kansas	mo.	100	5–100		5	
Kentucky	mo.	45	10–45	—	10	
Louisiana	mo.	50	50			
Maine	mo.	100	50–100	25–50	25	
Maryland	mo.	100	100	under 50		
Massachusetts	quar.	100	8.33–100	meals	8.33	
Michigan	mo.	200	16.67–200	—	16.67	
Minnesota	mo.	250	25–250		25	
Mississippi	mo.	50	50	wholesale tax	few cotton gins	

Missouri	quar.	150	15–150		15	M tax over 100
Nebraska	mo.	20–80	80		20	
Nevada	determined by firm					
New Jersey	quar.	50		under 50		
New Mexico	mo.	100,000	20.83–100,000		20.83	M taxes[c]
New York	quar.	25	25			
North Carolina	mo.	deling.				
North Dakota	quar.		standard	seasonal	1	credit if pay early
Ohio	semiann.	100	—	100		
Oklahoma	mo.	25	25			
Pennsylvania	quar.	200	75–200		few special seasonal	M tax over 2,000
Rhode Island	mo.	33	33[d]			
South Carolina	mo.	100	100			M tax over 12,500
South Dakota	quar.	few delinq.	standard	under 200 annual tax	under 100 annual tax	
Tennessee	mo.	100	100		41.66	option
Texas	quar.	1500	1500			special
Utah	quar.	few delinq.	over 8.33		under 8.33	
Vermont	quar.	500	—	use tax only	50.00	
Virginia	mo.	10	10			
Washington	quar.	150[e]	12.50–150[e]		12.50[e]	
West Virginia	mo.	10	10			
Wisconsin	—	166.67	25–166.67			
Wyoming	mo.	150	150		25	over 3,000 per quar.

[a] $100 in last quarter; if under $200 tax in last six months, semiann.
[b] Approximate; not a set figure.
[c] Required once a year on March 20, for estimated amount due for March.
[d] Six months liability under $200.
[e] Author's estimate; actual figures not released.

TABLE 6.2 Number of Sales Tax Vendors by Return Intervals, 1980–81

State	Mo.	Quar.	Prepay	Semiann.	Ann.	Special Seasonal
Alabama	49,222					
Arizona	63,000	12,000[a]				
Arkansas						
California	81,632	283,050	53,989	—	209,753[b]	
Colorado						
Connecticut	18,000	75,000				
Florida	—					
Georgia	75,000	28,000				
Hawaii	—	—				
Idaho	16,600	12,400				
Illinois	—	—				
Indiana	84,965	22,601		103	20,613	
Iowa	0	99,949	35,150	—	1,965	
Kansas	46,785	23,001			5,197	570
Kentucky	56,164	9,209			11,855	
Louisiana						
Maine	11,000	3,000		3,000[c]	2,000	3,600
Maryland	40,027	22,246			28,529[d]	
Massachusetts	25,999	40,403	2,808		41,808	3,813[c]
Michigan	77,335	47,439			17,168	
Minnesota	51,200	23,397			30,350	3,000
Mississippi	50,195	15,654				
Missouri	24,221	47,907			27,892	
Nebraska	30,379	18,221			7,000	
Nevada	11,000	9,000			200	
New Jersey						
New Mexico	62,602			23,085		
New York	11,000	339,000	11,000		100,000	
North Carolina	111,435	11,846				
North Dakota	50	20,700	800	4,500		
Ohio	87,282	—		142,214		
Oklahoma						
Pennsylvania	56,926	113,971		52,566	5,580	
Rhode Island	22,300	1,689				
South Carolina			3,027			
South Dakota	572	23,802		634	4,338	572
Tennessee	80,789[e]	20,605				
Texas	43,729	145,968		3,700	100,183	
Utah					7,000	
Vermont	5,316	10,407			3,007	
Virginia	60,000	20,000				
Washington[f]	34,000	79,000			44,000	
West Virginia	27,726	9,297				
Wisconsin	39,700	35,600	8,600		39,300	
Wyoming	27,755	10,215				
District of Columbia	—	32,000		2,000		

[a] Quar. and ann.
[b] Plus 1,119 on fiscal year.
[c] Included in ann.
[d] Includes seasonal and semiann. (as well as ann.).
[e] Plus 591 13-period filers.
[f] Figure estimates based on assumption that 72% of all active accounts are sales tax vendors. There are 217,670 accounts in total, including business and occupation, tobacco, and utility taxes.

quarterly period, moving most of these firms to semiannual in order to reduce paper and computer work and delinquency checks.

Prepayment

Several states employ a prepayment system. California, Iowa, New Jersey, and Rhode Island all primarily quarterly return states, require payment or deposit to be paid monthly, if the monthly tax is in excess of $1,020, $50, $100, and $2,000, respectively—thus ensuring early payment but avoiding the need for monthly returns. Illinois requires firms with monthly tax liability in excess of $10,000 to pay four times a month, and Massachusetts requires weekly deposit for firms with annual tax in excess of $25,000. The District of Columbia requires monthly deposits of all quarterly filers. In Georgia, if the monthly tax is over $2,500, the firm must pay one-half the estimated tax for the next month with the previous month's return. Indiana, South Carolina, and Wisconsin require an earlier filing date for larger firms. Texas gives a discount for early filing, which is not mandatory.

Several states, including Hawaii and Michigan, require an annual summary return. Such a return serves for internal review for selection of accounts for audit; this review can be done much more effectively annually than monthly or quarterly. With modern computers, however, if all information on the returns is transferred to memory, annual data can easily be created, and the additional work for the vendor can be avoided.

Seasonal Operation

One nuisance encountered by the states is the treatment of seasonal firms. If the former are handled as other vendors, they are not likely to file in the off months and thus appear as pseudo-delinquents, with time and money wasted to track them down. Their off-season addresses are often not available. The result is that many states try to code the seasonal firms separately and mail them returns only during the months they operate, but the periods are not necessarily the same each year because of weather conditions and other factors. West Virginia and Wisconsin code the seasonal firms and send them a packet of returns for each month during the season. Identifying the firms and getting the necessary information about months of operation are problems. Despite these problems, this solution is the most widely used. A few states expect the firm to notify the revenue department when it opens and closes, and place it on active status during this period. This procedure is really merely a variant of the first and appears to work no better.

Reclassification of Firms

The states vary in their approach to classification. Typically, the computer determines annually the firms that fall into each category, based on the tax due (in a few instances, sales) in the preceding periods. New firms are classified accordingly, as are firms moving from a longer to a shorter interval. To avoid borderline firms from shifting back and forth frequently, a range is often used; a firm will be moved into a longer interval period automatically but will not be moved back to a shorter interval on the basis of the experience of one period, and only when the tax exceeds a higher figure than the one which would move it into the shorter period. In several states—North Carolina and Oklahoma, for example—change to a longer interval is made only upon request of eligible firms. In most states, however, the change is made automatically, but most of these will allow a firm to remain on the monthly interval if it prefers, and a substantial number do. South Carolina is one of the few to give no choice.

Nevada alone gives the taxpayer complete choice between monthly and quarterly. The choice is made by the firm on the basis of the size of the required security, which all firms in the state must provide. Washington alone does not publicly reveal the figures used as a basis for classification; the figures given in table 6.1 are the authors' estimate of what is used.

Types of Equipment

In the earliest days of state sales tax operation, mechanical equipment was limited to bookkeeping machines and hand calculators. Many aspects of the tax operation were well suited to EDP, however, and gradually it was introduced. Computer technology has changed rapidly in the last three decades, and the systems in operation today are substantially different from those of even a decade ago. Most states have moved to sophisticated, third-generation computers.

As a decade ago, the dominant type of computer equipment is IBM, used by thirty-two states and the District of Columbia. Most states in recent years have been using the 370, which has replaced the 360 of a decade ago. Most states are using the 370/58,[9] but a number have moved to the 370/68,[10] whose performance is about 2.74 times as great (in million instruction units per second). The states are now commencing to move to the 3000 series units, which require less peripheral equipment, as more is inboard; also overall cost is less with the 3000 series. Louisiana uses a 3031, whose rating relative to the 360/58 is 1.7. The 3032 has about the same performance as the 370/68. Pennsylvania, Hawaii and Kentucky are using the 3033, which rates about 5.15 in performance relative to the 370/58.

---

[9]Arkansas, Colorado, Connecticut, Idaho, Iowa, Kansas, Louisiana, Maryland, Minnesota, Mississippi, Missouri, Nebraska, Nevada, New Jersey, New Mexico, North Carolina, North Dakota, Oklahoma, Pennsylvania, South Dakota, Tennessee, Texas, Utah (for a time an ITEL installation), Vermont, Virginia, West Virginia, and Wisconsin.

[10]For example, Hawaii, Minnesota, Mississippi, Oklahoma, Tennessee, and West Virginia. North Carolina uses a 370/148.

Seven states use UNIVAC: Alabama, Arizona, and California, the 9080, with performance about 0.74 times the IBM 370/58; Florida, the 1100-81, 1.7 times the performance of the 370/58; and Illinois, Massachusetts, and New York, the 1100-42, about 0.82 times the performance of a 370/58. Ohio and South Carolina use NCR systems, and the private firm that contracts to do the work for Indiana uses an NCR 200-01 installation. Maine uses a Honeywell system, Michigan, a Burroughs B 6700, and Wyoming, a Bell Telephone Data Speed 4540 installation.

Input

In the earlier years of computers, input was via the punching of cards, a slow process in itself. Verification and subsequent processing were also slow, and there was no means of direct access to information. Data could be obtained only sequentially. Today the standard method of entry is via key to disc, the keyboard frequently linked to a video screen (CRT). The data on the disc is then transferred to magnetic tape for entry into the computer memory with on-line direct access. The entry onto a disk (round diskssomewhat comparable to phonograph records in appearance, often called floppy disks), and then the transfer to a tape allows faster processing than the entry directly onto magnetic tape. The NCR systems provide input via key to a cassette, from which in turn the data are transferred to magnetic tape. A few states—Kentucky, New Jersey and Texas are examples—have added minicomputers to the input units; these check arithmetic and catch certain types of error before the data are entered into the main computer.

Direct Access

The most significant element of the modern computer systems is direct (often called random) access on-line—the ability, in the case of taxation, to retrieve information on the sales tax accounts instantly on video units, and, in most instances, by hard (printed) copy, if desired. In 1971, only ten states had direct access, and some of these for only limited data. As of 1981, only five states do not have on-line direct access—Hawaii, Missouri, Ohio, Utah, and Virginia—but they all have plans for it. Furthermore, at least twenty-three states have direct access (via CRT) units in the district offices: California, Colorado, Florida, Georgia, Idaho, Illinois, Iowa, (data for one year), Kentucky, Louisiana, Maryland, Massachusetts, Michigan, Minnesota, Mississippi (hard copy only), Nebraska, Nevada, New Mexico, New York, Pennsylvania (three cities only), Tennessee, Texas, Vermont, and Wisconsin.

In many states, not all the data on the returns—especially various categories of exempt sales—are entered into the system and therefore cannot be retrieved from the computer. Given the input, however, the systems allow speedy updating of files and the possibility of gaining instant information on the status of any account and the payment record for the past period. The data are kept from one to three years and then transferred to tape, with much slower retrieval.

Jurisdiction over Computer Facilities

In twenty-three states and the District of Columbia, all computer facilities are operated under the jurisdiction of a state central data processing agency.[11] In some of these states, the revenue departments do their own programming. In five additional states—Maryland, Michigan, New Jersey, Rhode Island, and South Dakota—the facilities are not in the revenue agency but in a state department of which revenue is a part. In sixteen states and the District of Columbia, the computer facilities are in the revenue department. In Indiana, the revenue department contracts for its own computer operations, provided by a private firm. In South Dakota, the department contracts with the University of South Dakota for computer work. The trend has been toward centralization of computer facilities, although Oklahoma moved the opposite way in 1977.

There are obvious advantages to the revenue department having complete control of its computer facilities, particularly the ability to schedule work to meet its own needs. Several of the tax units with central computer systems, for example, Idaho, Kansas, Minnesota, New Mexico, Utah, and Virginia, are by no means fully satisfied with the present relationships. They report inability to get work done when they need it and delays in getting necessary information. Kansas and Utah are particularly unhappy, and the latter hopes to get its own computer. Others, however, such as Iowa, Maine, Nebraska, Nevada, and Washington, report no difficulty in obtaining needed coordination.

The advantage of a central state system is the possibility of introducing and effectively using more advanced computer techniques. In the small states, centralization is imperative for economy and efficiency. In the largest states, tax operations alone can use modern equipment effectively. In the intermediate group, the relative gains and disadvantages must be balanced in reaching a decision.

PROCESSING OF RETURNS

The precise system of processing returns varies among the states and is conditioned by the data processing equipment. The basic patterns, however, are similar in most states.

[11] Arkansas, Connecticut, Georgia, Hawaii, Idaho, Iowa, Kansas, Kentucky, Maine, Minnesota, Mississippi, Missouri, Nebraska, Nevada, New Mexico, North Dakota, Tennessee, Utah, Vermont, Virginia, Washington, West Virginia, and Wyoming. Some of these states are small in population; none of the largest states are in the group. The issue of central jurisdiction over computer facilities is discussed in a series of papers in *Revenue Administration,* 1977, pp. 45-50.

Addressing and Mailing of Tax Return Forms

All but nine states mail the return forms to the registered firms a short time, often two or three weeks, before the returns are due in each reporting interval. In the most common form of operation, the computer equipment addresses either the return forms or the labels that are mechanically attached to the forms with information from the master file that identifies those to receive returns in the particular period when more than one reporting interval is used. The computer prints the name, address, account number, and often the month or quarter (in some states, this information is preprinted on the return forms). Typically, the return (including a duplicate for the vendor) is stuffed in a window envelope and mailed. A few states fold the return and mail it without an envelope. A return envelope, often with a distinctive color for each type of tax, is usually enclosed. In a few states using card return forms, the cards are prepunched with account numbers at the same time they are printed, but this is less common than it was in the past. The other states send out the forms in larger batches at less frequent intervals: twice a year in North Carolina; four times a year in Alabama, Hawaii, Massachusetts, and Rhode Island; every six months in New Jersey and North Carolina; every nine months in Oklahoma; and once a year in Michigan and Hawaii, where the vendor receives a packet of twelve monthly returns plus the annual return form. Wisconsin tried a longer interval and found it unsatisfactory.

There is merit in sending the returns each time period as a reminder that they are due. The only gain from mailing at less frequent intervals is that of the cost of preparing the returns for mailing and the postage. Only Alabama still addresses from addressograph plates, once the common practice.

Another question is the choice between bulk and first-class mail. Originally, the states used bulk, and most still do. Some are satisfied; many are not. Of a sample of twenty-nine states, seventeen use bulk[12] and ten, first class (several, presorted). New York uses first class on monthly returns, bulk on quarterly; North Carolina reverses this. Wisconsin sends the large account returns first class, the remainder, bulk. While first class is much more expensive, it ensures prompt delivery and forwarding. Since many small vendors are constantly on the move, forwarding aids the state in obtaining a correct current address. The greatest problem with bulk mail, however, is the unreliability of delivery within a reasonable time. Some states, when investigating, have found large stacks of bulk mail in post offices undelivered for months. In some instances, bulk mail is reportedly destroyed because of lack of personnel to deliver it. Some mail service has deteriorated substantially over the last two decades. Perhaps the need is for an intermediate class of mail, not requiring the priority of first class mail but with ensured delivery within some reasonable period. The alternative is general improvement in the mail service.

[12]Alabama, Colorado, Connecticut, Florida, Georgia, Kentucky, Louisiana, Michigan, Missouri, North Dakota, Oklahoma, Pennsylvania, Rhode Island, South Carolina, South Dakota, Tennessee, and Washington.

Initial Processing

In most states, all returns come to the revenue department, usually into a central mail room. A few may come into district offices and be forwarded to headquarters. Only in Hawaii and New York do the returns regularly come to the district offices, and some do in Nevada. The envelopes are opened mechanically and the returns usually segregated, the sales tax returns being separated from others and current returns from late returns of previous periods. Most states then give a brief preedit, to ensure that the amount of the check and the return are in agreement. Some offices check at this point for completeness of information. Check and return are pinned or laid together for transmission to the cashier. Returns are batched, from fifty to one hundred.

The second step in most states is validation. The cashier places a validation number on the check and the return, either by hand-numbering stamp, cash register, or newer techniques, and separates the return from the check. After separation, a deposit listing is prepared for the batch, often on a bookkeeping machine, the total is compared with the totals of tax due as reported on the returns, and the checks are sent to a bank. A number of states now prepare deposit listing by computer. Many states have sought to reduce the delay time in depositing by stressing speed in the handling of the checks themselves.

A few states, primarily larger ones, follow somewhat different patterns. In New York, the returns are initially processed by the banks rather than the revenue department. The returns come in to the district offices and are transmitted to a bank. The bank validates, prepares the deposit listing, credits the amounts to the state's account, and prepares a magnetic tape listing of the payments. The tape and the returns are then transmitted to the sales tax headquarters in Albany. The state regards this system as highly satisfactory. With banks doing a considerable portion of the work, money is deposited more quickly. In Washington, all returns come in to a Seattle bank, which performs much the same functions as the banks in New York; and in Michigan, larger returns and payments come to a Detroit bank, and returns are forwarded to the revenue department. Prepayment deposits now required in Massachusetts and the District of Columbia are made to a bank.

Some states that have commenced to microfilm the returns and the checks immediately after preediting do not batch; the returns go on to the computer system entry immediately. New Mexico and Texas are the prime examples. Colorado, Louisiana, Maryland, North Carolina, and Tennessee are also microfilming almost immediately after the returns are opened.

Basic Processing

A number of steps must be performed on returns following initial processing. Exact techniques vary and are constantly changing. The extent to which they are performed by computer varies among the states.

Check on Arithmetic.   Virtually all states check the accuracy of the arithmetic on the returns: addition and subtraction, application of percentage vendor discounts, application of tax rate, and other aspects. The check is made by the computer in most states, but still manually in at least five: Arizona, Colorado, Illinois, Oklahoma, and Utah.

Posting.   Before modern computers, most states used a system of visible ledger cards, one for each taxpayer, the periodic payments being entered on each card during the processing of returns, usually by bookkeeping machines. This was a slow process, in most states requiring the pulling of ledger cards from the files by hand. This system has been universally eliminated (only seven states were using it as long ago as 1970); the cards have been replaced by computer files. Current data from returns are now entered into the computer memory by the various input devices noted earlier in the chapter. Returns typically go to data processing immediately after validation.

Usually, only the basic data of gross sales (omitted in some states), total deductions, taxable sales, and tax paid are entered into the computer. Details of deductions are not required on the returns in a number of states and are not entered into the computer file in most of the others. Kentucky, New Jersey, Rhode Island, and South Dakota are among the few states to enter all details on deductions. Connecticut does so quarterly on a sample basis. Placing all information in the computer is expensive in operating time and storage required and not essential for most sales tax operations. As a result, however, the computer record is incomplete and continued reliance must be placed on other records. Detailed record is essential if EDP equipment is to be used for selection of accounts for audit. Entering monthly is unnecessary, however, and details can be processed from an annual return if one is required.

Data are usually accumulated in the computer for at least one year, and frequently for three years, the usual period of the statute of limitations and, thus, the basic audit period.

Preparation of Print-outs of Information.   With the modern video random access units, as described, data in the memory file on any account can be obtained instantaneously, and, with adequate equipment, hard copy can be printed. Thus, most states no longer print out periodically the data from all returns, as was common in earlier days of data processing.

Accounts Receivable.   Most states set up with varying degrees of sophistication an accounts receivable file, in which are listed amounts reported on returns but not paid, deficiencies assessed from office or field review or audit, and other items. These files are updated frequently. Accounts receivable were among the first files to be computerized.

Delinquency. As explained in the next chapter, in most states, delinquency is now ascertained from the records of filed returns, by data processing equipment.

Other Uses of the Computer System

1. Provides the necessary totals of amounts collected and performs a number of internal balancing functions.
2. Allocates collections to the various local governments in those states with state-collected local sales taxes or allocates a portion of the sales tax revenue to local governments on a formula.
3. Prepares statistics, by type of vendor, by county, and other criteria.
4. Selects accounts for audit, in a few states.

Storage of Returns

Initially, states filed manually the returns in account folders for storage. This procedure, still followed in thirteen states,[13] including California, is time consuming, laborious, and subject to many errors. Misplaced returns are extremely difficult to find. On the other hand, with this system, the returns for any account are always readily available, for check, for audit information, and for other purposes. Eighteen states now leave the returns in batches,[14] compared to seven in 1970. Although the returns are less readily available, this is now of less concern because of direct access in most computer systems. Kentucky destroys the returns after microfilming.

Microfilming

The most significant change from a decade ago is the shift toward "instant" microfilming, done at a very early stage in processing, often of both the return and the check. Data are then entered into the computer system from the returns and the latter either immediately shredded or kept for a few months in the event of any question about the microfilm. The microfilm provides the permanent record of the return. Fourteen states now follow this procedure: Arkansas, Colorado, Connecticut, Kentucky, Louisiana, Maryland, Minnesota, Nebraska, Nevada, North Carolina, Oklahoma, Tennessee, Texas, and Wyoming.

In addition to the states that do instant microfilming, a number of states microfilm the returns after two or three years to save storage space: Ala-

---

[13]Alabama, Arizona, California, Georgia, Illinois, Kentucky, Mississippi, Missouri, North Dakota, Pennsylvania, Utah, Washington, and Wisconsin.

[14]Florida, Hawaii, Idaho, Indiana, Iowa, Kansas, Kentucky, Maine, Michigan, New Jersey, New York, Ohio, Rhode Island, South Carolina, South Dakota, Vermont, Virginia, and West Virginia.

bama, Georgia, Idaho, Kansas, New Mexico (microfiche), Ohio, South Carolina, South Dakota, Utah, and Wyoming. The other states, roughly half, have not considered microfilming worthwhile, however. The objection long raised against microfilming is the greater difficulty in working with microfilmed material and the resulting eyestrain. But this argument is no longer nearly as serious, since the computer memory contains most information from the returns. The computer memory may contain data only for one or two years, whereas for some purposes a much longer record is required, and not all information on the returns is entered into the computer in many states. Ultimately, with still greater improvements in computer systems and use, all data on returns will be available from the computer for the necessary period of years—typically three to five—and the returns will have even less use than they now have. The microfilm or microfiche record is adequate for legal purposes.

Office Audit or Post Audit

Some states routinely review all returns, or, as in Washington, all return folders annually or biannually, to look for ones in which gross sales or various deductions appear to be out of line. This review is performed to some extent by computer in Florida, Kentucky, and Michigan, by office auditors who are not, in most states, trained auditors but senior clerical personnel, and by senior auditors in a few states, such as Indiana.

INFORMATION PROVIDED TO REGISTERED VENDORS

By far the most common practice currently is to provide all new taxpayers with a booklet explaining the tax and the requirements. These vary from brief instruction sheets to lengthy booklets. Most states do not give out copies of the act and regulations (although Virginia does give all new firms a copy of the rules and regulations), but many, for example, Maine, Minnesota, North Carolina, North Dakota, Texas, and Vermont will give copies of the act and regulations upon request.[15] North Carolina provides basic material and an order form for additional types. Usually the material is sent out with the permit; but Ohio provides it through the office of the county auditor when application is made for a permit. Several states provide circulars by type of business—Indiana, Kentucky, Maryland, Nevada, and Vermont, for example. Nebraska provides the regulations and then makes personal contact by phone. Other states hold periodic seminars for vendors in the various districts—Florida, New Jersey, New Mexico, and Texas, for example. California

[15]In Minnesota, about 7% of all new registrants do request this material.

has developed a detailed information service for its own internal use, but which it will sell to registered firms.

One of the chief problems is to keep the taxpayers acquainted with changes that are occurring. The province of Ontario has long provided a periodic bulletin sent to all vendors; Louisiana, Minnesota, North Dakota, and South Dakota issue a quarterly newsletter (figure 6.8), sent to all vendors; Wisconsin does so on a periodic basis; and Maine provides an annual summary of all changes. Many of the states develop circulars describing changes in certain lines of business, mailed with the tax returns; others provide brief instruction sheets indicating the changes, also mailed with the returns. Maryland provides a message line on the return form itself, on which any new information is printed by the computer and the Kentucky system is capable of doing so. Trade associations assist in circulating information on changes. The instructions on or accompanying the tax return forms provide basic information.

Information on particular questions is provided by phone or correspondence, or in some instances in person, from headquarters and in district offices in the states having such offices. Major questions of interpretation are answered by senior officials; some are referred to the legal staff or the director of revenue. In most states, answers to questions are readily available informally. One important change has been the provision of "800" telephone numbers, so that taxpayers can call in to the district office or headquarters without charge to obtain clarification.

On the whole, though some states are doing a good job of disseminating information, others are not. Successful operation of a retail sales tax requires

TABLE 6.3 Percentage of Total Sales Taxes Paid by Larger Vendors

State	% of Registered Vendors	% of Total Tax
Alabama	10.0–15.0	75.0–80.0
Arizona	0.8	60.0
Connecticut	0.2	28.0
Connecticut	3.0	61.0
Florida	2.0	52.0
Kentucky	1.0	45.0
Louisiana	20.0	70.0
Minnesota	0.6	35.0
Minnesota	10.0	79.0
North Carolina	10.0	81.0
North Carolina	44.0	98.0
Utah	1.0	40.0

Source: Supplied by state revenue departments.

North Dakota

Byron L. Dorgan
TAX COMMISSIONER

sales tax

VOLUME 6   MARCH, 1980   No. 1

Newsletter

GUN SHOWS AND ANTIQUE SHOWS ARE TAXABLE

We have had questions this winter regarding the taxability of goods sold or traded at gun shows and antique shows by "hobbyists." We regard the sale and trading of antiques, guns and other commodities by "hobbyists" to be a taxable transaction when these transactions take place at a public show or exhibition. We believe that when a "hobbyist" brings his goods and wares into a public place and exhibits them for sale to the general public, he or she has set himself/herself up as a retail merchant and any sales or trades which are made and at which the value of the particular items being sold or traded is ascertained, sales tax must be collected on all such sales and/or trades. Those people who are not in the habit of exhibiting their goods on a regular basis and holding themselves out to be retailers but who do take goods and wares to an occasional public showing or exhibition and offer them for sale can report the sales tax on all such sales on a one time basis to the Tax Department through the sponsor of the show. Further instructions are being issued now to sponsors of gun and antique shows and will be available to those people who wish to exhibit and sell at such sales.

LESS PAPERWORK

Beginning with this quarterly sales tax reporting form, you will note that we are no longer sending to our sales tax permit holders a schedule of deductions which has been an enclosure in the sales tax reporting forms for many years. On that schedule, we have asked permit holders to list specific details for certain deductions claimed on the reporting form. These included line 23 which is a miscellaneous deduction line and also line 25 which is a deduction for bad debts claimed. We found that most of the sales tax permit holders did not utilize the schedule of deductions and even for those that did, we very often had to write for further information. For those reasons and for the obvious cost savings of printing 25,000 of these additional schedules, we decided that we would eliminate the schedule of deductions from the enclosures which are mailed to each sales tax permit holder on a quarterly basis.

2% RATE APPLIES ONLY ON FARM MACHINERY FOR AGRICULTURAL PURPOSES

We continue to receive questions from contractors and others who purchase items of what would normally be considered farm machinery such as tractors and loaders who believe that they are eligible for the reduced 2% rate on the purchase price of these items. The initiated measure which reduced the sales tax to 2% on farm machinery specifies that the farm machinery must be used exclusively for agricultural purposes. Thus, under the provisions of that initiated measure which have been effective since January 1, 1977, a tractor sold to a farmer or rancher for exclusive agricultural purposes is taxed at a rate of 2% while the same tractor sold to a construction contractor would be subject to the 3% general sales tax rate since the tractor will obviously not be used exclusively for agricultural purposes.

RECEIPTS FROM COIN-OPERATED VENDING MACHINES

The receipts from coin-operated vending machines which dispense products selling for more than 15¢ are fully subject to North Dakota sales tax. The owner of the vending machine is responsible for that sales tax! We have had a number of inquiries from vending machine operators and from others around the state who ask us whether the receipts from a coin-operated vending machine which is located in an institution which is normally exempt from sales tax (such as a school, a state or federal building, or a hospital) should be subject to sales tax. Our response is very definitely yes! The gross receipts from all vending machines which dispense tangible personal property that sells for more than 15¢ are totally subject to sales tax and the owner of the coin-operated vending machine is responsible for the tax on those gross receipts. If the owner of the vending machine has a coin-operated machine in a state office building, for example, the receipts remain subject to sales tax because the owner of the vending machine is responsible for the tax and not the operator or manager of the state office building. The 3% general sales tax may be deducted from the total gross receipts of the vending machine prior to the time that the owner of the machine pays the percentage normally allowed to the location owner. Thus, if the receipts from a vending machine for a given length of time totaled $100, the owner of the machine would be allowed to deduct the tax from the $100 before dividing the proceeds with the location owner. He would report to us gross receipts of $97.09 upon which the sales tax would be remitted and he would then apply the normal location owner's percentage on the $97.09

FIGURE 6.8   SAMPLE PAGE OF SALES TAX NEWSLETTER, NORTH DAKOTA

that vendors be well informed and cooperative; thus, adequate information must be given to them. As a minimum, the following is suggested:

1. A single volume that contains the act and general regulations and rulings and is well indexed. Most of the current indexing leaves much to be desired. This volume would be available to all taxpayers on request, free of charge. There would be no need to mail a copy to each vendor when the permit is issued, as many would not make use of it.

2. A summary of the tax, with a listing of exemptions and other major features. This publication would be mailed to each new vendor. When changes occur in the tax, the summary would be reissued and mailed to all vendors.

3. Circulars that summarize provisions of the act and rulings applying to particular types of business. They would be mailed to all new firms and to all firms in a particular line of business when significant changes are made.

DISTRIBUTION OF TAX PAYMENTS BY MAGNITUDE OF PAYMENTS

In all states for which information is available, a very high percentage of the total tax liability is paid by a very small percentage of the total number of firms. Examples are given in table 6.3.

This sample suggests that 1% of the vendors pay around 40% of the tax; 10%, around 80%; and the upper half of the firms pay over 95% of the total.

7. State Control of Sales Tax-Delinquent Vendors

Enforcement of sales and use taxes involves two basic problems: the control and prevention of delinquency, in the sense of failure to file returns and pay tax reviewed in this chapter, and the ascertainment of the correctness of the reported tax.

DELINQUENCY PROCEDURE

Filing Requirements

All states require vendors to file returns and pay tax at specified dates for each period, as shown in table 7.1. Dates, except as indicated, are for the month following the period for which the return is due. States whose filing dates fall at the end of the month are concentrated primarily in the Midwest, along with a few others that initially had solely quarterly return periods. Not a single southern state east of Texas, except Florida, has a filing date beyond the 20th.

The noticeable tendency in the last decade is to provide later dates. The number of states using the 15th or the 20th has fallen from twelve in 1970 to six currently, and one of these, Arizona, in fact requires payment by the 20th, whereas the end of the month or later group has grown from eight in 1960 to sixteen in 1970 and to twenty in 1981. The earlier the date, the shorter the lapse of time before the state gets its money, the more interest gained, and the smaller the danger of default. The fifteenth is too early for many firms, however, especially chains or those whose accounting is done outside the state, and the states with this data are under great pressure to grant extensions. Some firms simply cannot meet the deadline. The end of the month date is more satisfactory from the vendor standpoint. Some states now require a deposit by large firms. Whereas most states use the postmark date, several, including Connecticut and New Jersey, require receipt of the return by the specified date.

Granting of Extensions

Most states will grant, upon prior request, some extension of time, either for individual requests during a particular return interval or, more permanently,

TABLE 7.1 Filing Dates for Sales Tax Returns

Day of the Month	State
15th	Arizona[a]
	Maine
	Michigan
	North Carolina
	Oklahoma
	West Virginia
20th	Alabama
	Arkansas
	Colorado
	Georgia
	Kentucky
	Louisiana
	Massachusetts
	Mississippi
	Missouri
	New Jersey
	New York
	Ohio
	Rhode Island
	South Carolina
	Tennessee
	Virginia
	Washington (15th after May 1983)
	Wisconsin (large accounts)
21st	Maryland
25th	Idaho
	Minnesota
	New Mexico
30th, 31st, or last day of the month	California
	Connecticut
	District of Columbia
	Florida
	Hawaii
	Illinois
	Indiana (30th)
	Iowa (30th)[b]
	Kansas
	Missouri (quar. returns)
	Nebraska
	Nevada
	North Dakota
	South Dakota
	Texas
	Utah (30th)
	Vermont (30th)
	Wisconsin (except large accounts)
	Wyoming
15th of the second succeeding month	Pennsylvania (mo. returns)[c]

[a] Delinquent 20th.

[b] Deposits due 20th.

[c] Quar. returns are due on the 15th of some months and the 20th of others (there are actually five periods); semiann. on the 20th of the succeeding months.

for firms which cannot easily meet the deadline. The policies, however, vary substantially. Some states, including Connecticut, Florida (to avoid paying a charge), and Georgia, require payment of estimated tax by the due date. Permanent extensions to a specified date are permitted in Arizona, Colorado, Florida, Kentucky, Michigan, New Mexico, Texas, Utah, Virginia, and Washington. At the other extreme, one group will either grant no extensions or grant them only rarely: Arkansas, Hawaii, Illinois, Maryland, Nebraska, and the District of Columbia. Extensions are rare in Idaho, Massachusetts, Rhode Island, South Dakota, and Vermont (the firm must pay an estimated amount).

When an extension is granted, penalty is waived, of course, and usually interest is waived for an extension of a few days, except where required by law. For more than a few days, however, and in some states even for any period, interest is applied because the vendor has had use of the money for a longer period. In most states, the vendor loses his discount (payment for collecting the tax) if he gets an extension.

Ascertainment of Nonfilers

The system of ascertainment of nonfilers has undergone drastic change over the last several decades. Initially, and even many as late as 1960, states ascertained nonfilers manually, by checking the ledger cards on which payments were recorded; addressograph plates were then pulled to mail delinquency notices. This gave way to punch card systems; data from returns were punched onto cards and the return cards were run against the master cards. The master cards with no accompanying return card were those of nonfilers; these were then run through the printer to address the delinquency notices.

With minor exceptions, all states are now determining delinquents from the computer memory. Data of payments are entered into the computer system as the returns come in; at the cutoff data the computer determines those firms that have not filed, addresses the delinquency notices, and, in most states, provides a print-out listing of the nonfilers. This can be done very quickly and thus delinquency notices prepared much sooner than in the past.

Date for Ascertaining Delinquents

The states vary somewhat in the time allowed to elapse between the due date and the date on which delinquents are ascertained as shown in table 7.2. The variation reflects partly differences in techniques employed and availability of computer time and partly deliberate policy. Some states seek to determine the delinquents as quickly as possible in the belief that revenue loss is minimized. Others emphasize the large number of returns filed shortly after the due date. Listing of these returns as delinquents is wasteful and a source of ill will and unnecessary correspondence.

Determination of the optimum interval is difficult. Any time lapse in excess

TABLE 7.2   Time Lapse between Due Date and Date of Ascertainment of Delinquents

Days	State
10–17	Florida, Maryland, Nebraska, Nevada, North Dakota, Rhode Island, South Dakota (10–15), Tennessee (all 10 except South Dakota)
18–20	Idaho (18), Kansas, Mississippi, South Carolina, Washington (all 20)
21–25	Alabama (20–24), Arkansas (2d–3d wk.), California (21), Colorado (25), Louisiana (25), Maine (21), Michigan (18–25), Minnesota (21), Vermont (3d wk.), Virginia (25)
26–31	Georgia (25–30), Indiana (30), Iowa (30), Kentucky (30), Ohio (30), Pennsylvania (25–30), Wisconsin (30), Wyoming (30)
35	Connecticut (mo. filers; 65 days quar.), North Carolina
45	Arizona, Hawaii, Illinois,[a] Oklahoma, Utah
45 to 60	New York
60	New Mexico, District of Columbia
30–40 from end of quar.	Missouri, New Jersey

[a] 45-day cycle; actual time depends on time in cycle.

of roughly a month appears excessive. But short of a month, the optimum is impossible to determine with current information and likely varies among the states. California, which has given this question more study than any other state, used a seven-working day rule in 1970 but later shifted to a three-week period. Virginia experimented with a ten-day interval but shifted to twenty-five because of the number of returns that came in during that time.

In all states, a number of vendors file during the period betwen the due date and the delinquency cutoff date. These vendors do not appear on the delinquency lists but are legally subject to interest, penalty, and loss of vendor discount, if any. Several states, without publicly announcing it, give two or three days grace before applying interest or penalty; at one point, several states applied no penalty up to the end of the month—thus in fact granting general extensions of filing time, but only Minnesota appears to do so currently.

Initial Action

In all states except two (Illinois and Mississippi), initial action consists of a notice to the vendor to file a return. This notice may be a form or a copy of the return, as shown in figures 7.1 and 7.2 for Nebraska and Virginia, or a computer prepared notice, or letter (figure 7.3). In Georgia, Hawaii, Ohio, Pennsylvania, Texas, and Virginia, a copy of the return form is sent (to facilitate filing). In Colorado, Missouri, and Utah, the notice includes an assessment of tax, based on the experience of recent months. In several states, such as Idaho, Nevada, New Mexico, North Dakota, and Virginia, the field district office is sent either a copy of the notice or a listing, and in Nebraska, Nevada, and New Mexico, the compliance officer is expected to contact the firm, usually by phone, immediately. In Maryland, Massachusetts, and Tennessee, the tax-

NEBRASKA NONFILER NOTICE FOR SALES AND USE TAX

nebraska
department
of revenue

Our records show that your Nebraska and City Sales and Use Tax Return, Form 10, for the tax period indicated in block 2 below has not been timely filed with this office. Returns must be filed every tax period even though there have been no sales. Returns not timely filed are subject to a penalty of five dollars or loss of collection fee, whichever is greater. Interest on the tax due at the rate of 14 percent per year is due from the original due date until paid. If you have filed your return after the due date and paid the tax due for the tax period shown, please disregard this notice. If you do not have a Nebraska and City Sales and Use Tax Return for the tax period shown, contact one of the offices of the Nebraska Department of Revenue listed on the reverse side of this notice.

NAME AND LOCATION ADDRESS

NAME AND MAILING ADDRESS

(1) Nebraska I.D. Number	(2) Tax Period	(3) Tax Category	(4) Date of Notice

6-049-70 Rev. 6-81 Supersedes 6-049-70 Rev. 6-80

FIGURE 7.1   NONFILER NOTICE FOR SALES AND USE TAX, NEBRASKA

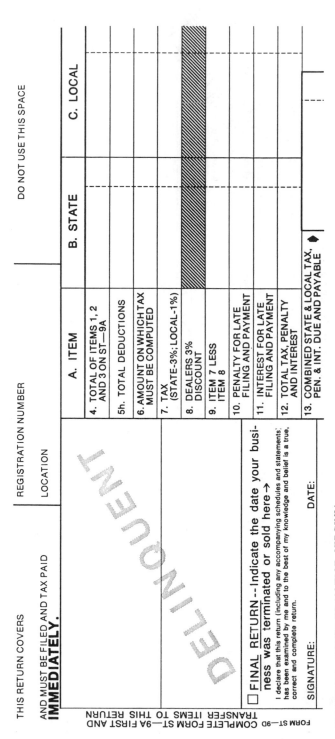

FIGURE 7.2 NONFILER NOTICE, VIRGINIA

payer is phoned from headquarters at the same time the notice is mailed. In Maine, the taxpayer is contacted by phone if the tax liability exceeds $500. In Rhode Island, the taxpayer is contacted directly by a revenue officer if the firm has a history of normally high sales tax liability.

Two states do not mail a notice. Illinois notifies the district office for contact (often by phone) by a compliance officer. In Mississippi, the procedure is similar, the compliance person in the area being required to contact the firm immediately by personal visit.

The widespread use of the mailed notice and the relatively good response to it confirm the desirability of using it initially rather than taking the time of compliance personnel. Increasingly, however, states are relying on "phone power."[1]

Second Action

The states differ widely in the choice of techniques for follow-up, the choice influenced to some extent by the nature of the initial action.

Second Notice. One group sends a second notice, usually worded in a much more demanding fashion than the first, before any additional action is taken:

Connecticut: A citation, with notice to appear, is mailed to quarterly filers; if this is ignored, a compliance officer contacts by phone or visit.

Louisiana: A proposed assessment, based on previous returns, is sent; if there is no response within thirty days, a final assessment is sent.

Minnesota: A second notice is sent; after four weeks, a final notice goes to the phone power unit.

New Jersey: Second notice, to field after thirty days.

New York: Second notice; if no response, district office is notified and contacts firm.

North Dakota: Second notice; phone call from headquarters if no response in ten days.

Ohio: A notice is mailed requiring the vendor to appear at the local field office; if this is not done, a compliance officer contacts.

Oklahoma: A ten-day letter is mailed, followed by a thirty-day notice of assessment (figure 7.4).

Rhode Island: A notice is mailed, followed if no response by a phone call and then a visit.

Utah: A warrant (lien) letter is sent, explaining the judgment lien and informing the vendor that the sheriff may be ordered to seize and sell the assets to satisfy the judgment.

[1]Note National Association of Tax Administrators, *Proceedings of the National Training Workshop on the Use of Phone Power in State Tax Administration,* Washington, 1979.

OKLAHOMA TAX COMMISSION

STATE OF OKLAHOMA

D. M. BERRY, Chairman
L. L. LEININGER, Vice-Chairman
J. L. MERRILL, Sec'y-Member

2501 LINCOLN BLVD.
OKLAHOMA CITY, OKLAHOMA 73194
September 21, 1976

SAMPLE

Sales/Use Tax

DIVISION
307992

Mr. John Doe
1521 Smith Street
Oklahoma City, Oklahoma 73106

Dear Mr. Doe:

Records in this Division indicate you are delinquent in the payment of sales tax for the period January 1, 1976 through June 30, 1976.

This is to advise that we shall expect you to prepare and mail to this Division immediately, a sales tax report, together with a remittance in payment of the tax, interest and penalty due. Should we not receive such report and remittance within a period of ten (10) days from date of this letter, the Commission will issue a notice directing you to appear before them and to show cause why your sales tax permit should not be cancelled and revoked.

Of this you will take due notice and be governed accordingly.

Yours very truly,

OKLAHOMA TAX COMMISSION

Everett Watkins, Director
Sales and Use Tax Division

EW:mbe

REMITTANCES SHOULD BE MADE TO THE OKLAHOMA TAX COMMISSION AND REFER TO DIVISION

FIGURE 7.3   INITIAL NONFILER NOTICE, OKLAHOMA

OKLAHOMA TAX COMMISSION
STATE OF OKLAHOMA

D. M. BERRY, Chairman
L. L. LEININGER, Vice-Chairman
J. L. MERRILL, Sec'y-Member

2501 LINCOLN BLVD.
OKLAHOMA CITY. OKLAHOMA 73194

September 21, 1976

SAMPLE

Sales/Use Tax

DIVISION

307992

CERTIFIED MAIL

Mr. John Doe
1521 Smith Street
Oklahoma City, Oklahoma 73106

Re: 30-Day Proposal to Assess Delinquent Sales Tax
Period: 1-1-76 through 6-30-76
Amount: $1,150.00

Dear Mr. Doe:

Records in this Division indicate you are delinquent in the payment of sales tax for the period January 1, 1976 through June 30, 1976. The estimated amount of tax due for the delinquent period is $1,000.00, plus interest of $50.00 and penalty of $100.00, which totals $1,150.00.

The Commission hereby proposes to assess sales tax against you, along with interest and penalty, as outlined. Please attach your remittance in the amount of $1,150.00 to the enclosed copy of this letter and mail to the Oklahoma Tax Commission at once.

If you do not agree to this proposed assessment, you must file reports and payment in full for all delinquent sales tax, including interest and penalties, subject to audit; or you must file a verified written protest, in triplicate, with the Oklahoma Tax Commission within thirty (30) days from the date of mailing of this letter. If you fail to file a verified written protest within the thirty day period, this proposed assessment will become final and absolute and a tax warrant will be filed with the Court Clerk and Sheriff of Oklahoma County as a lien against any property owned by you. The lien will remain on file accruing interest at the rate of twelve per cent (12%) per annum until paid in full.

This proposed assessment is made in accordance with the terms and provisions of House Bill 701 of the 30th Session of the Legislature, which Act now appears as Section 221 of Title 68, O. S. 1971, known as the Uniform Tax Procedure Act.

Very truly yours,

OKLAHOMA TAX COMMISSION

Everett Watkins, Director
Sales and Use Tax Division

EW:mbe   REMITTANCES SHOULD BE MADE TO THE OKLAHOMA TAX COMMISSION AND REFER TO DIVISION

FIGURE 7.4 NOTICE OF ASSESSMENT, OKLAHOMA

Wisconsin: A demand notice is sent, followed in fifteen days by an assessment.

District of Columbia: Assessment and bill are mailed; then to field.

Field Visit with Second Notice.   A second group sends a second notice, accompanied by a notice to the field to contact the delinquent:

Arizona

Tennessee: The second notice is followed by a ten-day demand to pay, followed by a levy.

Field Visit without Second Notice.   In the third group of states, the field is notified for immediate contact:

Alabama

Connecticut: Monthly filers.

Florida: Phone contact.

Georgia

Illinois

Iowa

Kansas: Phone contact.

Kentucky

Massachusetts

Michigan

Nebraska: Followed by notice from field, as illustrated in figure 7.5.

New Mexico: Phone contact, followed by provisional assessment.

North Carolina

Pennsylvania: Phone or visit, followed by assessment.

South Carolina

South Dakota: Phone or visit.

Texas: Phone or visit, then collection letter sent.

Washington: The compliance officer is provided with a detailed record of the firm via computer print-out.

West Virginia: Contact, followed by assessment.

Phone Call from Headquarters without Contacting Field.

Arkansas

Iowa: Followed by field visit.

Hawaii

Idaho

Maine

Maryland

Vermont

More Direct Techniques.
Phone Call from Headquarters and Notice to Field.
Virginia: Followed by a summons to appear at the field office.

Two sets of states use much more direct and demanding techniques:

California: The second notice is a notice to appear at a hearing to revoke the firm's sales tax permit.

Colorado and Mississippi: The second step is the issuance of a distraint warrant, a step taken in other states only as a final action.

Timing of the Second Action

Table 7.3 shows the typical elapsed time between the first and the second action. The interval is affected somewhat by the nature of the first action. States relying primarily on phone power initially tend to go to the second action sooner than the others.

There has been a definite tendency to lengthen the time interval; whereas twenty-two states waited less than a month in 1970, only sixteen states now do so.

The Iowa pattern follows from the initial phone contact system; if this brings no results, the state proceeds immediately to the next step. The philosophy still differs sharply among states; one group of states believes that losses of revenue are minimized by speedy action; the other is convinced that money is saved by delaying before more expensive action is undertaken, as many of the returns will come in anyway.

It is impossible to assess empirically the relative advantages of the alternative systems or the time intervals. Some states clearly allow unnecessarily long intervals, partly because of computer difficulties and lack of field personnel. Others have discovered that the use of too short an interval results in wasted effort. A number of firms will pay on the basis of the notice if given adequate time, and premature field visits waste time and money. On the other hand, immediate visits do bring in some money more quickly and lessen the danger of loss through bankruptcy or disappearance of the vendor. California, for example, has concluded that an interval of seventy days from the due date to actual revocation of the permit is optimal. When a shorter interval was used, there was substantial wasted effort from communications crossing in the mails and the like. An optimal cycle might be roughly as follows: due date, 30th; first notice mailed, 15th; refer to field, 10th of the following month.

Final Action

The aforementioned methods result in collection of tax from most of the initially delinquent vendors. In all states, however, a hard core fail to pay even after notices and field visits. Typically, they will be fewer than 1% of the ven-

STATE OF NEBRASKA DEPARTMENT OF REVENUE

Charles Thone, Governor

Fred A. Herrington, Tax Commissioner

Box 94818
Lincoln, NE 68509
Tel. (402) 471-2971

Name

Street or Other Mailing Address

City   State   Zip Code

Date:

**If You Inquire About Your Account
Refer To These Numbers**

Nebraska I.D. Number	
Due Date	

Dear Nebraska Taxpayer:

NOTICE OF DELINQUENCY

The records of the Nebraska Department of Revenue indicate your Nebraska tax account is delinquent as shown below. Failure to comply with this notice before the due date referenced above may result in tax assessments being made for nonfiled tax periods, tax liens being filed against your property rights for the balance(s) due, and other legal action which may include seizure of property. Nebraska tax returns must be filed even if there is no tax due to report.

NONFILED NEBRASKA TAX RETURNS

Type of Tax	Nonfiled Tax Periods

BALANCE(S) OF NEBRASKA TAX DUE	
Type of Tax	Balance Due
$	
TOTAL	$

If the above tax return(s) have been filed or the payment(s) remitted, send copies of the tax return(s) and both sides of your cancelled check(s) to this Department. A copy of this letter should accompany the information requested and be returned in the enclosed envelope.

This matter deserves your immediate attention.

FOR THE STATE TAX COMMISSIONER

Sincerely,

Revenue Agent
Field Services Division

Enclosure

FL 376 Rev. 3-81
Supersedes FL 376 Rev. 8-79

FIGURE 7.5   DELINQUENCY NOTICE, NEBRASKA

TABLE 7.3   Time Lapse between First Notice and Second Action, 1980-81

Under One Month	*Approximately One Month*	*Over One Month*
10–12 days	Arizona	*45 days*
Iowa	Arkansas	Utah
Maryland	Colorado	
Nebraska	Connecticut (25–35 days)	*60 days*
North Carolina	District of Columbia (30–60 days)	Georgia
Rhode Island	Florida	Illinois
South Carolina	Indiana	Maine
	Kentucky	Oklahoma
14–15 days	Louisiana	
Alabama	Michigan	*90 days*
Hawaii	Minnesota	Ohio
Idaho	Missouri (30–90 days)	
South Dakota	Nevada (30–90 days)	*Twice a year*
	New Jersey	West Virginia
20–21 days	New Mexico	
California	New York (3–12 wks.)	
Kansas	Pennsylvania (35 days)	
Mississippi	Tennessee	
North Dakota	Texas	
Wisconsin	Vermont	
	Virginia (25–30 days)	
	Washington	
	Wyoming	

dors. At any particular time, in a state with 50,000 vendors, there will be nearly 500 delinquent vendors. The states vary somewhat in their approach, depending upon the legislation and property laws of the state and their experience with different approaches.

Warrants.   In twenty-five states, primary, but not necessarily sole, reliance is placed on the use of a warrant, variously called a tax warrant or a distraint warrant, based upon an assessment (see figures 7.6 and 7.7). The warrant is usually prepared in the revenue department and then is transmitted to the sheriff of the county for execution through the seizure of property or other means. Thus, the sheriff can close the business and take possession of the assets. In some states, he can attach real property as well. A number of states report difficulties in obtaining the full cooperation of local sheriffs. In a few—Colorado, Connecticut, Georgia, Idaho, Kansas, Michigan, Minnesota, Mississippi, Nebraska, and New York—the revenue department has been given authority to execute warrants with its own personnel. Colorado has a reputation for being very strict. If payment is not made after the initial steps, a distraint warrant is prepared and turned over to the field division. If it cannot collect, the compliance officer padlocks the business and attaches the property. States emphasizing the warrant approach include Colorado, Connecticut, Florida, Georgia, Hawaii, Idaho, Illinois, Indiana, Kentucky, Louisiana, Michigan, Minnesota, Mississippi, Nevada, New Jersey, New Mexico, New York, Oklahoma, South Carolina, South Dakota, Utah, Virginia, Washington, Wisconsin, and Wyoming.

The District of Columbia uses a jeopardy assessment in much the same manner, seizing property and closing the business. A similar process is followed in Ohio and Pennsylvania. The revenue department obtains from a county court a judgment against the vendor, which is then enforced in the same fashion as are the warrants. This process is somewhat slower, but the courts normally cooperate.

In Tennessee, a levy (not a warrant) is executed by the department's own personnel; businesses can be padlocked or sold and bank accounts can be seized. Tangible personal and real property can be seized and sold.

Liens. In virtually all states, a lien is filed against the delinquent taxpayer. In some states, for example, Indiana, Minnesota, South Dakota, Utah, Virginia, Washington, and Wisconsin, the warrant automatically becomes a lien against the property. In others, such as Mississippi, Nebraska (figure 7.8), New York, and Tennessee, a lien is prepared separately from the warrant and filed in the county. States using the revocation technique usually prepare liens to protect revenue at the same time that they revoke or threaten to revoke permits.

Four states—Arizona, Nebraska, Pennsylvania, and South Carolina—rely almost entirely on the lien to bring about payment. When the taxpayer does not file or pay, an assessment is made and a lien prepared and filed with the county. Typically, the firm finds that the lien so hamstrings its operation that it takes action to clear it, even without action to seize property. Massachusetts is commencing to foreclose on the liens.

Revocation. A major group of states, now sixteen in number, stress the revocation—or, in practice, the threat of revocation—of the sales tax permit as the primary approach, although using the other techniques, particularly liens. These states include Arkansas, California (which pioneered this approach), Connecticut, Iowa, Kansas, Kentucky, Louisiana, Nevada, North Dakota, Oklahoma (figure 7.9), Rhode Island, South Carolina, South Dakota, Vermont, Wisconsin, and Wyoming. Threat of revocation is also used in Idaho, Illinois, Maryland, Minnesota, Missouri, Utah, Virginia, and Washington. Several of these states find revocation unsatisfactory, as firms continue to operate and local law enforcement officers and the courts do not cooperate. In California, if the vendor does not respond to the first notice within three weeks, the department prepares a citation to show cause why the permit should not be revoked and establishes a date and place of a hearing on revocation. After the notice is mailed, a compliance officer visits the firm to see if it is still in operation and, if it is, to try to collect. Twenty-eight days after the citation notice, the permit is revoked if payment has not been made. The taxpayer may, of course,

C4530 (REV. 3-79)

MICHIGAN DEPARTMENT OF TREASURY
TAX COLLECTION ENFORCEMENT DIVISION

WARRANT

Taxpayer Name and Address:

Date: \
Warrant No.: \
D/T: \
Acct. No.:

WHEREAS there is now due, owing and unpaid to the State of Michigan from the taxpayer whose name appears above the sum of $ _____ as said taxpayer has failed to pay the taxes, penalties, interest and/or costs as required by the provisions of Department of Revenue Act 122, P.A. 1941, as amended, and the following:

☐ Income Tax Act 281, P.A. 1967 as amended \
☐ Sales Tax Act 167, P.A. 1933 as amended \
☐ Single Business Tax Act 228, P.A. 1975 as amended

☐ Use Tax Act 94, P.A. 1937, as amended

ASSESSMENT NO.	TAX DUE	PENALTY	INTEREST	TOTAL

WARRANT PREPARATION COSTS

TOTAL AMOUNT DUE

WHEREAS the Revenue Division of the Department of Treasury administers the provisions of the above-mentioned act or acts and, in particular, the Commissioner may issue a warrant under the official seal of his office, the Commissioner through his authorized employees may levy upon all property and rights to property and all the real and personal property of the taxpayer, without exception, found within the state, for payment of the amount of the tax, the cost of executing the warrant and the added penalties and interest; and

WHEREAS demand has been made upon the taxpayer for the above amount and it has been determined that the amount is due and unpaid and constitutes a lien against all real and personal property of the taxpayer, and that the taxpayer has had due and proper notice of assessment and demand therefore and that the taxpayer has failed to comply within the time allowed by law.

NOW, THEREFORE, IN THE NAME OF THE PEOPLE OF THE STATE OF MICHIGAN, any authorized employee is commanded that from the goods and chattels of, and for want thereof, then the real property of the above named taxpayer within your jurisdiction, you shall cause to be made a sum equal to the above total tax, penalty and/or interest aforesaid, together with costs of this proceeding, by levying upon and seizing such goods, chattels and/or real estate and selling the same or such portion thereof as shall be necessary to satisfy this warrant, and that you remit the proceeds of such sale to the Department of Treasury in the City of Lansing within 90 days from the date hereof and for so doing this shall be your warrant.

Given under the official seal of the Revenue Division this _____ day of _____, A.D. 19___

_____
(Deputy) Commissioner

TAXPAYER

FIGURE 7.6 TAX COLLECTION WARRANT, MICHIGAN

C-4606 (REV 11-80)

MICHIGAN DEPARTMENT OF TREASURY
TAX COLLECTION ENFORCEMENT DIVISION

WARRANT – NOTICE OF LEVY

Date:

To:

Levy No:

D/T:

Acct. No:

YOU ARE NOTIFIED that the following amount is now due, owing and unpaid to the State of Michigan, from the person whose name appears below, as required by the provision of the Revenue Act (Act 162, Public Acts of 1980).

☐ Income Tax, see Act 281, P.A. 1967 as amended
☐ Sales Tax, see Act 167, P.A. 1933 as amended

☐ Use Tax, see Act 94, 1937 as amended
☐ Single Business Tax, see Act 228, P.A. 1975 as amended

ASSESSMENT NO. TYPE OF DEBT	TAX AMOUNT DUE	PENALTY	INTEREST	TOTAL

WARRANT COSTS

TOTAL AMOUNT DUE

YOU ARE FURTHER NOTIFIED that demand for payment of this amount was made upon the debtor as required. This notice constitutes a levy against all property and rights to property, real and personal, tangible and intangible, in your possession but belonging to the debtor (e.g. wages, credits, bank deposits or other monies).

ACT 162, P.A. 1980 provides that a person:

- who refuses or fails to surrender such property upon demand is personally liable to the state for this amount, plus interest at 9% per annum from the date of the levy, and/or 50% penalty.
- who surrenders such property discharges his/her obligation to the debtor for the same amount.

THEREFORE, IN THE NAME OF THE PEOPLE OF THE STATE OF MICHIGAN, Demand is hereby made upon you for the above amount, or for any lesser amount that you may hold.

Your Employee/Creditor	I certify that this notice of levy was served, delivering a copy of it to the person below.	Given under the official seal of the Revenue Division this _____ day of _____ , A.D. 19 ____ .
Identifying No. of Employee/Creditor	Name	
Taxpayer Name and Address	Title	
	Date	Time □ AM □ PM	
	Signature of Serving Officer	(Deputy) Commissioner

SERVICE COPY

FIGURE 7.7 NOTICE OF LEVY, MICHIGAN

nebraska department of revenue

Notice of State Tax Lien

• Read instructions on reverse side

Lien Serial Number	Lien Type ☐ Original ☐ Renewal	Date	Social Security Number
Nebraska I.D. No.	County	Lien Filed With ☐ Register of Deeds ☐ County Clerk	Spouse's Social Security Number

BUSINESS NAME AND LOCATION ADDRESS

Business Name

Street Address

City   State   Zip Code

TAXPAYER NAME AND MAILING ADDRESS

Name

Street or Other Mailing Address

City   State   Zip Code

Pursuant to the revenue laws of the State of Nebraska, notice is hereby given that taxes (including penalties, interest and additions) have been assessed and are due from the above taxpayer and remain unpaid after demand. These taxes constitute a lien upon property belonging to the taxpayer, or hereafter acquired by the taxpayer, and located in the above county. Liens for sales and use taxes only attach to the real property belonging to the taxpayer, or hereafter acquired by the taxpayer, and located in the above county.

Tax Category Number	Tax Period	Date of Assessment	Amount of Tax	Penalty	Interest	Additions	Balance of Assessment Due

						TOTAL	$

I hereby certify that the Nebraska Department of Revenue has complied with the revenue laws of the State of Nebraska in the determination of the amount shown to be due, and the taxpayer has failed to pay the amount due after demand. If this Notice of State Tax Lien is an extension of an effective lien it serves to continue the priority of the state's interest in the affected property of the taxpayer.

sign here ▶ Preparer's Signature _____ Title _____ Date _____

▶ Authorized Signature _____ Title _____ Date _____

FOR COUNTY OFFICIAL'S USE

NEBRASKA DEPARTMENT OF REVENUE — White and Canary Copies   TAXPAYER — Pink Copy   COUNTY OFFICE — Goldenrod Copy

4-494-74 Rev. 12-79
Supersedes 4-494-74 Rev. 5-79

FIGURE 7.8 NOTICE OF STATE TAX LIEN, NEBRASKA

STATE OF OKLAHOMA:

SAMPLE

TO: JOHN DOE
             1521 SMITH STREET
             OKLAHOMA CITY, OKLAHOMA 73106

GREETINGS: You will please take notice that the files and records of
the Oklahoma Tax Commission show that you have violated the Oklahoma
Sales Tax Law in this to-wit.

You have failed, neglected or refused to pay sales tax, interest and
penalty due as required by Law for the following period:

             January 1, 1976 through June 30, 1976.

You are therefore notified that on the_____day of_____,1976,
at 9:00 a. m., a hearing will be had before the Oklahoma Tax Commission
in its office in the M. C. Connors Building, 2501 Lincoln Boulevard,
Oklahoma City, Oklahoma, at which time you may appear and show cause why
your Sales Tax Permit #307992 should not be cancelled and revoked.

You may govern yourself accordingly.

DATED this 21st day of September, 1976.

(SEAL)

ATTEST: OKLAHOMA TAX COMMISSION

_____   _____
Secretary   Chairman

APPROVED AS TO FORM:

_____
Attorney

APPROVED:

_____
Director, Sales Tax Division

RAE:mbe

FIGURE 7.9   NOTICE TO SHOW CAUSE WHY SALES TAX PERMIT SHOULD NOT BE
CANCELLED, OKLAHOMA

then seek reinstatement, which may be granted upon payment of all monies due including a penalty.

If the firm continues to operate after revocation, criminal charges are brought through the local district attorney. In several other states, criminal prosecution for operating without a permit is brought if the firm continues to operate after revocation: Arkansas, South Carolina, and South Dakota. In Kansas, Rhode Island, and Vermont, a court injunction is obtained after revocation, and continued operation is held in contempt of court. Nevada and Oklahoma, however, do not use criminal prosecution but bring court action to close the business.

On the whole, the states that use the revocation system like it, despite the less than satisfactory experience of several states. The number of states emphasizing the system has increased between 1962, when only five states made significant use of it, and 1980. In these states, the threat of revocation, which would put the firm out of business, appears to be more effective than merely threatening legal action to enforce payment. If revocation actually becomes necessary, the success of the revenue department depends upon the ability to obtain the cooperation of the local prosecutor.

Criminal Prosecution. In all states, the sales tax legislation provides for criminal action for violation of the law. Only Maine, however, relies on this approach as the primary instrument of enforcement. Massachusetts also uses criminal prosecution to some extent. The District of Columbia, which once used it extensively, now does so rarely. In Maine, any firm not filing after the initial letters is summoned into court on a misdemeanor charge and upon conviction is fined for failure to file. The courts cooperate, and the state finds this to be an effective approach. If the vendor files but does not pay, this method is not successful because of the courts' reluctance to become money collectors. Virginia, which at first used the prosecution approach, abandoned it, as the courts did not cooperate adequately.

Criminal prosecution in other states is very limited. Alabama, Arkansas, and Connecticut make some use of it. In Alabama, the compliance officer can arrest the vendor. Some states such as Arkansas, California, South Carolina, and South Dakota, which stress the revocation technique, prosecute for operation after revocation, but even these cases are not numerous. Most states never prosecute on criminal grounds, though a few do in the event of deliberate fraud.

The limited use of the criminal approach reflects in part the reluctance of prosecuting officers and local courts to be concerned with questions of money collection, in part the revenue commissioners' fear of political repercussions. Commonly, it is felt that other methods are sufficiently effective to obviate the need to go to the trouble of prosecution in court. When outright fraud is suspected, generating proof to the satisfaction of the courts is difficult, and the severe penalties for fraud are of little significance.

Other Methods. Several states, particularly Georgia, Illinois, Kentucky, Massachusetts, Texas, and Utah, obtain cooperation from the liquor control agencies to revoke the liquor licenses of delinquents having such licenses—a very effective weapon.

Summary. Several methods work satisfactorily with hard core delinquents: the traditional warrant method for enforcing legal obligations, revocation of permits, and court orders to suspend operations for failure to file and pay. At least two states, Missouri and Oklahoma, lack power to close the business and seize property, however.

Some Examples

More detailed information for four states illustrates the procedures.

Connecticut.
1. Two mail notices are sent, the second, two weeks after the first.
2. The second notice, coming after the account is sixty days overdue, warns the taxpayer that enforcement action is pending.
3. The account is then referred to a revenue agent, who contacts the taxpayer by phone or letter.
4. If the vendor still does not file and pay, the following steps are taken:
   a. A tax warrant is prepared, which enables a serving officer to seize real or personal property, or garnish savings accounts or salaries. The tax warrants may be served by an employee of the department or a deputy sheriff.
   b. A lien is placed on the property.
   c. The taxpayer may be ordered to appear at a hearing to show cause why sales tax and other permits should not be revoked.

Texas.
1. One notice is sent to the taxpayer, a second copy of the return form.
2. The account is then referred to the field. An enforcement officer will follow these steps, not all being used in any particular case:
   a. Phone the taxpayer.
   b. Send a collection letter, and seek to track down the taxpayer if the letter is returned.
   c. Visit the taxpayer's place of business.
   d. Freeze liquid assets—bank accounts, accounts receivable, or other assets held by others.
   e. Notify the Alcoholic Beverage Commission, which will send the firm a notice of a hearing to cancel its liquor permit.
   f. Seize the money in the vendor's cash register.

g. Upon approval from headquarters, seize the taxpayer's business and padlock it.
h. Sell the assets at public auction.
i. If there are no assets to seize, the enforcement officer will certify the account to the attorney general, who will take legal action to ensure payment.

Washington.
Delinquents are divided into two classes, nonproductive and productive. The former, the smaller accounts, are handled in headquarters, with notices sent and, ultimately, phone contact. About 60% of these are cleared by the notices and most of the rest by phone. Often such accounts appear delinquent because they are out of business, the address is wrong, and other reasons.

The productive accounts, in turn, are grouped according to estimated tax liability. Immediate phone contact is made; this clears about 85% of the delinquents. Then follows a series of steps if the accounts are still not cleared:
1. Make a field visit.
2. Issue a summons to appear at the district office with records.
3. Send a notice of hearing to revoke. This is not widely used, but some certificates are revoked.
4. Issue a warrant for the estimated amount of tax; this constitutes a lien. The compliance officer holds the lien for thirty days; it can then be filed, and it becomes the basis for withholding amounts due the vendor. The compliance officer can also file a warrant, obtain a judgment, and seize the taxpayer's property.
5. If the permit is revoked and the firm operates, criminal action can be brought, but this is rare; local prosecutors often will not cooperate.

Nebraska.
Figure 7.10 outlines the steps in the Nebraska procedure.

The Time Lapse Allowed before Final Action is Commenced

In most states there is no precise interval of time before final action is started. Table 7.4 gives some indication of general patterns.

Wisconsin.
The Wisconsin schedule is more specifically defined than many:
1. First notice of delinquency: thirty days after due date.
2. Second notice: twenty days after first notice.
3. Assessment to taxpayer: fifteen days after second notice.
4. Official listing of taxpayer as delinquent: thirty days after assessment.

Field Services Division Generalized Collection Process

For Business Tax Programs

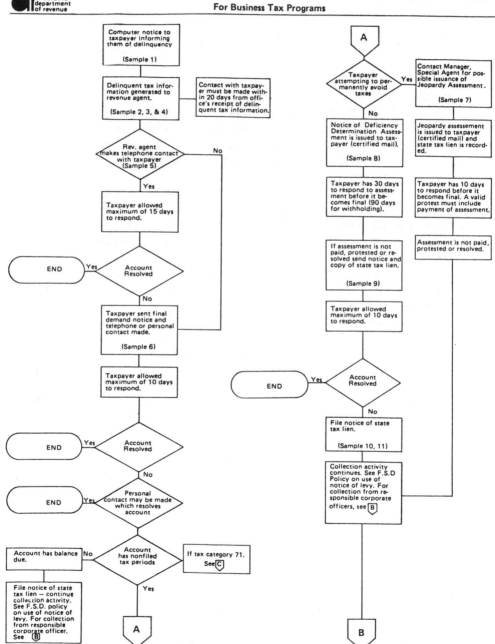

FIGURE 7.10   CHART OF COLLECTION PROCESS, NEBRASKA

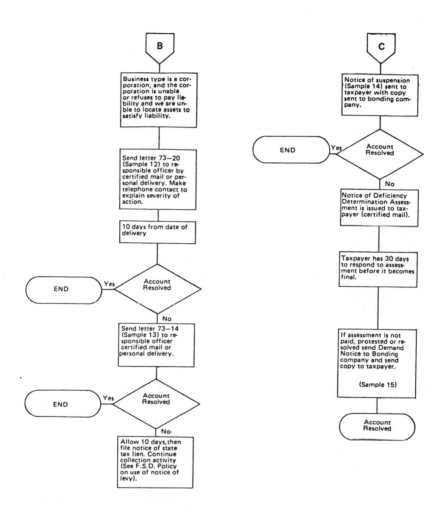

B

Business type is a corporation, and the corporation is unable or refuses to pay liability and we are unable to locate assets to satisfy liability.

Send letter 73—20 (Sample 12) to responsible officer by certified mail or personal delivery. Make telephone contact to explain severity of action.

10 days from date of delivery

Account Resolved — Yes → END

No

Send letter 73—14 (Sample 13) to responsible officer certified mail or personal delivery.

Account Resolved — Yes → END

No

Allow 10 days, then file notice of state tax lien. Continue collection activity (See F.S.D. Policy on use of notice of levy).

C

Notice of suspension (Sample 14) sent to taxpayer with copy sent to bonding company.

Account Resolved — Yes → END

No

Notice of Deficiency Determination Assessment is issued to taxpayer (certified mail).

Taxpayer has 30 days to respond to assessment before it becomes final.

If assessment is not paid, protested or resolved send Demand Notice to Bonding company and send copy to taxpayer.

(Sample 15)

Account Resolved

TABLE 7.4 Time Lapse before Final Action

Under 3 Months	3 to 4 Months	Other
California (1.5–2)	Georgia (4)	Kentucky: (3 mo. delinq.;
Colorado (2)	Indiana (3)	2 quar. delinq.)
Connecticut (2)	Louisiana (3)	
Mississippi (2)	Michigan (4)	
Rhode Island (2)	Nebraska (3)	
Utah (2)	New Jersey (4)	
Wyoming (2)		

5. Notice of warrant sent to taxpayer: thirty days after listing.
6. Recording of warrant: forty-five days after warrant sent to taxpayer.
Total days: 170

California.
The California cycle is as follows:
1. Notice of delinquency: three weeks after due date.
2. Notice of hearing to revoke: three weeks after notice of delinquency.
3. Date of revocation: day following hearing.
4. Notice of revocation: two weeks after revocation date.

DELINQUENCY EXPERIENCE

Experience with delinquency of forty of the forty-five states is shown in table 7.5. Information is not available from Colorado, Massachusetts, New Mexico, Tennessee, and Texas. The average for the forty states plus the District of Columbia is 9.9%; that is, of the returns mailed each period, 9.9% of the returns are not filed at the time the delinquency is determined and the notices sent. The figures are by no means entirely comparable among the states for several reasons. The time lapse between the due date and the date of ascertainment of delinquency varies, although there is little correlation between the time interval and the delinquency rate. Firms filing in the interval between the due date and the delinquency date are not included in the list of delinquents, but in most states they are billed for interest and penalty. Few states keep a record of the number of such firms.

Another source of variation is the extent to which states purge their files of nonactive accounts. States failing to do so will have high percentages of delinquencies because the firms that have become inactive or quit business will often not file returns. If the master file is kept carefully purged, but those firms coded as inactive are included in the total, the percentage of delinquency will appear artificially low because the base upon which the percentage is figured is higher than that in states calculating it on returns actually mailed. Another difference

TABLE 7.5 Delinquency Record by State, 1979-81

State	% of Vendors Delinquent			
	1st Notice	2d Action	3d Action	Final Action
Alabama	8.0–11.0	5.0–7.0		
Arizona	11.0	7.0		0.3
Arkansas	13.0	8.0		0.1
California				
mo.	8.0	3.0–4.0	1.2[a]	
quar.	13.0	5.0–6.0	2.0–3.0	0.2[b]
ann.	19.0	9.0–10.0	4.0–5.0	
Colorado	8.0–9.0	5.0–6.0		
Connecticut	10.0	6.0	3.0	0.2
Florida	13.0–18.0	11.0	4.0	
Georgia	7.0–9.0	5.0	0.5	0.3
Hawaii	20.0 est.			
Idaho	8.0[c]			
Illinois	10.0			0.2
Indiana	9.0	7.0	2.0[d]	
Iowa	10.0	7.0	3.0[e]	
Kansas	4.0–6.0	3.0	0.1[e]	0.01[f]
Kentucky	12.0	4.0	0.4[f]	
Louisiana	11.0	8.0–9.0		3.0–4.0[g]
Maine	10.0		1.0–2.0	0.03[h]
Maryland	9.0	4.0		0.2
Massachusetts				
mo.	6.0			
quar.	8.0			
ann.	11.0			
Michigan	5.0–7.0	2.5–3.5		
Minnesota	6.0	4.0	3.0	
Mississippi	14.0 est.			
Missouri	5.0		1.0[i]	
Nebraska	6.0	2.0		
Nevada	5.0–8.0	3.0		
New Jersey	10.0		1.0[j]	
New Mexico	9.0			
New York	15.0–16.0			
North Carolina	9.0			
North Dakota	5.7	3.3	1.5[k]	neg.[h]
Ohio	14.0	4.0–5.0	2.0–3.0[e]	
Oklahoma	26.0			
Pennsylvania	10.0	7.0		1.5[l]
Rhode Island	13.0	6.0	1][e]	
South Carolina	5.0	2.0	0.1[e]	0.02[f]
South Dakota	8.0	2.0	0.5	0.5[l]; 0.2[g]; 0.1[h]
Tennessee		2.7		
Texas		14.0		1.0
Utah	7.5	6.0	3.0	0.5[m]
Vermont				
mo.	5.0–8.0	3.0–5.0		
quar.	10.0	6.0		

TABLE 7.5 (*continued*)

State	% of Vendors Delinquent			
	1st Notice	*2d Action*	*3d Action*	*Final Action*
Virginia	7.3	3.6	3.0[e]	
Washington				
mo.	11.0		0.004[f]	
quar.	18.0			
ann.	26.0			
West Virginia	18.0			1.0
Wisconsin				
mo.	5.0	3.0	1.5	0.1[e]
mo. & quar.	6.0	3.0	1.5	0.06[f]
mo. & ann.	9.0	3.0	1.5	
Wyoming	5.0	2.0		0.2[n]
District of Columbia	10.0	4.0		0.1[m]

[a] Notice of hearing to revoke.
[b] Revocation—ann.
[c] No exact data; 8% of accounts delinq. at end of each mo.
[d] To collection division.
[e] Notices of hearing to revoke.
[f] Revoke.
[g] Issued warrants.
[h] Criminal action.
[i] To assessment.
[j] Five-day letter.
[k] To phone.
[l] To lien.
[m] Act to close.
[n] Seize property.

is in the treatment of multiple-unit vendors. These firms are less likely to be delinquent than others. The states counting each unit in the chain as a vendor will have, other things being equal, a lower percentage of delinquency than those listing the chains as one vendor. Complications have also been created by the transfer of some firms to longer return intervals. The larger-account monthly payment vendors will show less delinquency than the firms placed on the longer intervals. Transferring the small firms to longer intervals reduces the number of opportunities for them to be delinquent during the year.

Initial Delinquency Record

Table 7.6 shows the ranking of states by delinquency record. It must be stressed that small differences are not significant. Despite the problems of comparison, approximately half of the states (twenty-two) are in the range of 7% to 11%. The median is 10%. All but seven states are in the range of 5% to 15%. One group of states stands out at the high end, for reasons by no means

TABLE 7.6 Ranking of States by Delinquency Record, 1979-80

Level/State	1979-78	1969-70
High		
Oklahoma	26	12.5
Hawaii	20 est.	
West Virginia	18	10.0
Florida	15	2.0
New York	15	10.0
Ohio	14	6.5
Mississippi	14 est.	10.0
Arkansas	13	5.0
Typical		
Rhode Island	13	10.0
Kentucky	12	
Arizona	11	12.0
Louisiana	11	12.0
Washington (mo.)	11	10.0
Connecticut	10	5.0
Illinois	10	7.5
Iowa	10	11.0
Maine	10	3.5
New Jersey	10	10.0
Pennsylvania	10	10.5
Alabama	9	10.0
Indiana	9	
Maryland	9	8.0
New Mexico	9	
North Carolina	9	7.0
California (mo.)	8	6.0
Georgia	8	4.5
Idaho	8	
South Dakota	8	5.0
Utah	8	7.0
Massachusetts	8	
Low		
Nevada	7	10.0
Vermont (mo.)	7	7.0
Virginia	7	7.5
Nebraska	6	3.0
Michigan	6	5.0
Minnesota	6	7.0
North Dakota	6	5.0
Wisconsin (mo. & quar.)	6	
Kansas	5	5.0
Missouri	5	10.0
South Carolina	5	7.0
Wyoming	5	7.5

clear. Another group, in the 5% to 6% range, does noticeably better than the majority of the states. None of these states is east of Michigan, and South Carolina is the only southern state.

When comparison is made with figures of a decade earlier, the average has increased, from 7.7% in 1960-61, to 8.0% in 1970, to 9.9% currently. There is no obvious explanation for this increase. Fourteen states show a poorer record than a decade ago, the 1980 figure being more than two percentage points above the 1970 figure. Only Missouri, Nevada, and Wyoming improved their record by more than two points. There were very few surprising changes. Florida went from the best record to fifth from the worst; the 1970 record was suspect at the time. Arkansas, Georgia, Maine, New York, Ohio, Oklahoma, and West Virginia all showed substantial worsening of their percentage positions. Some of these differences undoubtedly reflect changes in reporting of delinquencies, but some inevitably show the effect of inadequate enforcement programs.

Table 7.5 shows the delinquency rate after the first action has been taken; on the average, the first action clears 43% of the delinquencies (many would clear themselves even if no action were taken).

Final Action Experience

Data on the extent to which final action is taken are not kept by many states, but as shown in table 7.5, the percentages are low. Limited as the data are, they show that for the returns for any month, rarely over 0.1% of the accounts will be subject to the final action—revocation, seizure, or the like. A few states have detailed information available, as indicated in table 7.7.

Despite all the possible sources of difference, one is inevitably led to conclude that the great difference between the high and the low states can be explained largely by enforcement policies that, over the years, have induced firms to be more careful in some states than in others. No significant difference occurs in penalties in the high and low states; rather, difference appears in the extent to which penalties are applied, and applied quickly, though the results cannot easily be measured. In Canada, a very sharp difference occurs between those provinces that have effective penalty systems and those that do not. The figures of the ineffective systems run to 20%.[2] No such difference appears in the United States.

ANALYSIS OF DELINQUENCY

Rarely have the states made any scientific study of delinquency to pinpoint frequency by type of business, size of business, location, and other elements in order to facilitate improved methods of control and cost reduction.

[2]J.F. Due, *Provincial Sales Tax*, rev. ed. (Toronto: Canadian Tax Foundation, 1964).

TABLE 7.7 Details of Final Action on Sales Tax Delinquents

State	Approximate No. of Vendors	Final Action
Connecticut	100,000	200 warrants a mo., 5-6 arrests a yr.
Kansas	75,000	80-90 notices of hearings to revoke a mo.; revoke about 6 a mo.
Maine	40,000	10-12 criminal prosecutions a mo.
North Dakota	26,000	200 a quar.—notice of hearing to revoke; 5-6 a yr. to criminal prosecution
Rhode Island	23,000	about 4 hearings a mo. to revoke; revoke about 20 a yr.
South Carolina	72,000	80 a mo. to show cause why license should not be revoked; revoke 15 a mo.
South Dakota	30,000	30 criminal actions (including NSF checks), 160 liens filed, 55 distress warrants a quar.
Washington	157,000	In a typical yr: 78 revocations of licenses; 20 seizures of property, 2 criminal prosecutions
Wisconsin	108,000	1978: for the yr., 1200 hearings to revoke; revoked 788
District of Columbia	33,000	25-30 closures of business a yr.

Type of Business

Despite the absence of exact data, administrators are well aware that the delinquency problem concentrates in certain fields. Small cafes, beer parlors and taverns, small grocery stores, and service stations are universally the worst offenders. These businesses are typically small, with inadequate bookkeeping help, inadequate capital, a high rate of store mortality, and low profit margins. In some lines the firms have been squeezed by competition with larger firms: chain stores and supermarkets, fast-food franchise restaurants. Fortunately, the amount of tax due is not great.

States reporting substantial concentration of delinquency in these fields include:

Beer parlors, taverns, and liquor stores: Alabama, Connecticut, Idaho, Louisiana, Maine, Michigan, Minnesota, Missouri, North Dakota, Ohio, Oklahoma, South Dakota, Tennessee, and Wisconsin.

Cafes, restaurants (usually small ones): Idaho, Louisiana, Michigan, Minnesota, Nebraska, Nevada, North Dakota, South Dakota, Vermont, and Washington.

Small grocery stores: Georgia, Louisiana, and Washington.

Service stations: Georgia, Idaho, Michigan, North Dakota, and Tennessee. The decline in the number of independent service stations has lessened the problem to some extent.

Mississippi and Louisiana have solved the service station problem in large part by collecting the tax, or most of it, from the wholesale suppliers of the stations; New Jersey has done the same with liquor.

Several states—Connecticut, Maine, Nevada, and Utah—report trouble with used-car dealers. In this field, the possible revenue loss is much greater. Other types of business mentioned include repair shops, services, and recreation (Iowa, Nevada, and Washington), door-to-door sellers (North Dakota), hobby shops (Nebraska), contracting (Vermont), and motels (Wisconsin). A few states note substantial geographical concentrations of delinquency—Las Vegas, Nevada, for example.

In general, the delinquents are small firms owing relatively small sums of money, but there are exceptions. Most states have had the experience of a large vendor suddenly going bankrupt with little or nothing in assets, with substantial loss of tax money.[3] Used-car dealers sometimes simply vanish, owing the state considerable money.

Causes of Delinquency

Little study has been made of the question, but several causes are obvious:[4]

Carelessness. Many small shopkeepers are hard pressed for time, have no regular bookkeeping help, and are not careful about records and deadlines generally. They do not bother to get the returns in promptly, postponing the work until they have more time, or they fail to file because they are ill, away on vacation, and the like. A number believe it is cheaper to pay penalties than to hire bookkeeping help to get reports ready on time.

Shortage of Funds. Many small operators are constantly at the margin. They use sales tax money to meet other obligations and thus do not have the money when the returns are due.

Use of Funds. Some firms delay paying simply to have the funds for a longer period, even though they are in good financial condition. Delay is espe-

---

[3]For example, a large department store in San Francisco a decade ago.

[4]Two earlier studies are still of some significance. A Kentucky study of the December 1960 returns showed that over one-third (34%) of all delinquent accounts showed no tax due, primarily because no operations or no taxable operations were carried on during the month. One-fifth (21%) paid in full; 3% paid in part or were unable to pay. Over one-third (37%) claimed that a return had been filed. The remaining 5% could not be found or refused to cooperate or give information. Average collections on delinquent accounts were only $9.81 per assignment. Obviously, it is uneconomical to send compliance personnel to visit firms that owe no tax if this fact can be ascertained by other means. The Kentucky department concluded that 63% of the field assignments might be eliminated by a prior mail notice (which the state did not then use).

A South Carolina study of the results of the first-notice mailing showed that of 2,903 notices mailed during the sample month, 26% were cleared after the first notice. Of the 635 who filed returns after receiving the notice, many indicated the reason for not filing earlier, typically: "I forgot," "I thought it had been filed," "I was sick," or "I was away." The post office returned seventy notices marked "addressee unknown." Some twenty-three firms that owed no tax filed returns, and twenty-eight notified that the return had been filed. This experience suggests that notices will get "forgetful" taxpayers to file, but not those who owe no tax and obviously not those who are out of money or are deliberately delinquent.

cially appealing when capital is difficult to raise. Current high interest rates aggravate this problem.

No-tax Firms. Such studies as have been made show that a substantial number of nonfilers owe no tax. They may be closed down temporarily or for the season, or they may make no taxable sales during the period even though they are operating. Tracking these firms down, of course, yields no revenue.

Errors on the Part of the State. Errors are made in recording of address changes, or the vendor may not report the change so the return is mailed to an incorrect address. Mistakes are also made in crediting payments to accounts, and mail sometimes simply goes astray.

Out of Business. A significant percentage of the delinquents have gone out of business and failed to notify the revenue department.

PENALTY AND INTEREST

Penalties

All states use an automatic penalty system for failure to file on time, the penalty applying without the need for court action. This significant feature is rarely found in other countries. Most states also charge interest for each month or fraction thereof that the account remains unpaid. A few states combine the penalty and interest into a single charge. Likewise, delinquents lose their vendor compensation if one is provided.

The penalty systems fall into two general groups. The first is a flat percentage, several states also having dollar minimum figures, regardless of the period of delinquency:

   5%: Florida ($5 minimum), Illinois, New Jersey, and North Dakota ($5 minimum)
   8%: West Virginia
  10%: Arizona, California, Colorado, Indiana, Kansas, Missouri (5% failure to pay, plus 5% failure to file), Nevada, Ohio ($50 minimum), Oklahoma, Rhode Island, South Dakota ($10 minimum), Utah, and Wyoming
  25%: Alabama (10% if failure to pay only), District of Columbia (plus 1% a month to 5%)
  50%: South Carolina

In the second group, the penalty increases with the period of time of delinquency:

10% to 35% ten days after first notice: Maryland

5% a month to 25%: Arkansas, Georgia ($5 minimum), Hawaii, Idaho ($10 minimum), Iowa, legally designated as interest (plus 5% for failure to pay), Kentucky ($10 minimum), Louisiana, Maine, Michigan, North Carolina ($5 minimum), Rhode Island ($2 minimum), Tennessee, Vermont ($2, then 5% a month to 25% after thirty days), Virginia, Washington (to 20% maximum), and Wisconsin ($10 minimum) plus $10 late filing fee

5% first month, 1% a month thereafter to 25%: New York

10% plus 5% to 25%: Minnesota

$2.50 plus 5% during the first period, 10% beyond: Connecticut

2% a month to 10%: New Mexico (or $5, whichever is greater)

$5.00 or collection fee: Nebraska

1% a month to 25%, plus 0.5% a month to 25% for failure to pay: District of Columbia

5% up to thirty days late, 10% if over thirty days late: Texas

5% plus $2.50 up to fifteen days, 10% plus $2.50 if over fifteen days: Connecticut

There is some indication of a trend toward the use of the 5% a month to 25% figure, and a few states use much higher figures than they did a decade ago. Many are still very low, however, compared to current market interest rates. The flat 5% figure is particularly inadequate to encourage firms to pay and file on time.

The use of a dollar minimum has great advantage, since many nonfilers owe no tax, yet cause the state substantial expense, and a percentage minimum is ineffective. Unfortunately, inflation has eroded the significance of these figures, just as high interest rates have eroded the effectiveness of the percentage penalties.

In most states, the revenue department can waive the penalty for cause, and many do rather widely. Several states hold waiver down to extreme cases, and thus, in practice, there are only a few. Four states—Hawaii, South Dakota, Washington, and West Virginia—will not waive, and waiving is very rare in Georgia, Nevada, and New Mexico. Florida will not waive the $5-minimum.

Interest

The usual pattern for the state is to charge interest for failure to pay on time, in addition to the penalty for late filing and payment. The interest, however, does not always commence until the end of the first month after the due date. The interest rates charged, as of 1980–81, are as follows, converted to a monthly basis for comparison:

0.5%: Arizona, Colorado, Idaho, Kansas, Nevada, New Mexico, North Carolina, and Tennessee

0.83%: Texas

0.67%: Arkansas, Hawaii, Kentucky, and Virginia

0.75%: Maine, Maryland, Michigan, and Pennsylvania

1.0%: Alabama, California, Connecticut, Florida, Georgia, Illinois, Indiana, Louisiana, Minnesota, Missippi, Missouri, New York, North Carolina, North Dakota, Oklahoma, Rhode Island, South Carolina, Utah, Vermont, and Wyoming

1.0625%: Nebraska

1.167%: New York, currently, basic figure of 1%, adjusted upward if bank rate exceeds 12%

1.25%: Connecticut

1.5%: New Jersey, Wisconsin

2.0%: South Dakota (minimum $5; 1% after six months)

Variable: Iowa, set annually at 2% less than the annualized prime rate for the previous year

Washington does not make an interest charge except on audit assessments; West Virginia uses a single 8% charge covering interest and penalty.

There has been some tendency to raise the interest charges in view of higher market rates; for example, only ten states still use the 0.5% rate, compared to twenty-five states in 1970. Given present rates, however, any figure below 1% a month is too low and encourages firms to delay payment, even if they file, to have more cheap working capital. Legislators, however, have been very slow to make the necessary charge.

In most states, interest cannot be waived, and quite appropriately so, since the firms have had money for a longer period. In the District of Columbia and in a few states, as for example, Arkansas, Idaho, Michigan, and Missouri, interest can be waived, but it is very rarely done. In New Jersey, New York, and South Carolina, the interest rate can be reduced.

BOND REQUIREMENTS

The states differ widely in policy with respect to requiring bond from vendors.

Bonding Not Used. Thirteen states do not make use of a bond requirement. Arizona has no power under the law to do so. Most of the rest have the legal power but do not use it—Colorado, Hawaii, Idaho (not used because of lack of staff to handle bonding), Indiana, Louisiana, Minnesota, Nebraska, New York, Ohio, Utah, Vermont, and Washington. The usual reason given is that the firms for which bond is needed cannot obtain a bond. This was reported by Indiana,

Nebraska, and Virginia, for example. Utah tried the system once and did not find it useful but is considering another attempt. Vermont tried with the room and meals tax but did not find it useful.

Limited Use.   Seventeen states make limited use, under a variety of circumstances:

Direct-pay permit-holders only: North Carolina

Jeopardy or appeals situations only: Michigan (jeopardy), New Jersey, (appeals), and West Virginia (jeopardy and appeals)

Special events, such as flea markets: Florida

Out-of-state contractors: Georgia and New Mexico

Street vendors: District of Columbia

No place of business in the state: Alabama (itinerant vendors—annual bond), Arkansas, Massachusetts, Mississippi (plus mobile-home dealers, larger contracts), Oklahoma, and Tennessee

Use with chronic delinquents: Iowa (quarterly filers—vendors twice delinquent in a two-year period, monthly filers if delinquent four times in two-year period, bond three times quarterly tax, release after two years), Kentucky (transient vendors), Maine, Massachusetts, New Mexico, Pennsylvania (if delinquent beyond thirty days three times), South Carolina (accounts with a bad history), and Wyoming (also nonresidents, or no real property)

Extensive Use.   Ten states make extensive but varied use of the bonding power and find that it contributes to effective enforcement:

California: Bond is required of about 65% of all new firms, when there is any question about the adequacy of assets to cover any tax liability. The amount required is three times the monthly liability, two times the quarterly, or equal to the prepayment amount. If the estimated amount is under $500 (formerly $100), no bond is required; the maximum that can be required is $10,000. Vendors are usually released from bond after three or four years of good records, except for corporations, since the officials of the latter are not responsible for the corporate tax liability. There is no complete uniformity among districts as to release from bonds. The usual types of bond are accepted: surety bond, personal guarantee, treasury bond, Time Deposit Certificate (TDC), savings and loan certificate.

Connecticut: Bond is required when there is a question about ability to remit taxes, to the extent of six times monthly estimated tax liability to $20,000.

Illinois: Bond is required of all new firms, to the extent of three times estimated monthly tax to $50,000. Firms are released after three years of good record. All usual forms are accepted.

Kansas: Bond is required of all corporations, unless net worth exceeds twelve months' tax liability or record is good. Firms, however, are not usually released once they are bonded.

Maryland: Bond is required, on recommendation of auditor or collections officer, of one-third of annual tax. Surety bond, passbook, or cash are accepted. Firms are usually released after one year if record is good.

Nevada: This is the only state to require permanent bond of all vendors. The amount is from $30 to $20,000, equal to three times the monthly estimated liability or twice the quarterly. An estimate is made by new firms; the figure is checked by compliance personnel. Various forms are accepted: TDC, the most popular; cash; surety bond; savings deposit; pledges of real property or a lien thereon. Check is made four times a year by the computer (one-fourth of the firms each quarter) to see if the amount is still adequate and, if not, a notice is sent of the additional assessment.

North Dakota: An office auditor reviews each request for a permit and decides whether a bond is required, on the basis of real estate in North Dakota, sales, and type of business. The requirement is automatic for out-of-state firms and for some types of in-state firm, such as bars. The amount is twice the estimated quarterly tax. Firms are released after one year if the record is good, but bond may be required of delinquents.

South Dakota: Bond is required of all corporations where officers do not accept personal liability and firms delinquent in two of the last four quarters. The corporations are never released; the delinquents, after a good record is established.

Texas: Bond is required of every new applicant and of any firm becoming delinquent; firms are released after two years of good record. Bond is two-thirds of estimated average tax per quarter. No bond is required if the amount is less than $100; minimum bond is $100.

Wisconsin: Bond is required if assets are limited relative to quarterly liability and record is poor. Firms with good records are released after two years. Bond required is equal to quarterly tax liability figure raised to nearest $100, with $1,000 minimum on surety bond.

There has not been any great change in bond requirements over the last decade, and the shifts have been marginal. Florida, Iowa, and Michigan appear to make less use of bonding; Connecticut, Maryland, North Dakota, and Texas, somewhat more.

BAD CHECKS

The states regard the bad check problem as a nuisance, but not a great deal of revenue is involved since the typical bad check is for a small amount. Issuance of bad checks by registered vendors rarely involves deliberate attempt to defraud; it is a product of carelessness or shortage of funds. The only exceptions are of firms going out of business or leaving the state. Table 7.8 shows the figures for a sample of states for which information is available. The figures are not entirely comparable, since in some states the actual figure of remittances was not available, and an estimate was made based upon the number of monthly, quarterly, and annual filers. Despite this problem, however, the percentages are remarkably uniform; ten of the nineteen states have figures between 0.3% and 0.5% of the checks received; four have figures of 0.6% or 0.7%, and only two are over 1%. Three have a 0.2% figure. There is no noticeable change in the pattern over the last decade. A few states show higher figures, some lower, but most have stayed within the same narrow range.

The procedures followed with bad checks vary among the states. Most states deposit the second time (Louisiana is an exception) and one, even three times. Beyond this, the typical pattern is to send a special notice and then, if the payment is not forthcoming, treat the firm as a delinquent, with the usual proce-

TABLE 7.8 Bad Checks as a Percentage of Total Remittances per Return Period

State	1969-70	1979-80
Alabama	1.0	1.0
Arizona		0.5
Connecticut		0.6
Georgia	0.4	
Iowa	0.2	
Kansas	0.5	
Kentucky	0.5	
Louisiana	0.8	0.4
Maine	0.3	
Maryland	0.3	0.5
Massachusetts	0.3	
Michigan	0.4	0.3
Mississippi	0.9	
Nevada	0.3	1.7
New Jersey	0.5	
New Mexico		0.3
Ohio		0.1
Oklahoma	0.5	0.5
Pennsylvania		0.4
Rhode Island	0.2	0.2
South Carolina		0.7
South Dakota		0.4
Tennessee		0.6
Texas	0.3	0.7
Virginia	0.2	
Washington		0.3
West Virginia		0.3
Wisconsin		0.4

dures. There is some variation, however: Louisiana, after a demand notice, goes directly to the warrant stage; New York, to assessment; South Dakota, to lien after ten days; Maine, to the sheriff for action; and Missouri, after a fifteen-day notice, to criminal prosecution. New Mexico, North Carolina, and Texas refer the checks to the district offices for collection (in Texas, if over $1,000; if under, directly to taxpayer); New Jersey, to the field after a ten-day notice. If immediate payment is not made, Iowa and Kentucky move directly to revocation of the license. Four states stress phone calls initially: Arizona (the calls clear about 90%), Florida, Georgia, and Iowa.

SUMMARY

Delinquency in its various forms is a never-ending problem with no complete, ideal solution. The four classes of delinquents are: the small, struggling firm short of money and bookkeeping help; the deliberate chiselers, seeking to use the state's money or disappear with it; the large firm failures; and the pseudo-delinquents, firms not filing but out of business, not currently operating or making taxable sales.

With some justification, many states tend to be somewhat lenient with the first group in the interest of aiding small, independent businessmen, often operating in low-income urban or rural areas. Yet there are limits as to how long these firms should be allowed to survive on public money. Fortunately, the amount of tax involved is often small. The second and third groups are the ones for which drastic action is needed and for which bonding requirements are particularly helpful. The final group results primarily from inadequate reporting and processing.

Several suggestions are offered:
1. In a few states, powers to enforce tax, now seriously inadequate, should be greatly strengthened. Oklahoma and Missouri are the worst.
2. A minimum dollar penalty is highly desirable to avoid the nuisance and cost of tracking firms owing little or no tax.
3. Progressive penalties for successive delinquencies and for added months of delinquency are useful in placing more pressure on the hard core delinquents and the chiselers.
4. A system of bonds for all selected new firms and chronic delinquents has proved useful in a number of states.
5. Placing small firms on quarterly or semiannual filing intervals reduces the total number of delinquencies but increases the potential loss per delinquent.
6. A faster cycle of operation is needed in some states. But if the cycle is too rapid, there will be extensive lost motion from contacting firms that have already paid.

7. Efforts should be made to eliminate pseudo-delinquents by greater care in handling business closures and change of address and in recording tax payments, and in techniques for handling firms registered but typically owing no tax, and seasonal operators.
8. Greater analysis of delinquencies is desirable to ascertain the characteristics of the delinquents. Use of a variety of techniques to deal with different types may be warranted. Very little study of delinquency has been made, yet present day computer systems make study relatively simple.

8. Sales Tax Audit Programs

Successful sales tax administration requires investigation to ensure that vendors report the correct amount of tax due. Such investigation, involving analysis of the firms' returns and records, is known as audit.

AUDIT ORGANIZATION

Separate or Integrated Audit

A basic issue in the organization and operation of the audit program is whether to operate sales tax audit separately from audit of other taxes, as was common in early years, or to integrate the sales and use tax audit with that of other taxes. Separate audit is almost inevitable if the sales tax is administered by a separate unit with its own audit staff. The reverse, however, is not necessarily true. Functional organization, with a single audit staff, does not ensure integrated audit.

The states can be classified into several groups with regard to integration: separation of sales tax audit, integration of sales tax audit with that of related taxes, nominal integration, limited integration, substantial integration, and complete integration.

Separation of Sales Tax Audit. The following states have maintained completely separate sales and use tax audit operations:

Arizona
Idaho (except a limited amount of audit of withholding tax)
Kansas (despite functional organization)
Maryland
Massachusetts (now occasionally auditing meals tax and withholding tax also)
Missouri
North Dakota (abandoned integrated audit as unsuccessful)
Ohio
Oklahoma
Tennessee
Wyoming (has no income taxes)

Integration of Sales Tax Audit with That of Related Taxes.   A second group of states has integrated sales tax audit with that of related levies, including withholding taxes, but not with income taxes. Several of these states (Connecticut, Nevada, South Dakota, Texas, and Washington) do not have general income taxes. The group is composed of:

California (income taxes administered by a separate state agency. Sales and use taxes account for most of the audit time, but audit also covers excise taxes.)

Connecticut

Nevada

Pennsylvania (withholding and fuels taxes)

Rhode Island (motor fuel, withholding, and certain corporate tax areas)

South Dakota (bank and related taxes)

Texas (franchise tax; sales and use taxes utilize 60% of audit time)

Washington (business and occupation tax and excises)

West Virginia (business and occupation tax)

Nominal Integration.   States that theoretically integrate sales tax audit with that of other taxes, but in fact do so only nominally are:

Iowa (though the intent is to integrate, and out-of-state offices are integrated. Corporate income tax audit is separate.)

Maine (auditors do not do personal and corporate income tax audit as routine procedure)

Minnesota (plans to use more integration)

Mississippi

New Jersey

Virginia

Limited Integration.   In the following states there is limited integration but substantial specialization by auditor:

Alabama (varies by region)

Florida (corporate income tax; no personal income tax; substantial specialization by auditors)

Georgia

Hawaii

New York (not all auditors are trained for all taxes)

Substantial Integration.   In two states there is substantial integration, with some specialization:

Arkansas (all auditors can do both taxes)

Utah (two sets of auditors, though in the same functional unit; but each does the other group's tax as well)

Complete Integration.   In general, with some exceptions, all auditors are trained to do both sales and income tax audits and routinely do both types in an audit in the following:

Colorado

District of Columbia (more of the time devoted to sales and use taxes)

Illinois (though most of the time goes to sales and use taxes)

Indiana

Kentucky

Michigan

Nebraska

New Mexico

North Carolina

Vermont (most of time to sales and use taxes)

Wisconsin (audits do not always include both sales and income taxes)

Several of these states, for example, Michigan and Nebraska, express the view that integration has been a complete success.

Without question, the trend has been toward integration. Nineteen states reported no integration in 1970, compared to eleven in 1980. Eleven states reported complete integration in 1980, compared to five in 1970. Four of those five—Indiana, Kentucky, Michigan, and Nebraska—were the pioneers in integration, together with Utah, the fifth, which has integration but separate income and sales tax audit units. The trend has been strengthened by the tendency of management consulting firms to favor this approach, which appears to be more logical.

The approach has several potential advantages. First, less nuisance is created for the taxpayer. With nonintegrated audit, the taxpayer may be visited by a sales tax auditor one week and an income tax auditor the next, with the need for making various records and time of personnel available (although in most states, the audit coverage is so limited that this danger is not very real, except for a few large companies). Second, travel time for auditors and wasted time in waiting for access to records and other activities are reduced. Third, since some data checked for both taxes are the same, greater efficiency in audit should result from integration. A check of gross receipts is required for both taxes, for example, and a cross-check of figures reported on the two returns is helpful. A check on capital equipment purchases for income tax purposes sometimes leads to the discovery of possible avoidance of the use tax.

In practice, however, the advantages appear typically not to be fully realized. One problem relates to selection of accounts for audit, since criteria differ in selection. If either tax dominates, firms warranting audit under the other levy are neglected. Second, the emphasis in audit is different, though some figures are required in common. Much sales tax audit is designed to uncover purchases on which tax has not been paid and to check on the accuracy of reported nontaxable sales. Neither of these items is of any concern for income tax audit.

Partly because of these differences, most auditors appear to prefer to work on one tax or the other. Training poses similar problems. Competence in audit of both taxes requires more extensive training, and many auditors never gain equal competence in both. The tax field in which a person is most competent and most interested will get the most effective audit.

One limiting factor on true audit integration is that many states do little income tax audit, relying primarily upon federal audits. This is true of both the personal income tax and the corporate tax on firms doing business solely within the state. Such audit of corporations as is done is concerned primarily with interstate allocation of income, an issue of little concern for sales tax purposes.

On the whole, the net advantage from integrating sales and income tax audit is unclear, though close cooperation is desirable. The best solution in a particular state depends upon a number of factors: the geographical dispersion of firms, which affects travel time and cost; the nature of the sales tax, which affects emphasis in sales tax audit; the willingness of the state to rely primarily upon federal audit for income tax purposes; the ability to establish satisfactory working relations between senior sales tax personnel and field division personnel; the general competence of auditors; the willingness to cross-train auditors for multiple taxes; and other considerations.

By contrast, integrating audit of the sales tax and any closely related levy, such as a business gross receipts tax, is desirable, since the audit procedures are very similar. Integrating specialized taxes, such as those on insurance premiums or pari-mutuel betting with the sales tax, is not particularly significant, since relatively few taxpayers and specialized personnel are involved.

Responsibility of Selection of Accounts for Audit

The general pattern remains the same as that of ten years ago: primary responsibility for the selection of accounts for audit rests with headquarters, not the district offices, and usually with the field audit unit.

Headquarters Selection.   Some twenty-seven states place the responsibility for audit selection on headquarters. There are several reasons. Complete data on the performance of the firm are located in headquarters; even with video terminals in district offices, all information desired for audit selection is not available. There is also the belief that more satisfactory comparisons of potential audit productivity can be made on a centralized basis, with experienced personnel.

The exact location of responsibility varies. At least six states, plus the District of Columbia, use a selection committee or unit system—Colorado, Connecticut, Kentucky, Louisiana, Michigan, and New Jersey. The committee is made of senior audit staff. In many of the less populous states, the responsibility rests with the chief auditor: Arizona, Idaho, Kansas, Maryland, Nebraska, North Dakota, Oklahoma, Rhode Island, South Carolina (chief of the sales tax audit group), and Wyoming. In Virginia, one-third of the audits are selected by the sales tax unit, two-thirds, by the field unit. Other states with selection in headquarters include Florida, Hawaii, Massachusetts, Minnesota, New York, Washington, West Virginia, and Wisconsin. In all of these states with central selection, requests for selection and leads are fed back to head-quarters from auditors and district officers, but no selection occurs except at headquarters.

Headquarters and District Offices. In seven states, the responsibility is divided between headquarters and district offices: Alabama, Arkansas, Maine, Minnesota, Missouri, Nevada (headquarters prepares lists with priorities which go to district offices), and Texas.

District Offices. In eleven states, primary responsibility rests at the district level, although guidelines, priorities, and, often, lists of vendors are sent from headquarters: California, Georgia, Illinois, Indiana, Iowa, Mississippi, New Mexico, North Carolina, Ohio, Tennessee, and Vermont.

In three of these states, substantial responsibility is placed on the auditors for selection. In Mississippi, they have primary responsibility for selection and do not require approval of higher authority. In North Carolina, responsibility rests primarily on the auditors.

Field Audit Personnel

Field auditing, once performed in part by compliance personnel, is now performed solely by the audit staffs except in very limited instances. In states with a single class of field personnel—Alabama, Hawaii, Maine, Minnesota, Ohio, and Vermont—there is some overlap of functions, but in general, the junior personnel do the compliance work; the more senior, the audit work.

METHODS OF SELECTION OF ACCOUNTS FOR AUDIT

The states have never had the personnel to audit all firms within the period of the statute of limitations and would not find it worthwhile to do so, as experience has shown that many accounts will yield little or no additional revenue from audit.[1] Many of the registered firms owe so little total annual tax that audit could not possibly pay for itself. Accordingly the methods for selection of accounts for audit are highly important, if the limited audit program is to offer maximum effectiveness. The states have struggled for years to determine the optimal method. The great majority of states still feel that their methods are

---

[1] A series of papers on audit selection methods included in *Revenue Administration,* 1977, pp. 193–211.

not very scientific—that the simplest methods will reveal sufficient profitable audits to occupy the time of the available personnel. Several states, however, have made extended efforts to find the most effective selection methods, including experimentation with EDP.

Most states use more than one method of selection, and thus the following lists are not mutually exclusive.

Leads. Most states rely, at least in part and many primarily, on leads—especially those unearthed in other audits. In a sense these may be considered spinoffs from other sales tax audits, or, in some instances, income tax audits, (in Hawaii, for example). Among the states that emphasize leads as the primary basis for selection are Arizona, Florida, Idaho, Indiana, Iowa (60% of the selection from leads), Kansas, Massachusetts, Missouri (95% from leads), and North Carolina, plus the District of Columbia.[2] As an example, audit of one type of retailer shows that the store bought taxable office equipment from a supplier under a resale certificate. Audit of the supplier will likely show that the supplier was not careful about checking upon resale certificates. Audit of a sheet metal firm may show misapplication of tax to shop-built downspouts; this will lead to audit of other sheet metal shops.

Office Audit

In earlier years of the sales tax, selection of accounts for audit was based primarily upon office audit—of examination of returns, usually by senior clerical personnel, to discover those that appeared to be out of line and therefore warranted field audit.

This procedure is still followed in twelve states to some extent. In Hawaii, annual and monthly returns are checked; in Wisconsin, only annual returns. Detailed examination of all returns is made in Iowa, Kansas (the office auditors will often contact the vendor for clarification), Minnesota, New Jersey, North Dakota, Ohio, Oklahoma, South Carolina, Virginia, and Washington, and this constitutes one source of leads for field audit. Colorado plans such a system.

A second group of states makes a less complete review, checking certain transactions only: Alabama, Idaho (automobile sales, contractors), Illinois, Indiana (exempt purchasers especially), Kentucky, Louisiana, Maryland, Michigan (bankruptcies, etc.), Missouri, North Carolina, and West Virginia. Only clerical review is given in Arizona, Connecticut, Georgia, Utah, and Vermont. The District of Columbia desk-audits returns of certain business classifications prone to error or affected by recent law changes, and firms whose pre-

---

[2]Other states noting leads as a significant source are Alabama, Arkansas, Colorado, Connecticut, Kentucky, Maine, Maryland, Minnesota, Nebraska, Nevada, New Jersey, New Mexico, North Dakota, Oklahoma, Rhode Island, South Carolina, South Dakota, Vermont, Virginia, and Wyoming.

vious audit results were favorable. Ohio office-audits returns on which the computer has shown a variance.

The remaining states make no office audit at all (returns are, of course, checked for completeness before entry into the computer system, and the computer checks arithmetic): Arkansas, California, Florida, Iowa, Maine, Massachusetts, Nebraska, Nevada, New Mexico, Pennsylvania, Rhode Island (except boat sales), South Dakota, Tennessee, and Texas.

Classification of Firms: Industry-wide Selection and the Cell System

The states discovered very early that some types of business are more prone to errors than other types; for example, plumbing and electrical shops make more errors than shoe stores, simply because they have relatively more exempt transactions and those of a borderline nature. A store selling only shoes and related items, such as shoelaces and shoe polish, makes only taxable sales, and chances for error are slight. By contrast, an office supply and print shop makes some taxable sales, some exempt sales, renders services that may not be taxable, buys some goods for taxable purposes, buys others for nontaxable ones, and makes sales to churches and other exempt institutions. The chances for error are great. Thus, some states make some audit selections simply on an industry-wide basis: Alabama, Colorado, Connecticut (for example, car dealers), Iowa, Mississippi, Nevada, and West Virginia. Used-car dealers are a particular favorite. Nevada has a special program for casinos, auditing the larger ones every eighteen months, the smaller, every two years.

Several states have sought to go beyond this simple approach, classifying firms by industry and sales volume into cells, on the basis of experience built up from previous audit, to establish priorities for selection. The pioneer was California, which began the system about twenty years ago and has continued to update and improve it. The basic system remains largely the same. Firms are classified into 16 cells on the basis of experience with audit productivity as revealed by the EDP system, according to type of business and volume of sales, plus two additional: 17, closeouts, and 18, no seller permit. Headquarters sends detailed information to the district offices on the firms in the top six cells, for a three-year period; the district office is expected to look at the records of these firms in the top five and select particular firms for audit. Information on firms in cells 7 to 16 are sent only on request, but a print-out of all firms "ripe" for audit goes out annually to the district offices. Although priority is attached to the top five, some coverage of all cells is expected.

Michigan uses a simplified version of the cell system; firms are classified into three groups, based largely on potential revenues. As explained shortly, Michigan was a pioneer in the experiments with EDP selection based on norms but abandoned it for the cell approach. In New York a basically similar system is used; firms are grouped into cells on the basis of probable audit productivity and audit assignments are developed accordingly. Idaho classifies firms by gross annual sales into four groups and assigns them to auditors by rank. Texas has sought to refine the California system, which it adopted in 1975, by seeking to computerize the information that personnel now use in the final selection.

EDP Selection Based upon Norms Developed from Experience

The cell systems involve substantial use of EDP equipment, to build up information on past audits and to classify firms into the cells established. A number of other states are making some use of data processing in selection of accounts for audit in other ways; most of these, at present, involve simply the preparation of listings of firms by type of industry, volume of tax liability, or both, to facilitate selection of the accounts to receive priority in audit. These include the following:

Colorado

Illinois (the print-outs showing tax liability by firm)

Kentucky (print-outs showing receipts, deductions, and accounts subject to use tax over $10,000)

Mississippi (providing computer print-outs to the district offices to aid in selection)

Nebraska (print-outs showing firms with large tax liability)

Pennsylvania

Rhode Island (print-outs showing firms with large tax liability)

Texas (each taxpayer is scored based on several factors)

Arkansas, Indiana, Iowa, Maine, and Wisconsin have plans for use of EDP in selection.

A second group of states seeks to go beyond mere listing by tax liability, location, and similar factors to show deviations from established norms. States began experimenting with this approach two decades ago, commencing with Michigan. The principle is to develop norms on the basis of experience, as, for example, typical gross sales for particular types of stores in cities of a given size and typical figures of deductions of various types as a percentage of gross sales by type of business. The computer then determines those firms that deviate by a specified percentage from the norms; these represent prime candidates for audit selection. States making some use of this approach include:

Connecticut (in which the computer is used to call attention to firms departing substantially from the norms)

Florida (in which the computer determines the ratio of tax to gross sales; the primary selection, however, is on the basis of leads)

Iowa

Minnesota (using EDP prepared print-outs, showing, for example, deductions as a percentage of gross sales, etc.)

North Dakota (EDP provides listings of volume of tax by city size, percentage of deductions of various types, etc.)

Washington (with EDP-supplied figures of volume of sales by type of business, deduction percentages, etc.)

None of these states, however, relies primarily upon EDP selection, as was hoped a decade ago. There are several difficulties. One is that of appropriate classification of firms, given the diversity in various types of businesses and the changing patterns over time. Some drugstores carry a wide range of nondrug items, for example. There are many individual circumstances affecting both gross sales and deductions. Nevertheless, the computer system can develop leads that indicate potential for audit more cheaply and satisfactorily than can other means.

Other Methods

Complaints and Informers. Several states make some selection on the basis of complaints—usually from competitors or from disgruntled employees—Colorado, Connecticut, Hawaii, Iowa, New York, Virginia, and Washington, for example.

Previous Audit Experience. Several states give substantial attention to the productivity of past audits—Alabama, Arkansas, Florida, Illinois, Kentucky, Maryland, Minnesota, Nevada, New York, Rhode Island, and South Carolina. Many firms do not appear to learn from experience. In several states, continued delinquency, especially on the part of larger firms, results in audit.

Large Firms. The cell systems tend to place substantial stress on the larger firms, but a number of other states set up priority systems for such firms, since the dollar productivity of audit is likely to be high. The following states particularly stress the importance of auditing large firms (the figures in parentheses indicate the interval in which they seek to audit all large firms): Idaho (three years), Kentucky (four years), Louisiana (yearly), New Mexico, Nebraska, New York (five years), Oklahoma (three years), Rhode Island (three years), Texas (four years), Maine, Wisconsin (four years), Wyoming (five years). Several states audit all direct-pay permit-holders at frequent intervals.

Random. With the usual system of audit selection, smaller firms in some lines of business will never be audited as the potential productivity is far too low. If this word gets around, obviously the firms have little incentive to apply the tax correctly. Thus, a few states do some strictly random audit—California, under its cell system, Kentucky, New Mexico, and Texas. Most states do not bother, however, concentrating their efforts on the productive audits.

As the primary methods of selection suggest, the foremost objective in audit selection is to maximize the recovery of tax revenue. Some states explicitly state this as the primary goal, for example, Georgia, Nebraska, New Jersey, Oklahoma, Rhode Island, Utah, and Washington. But in fact, most other states do so as well—though it is difficult, as a rule, to get a positive statement of objectives out of the revenue department. Apart from revenue, however, some states do indicate the desirability of ensuring overall compliance with the law on the part of all firms; Maryland, for example, now stresses compliance.

AUDIT APPROACHES AND PROCEDURES

Guidance and Information for Auditors

The majority of states, currently twenty-eight, have relatively up-to-date manuals as a guide for auditors.[3] These vary in completeness, but in general, they outline the steps to be taken in the audit procedure and serve as guides for the conduct of the audit itself. Many of them provide information relating to various types of industry. In addition to this group, Wisconsin has a manual for training purposes only. New manuals are being developed in Florida, Georgia, New Mexico, New York, and North Carolina.

The states differ in what the auditors take with them on audits. The most common approach now is to provide the auditor with a computer print-out of the information from the returns for the past several years, often three. This is easily generated—so long as this information is in the computer memory. But the memory often does not include the full period, and details of deductions by type are often not entered into the memory. The print-out approach is used in, among others, Kansas, Kentucky (current year), Illinois, Louisiana, Maine, Minnesota, Mississippi (sent by telex), Nebraska, New York, North Carolina, South Carolina, and Vermont. With states with video units in the district offices, the auditors can, of course, gain access to information the computer memory contains on a video screen or direct print-out. The major alternative is to send copies of the returns, produced in some states from microfilm or microfiche. Idaho, Indiana, Kentucky (previous years), Michigan, Nebraska, South Dakota, and Wisconsin send the original file. Iowa provides a summary of the record.

Several states emphasize checks on all material in the vendor's file; returns, results of past audits, correspondence, etc.—Georgia, Maryland, Michigan, New Jersey, and West Virginia. This is not possible in states with large geographical areas with auditors assigned to districts.

Missouri provides nothing to the auditor, who must work from the vendor records, and Utah does not provide the account history.

[3]Arizona, Arkansas, California, Connecticut, Idaho, Illinois, Indiana, Kentucky, Louisiana, Maryland, Michigan, Minnesota, Missouri, Nebraska, New Jersey, New Mexico, New York, North Dakota, Ohio, Pennsylvania, South Dakota, Tennessee, Texas, Utah, Virginia, Washington, West Virginia, and Wyoming. Colorado, Iowa, Maine, and South Carolina have manuals, but they are out of date. Massachusetts has just issued a new manual. The District of Columbia also has a manual.

Initial Steps in Audit

Typically, when auditors commence assignments, they contact the vendor in advance for an appointment and then review with the appropriate person the nature of the accounting system. If the taxpayer is a vendor with a substantial volume of business, some states require a preliminary test check to determine the desirability of a complete audit. Even in the large firms, a test check lasts only two or three days.

If a more complete audit is scheduled as a result of the preliminary check, or a thorough audit is undertaken as a matter of policy without a preliminary check, a test period is selected for the typical retail business. This period is often one month during a year. Results are then projected for the entire period, back to the previous audit or over the period allowed by the statute of limitations. Attempts are almost always made to get the vendor to agree to accept the test period, and in order to get this agreement the auditor may make adjustments in the exact period to be used. It is normally to the vendor's advantage to agree; otherwise, the firm may be subjected to a much longer and more careful audit, a source of inconvenience. Failure of the vendor to agree to a particular period creates the danger that the vendor will challenge in court the validity of the selected test period in the event of disagreement with the assessment based upon the audit.

A great increase is reported in use of statistical sampling techniques in selecting test data and establishment of confidence levels. This was particularly noted in California, Colorado, Florida, Indiana, Maryland, Michigan, New York, Ohio, Texas, West Virginia, and Wisconsin.[4]

The test period check is unsuitable for certain firms: contractors, sellers of high-value items, such as motor vehicle dealers; manufacturers, whose liability is mostly on purchases from out of the state; and businesses with sales, often large in amount, that are made for exempt purposes other than resale.

Approaches to Audit

States differ somewhat in approaches to audit, particularly on emphasis, but the same techniques are almost always used. There are several major elements in sales and use tax audit.

Taxable Purchases by Vendor. Business firms frequently make out-of-state purchases of equipment, supplies, and other taxable items tax free and fail to pay use tax, or purchase such goods in-state under exemption certificate and fail to account for tax themselves. One of the principal audit checks is to ascertain failure to pay tax on these purchases. Asset accounts, depreciation accounts, and depreciation schedules are examined to ascertain taxable

[4]J.A. Heintz, "Applying Statistical Sampling in Use Tax Audits," *Proceedings of the National Tax Association for 1979,* pp. 190–94.

items, and frequently purchase invoices are checked to see whether tax was applied by the supplier. Examination of income tax returns aids in revealing purchases on which tax should have been paid. A number of states report this activity as constituting a large portion of audit work: Georgia, Indiana, Kansas, Michigan, Nevada, North Carolina, North Dakota, Rhode Island, South Dakota, Texas, Utah, Vermont, Washington, and Wisconsin.

Reported Sales.   Initially, the auditors will check the sales account in the general ledger or the general journal to compare these sale figures with figures reported on the tax returns. They will also examine other accounts in the general ledger to ascertain taxable sales that do not appear in the sales account, such as provision of meals to employees. Likewise the data in the sales and use tax accounts in the general ledger will be compared with the figures shown on the returns, especially in the states that stress reporting of exact amounts of tax collected. Some check, at least a sampling, will be made of sales invoices to see that the tax has been properly applied and posted. When only cash register tapes are available, sometimes a quick check on the application of the tax will be made, but for the most part the tapes are useless for audit.

Although these checks will give some indication of proper procedures and application of tax, they will not reveal underreporting of gross sales if the sales invoices are missing or if they take the form of only cash register tapes. Since careful comparison is difficult, a number of states utilize secondary audit checks, either as a routine matter on a sample basis or where irregularities are suspected. There are four types of check:

1. *Review of purchase records:* A check is made of figures reported in the accounts against purchase invoices, to ascertain total cost of goods sold. A markup figure is then employed, either standard for the type of retailing or one based on a shelf test, to see what the volume of sales should have been. If a wide discrepancy occurs between this and reported sales, further check will be made.

   This method produces accurate results only if purchase records are complete. A firm wishing to evade will dispose of some of the purchase invoices. The only further check (apart from income tax records noted below) is to obtain information from the firm's supplier. This check is relatively easy in some instances, but for many states in which retailers are largely supplied by out-of-state firms, this check is laborious and expensive and resorted to only in extreme cases. The fact that this method can be used, however, serves to make retailers more careful than they would otherwise be about attempting to conceal purchases. Some states find it worthwhile to calculate the markup as shown by the purchase and sales figures. If the figure departs substantially from the usual markups, further investigation is made.

2. *Income tax returns:* Most states now make some check of figures of sales reported on sales tax returns with reported sales on income tax returns. The income tax returns are often prepared by public accounting firms, and so

the danger of outright evasion is less than with the sales tax returns. The income tax returns also show the cost of goods sold. Firms seek to maximize these figures for income tax, whereas they wish to minimize them for sales tax if they are underreporting sales. Discrepancies suggest understatement of purchases in the purchase records. The income tax returns also reveal capital account purchases on which use tax may be due, as noted above. Otherwise, they provide little assistance for sales tax audit.

3. *Cash analysis:* A few states place greater emphasis on analysis of bank deposits and cash flows to check the accuracy of reported sales and purchase figures.

4. *Special:* Minnesota attempts to check the accuracy of reported liquor sales by checking liquor purchases and drinks per bottle.

Deductions. A large portion of audit effort is devoted to check on the accuracy of deductions from gross sales. There are several types of deductions, and the approaches to checking differ somewhat:

1. *Sales for resale:* Audit of firms doing any wholesale business requires check on the accuracy of reported sales for resale. Check is made against the file of resale certificates the vendor (in almost all states) is required to keep on hand. If the vendor does not have a certificate for a particular sale he is frequently given time, a week or so, to obtain one. Likewise, the auditor considers the reasonableness of the claim of sale for resale. If, for instance, furniture is sold to a bakery under a resale certificate, the claim is almost certainly invalid. When necessary, the auditor will suggest that investigation be made of the purchasing firm that gave the certificate. There is no other effective means of auditing sales for resale. Norms are useless because of wide variations in the extent of wholesale sales.

2. *Sales for out-of-state delivery:* Audit of reported sales for out-of-state delivery requires check upon the sales invoices and, in the event of doubt, upon the evidence of out-of-state delivery such as postal receipts or truck or rail bills of lading, or, in the event of delivery by the firm's own truck, some type of log of such deliveries. Perfect check on the firm's own truck deliveries is impossible, but leakage is probably not great. Unless evidence of delivery is checked, firms may write "Out-of-State Delivery" on sales invoices even though the customer takes delivery across the counter.

3. *Sales to exempt buyers:* Sales to various exempt purchasers, such as governmental units and religious and charitable organizations in many states and to farmers when the exemptions are conditional on the purchaser being a bona fide farmer, require some check against invoices and upon certificates where they are required. In many states where no certificate is used, an invoice must be issued with name and nature of the exempt purchaser. The auditor, as a rule, will make little further check unless large items are involved, in which case the purchaser will be contacted. On sales to farmers, little investigation is made beyond the invoice to determine if the purchaser

appears to be a farmer. Actually, with most sales of farm supplies, eligibility is obvious from the product sold. Individuals, for example, do not buy twenty sacks of hog food for personal use.

4. *Commodity exemptions:* Firms have incentive to report sales of taxable commodities as sales of exempt ones, whether or not they collect the tax from the customer. One step is to examine the general ledger and the sales tax account and returns to be sure that tax is paid on the amounts posted as taxable sales. This figure does not always appear in the accounts. A second check is to sample sales invoices to see if the firm is applying the tax correctly, distinguishing properly between exempt and taxable goods, and then correctly totaling the sales of taxable goods for tax calculation.

   With cash register tapes, this type of check is virtually impossible. Modern cash registers allow identification of taxable and exempt sales, but there is no assurance of proper punching of the register and no simple way to check. Only with the newest scanner computer-linked checkout systems in supermarkets is there almost certain assurance of correct application of tax. Older cash registers either do not identify taxable and exempt sales or have no tape at all. Some small firms use neither invoices nor cash registers. Even invoices, of course, may be in error.

   Auditors use several approaches to check upon the accuracy of the figures shown on the invoices or to check where invoices are unavailable. The most common is to review the purchase invoices of the firm. If, on the average, 20% of a firm's sales consist of exempt goods, and markup percentages are the same on taxable and exempt goods, 20% of the sales should consist of exempt goods. If the accuracy and completeness of the purchase invoices are doubted, the auditor may check back on the supplier, but in most states this check is difficult, costly, and resorted to only in extreme cases. The auditor will frequently check the ratio of exempt to taxable sales and compare it with past years for the firm and for the typical figure in the industry. Any significant departure from the norm will result in more careful audit.

   As a final resort in a few states, a cash register test will be made. For a sample period, an agent will stay at the cash register and watch the accuracy of recording and the percentage of taxable and exempt sales. This process is costly, and most states avoid it in preference to other means.

5. *Other deductions:* Check is frequently made on a sample basis of correct treatment of freight, interest, installation charges, and other elements in price. These problems most commonly arise with manufacturers.

   In states in which sales under a specified figure arc exempt, check must be made of the accuracy of the reported volume of these sales. Similarly, in states that require the vendor to pay the exact amount of tax received from the customer when this amount exceeds the product of tax rate times taxable sales, check must be made. Georgia and Ohio are examples. This check is frequently done by sampling through review of invoices and cash register tapes (which identify small sales) and, if necessary, through the type of actual test check at the cash register as noted. This process can be time consuming, with little revenue gain. In these instances also, norms are frequently employed, best developed from experience. Only firms departing significantly from the norms are investigated.

Ascertainment of correct reporting of exempt sales and other deductions is not aided by income tax returns, since taxable and exempt sales are treated in the same fashion for income tax.

Firms without Records

A problem of diminishing importance is the small vendor without records or with seriously inadequate records. Most states report few firms of this type. They are encountered primarily in rural areas in the South and low income areas of large cities. Pressure for records for other taxes plus general improvements in retail bookkeeping have materially reduced the problem. All states, however, encounter some stores of this character. The most common approach is to ascertain the stores' purchases from suppliers and then apply a standard markup, or to obtain a figure of markup by a shelf test. Tennessee and Michigan, for example, report primary reliance on this approach, but the latter also uses cash analysis. North Dakota relies on bank statements and income tax returns, partly because of the difficulty in contacting suppliers.

Other techniques are occasionally used. Projection of sales from earlier periods for which figures are available is a relatively simple method. In other instances, the sales-in-progress test mentioned earlier will be used to ascertain actual gross and taxable sales and actual tax collected (if this figure is required) for a short period and then the figures will be extended to the entire period. This technique is relatively costly.

Court attitudes toward constructive assessments based on purchase invoices and markup and other secondary indexes and test periods vary considerably. Usually, there is no problem if the vendor cannot produce records.

Audit of Firms Other than Retailers

A substantial amount of audit time is devoted to manufacturers, wholesalers, and other nonretail firms. Most sales of firms in these categories are not taxable, but a spot check will be made of sales invoices to see if tax is being reported on sales that are. The audit approach is frequently through a check on taxable sales rather than gross sales less deductions, since few sales are taxable. As noted, review is made of resale certificates to ensure that they have been validly executed and that the firms issuing them are actually registered. Audits of wholesalers pick up little tax, but they suggest audits of customers apparently misusing their certificates and make the wholesalers more careful about obtaining resale certificates.

Most errors by manufacturers arise from failure to apply use tax to purchases from out of state or to items legitimately purchased under resale certificate and then used for taxable purposes. Audit therefore centers around purchase account records and invoices, internal transfer orders, depreciation accounts, and inventory records.

Audit of contractors involves primarily a check to ensure that use tax has been paid on items bought from out of state or bought tax free under registration number. Dual contractor-retailer and contractor-manufacturer businesses involve some of the most complicated audits, involving careful check to ensure that tax has been applied properly on the suitable price figure for both contract work and retail sales.

Summary of Major Sources of Error

The relative importance of various types of error uncovered in audit varies among the states with the structure of the tax, the nature of the economy, the emphasis in the audit program, and other considerations. Substantial agreement occurs however, on the importance of several sources of error.

Tax on Purchases.   All states report that failure to report tax on taxable purchases is a major source of audit assessment. In many states, tax assessments on purchases exceed tax assessments on sales. In Iowa, for example, two-thirds of the additional revenue from audit is from use tax on purchases. In Illinois, the figure is 40%.

1. *Out-of-state purchases:* Firms may fail to account for and pay use tax on taxable items purchased from outside the state. Firms of any size will make some purchases from out-of-state vendors, and many are careless about establishing a satisfactory system for accounting for tax on taxable purchases of this character. Frequently, operators of smaller firms never think of the question or fail to examine purchase invoices to ensure that tax has been paid. Many larger firms have not developed satisfactory control systems to ensure that tax is accounted for on all taxable out-of-state purchases.

2. *Purchases under certificate:* Closely related to the first source of error is failure to account for tax on purchases made tax free under resale certificate and then used for taxable purposes. To some extent, particularly with smaller firms, deliberate misuse occurs. A store will issue a resale certificate to purchase an item intended for taxable use by the store or by the owner, for example, a refrigerator. Few suppliers will question a certificate. In fact, they cannot be expected to do so except in the most obvious cases.

Far more common than the cases of deliberate abuse are those of simple failure to account for tax when items are used for taxable purposes. In smaller stores, owners frequently divert store purchases to personal use and fail to record the transaction or report tax. Most businesses, large or small, use some items purchased for resale: light bulbs, stationery, cleaning compounds, and a thousand and one other items. Few appear to have devised internal control systems adequate to pick up tax on all these transfers from stock to store use, and many smaller establishments do not even consider the question.

A related situation occurs when a firm purchases from the same suppliers articles used partly for resale, partly to render service activities, and partly for taxable use by the firm. Automobile paint purchased by a garage that does body refinishing work for customers and prepares used cars for resale is a good example. The garage is also likely to sell such paint to customers and to use it on its own trucks. Obviously, the garage must be allowed to buy all of the paint tax free. Ensuring correct application of tax is difficult, even if the garage has an entirely satisfactory record system. Audit does not always reveal errors of this type, at least without a careful, time-consuming check.

Nontaxable Sales.   Most errors relating to sales tax, per se, center around exempt sales. Firms may deliberately overreport nontaxable sales, but more commonly they are not careful about keeping an exact record of such sales and are inclined to overstate them. Sometimes sales are made tax free when they should not be. Often error is due to honest misinterpretation of the law. In other cases clerks are careless or are not well instructed on taxable and exempt sales.

Michigan, Rhode Island, and Utah find errors with nontaxable sales generally; Georgia, with exemption certificates; Arizona, Indiana, Kentucky, Nebraska, and Washington, with sales for resale; North Dakota, Vermont, and Washington, with sales for out-of-state delivery. Exempt farm supplies are a major source of error in Idaho; sales to the federal government, in Arizona; application of tax to services, in Iowa and New Mexico; exemption of machinery, in Georgia and Idaho.

Two specific examples of errors can be given. Kentucky lists five categories of major tax misapplication: exempt purchases by manufacturers and sales for resale; purchases by contractors; out of state purchases of supplies by banks; lack of exemption certificates on exempt sales; and firms with no records.

Illinois reports that 60% of the amount of assessments from audit are on sales (retailers occupation tax) errors, 40% on use tax. Of the 60% on sales tax, 30% involved unreported receipts, 70%, deductions.

Underreporting of Gross Sales.   Normally, auditors test check reported gross sales figures, but errors are relatively rare except in very small firms. The gross sales figure, which is required for federal income tax, is provided by the most elementary bookkeeping system if sales are recorded. The figure is subject to check in audit by CPA firms, whereas the breakdown between taxable and exempt sales is not. Only the small family business with few records of any kind and no clear segregation of business and household receipts is likely to lack a reasonably accurate figure of gross sales. State experience now shows that these businesses are of no major concern. Only Michigan notes understatement of gross sales as a significant problem. Tax treatment of contractors is always a fertile field for misapplication of tax because of the interpretative questions on tax base and the dual operations of many firms.

Completion of Audit

The experienced auditor develops a feel for the extent to which the conduct of the audit is justified and brings it to a conclusion when the optimal point is reached, making the tentative assessment or credit. Most states are careful to ensure that credit is given for any net overpayment.

In virtually all states the auditors are required to discuss their findings with the vendors to obtain their approval. In a surprising number of cases, the auditors receive approval—usually around 90%. States, however, differ sharply on the instructions to the auditors on collecting an amount owed. Collection is prohibited in Arkansas, California, Colorado, Connecticut, Kansas, Louisiana, New Mexico, North Dakota, Ohio, Oklahoma, Rhode Island, West Virginia, and Wisconsin. Two reasons are the desire to avoid subsequent changes following review of the audit, and the belief that collection may lead to wrong impressions on the part of the taxpayer and possible improper negotiations between auditor and taxpayer. Collection is discouraged in Maryland. It is permitted, but not encouraged, in Arizona, Idaho, Indiana, Iowa, Maine, New Jersey, Texas, Vermont and Washington. By contrast, collection is actively encouraged in Alabama, Florida, Georgia, Kentucky, Massachusetts, Michigan (about one-third is collected), Minnesota, Mississippi, Missouri, Nebraska, New York, North Carolina, Pennsylvania, South Carolina, South Dakota, Tennessee, and Virginia.

The auditor must submit a formal report to his supervisor. Typically, a form is provided to show whether a check was made on various items, the nature of the deficiency, and the apparent reasons for it. Summaries of sales and tax data by month or quarter are frequently required, as are calculated data for sales, the relationship of purchases and sales, and inventory markup. The aim is to ensure adequate information for review of the audit.

Audit Assessment

While the auditors universally recommend the amount of the assessment if they conclude that additional tax is due, location of responsibility for legal assessment of additional tax as a result of audit varies among the states. Assessment is made by the chief of audit in Arizona, Kansas, Mississippi, North Dakota, Utah, Wyoming, and by the audit branch in Kentucky. It is made by the sales tax division in Alabama, California (business tax division), Colorado, Louisiana, Michigan, Missouri, Ohio, South Carolina, and West Virginia (business tax division), and by the tax division in Iowa and North Carolina. In most other states, the assessment is also made in headquarters.[5]

By contrast, assessment is made in the district office in Arkansas, and by the auditors themselves (subject to possible charge upon review) in Illinois (if the taxpayer agrees with the audit findings), Indiana, Minnesota, New York, South Dakota, Tennessee, and Virginia.

Interest and Penalty

In most states, the same rules on interest and penalty apply as for delinquency, but the penalty may be waived on application and very commonly is. Waiving may be recommended by the auditor, or it may occur only on the request of the vendors. Usually only penalty, not interest, is waived, but in a few states, such as New Jersey, both can be waived. Maryland can waive interest but rarely does. Tennessee is one of the few states in which the auditor can waive penalty; in other states the auditor merely recommends. Ohio (15% penalty) and Iowa do not waive, and Idaho and Rhode Island, only rarely. Arizona does so on occasion. In Arizona the chief auditor may apply a 25% fraud penalty on recommendation of the auditor.

By contrast, one group of states does not apply penalty so long as the return has been filed and audit assessments are paid by the specified date: Arizona, Minnesota, Nevada, Vermont, and Washington.

Review of Audit

All states provide some type of review of each audit, but the states vary in the relative responsibility placed on the district office and headquarters.

District Office. In eight states, almost sole responsibility for audit review is placed on the audit supervisor in the district office, with little or no review at headquarters:
Colorado (audit group leader)
Georgia
Hawaii
Illinois
Maine
Mississippi
New Mexico (a few to headquarters for review)
New York (some to headquarters)

[5]Colorado, Connecticut, Florida (board of audit selection), Georgia, Hawaii, Maine, Maryland, (assessment section), Massachusetts, Nebraska, New Jersey (central review group), New Mexico, Oklahoma, Pennsylvania (Bureau of Accounts Settlement), Rhode Island, Texas, Vermont, Washington, and Wisconsin.

District Office, and to Audit Division.   In eight states the review starts in the district office and then is sent to the audit division in headquarters:
California (group supervisor, district review officer in detail, district principal auditor, audit review unit in headquarters)
Massachusetts
Missouri
Nebraska
Pennsylvania
Texas
Vermont
Washington

District Office and to Sales Tax Division.   In six states, the review starts in the district office and then is sent to the sales tax division in headquarters:
Alabama
Iowa (excise tax policy division)
North Carolina
Ohio (to audit review group)
Tennessee
Virginia

Headquarters.   In the following states, primary review is in headquarters.
1. *By the chief auditor* (in some states, a part of the work is done by senior auditors working under the chief):
Arizona
Connecticut
Idaho
Kansas
Louisiana (then to sales tax division)
Maryland
Nevada
North Dakota
Oklahoma
Rhode Island
South Carolina (field audit section)
South Dakota
Utah
West Virginia
2. *Audit division, then to sales tax division:*
Michigan
3. *Sales tax division:*
Minnesota

4. *Special audit group in headquarters:*
   Florida
   Indiana
   New Jersey
   Wisconsin
   District of Columbia

Audit review serves primarily to ensure that the audit is correct, but it also serves as a check on the competence of particular auditors and aids in maintaining greater uniformity of interpretation among auditors.

APPEAL FROM AUDIT

Of constitutional necessity, states must provide for right of appeal from audit determination. In all states, some form of administrative appeal is authorized, formally or informally, to minimize the number of cases going to the courts. Frequently, there are two levels of administrative appeal and in some states as many as four prior to court appeal, though taxpayers do not necessarily go through all steps.

Initial Appeal

The taxpayer usually has thirty days to appeal the audit assessment. The figure is fifteen in Louisiana, twenty in Illinois and Michigan, and sixty in West Virginia and Wisconsin. A hearing must be requested, usually by mail, but request may often be made by phone or personal appearance. Initially, the appeal is highly informal. The exact procedure, however, varies among the states.

Primary Appeal at the District Level: In the states with decentralized administration, and particularly California, South Carolina, and Texas, initial appeal is at the district level. In California, for example, the vendor has ten days in which to file an appeal with the audit supervisor in the district office. The firm is then billed for the additional amount and has thirty days to appeal to headquarters, specifically, to the petitions unit, in the business tax division. A hearings officer, who is a lawyer or auditor on the legal staff, an administration unit not under the business tax staff, hears the appeal in the district office and reaches the decision. Further appeal is noted by the following methods:

Appeal to the Audit Division.   Appeal is made to the audit division, that is, to the chief auditor or his subordinates in headquarters, in several states and the District of Columbia: Kansas, Maine, North Carolina, North Dakota, Tennessee, and Utah (supervisor of audit selection and review section).

Appeal to Sales Tax or Tax Division. Appeal is made to the sales and use tax division in Georgia, Indiana, Massachusetts, Minnesota, North Carolina, Oklahoma, and Virginia; to the tax division in Iowa, Rhode Island, and Wyoming; and to the tax policy division in Nebraska.

Appeal to the Director of Revenue. Either initially or, more commonly, after appeal to one of the units noted, appeal is made to the director of the revenue department in Arizona, Colorado, Georgia, Hawaii, Idaho (the commissioner in charge of sales tax), Minnesota, Nevada, North Carolina, South Dakota, Vermont, Virginia, and Washington. The hearing may be conducted by the director himself, or by the deputy director, or by designated persons. These hearings are usually informal.

Appeal Handled by Hearing Officers. In several states, though the appeal is technically made to the director of revenue, it is handled by a hearings officer, as noted earlier for California. These are almost always lawyers, usually on the staff of the revenue department, but in some instances outside lawyers are hired on a case-by-case basis for this purpose. These states include Alabama, California (no outside lawyers are used), Maryland, Missouri, New Jersey, New Mexico, North Dakota, Ohio, Rhode Island, Washington, and West Virginia. In Arizona, appeal is made to the hearings office, which holds the hearings. The taxpayer may then appeal to the director.

At least four states—Iowa, Massachusetts, Mississippi, and New York—have established audit review boards within the revenue department. Wisconsin has established a separate Appellate Review Board within the department to handle initial appeals.

Final Administrative Review

If the vendor is still dissatisfied after the hearings noted, several states provide for formal administrative review.

Commission. In states still placing tax administration under a commission, this commission serves as the final administrative review agency—California (State Board of Equalization), Mississippi, Nevada, South Carolina, Utah, and Wyoming. The exception is Idaho, the other commission state, where the commission is an element in the revenue administration but is substantially removed from everyday involvement in administration of the taxes.

Independent Review Agency. Seventeen of the sales tax states, plus several others, have established independent tax appeals agencies, completely separate from revenue administration.[6] The members, usually appointed by the governor, have training and experience in the tax field. Membership on the board is not a full-time job as a rule. The most common title for such agencies is Board of Tax Appeals (in Arizona, Idaho, Kansas, Kentucky, Louisiana, Ohio, and Washington). The term is Board of Tax Review in Iowa (which has broader functions than only appeal), Appellate Tax Board in Massachusetts, Tax Tribunal in Michigan, Division of Tax Appeals in New Jersey, Tax Review Board in North Carolina, and Tax Appeals Commission in Wisconsin. The tax court form will be noted shortly.

Appeal to the Courts

The taxpayer has, of course, the constitutional right to appeal the findings to court. An appeal may be against the administrative findings, or a suit filed to recover the sum after payment. In most states, appeal is made initially to the principal court at the county level, often known as a superior court, or to a circuit or district court. Appeal is then normally directed to the state supreme court. In a few states, the initial action may be brought in the state supreme court (Ohio and Oklahoma). In New Mexico the initial action is brought in the appellate court. Only Hawaii, Maryland, and Minnesota have tax courts on the model of the federal system.

Frequency of Appeals

Most states do not keep records of the number of appeals, and available figures are largely estimates.

California: About 10% of the audits are disputed. The principal auditor in the district settles 80%; headquarters, 60% of the remainder. The Board of Equalization holds 300 to 350 hearings a year on sales tax audits.

Indiana: In 1979, 15% of the audits were protested; assessment was upheld on 36%, partially modified on 43%, and protest was upheld on 21%.

Iowa: 80% of the protests are resolved within thirty days; five a year go to court.

South Dakota: In 1979, thirty-eight appeals went to formal hearing by the commissioner; ten, to circuit court.

Texas: 5% to 6% of audits go to legal section for hearing.

Vermont: 10% of audits are appealed to the commissioner; 2%, to formal hearing.

Thus, in general, the number going beyond the initial appeal (records of which are never kept) is very small, constituting only a small fraction of the audits. Auditors usually can satisfy taxpayers that audits are correct. If they do

[6]Note the article "Twenty-one States Have Independent Review Agencies," in *Tax Administrators News* 42 (August 1978): 86–87.

not succeed, the initial appeal step usually does, or the taxpayer feels that appealing further is not worth the time and effort.

The system of a simple initial source of appeal with very informal, nonadversary proceedings has obvious merit, and most states provide this. Whether this initial hearing should be before the sales tax director (if any), chief of audit, or hearing officer is largely a matter of the administrative organization in the state and the number of taxpayers. In a second (or, in larger states, third) step, there is merit in allowing appeal to a special board, preferably external to the department but made up of knowledgeable persons, to give the taxpayer an objective hearing in a relatively informal way by persons not directly involved in the administrative actions. Such a procedure assures the taxpayer of a fair hearing without need to resort to the courts and is likely to produce better results than the courts, where the judges are not trained in tax law or audit. In most states the number of cases going to the courts is not sufficient to warrant a separate tax court.

OUT-OF-STATE AUDIT

All states send auditors out of the state occasionally to audit out-of-state vendors, primarily for use tax collection. The extent of this work varies among states and is somewhat difficult to measure and compare. In most states the task is assigned to various senior auditors on a rotating basis. Several states, however, have a separate audit section for the purpose: California, Florida, Indiana, Pennsylvania, and Virginia, for example. The common pattern is to send one person or a team two or three times a year to particular areas where most out-of-state firms are located and audit them during two or three weeks.

Ten states now keep auditors permanently located out-of-state. These states often recruit for the positions in the states where the auditors are stationed. California was the pioneer in this endeavor, now keeping auditors in Chicago, New York, and Houston, and sending others out from Sacramento from time to time. Illinois has auditors stationed in the New York area and Dallas and plans an office in Los Angeles. Tennessee has nine auditors stationed outside the state, in Chicago, New York, and Atlanta. Wisconsin has an extensive out-of-state system, with five auditors in New York, two in Minneapolis, three in Chicago, two in Dallas, and two in California. Michigan has eight auditors out-of-state, in New York, Cleveland, Chicago, Minneapolis, and Los Angeles. Louisiana has offices in Atlanta, New York, Chicago, Dallas, Houston, San Francisco, and Tulsa. Indiana has forty-eight auditors (all CPAs) located out of the state (New York, Chicago, Atlanta, Houston, Dallas, San Francisco, Los Angeles, and Milwaukee); they generate about 50% of total audit assessments. New York has an office in Chicago with a branch in Los Angeles. Massachusetts has offices in New York, Houston, Chicago, and Los Angeles; Washington has ten auditors located out-of-state, in San Francisco, Los Angeles, Dallas, Cleveland, and Minneapolis. Minnesota discontinued out-of-state audit offices because of personnel problems. Texas currently has audit offices in New York, Chicago, Los Angeles, San Francisco, Atlanta, and Tulsa; more are scheduled in the future. Iowa has offices in Dallas, Cleveland, New York, Kansas City, Los Angeles, Chicago, and Minneapolis.

Some states mention completely inadequate travel budgets for out-of-state audit work. Such a state policy is extremely short-sighted, since out-of-state audits are among the most productive. Failure of administrative officers to distinguish between this form of out-of-state travel and others is an example of bureaucracy at its worst.

Number of Accounts Audited

Table 8.1 shows the percentage of total sales and use tax accounts audited in 1979. Table 8.2 groups the states by percentage audited. The range is very substantial. Eleven states audit 4% or more of the accounts annually. Eight states audit under 1% of the accounts.

The highest group, which is likely to be attaining near-optimal coverage, is made up of two geographically distinct sets of states; four from the west coast and mountain areas, six from the deep south and southwest, plus Rhode Island (and the District of Columbia). With one exception, these states have had persistently high coverage over two decades or more.

The low figure on Connecticut is apparently the result of departmental reorganization in 1979 and is not typical. Most of the other states in the lowest group (Minnesota is an exception) have had consistently low coverage.

Precise comparison of the audit coverage of the states on the basis of these figures is not possible. The reported numbers of accounts are not entirely comparable. Some states include a separate figure for each store in a chain system; others do not. The extent to which consumers purchasing from nonregistered vendors (mostly out-of-state) are registered varies. Some states are much more careful to transfer inactive accounts from the active file than are others; some are more careful in eliminating out-of-business firms from the files. The larger the listed number of accounts for a given number of businesses, the lower the percentage of firms audited.

Furthermore, the percentage of accounts covered is by no means an adequate measure of the effectiveness of the audit program. The percentage figure is raised sharply by a large number of audits of small firms. Some indication of this is given by the column in table 8.1 showing the number of field audits per auditor; unfortunately, data are not available for many states because of integrated audit staffs. The average for the twenty-nine states for which data are available is thirty-three; the average number in the top coverage group was fifty-eight, in the lowest group, 8. Optimal selection of accounts for audit is of

TABLE 8.1 State Sales Tax Audit Coverage

State	Active Accounts, 1979–80	Annual Field Audits, 1979–81	Field Audits per Auditor	% of Accounts Audited Annually 1979–81	1969	1962
Alabama	63,634	2,938	—	4.6	6.6	5.3
Arizona	75,000	1,800	44	2.4	3.5	
Arkansas	56,56$	4,010	—	7.1	5.0	13.2
California	583,690	23,648	33	4.1	6.2	11.6
Colorado	91,200	3,840	—	4.2	6.9	2.3
Connecticut	100,000	430	6	0.4	4.3	4.2
Florida	295,254	3,423	—	1.2	0.8	1.2
Georgia	106,000	2,148	—	2.0	1.5	
Hawaii	60,000	1,200	—	2.0	3.0	
Idaho	31,000	209	12	0.7	0.8	—
Illinois	164,297	6,000	28	3.7	2.8	1.5
Indiana	137,723	1,769	—	1.3	5.9	—
Iowa	99,995	1,156	12	1.2	0.6	2.6
Kansas	75,493	900	50	1.3	0.8	0.4
Kentucky	76,820	1,106	—	1.4	1.0	
Louisiana	78,000	973	—	1.3	8.0	3.6
Maine	39,597	981	39	2.6	6.7	5.7
Maryland	91,802	1,340	15	1.5	4.5	7.1
Massachusetts	114,827	1,200	14	1.1	0.4	—
Michigan	138,000	3,674	—	2.7	2.0	6.1
Minnesota	105,000	474	12	0.5	3.9	—
Mississippi	73,554	6,483	81	8.8	4.3	6.9
Missouri	100,020	2,300	—	2.3	2.5	
Nebraska	56,000	220	7	0.4	0.4	—
Nevada	20,500	947	53	4.6	5.7	1.7
New Jersey	177,235	3,728	—	2.1	0.7	—
New Mexico	85,651	839	38	0.9[a]	3.1	—
New York	450,358	8,100	—	1.8	1.4	—
North Carolina	134,000	4,285	—	3.2	4.1	6.2
North Dakota	26,000	600	40	2.3	1.4	
Ohio	247,114	1,559	7	0.6	1.3	1.5
Oklahoma	56,000	3,879	79	6.9		3.2
Pennsylvania	229,039	3,000	—	1.3	1.6	0.6
Rhode Island	23,000	1,263	34	5.5	9.7	23.8
South Carolina	71,804	931	18	1.3	3.4	4.1
South Dakota	29,756	640	39	2.0	1.7	1.5
Tennessee	101,983	4,268	46	4.2	4.8	1.4
Texas	287,980	6,860	17	2.4		—
Utah	40,900	3,300	94	8.1	8.7	8.3
Vermont	20,880	331	20	1.6	—	—
Virginia	80,000	3,000	38	3.8	2.0	—
Washington	157,000	5,194	40	3.3	5.8	3.5
West Virginia	39,505	139	3	0.4	0.6	1.7
Wisconsin	108,000	1,080	18	1.0		—
Wyoming	28,073	231	23	0.8		1.8
District of Columbia	19,000	400		2.1	3.4	
Total	5,252,000			2.3	3.4	4.9

[a] 2.1 in 1979–80.

TABLE 8.2   Ranking of States by Audit Coverage

4% or over:	Mississippi 8.8		1–1.9%:	New York 1.8
	Utah 8.1			Vermont 1.6
	Arkansas 7.1			Maryland 1.5
	Oklahoma 6.9			Vermont 1.6
	Rhode Island 5.5			Kentucky 1.4
	Nevada 4.6			Pennsylvania 1.3
	Alabama 4.6			Indiana 1.3
	Tennessee 4.6			South Carolina 1.3
	Tennessee 4.2			Kansas 1.3
	Colorado 4.2			Louisiana 1.3
	California 4.1			Iowa 1.2
				Florida 1.2
3–3.9%:	Virginia 3.8			Massachusetts 1.1
	Illinois 3.7			Wisconsin 1.0
	Washington 3.3			
	North Carolina 3.2		Under 1%:	New Mexico 0.9
				Wyoming 0.8
2–2.9%:	Michigan 2.7			Idaho 0.7
	Maine 2.6			Ohio 0.6
	Arizona 2.4			Minnesota 0.5
	Texas 2.4			Connecticut 0.4
	Missouri 2.3			West Virginia 0.4
	North Dakota 2.3			Nebraska 0.4
	New Jersey 2.1			
	Georgia 2.0			
	Hawaii 2.0			
	South Dakota 2.0			

even greater significance than mere percentages covered, but the percentages are so low in a number of states that almost inevitably the coverage is far too low.

Recovery from Audit

The figures on revenues recovered from audit are shown in table 8.3.[7] On the average, recovery from audit as a percentage of total revenue is much higher in states with broad coverage than in states with limited coverage. The average for the top eleven in coverage is 2.45%; for the bottom six, 0.9%. There are some individual variations from the typical pattern. But the recovery percentage for the top group is less than three times that for the lowest, whereas the audit coverage is nine times as great. Productivity per audit decreases considerably as audit is extended. This result is, of course, to be expected. When audit selection programs work effectively, audit is concentrated first on the most productive accounts.

[7]These figures show actual recovery. Audit assessments are often as much as twice the recovery figures.

TABLE 8.3 Annual Recovery from Audit, 1979–81

State	Sales and Use Tax Audit Recovery Millions of $	Sales and Use Tax Recovery as % of Sales-Use Tax Revenue	Recovery per Auditor $	Recovery per Audit $
Alabama	7.1	1.3		2,417
Arizona	4.0[a]	0.5	97,907	2,417
Arkansas	8.5	2.5		2,120
California	107.2	1.3	149,000	4,533
Colorado	12.5	2.4		3,255
Connecticut	4.76	0.6	68,000	11,070
Florida	15.095	0.8	—	4,410
Georgia	14.0	1.6	83,865	—
Hawaii	—	—		
Idaho	1.5	1.2	83,333	7,177
Illinois	17.2	3.0	79,630	2,867
Indiana	10.0	0.8		5,653
Iowa	10.5		48.864	3,941
Kansas	1.9	0.5	146,154	2,111
Kentucky	4.6	0.8	53,000	4,186
New York	11.7	2.0		10,579
Louisiana	9.14	1.4		9,394
Maine	2.25	1.1	90,000	2,294
Maryland	7.7	1.1	85,555	5,746
Massachusetts	9.6[b]	2.4	151,000	
Michigan	20.1	1.2		5,471
Minnesota	14.0	neg.	350,000	2,954
Mississippi	15.0	2.5	187,500	231
Missouri	3.5	0.5		1,522
Nebraska	—	—		
Nevada	1.9	1.1	105,556	2,006
New Jersey	11.02	1.0		2,956
New Mexico	9.9	1.5	260,677	11,807
New York	140.0	5.4		17,284
North Carolina	—	—		
North Dakota	1.5	1.4	100,000	2,500
Ohio	27.8	2.1	115,833	17,832
Oklahoma	4.0	1.4	81,633	1,031
Pennsylvania	26.0	1.4		8,667
Rhode Island	4.4	2.8		
South Carolina	6.6	1.3	126,923	7,089
South Dakota	1.0	0.8	58,824	1,515
Tennessee	18.5	2.0	201,483	4,328
Texas	46.4	2.1	116,000	6,764
Utah	5.1	1.4		
Vermont	1.3	3.1	75,592	4,130
Virginia	4.3	0.8	53,750	1,433
Washington	44.1[c]	2.6	34,860	8,500
West Virginia	1.8	1.1	45,000	12,950
Wisconsin	10.2	1.2	170,000	9,444
Wyoming	0.73	0.5	73,000	3,160
District of Columbia	2.7	1.6	195,544	6,844

[a] Assessment was $15.7 million.
[b] Including the very productive meals tax audit.
[c] Includes B & O tax recovery.

Recovery per auditor is also shown in table 8.3. The figures range from $35,000 to $350,000, but only two are less than $50,000 and only two exceed $200,000. The average is $113,000 for the states (twenty-five) for which this information is available. This compares with $45,000 in 1969; the increase is greater than that of the general price level. Variations among states can be attributed to several sources:

1. The economy of the state; a state with extensive industry is more productive of audit than a largely rural state.
2. The extent to which audit is extended; the greater the coverage, the less will be the recovery per auditor (with a satisfactory audit selection system).
3. The effectiveness of the audit selection program.
4. The complexities of the tax, which give rise to errors in reporting.
5. The rate of the tax.

States with very high figures can almost certainly profit substantially from extension of audit coverage; those with low figures and limited coverage would do well to review their audit selection processes, unless the difference is clearly attributable to the nature of the economy of the state.

Table 8.3 also includes the data of recovery per audit, which show similar net results. The average for the thirty-eight states for which this information is available is $4,990. The six states with the broadest coverage show an average recovery per audit of $1,792, the lowest six, $7,774. There are individual exceptions however: Washington, with broad coverage, shows a figure of $8,500 (this figure includes business and occupation tax revenue); at the other end, Wyoming has a low ($3,160) figure despite limited coverage. This reflects in part the nature of the economy of the state.

A few states compile more detailed information on audit recovery:

Arizona: 8 to 1 dollar recovery from audit
Illinois: 66% of the audits result in additional assessment
New Mexico: 66.9% of the audits yield additional revenue
Rhode Island: 85% of the audits produce revenue

Trends

Comparison of audit programs with those of a decade ago is not encouraging. Progress in data processing has not been matched by similar progress in audit programs. The overall audit coverage was 4.9% of the accounts in 1959, 3.4% in 1969, and 2.3% in 1979. Of the thirty-nine states for which comparable data are available, fourteen showed an increased coverage from 1969 to 1979, twenty-five, a reduced coverage. In some states this reflects the belief that the initial high coverage was no longer necessary or optimal, but in most it reflects primarily a rapid growth in the number of registered firms without a comparable increase in audit staff. Mississippi and New Jersey appear to have made the greatest relative improvement in coverage.

Attitudes of Administrators toward Adequacy of Audit

When the question was raised, the officials in the following states indicated that additional audits were needed:

California
Colorado
Florida (aim for 4% coverage)
Idaho
Kentucky (need about double coverage)
Maine
Massachusetts
Missouri (prefer 5% coverage)
Nevada
New Jersey (aim for 2% coverage)
North Dakota
Rhode Island (a few more)
South Carolina (a few more)
South Dakota
Texas
Wisconsin (aim for 1.2% coverage)
Wyoming
District of Columbia (need many more, but number is being cut)
Only four states indicate that this coverage is adequate or more than adequate:
Kansas
New Mexico (24.6% of the audit show no change and 7.3% resulted in refunds. This is of course not conclusive that the audit coverage is too great.)
Vermont
Virginia

AN OPTIMAL AUDIT PROGRAM

It is impossible to determine exactly the optimal coverage figure; California has attempted to do so more scientifically than other states. There are several problems. First is the issue of the definition of the optimum. In many states this is defined as the coverage yielding the maximum net direct return from audit as noted above; thus, the audit coverage should be extended to the level at which the gain from additional audit hours just equals the cost of providing the additional hours. This figure is difficult to ascertain, but the high return from hour of audit activities at present suggests that most states are well below this level. Furthermore, additional audit presumably results in improved voluntary performance, both on the part of the audited firms and those that learn about the audits of others. These amounts are very difficult to estimate, but the likelihood of such indirect gain suggests that the optimal level is somewhat beyond that of the direct monetary gain. The argument can also be advanced that in the interests of equity, states have an obligation to cover all firms over an interval of several years. Given the scarcity of state resources, however, no state in fact attempts to do this.

Examination of the experience suggests several guides to decisions about coverage of audit programs.

1. Present audit programs in all instances yield substantially more than they cost, from twice as much to fifteen times as much.
2. The return per hour of audit diminishes as audit coverage is extended, since in general the most productive audits are selected first. This principle is true even with primitive selection programs, since some accounts are so obviously in need of audit.
3. Starting from a relatively low audit coverage of 0.6%, a state can roughly double its revenue recovery by tripling its audit coverage in numbers of accounts, though not much more is required than doubling the audit staff.

    Thus, for example, a state with 0.6% of the accounts audited annually and recovering $1 million can, by doubling the number of its auditors, obtain another million in revenue (at a cost of perhaps $250,000), with an increase in coverage to perhaps 2.4%. To obtain another million would require nearly doubling the audit staff again, at a cost of perhaps $500,000. The precise results will vary with conditions in the state.
4. Because the most complex audits are the most productive and are made first, the number of audits per auditor increases rapidly as the size of the staff increases, and thus the audit coverage as a percentage of total accounts rises much faster than the number of auditors.
5. The absolute recovery depends on the rate of the tax. A given audit program will recover twice as much money, more or less, with a 6% rate as with a 3% rate. These rates do not affect the figures of return from audit as a percentage of revenue but do alter the optimum point. As the rate rises, extending audit coverage further is advantageous, since the yield per dollar of cost rises. This advantage is strengthened by the effect the high rate may have in giving firms greater incentive to underreport tax.
6. Optimal coverage in a particular state depends on several considerations:
    a. Rate of the tax.
    b. Complexity of tax structure. Exemptions necessitate additional audit effort as the opportunities for misreporting are greater.
    c. Complexity of the economy. Much more audit time is required for audit of complex manufacturing firms than for the typical small vendor. On the other hand, per dollar of volume and tax, large chain systems can be audited more quickly than a number of independent merchants scattered around in different localities.
    d. Quality of vendor record systems.
    e. Competency and training of the auditors.
7. The state audit officials unanimously agree that most underreporting of tax

discovered in audit is not the result of deliberate evasion but of misunderstanding, simple mistakes, and negligence. There are, however, a few deliberate evaders.

8. Audit experience suggests that underreporting of tax is not more than 3% of the tax due with a minimum audit program and not more than 0.5% with a good program.

Summary

Most states have made relatively little progress in audit, though a few states have made good progress. Thus, the same conclusions are reached as were a decade ago. Only a small group of states—Alabama, Arkansas, California, Colorado, Mississippi, Nevada, Oklahoma, Rhode Island, Tennessee, Utah, and Washington—approaches reasonably adequate audit programs. The coverage is little better than nominal in a number of states. Some of these have good audit staffs but completely inadequate numbers. The states as a whole are losing at least $400 million and possibly as much as $800 million because they fail to extend audit to optimal levels. Most states need to at least double their audit staffs, increasing their audit coverage threefold to maximize revenue. Even so, the total losses are only a small fraction of tax due. Failure to establish an adequate audit program is not only costly of revenue, but it is grossly unfair to those vendors who pay correct amounts of tax.

9. Use Taxes

When the states first imposed their sales taxes, they were concerned about the potential loss of revenue from out-of-state purchasing, to which the sales tax, as such, could not be applied for constitutional reasons. In 1935, California and Washington developed the expedient of imposing use taxes upon the initial use of goods purchased outside the state and brought in for use in the state. Such practice had previously been upheld by the courts with respect to gasoline taxes. The U.S. Supreme Court upheld the Washington use tax in the case of *Henneford* v. *Silas Mason Co., Inc.,*[1] on the basis that the tax was imposed not upon interstate commerce, as such, but upon the privilege of use after interstate commerce was completed. Accordingly, the tax was valid, so long as it was not discriminatory against interstate commerce. This case was of key importance, and other states quickly imposed the tax. Had the tax not been upheld, the consequences for the states would have been very serious.[2] With the power to impose the use tax upheld, later cases have centered around the power to collect tax from out-of-state vendors. These cases are reviewed later.

STRUCTURE OF USE TAXES

Since the early sixties, all states imposing sales taxes also have imposed use taxes. As explained in chapter 10, use tax complements to local sales taxes are imposed in some states and not in others.

Single versus Dual Acts

Sales taxes were first introduced in the thirties without use taxes. When these states imposed the use tax, they usually enacted a separate use tax law.

---

[1]300 U.S. 577 (1937).

[2]In *McGoldrick* v. *Berwind-White Coal Mining Co.*, 309 U.S. 33 (1940), the right to apply the sales tax to deliveries from outside the state was upheld if the transaction was completed in the state, and it appeared that the sales tax itself might be used in lieu of a use tax. But an attempt to apply the sales tax to transactions made outside the state for delivery in the state was held invalid in *McLeod* v. *J.F. Dilworth*, 323 U.S. 327 (1944). Application of the Arkansas sales tax to an out-of-state vendor was held to violate the commerce clause.

Some of these states ultimately merged the two taxes into a single law, and all states imposing the tax after World War II did so in a single act but usually with separate sections. In all states there are two separate taxes, whereas in the Canadian provinces the same tax applies to sales in the province and to goods brought into the province. Arkansas, Kansas, New Mexico, and North Dakota still use the term *compensating tax* for the use tax; Washington once did so as well.

The systems operate much the same whether by single act or two acts. In earlier years, they differed in some states, but such differences have been eliminated almost entirely. In fact, as noted earlier, in most states no sharp distinction is made between the two in processing or handling of revenues. In Arizona, Michigan, Ohio, and Oklahoma a distinction is necessary, since the revenues are allocated differently. In Mississippi there is a sharp distinction; in-state firms must be registered separately for sales and use tax and file separate returns for each, if they are subject to both levies. Use tax supplements to the wholesale elements in the sales taxes of Mississippi and Hawaii are imposed.

Legal Nature of Use Taxes

Technically, most use taxes are imposed upon the storage, use, or consumption of tangible personal property within the state, property upon which sales tax has been paid being exempt. The net effect, therefore, is to confine the taxes to initial use of goods purchased from outside the state and brought into the state for use, plus, in some states, goods bought tax free within the state and then used for taxable purposes. The exception to this general rule is Illinois, although that state's use tax in practice operates much like the others.[3] Some states confine the tax to purchases made from a vendor selling at retail and thus exclude from the tax the use of goods obtained through casual purchases.

Some states, as for example, New Mexico, apply the use tax to taxable services. Others, such as South Dakota, do not because of problems of enforcement.

Basis of Liability: Place of Intended Use

States follow two patterns on the issue of intended use. One group of states imposes liability on goods "purchased for use" within the state. Accordingly, if a person can give evidence that an article was purchased for use in another state and only subsequently brought to the state, he is not subject to tax.[4] To

[3]In Illinois, in-state sales are subject to both sales (retailers occupation) and use tax, but the former, for the vendor, is a credit against the latter.

[4]Including Alabama, California, Colorado, Connecticut, Florida, Idaho, Illinois, Iowa, Kentucky, Maine, Michigan, Nebraska, Nevada, New Mexico, North Carolina, Ohio, Rhode Island, South Carolina, South Dakota, Utah, Vermont, West Virginia, and Wyoming.

simplify interpretation, some of these states establish a time period. If the article was purchased and used a certain length of time before being brought to the state, it is tax free. For example, Idaho and Maine use ninety days; Massachusetts and Vermont, six months.

Other states, about equal in number, apply the tax to any goods brought into the state for use, consumption, or storage in the state and thus regardless of whether or not they were originally bought for use in the state.[5] Frequently, however, these states will tax on the depreciated value (Maryland allows 10% a year), and a number of them follow a rule similar to that of the "bought for use" states. They exempt property owned more than a certain period of time—ninety days in Wisconsin, six months in Pennsylvania and Tennessee. Many of these states also exempt "settlers' effects"—goods belonging to persons moving to the state. States using the "brought in" rule almost universally tax all goods brought in by business firms but usually on depreciated value. West Virginia applies the use tax only to goods purchased for delivery by the vendor into the state.

Credit for Sales Taxes Paid to Other States

Initially, most states did not give credit for sales tax that had been paid to another state, and therefore, there was potential double taxation. The principal difficulty arose with goods used by a business firm in one state and then transferred to another state. Inevitably, complaints were raised about this treatment, and some states began to provide credit. The trend increased sharply as a result of the report of the Willis Subcommittee discussed later in the chapter and proposed federal legislation. As a consequence, credit is now given for sales taxes paid other states with relatively few exceptions:

General Credit. Twenty-six states and the District of Columbia give credit for sales tax paid to another state, whether or not the other state does.

Reciprocal Credit. Fifteen states—Alabama, Georgia, Kentucky, Louisiana, Massachusetts, Michigan, Nebraska, New Jersey, New York, North Dakota, Oklahoma, Pennsylvania, South Dakota, Texas, and Vermont— provide credit for sales tax paid to those states that also provide credit. In view of the broad provision of credit, this limitation is much less serious now, but still has significance for some states.

No Credit. Arkansas, South Carolina, and West Virginia have never allowed credit (except in South Carolina, for contractor equipment). Nevada had provided credit for sales tax paid states that were members of the Multi

---

[5]Including Arizona, Arkansas, Georgia, Hawaii, Kansas, Louisiana, Maryland, Missouri, New York, North Dakota, Oklahoma, Pennsylvania, Tennessee, Washington, and Wisconsin. Mississippi taxes "the privilege of using."

State Tax Compact. But when Nevada withdrew from the compact in 1981, this ended credit.

Restriction of Credit on Motor Vehicles. Four states—Maryland, Missouri, Oklahoma, and Vermont—provide no credit on motor vehicle purchases. These are states using special levies on motor vehicles in lieu of the sales tax. Oklahoma does not apply tax, however, if the vehicle has been used at least sixty days in another state.

Logically, under the philosophy of a sales tax as a levy on the final consumer, the tax should belong to the state of final use. If a person buys an article in one state, pays tax, and immediately transfers it to another, he should receive a refund from the former and pay tax to the latter. But this procedure is far too much of a nuisance to warrant use. Since transactions are constantly going both ways across state lines, allowing the original state to retain the tax, with credit by the second, is far easier, although some states do experience some net loss in revenue. Failure to allow credit creates gross discrimination against interstate commerce. It is one of the prime sources of complaint by business groups and a prime reason for potential adverse federal interference in state taxing powers. Unfortunately, four states still fail to provide the credit. West Virginia, however, argues that since its use tax applies only to purchases delivered across the state line, there should be no double taxation.

Differences between Sales and Use Taxes

In the earlier days of the use taxes, some differences occurred in coverage. A few states, for example, exempted certain forms of industrial machinery from use tax but not from sales tax if these forms were not readily available in the state. These features were ultimately eliminated. Similar features in reverse—exempting goods from sales tax but not from use tax—were struck down by the courts as obvious violations of the interstate commerce clause. The differences today are minor.

Trade-in Allowance. Mississippi allows deduction of trade-in allowances only on in-state purchases. This rule is clearly discriminatory against interstate commerce, and similar provisions have been eliminated in several states by court action. In Pennsylvania, where this rule was followed on motor vehicles, the state courts held the rule invalid and extended the allowance also to out-of-state purchases.

Services. Use tax has somewhat different significance for services than for commodities, as service is not "brought into the state" or "bought for use in the state." A person may go to another state for a haircut, but he does not bring the service, per se, back. Several states, including Iowa, do extend their use taxes to services; others, such as South Dakota, do not. Any attempt to do so is almost futile from the standpoint of enforcement, except for repair in another state of equipment owned by business firms in the state. Since most states do not yet tax services but instead tax the materials used to produce them, multiple taxation will result. On the whole, not trying to apply use tax appears preferable, but this policy admittedly encourages some persons to obtain services outside the state.

Dollar Exemption. Since small transactions cannot be reached, a few states have sought to legalize the avoidance of use tax by exempting certain dollar amounts: Colorado, for example, exempts the first $100 of out-of-state purchases by individuals: Connecticut taxes only purchases in excess of $25. Most states, however, have been reluctant to introduce such rules because of possible administrative complications.

Rates. Oklahoma in 1977 raised the rate of the use tax to 4%, leaving the sales tax at 2%, on the grounds that virtually all local governments had sales taxes but no use tax. The Oklahoma Supreme Court held this action to be unconstitutional.[6]

COLLECTION OF USE TAXES

Use taxes are collected from those out-of-state vendors who are required by the state to register and collect use taxes, from out-of-state vendors who are under no legal obligation to collect tax but register voluntarily, and from the purchaser in the state.

In general, the out-of-state vendors can be required to register as use-tax vendors and collect and remit tax constitutionally, without violating the Due Process Clause of the Fourteenth Amendment and the Interstate Commerce Clause, only if sufficient nexus exists between the state and these firms. Nexus may arise from several sources.

Place of Business

Vendors who have any places of business within the state, such as a store, office, warehouse, or display room, are required to register and collect tax on all sales for delivery into the state, even if they are made independently of the local place of business. This rule has been sanctioned by the courts since the earliest days of use taxes. It was specifically upheld in two Iowa cases in 1941 involving mail order sales by firms also in retail business in the state.[7] This

[6]*Phillips* v. *Oklahoma Tax Commission,* March 14, 1978.
[7]*Nelson* v. *Sears, Roebuck & Co.,* 312 U.S. 359 (1941), and *Nelson* v. *Montgomery Ward and Co.,* 312 U.S. 373 (1941).

rule is supplemented in several states, including Alabama, Arizona, and South Carolina, by a rule that firms qualified to do business in the state must register. Alabama and Louisiana require registration only if the firm actually has a place of business in the state.

Solicitation of Business by Representatives

Most states require registration of firms that solicit business in the state by representatives, salesmen, agents, or independent firms soliciting orders for the firms. This power was upheld in a series of Supreme Court cases.

In 1939, in the *Felt and Tarrant* case, the court upheld the right of California to require registration of an out-of-state firm selling through agents in the state who maintained offices paid for by the out-of-state firm. In such circumstances the firm was considered to maintain a place of business in the state.[8] In 1944, the power was further extended in the *General Trading Company* case to apply to a firm selling in the state through traveling salesmen who maintained no offices in the state. This practice was likewise interpreted as "maintaining a place of business in the state."[9]

In 1960, in the case of *Scripto, Inc., v. Carson,* the Supreme Court upheld Florida's right to require registration and payment of tax by an Atlanta firm that had neither a place of business nor any agents in Florida.[10] Selling was carried on through independent wholesalers and jobbers in Florida who solicited orders for the firm and sent the orders to Atlanta to be filled. Solicitation by an independent broker rather than be a representative of the firm, the Supreme Court held, did not alter the tax status.

Solicitation of Business through Advertising

After 1960 many states extended their requirements for registration to include firms soliciting business in the state by mailing catalogs and other mail solicitations into the state, and, in some states, advertising through billboards, newspapers, magazines published in the state, radio, or TV stations in the state.

The first inkling that the courts might not uphold this extension of power came when the Alabama Supreme Court, in *State of Alabama* v. *Lane Bryant,* held that the mere mailing of catalogs to customers in the state did not establish sufficient nexus to bring the firm within the scope of the law.[11] The principal case arose in Illinois, out of the effort of that state to enforce payment of tax by National Bellas Hess, a mail order house located in North Kansas City, Missouri, regularly mailing catalogs to Illinois residents and

---

[8]*Felt and Tarrant Manufacturing Co.* v. *Gallagher,* 306 U.S. 62 (1939).
[9]*General Trading Co.* v. *State Tax Commission,* 322 U.S. 335, 64 S. Ct. 1028, 1944.
[10]362 U.S. 207 (1960).
[11]27 Ala. 385, 171 2d 91, 1965.

selling by mail, but having no place of business in Illinois. The Illinois Supreme Court upheld the state position that regular solicitation of business in the state by catalog did constitute "doing business in the state" and gave the state the power to require collection and remittance of tax.[12] Upon appeal to the United States Supreme Court, the decision of the Illinois Supreme Court was reversed, by a 6 to 3 decision.[13] The U.S. Supreme Court stressed the difference between this case and the previous ones in which the power of the states had been upheld; in the others the vendor had retail outlets, agents, or solicitors in the state, whereas in this instance the vendor merely communicated with the customer by mail or common carrier. To the majority of the U.S. Supreme Court this difference was crucial and controlling. The opinion went on to say that were the power of Illinois to tax upheld in this instance, the vendor could be entangled in a welter of complicated obligations to local jurisdictions, contrary to the intent of the Interstate Commerce Clause to ensure a national economy free of such interferences.

The dissenting opinion, written by Mr. Justice Fortas, with the concurrence of Justices Black and Douglas, took serious objection to the majority position, on the grounds that the large-scale systematic exploitation of the Illinois consumer market constituted adequate nexus to justify the requirement for collection of tax. The opinion noted that National Bellas Hess enjoys the facilities nurtured by the state of Illinois just as much as retailers located in the state and that failure to require the firm to collect use tax penalizes firms in the state subject to the tax. Although the opinion granted that payment of tax is not feasible on interstate sales of casual irregular nature, it noted that in this case solicitation was substantial, regular, and more pervasive and comprehensive than it had been in the *Scripto* case. The opinion concludes with the argument that the burden placed on the firm would be no greater than that on a mail order firm located within the state and not much more than that on any retailer.

Delivery

Several states sought to require firms regularly delivering into the state to collect and remit tax. Other states required registration even if firms did nothing else to solicit business. In 1954, however, in the *Miller Brothers* case, the Supreme Court denied the right of Maryland to require collection of tax by a store in Wilmington, Delaware, that made deliveries into Maryland in its own trucks but did not otherwise solicit business in the state.[14] Thus, delivery alone is insufficient for enforcement of tax. Some states still have the

[12]*National Bellas Hess, Inc.* v. *Department of Revenue of the State of Illinois,* 34 Ill. 2d 164, 214 NG 2d 755, 1967.
[13]*National Bellas Hess, Inc.* v. *Department of Revenue of the State of Illinois,* 386 U.S. 753, 1967.
[14]*Miller Bros.* v. *Maryland,* 347 U.S. 340, 1954.

rule in their acts, but it does them little good. A few actively seek to locate firms regularly delivering into the state and to persuade them to register to avoid nuisance for their customers. Some states are convinced that eventually *Miller Brothers* will be reversed. The Vermont Supreme Court, in *Rose-Genereux, Inc.* v. *Vermont Department of Taxes* (February 8, 1980) held that a New Hampshire department store delivering into Vermont, advertising in Vermont, and retaining security interest in goods in Vermont was subject to Vermont use tax.

In 1979, the South Dakota Supreme Court held that an out-of-state vendor delivering into South Dakota on a regular basis was required to collect South Dakota use tax (*in the matter of Webber Furniture,* decided April 9, 1979). The court distinguished this case from *Miller Brothers* on the basis of the much greater volume of business that Webber did in the state, relative to that done by Miller, and the work of the deliverymen in the state.

Credit Sales

California sought to require chain store systems doing business in California and registered as vendors in that state to collect and remit tax on credit sales made over-the-counter in Oregon and Nevada to customers having addresses in California. The U.S. Supreme Court ruled, in 1969, that this action was invalid.[15] Due process was violated because the out-of-state stores did not, through their activities, receive sufficient benefits from California to warrant that state's requiring them to collect tax. The Interstate Commerce Clause was violated because during the period California gave no credit for Nevada tax and thus interstate commerce was discriminated against compared to intrastate commerce. Finally, equal protection was denied because only branches of nationwide store systems, not local stores, were affected.

Nonsales Activities in the State: National Geographic

The National Geographic Society is a nonprofit enterprise located in Washington, D.C. In addition to its magazine it sells, by mail order, books, atlases, maps, and the like. It maintains in California two offices (with four persons in each) for soliciting advertising for the magazine. The state assessed tax on the mail order sales on the grounds that these two offices provided adequate nexus, even though the magazine operation is a department distinct from the mail order sales. *National Geographic* maintained that since the parts of its activity were distinct, the existence of the offices did not establish nexus adequate to require the Society to collect and remit tax on the mail order sales.

The California Supreme Court upheld the state, and the Society appealed

[15]*Montgomery Ward and Co.* v. *State Board of Equalization,* 272 ACA 823, 78 Cal. Rptr. 373 (1969).

to the U.S. Supreme Court, which unanimously (two justices not participating) upheld the decision of the State Supreme Court, that the maintenance of the two offices established adequate nexus, and that neither Due Process nor Commerce clauses were violated. The two offices enjoy the benefits of the state's activities; adequate nexus was established; there is no danger of double taxation. The key point is that nexus need not be established for the particular activity, but for the firm, considering all its activities. The Court stressed the similarity between this case and the *Sears* and *Wards* cases of 1941 and the difference from *Miller Brothers* and *Bellas Hess,* where the firms had no offices or agents in the state. The court pointed out that the Society encountered no risk of bearing the tax itself so long as it collected from its customers.

The states had little to gain and much to lose in this case; had the Supreme Court held that nexus was inadequate, the powers of the states would have been weakened, and numerous cases would likely have arisen. The court action reaffirmed the concept of nexus as applying to the firm's activities as a whole, not to the particular mail order activity, in a situation less clear cut than the *Sears* and *Wards* cases, in which the firms operated a number of stores in the state. The decision therefore was at least a minor step forward for the states.

More significant than the decision, however, were two statements in the decision. The first was the comment on the California Supreme Court's statement that the "slightest presence" of the seller in the state established adequate nexus:

> We are satisfied that from the above cited decisions the following principle can be distilled, and we thus hold: Where an out-of-state seller conducts a substantial mail order business with residents of a state imposing a use tax on such purchasers and the sellers connection with the taxing state is *not* exclusively by means of the instruments of interstate commerce, the *slightest presence* within such taxing state independent of any connection through interstate commerce will permit the state constitutionally to impose on the seller the duty of collecting the use tax from such mail order purchasers and the liability for failure to do so. [Emphasis supplied by the U.S. Supreme Court]

The U.S. Supreme Court's comment was:

> Our affirmance of the California Supreme Court is not to be understood as implying agreement with that court's "slightest presence" standard of constitutional nexus. Appellant's maintenance of two offices in the State and solicitation by employees assigned to those offices of advertising copy in the range of one million dollars annually, . . . establish a much more substantial presence than the expression "slightest presence" connotes.

The second was the emphasis placed by the Court on the difference between this case and *Miller Brothers,* and particularly that in *Miller Brothers* the seller could not know whether the goods were used in Delaware prior to transport to Maryland. This emphasis constitutes in effect a reaffirmation of the *Miller Brothers* decision, suggesting that a reversal is most unlikely. The statement led Justice Blackmun to write a separate opinion, although concurring in the decision of the Court, in which he indicated that he could not see the Court's distinction between this case and *Miller Brothers*. The statement about not knowing whether the goods were used in Delaware was not valid for those delivered by *Miller Brothers*. He concludes: "If, as I suspect, the result today is not fully consistent with the result in Miller, I am content to let Miller go."

Related Cases: Standard Pressed Steel and Complete Auto Transit

There have been two other significant Supreme Court decisions in recent years relating to sales and related taxes, although not involving the question of liability of out-of-state vendors to collect use tax.

The case of *Standard Pressed Steel Co.* v. *Department of Revenue of Washington,* 419 U.S. 560 (1975) involved the state's gross receipts business occupation tax rather than the sales or use tax, but the decision is relevant for sales taxes as well; it was specifically referred to as a precedent in *National Geographic*. The company was a supplier of airframe fastenings (nuts and bolts mainly) to Boeing, from plants in California and Pennsylvania. Standard maintained one employee in Seattle, an engineer, who worked from his home, serving as a consultant to Boeing, and aided in projecting the needs of Boeing over coming months. He did not take orders. The state argued that the existence of this employee constituted adequate nexus for application of the gross receipts tax to the receipts of Standard from the sales to Boeing. Standard argued that this was not sufficient to provide nexus. The Supreme Court accepted the state's position, upholding application of the tax because Standard maintained an employee in the state whose activity was important to the company's sales and received benefits from the state's activities. In a sense *Standard Pressed Steel* and *National Geographic* are mutually reinforcing, although concerned with different taxes; both help to clarify the requirements for nexus for sales, use, and related taxes.

The *Complete Auto Transit (Complete Auto Transit, Inc.,* v. *Brady, Chairman, Mississippi State Tax Commission,* 430 U.S. 274, 1977) case related to the delineation of interstate and intrastate commerce; where does the former end and the latter begin? Complete Auto Transit is a Michigan corporation doing business in a number of states. Under contract for General Motors, it picked up new General Motors cars brought into Jackson, Mississippi, by rail from out-of-state and delivered them by truck to dealers around the state. Mississippi assessed against the company for the years 1968–72 a 5% tax that was a portion of the state sales tax structure. It was technically a privilege tax, for the privilege of doing business in the state (the application of the tax to the transport of freight was repealed in 1972). Auto Transit maintained that on the basis of the Supreme Court decision in the Spector case *(Spector Motor Service* v. *O'Connor,* 340 U.S. 603, 1951), the tax was not applicable because the movement by truck was a portion of the interstate movement. The state argued that in cases subsequent to Spector the Supreme Court had sanctioned similar taxes imposed as a franchise tax, rather than as a privilege tax, on activities in the state, and that there was no difference in substance between such a tax called a franchise tax and one called a privilege tax.

The Supreme Court accepted the state's argument, upheld the decision of the Supreme Court of Mississippi, and specifically overruled the *Spector* decision, on the grounds that there was adequate nexus, the firm received benefits from the state, and the distinction between a privilege tax and a franchise tax is a purely terminological difference, not one of substance.

This decision is likely to prove of greater significance than *National Geographic,* in suggesting that the Supreme Court in the future will give much more attention to substance in tax cases and much less to terminology, per se.[16]

Movable Equipment in Interstate Commerce

Major constitutional questions arise with equipment used in interstate transportation. As a general rule, equipment, such as railroad freight cars, used continuously in interstate commerce cannot be taxed by any of the states. But if the equipment is "stored" in the state before use in interstate commerce—as, for example, for installation of parts—then, the Supreme Court held in the *Southern Pacific* case in 1939, it is subject to tax.[17] This rule has been upheld in other cases, as, for example, *Aspen Airways.*[18] Usually, however, firms in the industry are careful to ensure that the equipment is engaged in interstate commerce on its way to the state and is used thenceforth for interstate activities, thus being free of tax.

Legal Ability to Collect

To establish legal jurisdiction over the out-of-state vendor does not necessarily ensure that collection of tax can be enforced. If difficulties arise, there are several possibilities.[19]

1. If the vendor owns property in the state, judgment can be obtained and enforcement realized by exercise of *in rem* jurisdiction.
2. If the vendor owns no property in the state, there may be serious difficulty

---

[16]This section is based on the article by J.F. Due, "Nexus for Use Taxes and National Geographic," and reproduced by permission of the *National Tax Journal.*

[17]*Southern Pacific Co.* v. *Gallagher,* 306 US 167.

[18]*Aspen Airways* v. *Heckers.* Note the paper by R.J. Krol, "Current Developments: Taxation of Movable Equipment in Interstate Commerce," *Proceedings of the National Tax Association for 1976,* pp. 153-57.

[19]See L.E. Kust and G. Sale, Jr., "State Taxation of Interstate Sales," *Virginia Law Review* 46 (October 1960): 1290-1326.

in obtaining *in personam* jurisdiction on the basis of a valid service of process. A few states have so-called long-arm service-of-process statutes that make this possible. Whether the U.S. Supreme Court would uphold their validity for use tax collection remains to be seen. Even if it does, the task remains of bringing suit in the seller's state to enforce, a time-consuming process.

3. If the two states have reciprocal enforcement statutes, one state can immediately institute suit to enforce payment in the courts of the other. In many instances, this approach would be the simplest and most satisfactory. Nearly three-fourths of the states have such statutes.

States without reciprocal enforcement statutes could, of course, attempt to sue in the courts of the other state involved, but these courts would likely reject the suit.

ACTUAL ENFORCEMENT POLICIES

States differ materially in enforcing their use tax laws.

Mandatory Registrants

Most states make at least some effort to ensure that out-of-state firms subject to the registration requirement register and collect tax, but they differ in the zeal with which they pursue the objective. Many such firms are noted in audit of in-state firms. Purchase invoices indicate out-of-state suppliers from which the firm is buying, and check is then made to see if they are subject to the registration requirement or are registered. Historically, Florida pursued the firms more seriously than any other state, seeking firms that must register, plus others that may be persuaded to do so, by check of waybills of all freight coming into the state and checking trucks entering the state. Geographically, such a procedure is much easier for Florida than most states. Other states following aggressive policies include California, Idaho, Louisiana, Michigan, Mississippi, New Mexico, Washington, Wisconsin, and Wyoming. Hawaii has an even better control; it can enforce payment through the importing firms. Other states, though not publicizing the fact, check much less carefully, simply registering those that request registration or appear in routine audit review.

Firms subject to mandatory registration are handled in the same fashion as in-state firms, except that frequently no fee is required for registration.

Voluntary Registration

All states find that some out-of-state vendors register voluntarily even though not required to do so, and some states have carried on an active campaign to increase the number of voluntary registrants. These firms fall into two groups: supply firms of a wide variety of types, and department stores in nearby states. Supply firms include those serving manufacturers and other forms of business, and professionals: medical, dental, etc. Many supply firms are willing to register to avoid having their customers file use tax returns and pay tax or possibly incur substantial penalties for not doing so. Not infrequently, the customers will urge their suppliers to register and collect tax.

This same consideration does not apply, however, to department stores and other retailers selling to the public or to farm supply firms, since their customers are not subject to sales tax audit. Few, therefore, have registered voluntarily, except through strong efforts of the states. A number of states have actively encouraged them to register, in some cases offering certain concessions (such as a promise not to audit) and in others applying a certain amount of pressure such as a threat to follow their delivery trucks and assess their customers.

The states report widely varying success with both groups. Among those that have had considerable success include:

Arizona

California: success with various supply firms.

Kansas

Kentucky: substantial success with stores.

Maryland and Virginia: good success with District of Columbia department and other stores; most regularly delivering into these states have registered. Maryland has had no success at all with Wilmington stores; Delaware has no tax.

Mississippi: substantial success with New Orleans, Memphis, and Mobile stores, but not those in Atlanta.

Nebraska

Nevada

New Mexico: success with supply firms, El Paso department stores. Careful check is made on delivery into the state.

North Dakota: success with stores in border cities, not others.

Rhode Island: some success reported with department stores.

Washington: some success, particularly with Portland department stores, even though Oregon has no tax, in the past, but very few registered now.

District of Columbia: success with firms operating in the District and adjacent states; little cooperation otherwise.

Several states report limited success, particularly with stores: Hawaii, Illinois, Indiana, Iowa, Nebraska, Rhode Island, and Wisconsin. Several states reporting little or no success with out-of-state retail stores have relatively little direct competition from such stores, for example, Arizona. The problem is much more significant for a state, such as Mississippi, with major shopping centers located outside the state but close to its borders than for a state with shopping centers in the state (e.g., Tennessee), or remote from those in other states.

Individual Customers

States also vary in their efforts to require payment from individual purchasers. Two groups are systematically controlled: business firms subject to sales tax audit and purchasers of motor vehicles that must be registered. Because of limited audit coverage, not all business purchases are caught, but at least they are potentially subject to control.

Most states make no effort to catch individual purchasers on goods bought outside the state. Administrators regard any effort as not worth the trouble. Commonly, tax will have been paid to the other state, and little or no revenue loss is involved.

There are, however, exceptions:

1. *Other registered items:* In states where certain other expensive items are registered, check is frequently made and the customer billed, or the tax collected with registration:
   a. Boats: California, Kentucky, Maine, Maryland, Michigan, and Missouri.
   b. Planes: Kentucky, Maine, and Maryland.
   c. Snowmobiles: Vermont.
   d. General: Arizona and Tennessee.
2. *Farm equipment:* A number of states attempt to discover out-of-state purchases of farm machinery, particularly when neighboring states do not tax it. These are now very expensive items and the amount of tax is substantial. California, Iowa, Nebraska, and Utah particularly note efforts to reach these items. Various methods are used, including ones also applied to other large item purchases as well—recording of chattel mortgages and liens (Maine, Utah), property tax rolls (Utah, Washington), truck weigh stations, as noted below, and observation by compliance officers.
3. *Mobile homes:* Kentucky and some other states.
4. *Check at truck weigh stations:* A few states systematically check trucks at weigh stations near the borders. Wyoming has a program of checking all bills of lading on trucks to determine destination of major items. Small delivery trucks are not stopped.
5. *Customs:* At least three states make use of information from U.S. Customs offices at border points: Maine, North Dakota, and Vermont. In the past there was not always complete willingness to cooperate on the part of U.S. Customs.
6. *Contractors:* A number of states gives particular attention to out-of-state contractors performing contracts within the state, using Dodge Reports and other sources: Alabama, Arkansas, Maryland, North Carolina, and South Carolina, among others.

Indiana has an unusual policy; a separate line on the individual income tax return requests the taxpayer to list use tax due on out-of-state purchases during the year. The state collects about $250,000 a year from this line. New Jersey, as of 1982, includes a use tax return with the income tax return.

Informal Agreements among States to Exchange Information

A decade ago, there was substantial interest in informal agreements among states to exchange information on sales made in one state for delivery in another, particularly in the central midwest. These agreements have become essentially dead letters. Information is exchanged among some states, it is true—but in a very limited way. Michigan, for example, reports exchange of information, especially on boats, with its neighbors. Kansas provides information to Nebraska and Missouri. Idaho exchanges information with its two sales tax neighbors—Washington and Utah. In 1980, New York signed agreements with Pennsylvania and Vermont, and in 1981 with Massachusetts. There are others as well, but the hope of more formal and lasting agreements of a decade ago has not been realized; concentrating on their own activities, many revenue officials apparently did not find cooperation worthwhile. Federal confidentiality legislation has made exchange more difficult. The shift toward functionalization may also have contributed to the demise of sales tax cooperative effort.

USE TAX LEAKAGE AND LOSS OF BUSINESS TO OTHER STATES

If the use tax were fully effective, sales tax would not cause loss of business to other states, certainly so long as the tax is confined to consumer goods, except possibly through migration of population or industrial activity, rather remote possibilities. But since use taxes are not fully effective, the fear has been that some business would be diverted to retailers or mail order sellers located beyond the borders of the state. The problem has, of course, diminished as the sales tax has spread. Now a person can buy tax free in fewer places. Two of these states, Alaska and Montana, are so remote as to be of little consequence. However, some differences in coverage and rates may lead to diversion, plus purchases by mail or for delivery in another state.

The state administrators responsible for sales taxation in general do not regard the loss of business to other states as serious. This includes such jurisdictions as the District of Columbia, despite a higher rate than the adjacent states, and Vermont—in which border merchants regard the loss to New Hampshire as serious but the state tax officials do not.

There are, however, exceptions, primarily, but not solely, in states bordering on ones without a sales tax.

Idaho: The chief area of loss is in the west, in the area adjacent to Ontario, Oregon, which does not have a sales tax. According to Idaho revenue officials, Ontario has been booming as a shopping center whereas the adjacent Idaho area, particularly Washington County, has been experiencing a decline in sales.

Maine and Massachusetts: Both states are convinced that they lose a substantial volume of business and thus of tax revenue to New Hampshire, which does not have a tax. New Hampshire merchants do their best to lure persons from the other states to buy—and will not register to collect and remit use tax. There is a substantial population in Massachusetts not far from major shopping centers in southern New Hampshire.

Maryland: The state is convinced that there is very substantial loss of business to Wilmington—in which merchants stress in their advertising the ability to escape sales tax by buying in Delaware. Apparently, part of the opposition to a sales tax in Delaware arises from the desire of Wilmington merchants to keep the Maryland business. Pennsylvania, which has had concern in the past, currently expresses less fear of Delaware than does Maryland.

Michigan: Although all of the bordering states have a sales tax, Michigan is convinced that there is substantial loss of business to the Toledo area for delivery into the state, and through catalog orders from nonregistered firms.

Ohio: Although apparently gaining from Michigan, Ohio in turn is concerned about losses to West Virginia (Wheeling area), Kentucky (across from Cincinnati), and Indiana (Union City). This, again, is delivery-type business in larger items.

Wyoming: The state is convinced of considerable loss, primarily to Montana in the north.

A second group of states believes that there is some loss, usually confined to particular lines of business:

Louisiana: heavy equipment, farm equipment.

Minnesota: farm equipment, and some loss in the Fargo area.

Nebraska: some loss in farm equipment sales to Kansas.

Nevada: McDermitt, a small town on the Idaho border, where sales tax collection is very difficult, and mail order purchases in California for delivery in Nevada.

New Mexico: mainly in the El Paso area, despite strong efforts to check it.

New York: loss in the New York City area, partly because of the high combined rate in New York City.

South Dakota: furniture to Sioux City, Iowa.

Tennessee

Texas: in the Roswell area.

Utah: farm equipment, to Idaho.

Washington: some loss to Oregon, but not thought to be as serious as in the past.

Wisconsin: catalog order sales.

The general attitudes of the states have not changed materially over the last decade, though some problems have been eliminated (e.g., Nevada, having exempted food, no longer loses food sales to California in the Lake Tahoe area).

Two states have taken measures to avoid loss of business in border communities from residents of other states and to lessen demand for delivery. Washington allows residents of states not imposing the sales tax to buy for $1 a permit that allows them to buy tax free over-the-counter in Washington. In practice this is significant for Oregon residents in border communities along the Columbia. There is probably some evasion resulting from use of the permits by Washington residents. North Dakota follows the same policy: nonsales-tax-state residents (in practice, Montana) can buy tax free in the state if the purchase exceeds $25. The state estimates that it loses about $2 million a year revenue as a result.

Attempts to measure actual sales loss have been limited in number. They are reviewed in the next chapter, since they have even greater relevance for municipal sales taxes.[20]

SALES FOR DELIVERY OUTSIDE THE STATE

Most states exempt from tax all sales for delivery outside the state. Arizona and Mississippi tax such sales when the sale itself has been made within the state. If the order comes from outside the state and delivery is made to a point outside the state, the state cannot apply its tax under court interpretation of the interstate commerce clause. The more usual policy of exempting all such sales is preferable. Taxation of sales for out-of-state delivery either takes revenue that is rightfully due the other state or, in a few instances, may result in double taxation.

PROPOSALS FOR FEDERAL LEGISLATION

Following the Supreme Court decision in the *Scripto* case, various business groups became concerned about the increased state power in this field and sought federal legislation to reduce this power. Congress provided for investigation of the question, which was conducted by the staff of the Subcommittee on State Taxation of Interstate Commerce of the House Judiciary Com-

[20]The most troublesome case of this type in North America is Lloydminster, which straddles the Alberta-Saskatchewan border. Saskatchewan has a sales tax; Alberta does not. Merchants on the Saskatchewan side of the border cannot collect the tax, and the province cannot enforce that tax in the city, though there is no legal exemption. After forty-five years the problem is just as serious as it ever was, giving rise to continued grievances.

mittee, known as the Willis Subcommittee. In a massive report submitted in 1965 and 1966, the subcommittee reviewed the problem at great length and made specific proposals for lessening the problems.[21]

Principal complaints of business firms, primarily firms selling in a number of states, were as follows:

1. Variation in state sales tax legislation is substantial and adds greatly to the tasks of firms subject to tax in more than one state.
2. Nuisance of complying with the sales tax laws of a number of states was significant, yet the amounts of tax owed were often very small. Return intervals vary. Firms could be subjected to audit by several states. A few states charged firms for out-of-state audits.
3. Some discrimination was occurring against interstate commerce, particularly from failure to allow credit for sales tax paid other states and different treatment of trade-in allowances.
4. The rapid spread of local sales taxes had added greatly to the complications for interstate sellers.

Willis Subcommittee Proposals

The subcommittee proposed a voluntary joint federal-state system for collection; first, the Treasury would supervise collection from out-of-state firms provided that the states would adjust their taxes to conform with a standard model. Second, states not joining the system would be denied the right to require out-of-state firms to collect and remit tax except when the vendor was (1) doing business in the state, in the sense of owning or leasing property or having full-time employees, or (2) making regular deliveries into the state. Finally, all states, whether or not they joined the cooperative system, would be subjected to various rules on interstate transactions, the most important of which would have freed the vendor from tax on the first $100 of taxable sales in any reporting period.

The subcommittee proposals encountered violent objection from the states, in part because the report disregarded their legitimate interests, and from some other groups. Consequently, the proposed federal collection system was abandoned, and a new Willis bill was introduced embodying the other proposals (and ones on income tax). In one respect, the powers of the states were restricted still more, since merely having salesmen in the state would not subject firms to the registration requirement.

The proposed legislation was passed by the House, but not by the Senate. It was ultimately revived as the Rodino Bill (H.R. 7906), which was passed by

---

[21]U.S., Congress, House, Committee on Judiciary, *State Taxation of Interstate Commerce: Report of the Special Subcommittee on State Taxation of Interstate Commerce,* H.R. 565, 89th Cong., 1st sess., 1965, Vol. 3. This report is summarized in J.F. Due, "State Taxation of Interstate Commerce."

the House, but not by the Senate.[22] It was reintroduced in 1971 (H.R. 1538). The Rodino bill would have restricted the powers of the states to require collection to those out-of-state vendors owning or renting real property in the state, having one or more employees in the state other than salesmen, maintaining a stock of goods in the state, or regularly making household deliveries to the state. Furthermore, a purchaser would be subject to use tax as a consumer only if he had a place of business or dwelling in a state.

The states continued to fight these bills, in a remarkable show of unanimity among states with varying political philosophies and economic interests, and blocked passage in the Senate. States were hindered by the *National Bellas Hess* decision in enforcing their taxes, but the decision lessened the pressure for adverse federal legislation. The states in turn in 1970 sponsored the Murphy-Cranston Bill (S. 3368), which would have codified the existing situation, and not extend the powers of the states except on deliveries, but it did not restrict present powers.

In more recent years, bills have been introduced by Senator Mathias of Maryland but have not been seriously considered.

Multistate Tax Compact

The states, in an effort to take more positive action, created in 1967 the Multistate Tax Compact, which is designed to bring greater uniformity of state action in the tax field. As of January 1, 1982, there are twenty members. Several states have withdrawn in recent years, some because of the dislike of giving credit for sales tax paid other states, some because of pressure of business interests unhappy with the Multistate commission income tax audits.

The commission has not been actively involved in sales tax audit. Three commission auditors located in New York do fifteen to twenty sales tax audits a year, of multistate firms with headquarters in New York. The commission also experimented with data processing for member states but this did not prove successful and was closed out.

The compact provides on sales taxes that:
1. All states shall give credit for sales tax paid another state.
2. Exemption certificates accepted by a vendor in good faith shall free him from future liability should the purchaser use items for taxable purposes.

Twenty years have elapsed since Congress first considered the problem of sales taxation of interstate sales. A great deal of controversy was stirred up, in part by the unfortunate tenor and proposals of the Willis Subcommittee Reports. Restrictive federal legislation has thus far been averted, but it may

---

[22]C.F. Conlon, "Interstate Taxation Bills and Proposals," paper presented to the annual meeting of National Association of Tax Administrators, Detroit, 1970; *Taxation of Interstate Business* (New York: Tax Foundation, 1970).

not be indefinitely so. Interstate agreements have accomplished something but not much in most cases. The multistate compact has attracted a number of states, but not the large industrial states (other than Michigan) necessary for its successful operation, and some states have withdrawn in recent years. Question about its legal authority without congressional action, which is not yet forthcoming, was settled in the *United States Steel* case.[23] Unless its membership is complete, it cannot in any event fulfill the goals.

In summary, the present state of affairs for interstate use taxes is better in some respects than it was, but is by no means perfect. States have been denied the right to require mail order sellers to collect and remit tax, and this type of business has expanded in recent years. Yet many of these firms could not easily comply with the sales tax laws of a large number of states even if they wished to. Some system of option must be provided these firms, such as paying the sales tax either of the destination state or of their home state, particularly for stores making a few mail order sales into a number of other states. The growth in the number of states using the sales tax has reduced leakage on over-the-counter sales, but there is still some in view of rate and exemption differences. The worst abuses of failure to allow credit and discrimination against interstate activity have been greatly reduced, but a few states refuse to act.

SUMMARY

Use tax remains the weak link in state sales tax administration, though total revenue loss is probably not great. From the state's standpoint, some leakage of revenue occurs, primarily on mail order sales by the catalog type of mail order house not operating retail stores, retailers doing some casual mail order business, and to some extent by purchase of consumer durables for delivery in the other state. The states can reach motor vehicles, other registered items, purchases through the large mail order houses also having stores in the states, and purchases by business firms subject to audit (though many of these purchases are not caught).

At the same time, some business firms selling in small amounts into large numbers of states are either violating the law, or, if they do register, are being put to substantial expense and nuisance in complying with the sales tax laws of a number of states.

Further restriction of powers of the states in the field is clearly undesirable. Legislation that would allow the states to make enforceable agreements with one another would greatly reduce the problem of escape of deliveries across

[23] *U.S. Steel et al.* v. *Multi State Tax Commission et al.* 434 U.S. 452 (1978).

state lines and some mail order purchases. The only ultimate solution for the widely selling mail order firms is to give them, by federal legislation, the option of paying tax to their home state or to the state of destination. Fortunately, the states have moved rapidly in the direction of providing credits for sales taxes paid other states and of eliminating various forms of discrimination against interstate commerce.

10. Local Government Sales Taxes

Local governments can levy sales taxes only when specifically or implicitly authorized by state constitution or statute. This authorization can be in the form of home rule charter powers, general licensing powers, or specific state legislation. Most localities have acted through specific authorization, as table 10.3 indicates.

As of January 1, 1982, local governments in twenty-seven states plus the District of Columbia are levying sales taxes. The District levy has been covered in the chapters dealing with state taxes and is not included here. Three other states—Florida, Kentucky, and Wisconsin—had authorized local sales taxes, but no localities in them have adopted sales taxes under that authority. Ten years ago, California and Georgia authorized transit district taxes; now the group includes eight more states (Colorado, Florida, Illinois, Kentucky, Missouri, New York, Ohio, and Texas), although not all use the authorization. Of states with localities using sales taxes, only four—Mississippi, Nevada, New Mexico, and Wyoming—have abandoned portions of local sales tax authority.[1] Each substituted locally shared increases in the state sales tax. Both New Mexico and Wyoming renewed authorization in one form or another. Nevada added authorization for county sales taxes for mass transportation. Mississippi renewed authorization for one city tax—Bay St. Louis—long enough to accumulate sufficient revenue to satisfy a judgment in a municipal swimming pool accident. Local sales taxes afford state legislatures a method of assisting local jurisdictions without placing responsibility for taxation on the state, hence the popularity of this revenue device.

In January 1981, of the 161 municipalities with population in excess of 100,000, 83 were receiving revenue from their own sales tax; 21 additional were located in counties or transit districts using the tax, and a number received a share of that tax. In fiscal year 1980, for all municipalities, the sales tax provided about 16% of the total tax revenue (from about 10% in

[1]The change was made in Mississippi in 1968; 20.5% of the state sales tax revenue collected in cities is given to the cities based on the place of collection. In rural areas, the state keeps the entire amount, but contributes to the local road fund. The change was made because the local taxes had become almost universal and were causing unnecessary compliance and administrative difficulties.

1969); local governments as a whole received about 9% of their total tax revenues from sales taxes, or about 3.5% of their total general revenue, including grants (compared to 4% and 3%, respectively, in 1969).[2] Table 10.1 indicates the use and revenue importance of local sales taxes today in cities of over 100,000 population.

The pioneer in local sales taxation in the United States was New York City, which introduced the tax in 1934. New Orleans introduced a tax of limited scope in 1936 and extended the coverage to that of a typical sales tax in 1938. Several states adopted local sales taxes in the postwar 1940s and 1950s, with major adoptions in California and Illinois. A key development in the history of local sales taxes was the introduction of state-administered local sales taxes by Mississippi in 1950, a technique that made effective use of the taxes possible. The fastest interstate spread of these taxes, however, occurred in the 1960s. In 1963, twelve states had authorized local sales taxes, and by mid-1970, twenty-five states had authorized them. Thirty states had authorized them by 1980. Much of this growth can be attributed to greater demand for local government services combined with continued dissatisfaction with local property taxes, and the reluctance of legislators to raise state tax rates.

Many local government sales taxes create sharp rate differentials at jurisdiction borders, just as state sales taxes do when a state with a high sales tax rate adjoins a state with a low sales tax rate. Businessmen often fear that rate differentials will depress retail sales and object to sales taxes for this reason. As local sales taxes often create this differential, the "border city" problem will be examined along with the specific features of these taxes.

Of the thirty states that authorize local sales taxes, twenty-three provide only state administration, three have local administration, and four have both state and local administration.[3] Table 10.2 indicates major features in each state. States have somewhat different administrative structures, but it is convenient to categorize them according to the principal unit of administration, the locality, or the state. Crucial elements of design—the rates employed, the situs rule, the application of use taxes, the coordination devices used, and the sharing of revenue between localities—are enumerated for easy cross-reference and comparison in other tables.

LOCAL ADMINISTRATION OF LOCAL SALES TAXES

Five states had no state sales taxes in January 1981. Of these states, only Alaska had local sales taxes. Hence, for the most part, local administration

[2]U.S., Bureau of the Census, *Governmental Finances in 1979–80; City Government Finances in 1979–80* and similar volumes for 1968–69.

[3]The municipal business and occupation taxes in West Virginia are excluded from this analysis, as is the Panama City, Florida, gross receipts tax.

TABLE 10.1 Sales Taxes in Cities of over 100,000 Population, January 1, 1981

State	City	Sales Tax Rate (%)					Sales Tax Revenue as % of Municipal Tax Revenue, 1980
		State	City	Other Local[a]	Combined Local[b]	Total Rate (%)	
Alabama	Birmingham	4	1	1		6	14c
	Huntsville	4	2			6	50c
	Mobile	4	2			6	55c
	Montgomery	4	2	1		7	51c
Arizona	Mesa	4	1			5	80c
	Phoenix	4	1			5	45
	Tucson	4	1			5	66c
California	Anaheim	4.75			1.25	6	34c
	Berkeley	4.75		0.5	1.25	6.5	19c
	Fremont	4.75		0.5	1.25	6.5	28c
	Fresno	4.75			1.25	6	33c
	Garden Grove	4.75			1.25	6	35c
	Glendale	4.75			1.25	6	38c
	Huntington Beach	4.75			1.25	6	22c
	Long Beach	4.75			1.25	6	28
	Los Angeles	4.75			1.25	6	25
	Oakland	4.75		0.5	1.25	6.5	26
	Pasadena	4.75			1.25	6	25c
	Riverside	4.75			1.25	6	37c
	Sacramento	4.75			1.25	6	29c
	San Bernardino	4.75			1.25	6	40c
	San Diego	4.75			1.25	6	41
	San Francisco	4.75		0.5	1.25	6.5	15
	San Jose	4.75		0.5	1.25	6.5	30
	Santa Ana	4.75			1.25	6	40c

State	City						
	Stockton	4.75			1.25	6	32[c]
	Sunnyvale	4.75		0.5	1.25	6.5	34[c]
	Torrance	4.75			1.25	6	34[c]
Colorado	Aurora	3	3	0.5		6.5	64[c]
	Denver	3	3	0.5		6.5	46
	Colorado Springs	3	2			5	58[c]
	Lakewood	3	2	0.5, 0.5		6	74[c]
	Pueblo	3	3			6	64[c]
Georgia	Atlanta	3		1		4	29[c]
	Columbus	3			1	4	10[c]
	Macon	3			1	4	
	Savannah	3			1	4	
Illinois	Chicago	4	1	1		6	15
	Peoria	4	1			5	38[c]
	Rockford	4	1			5	36[c]
Kansas	Kansas City	3	0.5	0.5		4	20[c]
	Topeka	3	0.5			3.5	
Louisiana	Baton Rouge	3	2.5	1		6	60[c]
	New Orleans	3	2.5	1.5		7	42
	Shreveport	3	1	1		5	37[c]
Missouri	Independence	3.125	1	0.5		4.625	37[c]
	Kansas City	3.125	0.5	0.5		4.125	18
	St. Louis	3.125	1.5			4.625	19
	Springfield	3.125	1			4.125	
Nebraska	Lincoln	3	1			4	29[c]
	Omaha	3	1.5			4.5	42
Nevada	Las Vegas	3		0.5		3.5	
New Mexico	Albuquerque	3.75		0.25		4	16[c]

TABLE 10.1 (continued)

		Sales Tax Rate (%)				
State	City	State	City	Other Local[a]	Combined Local[b]	Total Rate (%)	Sales Tax Revenue as % of Municipal Tax Revenue, 1980
New York	Albany	4		3		7	
	Buffalo	4		3		7	
	Rochester	4		3		7	
	New York City	4	4			8	17
	Syracuse	4		3		7	
	Yonkers	4	3	1		8	23[c]
North Carolina	Charlotte	3		1		4	
	Durham	3		1		4	
	Greensboro	3		1		4	
	Raleigh	3		1		4	
	Winston-Salem	3		1		4	
Ohio	Cincinnati	5		0.5		5.5	
	Cleveland	5		0.5, 1		6.5	
	Columbus	5		0.5		5.5	
	Dayton	5		0.5, 0.5		6	
	Toledo	5		0.5		5.5	
Oklahoma	Oklahoma City	2	2			4	61
	Tulsa	2	3			5	73
Tennessee	Chattanooga	4.5		1.75		6.25	
	Knoxville	4.5		1.5		6	
	Memphis	4.5		1.5		6	
	Nashville	4.5			2.25	6.75	25
	Davidson Co.						
Texas	Amarillo	4	1			5	24[c]
	Arlington	4	1			5	31[c]

Austin	4	1	5	28
Beaumont	4	1	5	30[c]
Corpus Christi	4	1	5	25[c]
Dallas	4	1	5	25
El Paso	4	1	5	27
Fort Worth	4	1	5	28
Garland	4	1	5	26[c]
Houston	4	1	1	6	28
Irving	4	1	5	20[c]
Lubbock	4	1	5	29[c]
Pasadena	4	1	5	27[c]
San Antonio	4	1	0.5	5.5	34
Waco	4	1	5	29[c]
Utah				
Salt Lake City	4		0.75, 0.25	5	40[c]
Virginia				
Alexandria	3	1	4	8[c]
Chesapeake	3	1	4	7[c]
Hampton	3	1	4	11[c]
Newport News	3	1	4	8[c]
Norfolk	3	1	4	12[c]
Portsmouth	3	1	4	10[c]
Richmond	3	1	4	9[c]
Virginia Beach	3	1	4	10[c]
Washington				
Seattle	4.5	0.5, 0.3	5.3	19
Spokane	4.5	0.5	5	22[c]
Tacoma	4.5	0.5, 0.3	5.3	16[c]
District of Columbia	6		6	21

Sources: U.S., Bureau of the Census. *City Government Finances in 1979–80* (Washington: G, 1981), and note c below.

[a] Rate to which sales within the city are also subject.
[b] Rate imposed jointly for city and other local use.
[c] U.S. Bureau of the Census, 1977 Census of Governments, Volume 4, Governmental Finances, Number 4, Finances of Municipalities and Township Governments (Washington: US6PO, 1979).

TABLE 10.2 Statutory and Administrative Features of Local Sales Taxes, February 1982

State/Jurisdictions	Approximate Number Using	Source of Authority	Referendum Requirement	Administration	Charge for Collection (%)
Alabama					
Municipalities	264	licensing	no	state	cost[a]
Municipalities	24	licensing	no	local	—
Counties	39	specific	usually	state	cost[a]
Counties	3	specific	no	local	—
Alaska					
Municipalities	85	specific	no	local	—
Boroughs	7	specific	yes	local	—
Arizona					
Municipalities	52	licensing	no	state	none
Municipalities	15	licensing	no	local	—
Arkansas					
Municipalities	13	specific	yes[c]	state (required)	2.0
Counties	4	specific	yes	state (required)	2.0
California					
Municipalities	381	specific	no	state	0.82
Counties	58[f]	specific	no	state	0.82
Transit districts	3	specific	sometimes	state	0.82
Colorado					
Municipalities	131	specific	yes	state	none
Municipalities	31	home rule	no	local	—
Counties	25	specific	yes	state (required)	none
Regional transit districts	1	specific	yes	state (required)	none
Florida					
Counties	0	specific[j]	yes	state (required)	
Georgia					
Joint county-municipality	111	specific	yes	state (required)	1
Regional transit authorities	1[h]	specific	i	state (required)	

Illinois					
Municipalities	1,250	specific	no	state	2
Counties	102	specific	no	state	2
Regional transit authorities	2	specific	no[k]	state	
Municipalities	1	home rule	no	local	
Kansas					
Municipalities	47	specific	yes	state	0
Counties	7	specific	yes	state	0
Kentucky					
Transit authorities	0	specific	yes	state (required)	
Louisiana					
Municipalities	154	specific	yes	local[m]	—
Parishes (parish or school board)	63	specific	yes	local[n]	—
Minnesota					
Municipality	1	specific	yes	local	—
Mississippi					
Municipality	1	specific	no	state	none
Missouri					
Municipalities	294	specific	yes	state (required)	1
Counties	33	specific	yes	state (required)	1
Transportation	3	specific	yes	state (required)	1
Nebraska					
Municipalities	7	specific	yes[n]	state (required)	3
Nevada					
Counties (for mass transit)	0	specific	yes	state	1
New Mexico					
Municipalities	95	specific	optional	state (required)	cost to 3 (1.2)
Counties	8	specific	yes	state (required)	cost to 3 (1.2)
New York					
Municipalities	28	specific	no	state (required)	cost (about 0.75)
Counties	48	specific	no	state (required)	cost (about 0.75)
Transit districts	1	specific	no	state	cost (about 0.75)

TABLE 10.2 (continued)

State/Jurisdictions	Approximate Number Using	Source of Authority	Referendum Requirement	Administration	Charge for Collection (%)
North Carolina					
Counties	99	specific	optional	state (optional)	cost (0.862)
Ohio					
Counties	55	specific	optional	state	0
Transit districts	3	specific	yes	state	1
Oklahoma					
Municipalities	424	specific	yes	state (optional)	p
South Dakota					
Municipalities	62	specific	yes	state (required)	cost (1)
Tennessee					
Municipalities	12	specific	yes	state (optional)	cost (1.5)
Counties	94	specific	yes	state (optional)	cost (1.5)
Texas					
Municipalities	945	specific	yes	state (required)	2
Transit authorities	2	specific	yes	state (required)	2
Utah					
Municipalities	all	specific	no	state	cost to 2.5
Counties	29[f]	specific	no	state (optional)	cost to 2.5
Transit districts	4	specific	yes	state	cost to 2.5
Virginia					
Independent cities	41[f]	specific	no	state (required)	0
Counties	95[f]	specific	no	state (required)	0
Washington					
Municipalities	266	specific	no	state (required)	not to exceed 2
Counties	38	specific	no	state (required)	
Transit	8	specific	yes	state (required)	

State/Jurisdictions	Frequency of Remittance	Rate Limit (%)	Range of Actual Rates (%)	Local Use Tax	Location of Liability	Vendor Compensation (%)
Wisconsin Counties	0	specific	no	state		
Wyoming Counties	16	specific	yes		state (required)	1
Alabama						
Municipalities	mo.	none	1-3	sometimes	delivery	usually—same as state
Municipalities	—	none	1-2.5	sometimes	delivery	yes—varies
Counties	—	2	.5-2	usually	delivery	usually—same as state
Counties	—	none	1-2	yes	delivery	
Alaska						
Municipalities	—	up to 6	1-5	sometimes		yes
Boroughs	—	up to 6	1-4	sometimes		yes
Arizona						
Municipalities	wk.	none	1-2	sometimes	vendor	no
Municipalities	—	none	1-2	sometimes	vendor	no
Arkansas						
Municipalities	mo.[b]	to 1	1	usually yes	vendor[d]	
Counties		to 2	1			
California						
Municipalities	mo.	1	1	yes[e]	vendor	no
Counties	mo.	1.25	1.25	yes[e]	vendor	no
Transit districts	mo.	1.25 or .5	.5	yes[e]	delivery	no
Colorado						
Municipalities	mo.	7 combined state, county, and city	1-4	sometimes[g]	delivery	0-5
Municipalities	—		1-3	usually	delivery	0-5
Counties	mo.		.5-2	sometimes[g]	delivery	0-3.33
Regional transit districts	mo.	1.25	.5	no	delivery	3.33

TABLE 10.2 (continued)

State/Jurisdictions	Frequency of Remittance	Rate Limit (%)	Range of Actual Rates (%)	Local Use Tax	Location of Liability	Vendor Compensation (%)
Florida						
Counties	as soon as practicable collection	1		yes		
Georgia						
Joint county-municipality		1	1	yes	delivery	yes—same as state
Regional transit authorities		1	1	yes	delivery	yes—same as state
Illinois						
Municipalities	mo.	up to 1	.5–1	yes[k]	vendor	no
Counties	mo.	up to 1	.5–1	yes[k]	vendor	no
Regional transit authorities	mo.	1	1; .25	yes[k]	vendor	no
Municipalities		1	1	no	delivery	2
Kansas						
Municipalities	at least quar.	.5	.5	no	vendor	no
Counties		.5 or 1	.5–1	no	vendor	no
Kentucky						
Transit authorities		up to .5	—	no		
Louisiana						
Municipalities	—	to 3 combined[n]	.5–2.5	yes	delivery	yes
Parishes (parish or school board)	—		1–3	yes	delivery	yes
Minnesota						
Municipality	—	1	1	yes	delivery	no
Mississippi						
Municipality		.5	.5	no		yes(2% to $50 per mo.)

Jurisdiction						
Missouri						
Municipalities	mo.	.05, .875, or 1	.5–1	no	vendor	yes (2)
Counties	mo.	.25, .375, or .5	.5	no	vendor	yes (2)
Transportation	mo.	up to .5	.5	no	vendor	yes (2)
Nebraska						
Municipalities	mo.	.5 or 1 (Omaha—1.5)	1–1.5	yes	delivery	yes (3)
Nevada						
Counties (for mass transit)		.5 to 2.5		yes		
New Mexico						
Municipalities	mo.	1 to .75	.5–7.5	no	vendor	no
Counties	mo.	.25	.25	no	vendor	no
New York						
Municipalities	mo.	3[o]	0–4	yes	delivery	no
Counties	mo.	3.25	1–3	yes	delivery	no
Transit districts		.25	.25	yes		
North Carolina						
Counties	quar.	1	1	yes	delivery	yes (3)
Ohio						
Counties	mo.	.5 or 1	.5	yes	vendor	yes (1)
Transit districts	mo.	.5, 1, 1.5	.5–1	yes	vendor	yes (1)
Oklahoma						
Municipalities	mo.	none	1–3	sometimes	vendor	yes[a]
South Dakota						
Municipalities	within 30 days collection	1[a]	1–2	yes	delivery	no
Tennessee						
Municipalities	mo.	up to 2.25	1–2.5	yes	vendor	yes[r]
Counties	mo.		1–1.5	yes	vendor	yes[r]

TABLE 10.2 (continued)

State/Jurisdictions	Frequency of Remittance	Rate Limit (%)	Range of Actual Rates (%)	Local Use Tax	Location of Liability	Vendor Compensation (%)
Texas						
Municipalities	mo.[s]	1	1	yes	vendor	yes (1)
Transit authorities	mo.[s]	.5 or 1	.5, 1	yes	vendor	yes (1)
Utah						
Municipalities	quar.	.75	.75	yes	vendor	no
Counties	quar.	.75	.75	yes	vendor	no
Transit districts	quar.	.25	.25	yes	vendor	no
Virginia						
Independent cities	mo.	1	1	yes	vendor	no
Counties	mo.	1	1	yes	vendor	no
Washington						
Municipalities	bimo.	up to .5	4.25–.5	yes	vendor	no
Counties	bimo.	.5	.5	yes	vendor	no
Transit	bimo.	.1 to .6	.2–.3	yes	vendor	no
Wisconsin						
Counties		.5		no	vendor	

Wyoming						
Counties	mo.	.5 or 1	1	yes	delivery	no

— Does not apply.

[a] Cities and newer county adoptions charged on number of accounts or fixed percentage (5% smaller units, 10% larger). Others charged percentage of state collection cost.

[b] When state sales tax receipts are remitted to state treasury (mo.).

[c] Texarkana had no use tax, Siloam Springs did initially.

[d] Motor vehicles taxable at registration.

[e] Use tax on instate purchases only.

[f] All units levy the tax.

[g] Use tax limited to motor vehicles and building materials.

[h] Metropolitan Atlanta Regional Transit Authority in Fulton and DeKalb Counties.

[i] Referendum required for initial counties; more may join MARTA (and become subject to the tax) without voter approval.

[j] For fixed guideway rapid transit only.

[k] A referendum on the RTA tax was held unconstitutionally vague.

[l] To 1% in Cook County and .25% in other counties of the district.

[m] A state agency administers the local motor vehicle sales tax.

[n] May exceed the limit.

[o] After 1978.

[p] Except New York City (4%) and Yonkers (city at 3% and county at 1%). With those exceptions, the local total (city plus county) cannot exceed 3%.

[q] 2.5% from 1% rate; 1.5% from 2% rate; 1% from 3% rate.

[r] Limit for taxes enacted after July 1, 1977.

[s] 2% on first $2,000 combined state and local tax, 1.5% above that.

[t] Required to remit at least twice a year.

of local sales taxes implies the existence of dual state and local administrative structures. The trend is clearly away from this administrative form. Three states (Alabama, Arizona, and Colorado) employing local administration have instituted procedures to permit state administration. Only Illinois and Minnesota have opted for local administration in the past thirty years. Illinois, which had only a state administration, now also permits local administration as well.

Locally Administered Taxes by State

Local administration in states with sales tax has created substantial problems in virtually every application. Current experience in Alabama and early experience in California clearly demonstrate the difficulties.[4] Colorado has experienced similar problems, but in Arizona and Louisiana, they have been less troublesome. Larger Arizona municipalities have, until recently, patterned their taxes after the state tax, and most smaller cities have selected state administration. Louisiana legislation has introduced some interlocal tax coordination. Potential dangers, however, remain in each state.

Alabama. Cities in Alabama have used sales taxes for about thirty-five years. As the taxes originally were all based on local licensing powers, the state has been unable to coordinate the local legislation and has never administered the sales taxes used by the largest cities. Counties have received specific sales taxing authority, originally on a county-to-county basis, and a few continue to administer their own taxes. City and county taxes frequently overlap. The 1965 Alabama legislature provided voluntary state administration of municipal sales taxes if the tax paralleled the state tax, but this option proved attractive only for smaller cities. The 1969 legislature passed specific authorization for state administration of city and county sales and use taxes patterned after the state tax, but the coordinating impact has been limited as larger cities and several counties continue locally administered taxes. The taxes levied under the recent legislation are technically sales taxes, not the license taxes used previously, to ensure that individual taxpayers can deduct them on their federal income tax returns.

Several problems with local administration in a sales tax state exist in exaggerated form in Alabama because of the widespread use of the taxes, the various authorizations of the taxes, and the peculiarities of the state laws. Some difficulties and complexities have been reduced by the continuing unification of state and local taxes under state administration, but several problems remain.

1. Local rates vary from 0.5% to 3.0% (a reflection of differing revenue

---

[4]Let's Make Sense Out of Local Sales Taxes (San Francisco; California Retailers Association, 1955), and California Senate Interim Committee on State and Local Taxation, *State and Local Sales and Use Taxes in California* (Sacramento, 1953).

needs) and coverage of the locally imposed taxes varies somewhat. Some tendency exists for them to follow the state sales tax base, though not all localities are equally concerned with this addition to compliance ease. State administration legislation requires base similarity as a price of state administration, yet previously existing authorization continues, and only a few larger cities have chosen state administration.

2. Questions arise about the extent of municipal authority over certain types of transaction.
3. A few county taxes do not apply in areas subject to a city tax (or apply at reduced rates) but some do, bringing the effective sales tax rate to 7% in some areas. Not only can the rate structure become complicated, but the reward for avoiding the local tax can be high, leading to tax-induced shifts in retail purchases. Jefferson County (Birmingham) has state-, city-, and county-administered sales taxes. Up to one-half of the city tax rate can be applied to its police jurisdiction—an area within three miles of the corporation limit in cities with population of 6,000 or more and within one and one-half miles of the corporation limit for smaller cities.
4. The locally administered taxes, based on licensing powers, are interpreted as vendor levies, and the amount collected by the retailers to compensate for the tax is included in the taxable price. Recent state legislation has attempted a shift to the use of true sales taxes but with little impact so far.
5. Enforcement effort varies widely among the localities administering their own taxes, with the result that the certainty of tax liability depends on the jurisdiction.
6. Use taxes apply to both interstate and intrastate purchases brought into localities. Hence, the state and local use tax bases do not coincide, producing both administrative and compliance difficulty. Not all localities, however, levy use taxes.
7. Rates vary within localities, with special treatment for purchases of automobiles, machinery, and farm equipment—although not in a uniform pattern.

In addition to the difficulties directly related to local administration, liability for local taxes, state-administered as well as locally administered, is determined by the jurisdiction to which delivery, if any, is made. Such a situs rule makes vendor compliance more difficult and potentially increases the demand for delivery. Allocation problems can become serious as the system becomes more unified, and vendors actually are required to determine liability. Many localities have pledged local sales tax revenue for retirement of bonded indebtedness. These pledges make any change in the taxes (including state administration) difficult.

The 6% combined rate applies to over 70% of the population. The rate reaches 7% in Montgomery, but there is neither city nor county tax in Gadsden; the 6% rate split variously between city and county applies in other major cities.

Alaska. Localities in Alaska had sales taxes at the time of statehood, and this specific authorization has continued. As the state has no sales tax, coordination is between borough and city only. The Anchorage area, the most populous portion of the state, has no sales tax. Many problems of sales allocation, sales deflection, and liability determination are reduced by the low population density where the taxes are used. City rates range from 1% to 5%, with 2% and 3% as most common. Borough rates range from 1% to 4%. Revenues are frequently earmarked for specific purposes (often hospital facilities), and borough rates apply in cities with sales taxes. Similarities appear among the taxes (food sales are taxed, medical services are exempt, prescription medicine is often exempt). Exemption of business purchases is limited, and most taxes apply to a broad range of services. As no state tax layer is common to all localities, differences are not surprising. Coordination is simplified since the retailer must be familiar only with local regulations. Some localities have use taxes. Since 1972, boroughs have been required to collect any sales and use tax levied by a city within its boundaries. The city tax must apply to the same base as the borough tax. Thus, many city taxes are piggybacked. In the absence of a state tax, further coordination is difficult. Some Alaska localities have granted exemption to purchases by older residents—identification cards are provided and purchases made by cardholders are not subject to tax. Vendors must then report such purchases with their return. The problems with compliance and administration are substantial.

Arizona. Cities in Arizona possess broad home rule licensing powers that translate into general sales taxes patterned after the state sales tax. All city taxes were initially locally administered, but state collection was authorized in 1972. In the early period, the state administered only taxes levied by the small cities, with the larger cities administering their own taxes. By April 1982, fifteen cities were administering their own tax and fifty-two cities were using state administration; ten years ago, all Arizona city sales taxes were locally administered. Major cities usually follow the broad state coverage (although not all follow state exemption of food and there are varied treatments of apartment rentals), thus reducing the major compliance, administration, and coordination problems found in other sales tax states with local administration. Liability is vendor-based. Tucson exempted food for a number of years prior to state exemption and still does; Phoenix exempted food for a while, restoring coverage to food at a charter amendment election that repealed the second percent of the city sales tax rate (the rate was 2% from November 1976 to February 1977).

A second lack of uniformity in the local taxes is the application of use taxes in some cities (including Phoenix) but not everywhere. Lack of conformity is not surprising when the taxes are locally administered on the authority of local licensing provisions. The Arizona League of Cities and Towns has attempted some coordination (by providing a model local transaction privilege tax ordinance patterned after the state tax), but further unification awaits state action, which is limited by local home rule charters. The state would prefer state administration for efficiency and uniformity, but the cities resist it because they wish autonomy of rates and bases and because they believe they do a more effective job. Cities particularly fear the state will reduce their base coverage. The cities and the state do exchange information and there appears to be no municipal double taxation. As opposed to the practice in other states, larger Arizona cities, especially Phoenix and Tucson, conduct substantial auditing programs to ensure tax compliance.

Colorado. Numerous cities in Colorado have used home rule authority to levy and administer local sales taxes. Along with its own tax, the state collects county sales taxes, the Denver area Regional Transit District tax, city sales taxes levied under specific (not home rule) authority, and sales taxes of home rule cities that choose that option. Since nuisances are obvious, the state has attempted to encourage administration of all local sales taxes, even providing administration at no charge to the locality, to obtain greater uniformity among the taxes. The attempt has not been completely successful, as a large number of cities retain local administration. Several forces contribute to that situation. Localities with state administration are limited to use taxes on building materials and motor vehicles only; home rule taxes can have use taxes on all purchases. Localities have feared that revenue return from the state will be erratic in comparison to the immediate revenue from local administration. Moreover, localities must adopt state administration by referendum, a requirement not present for local administration by home rule cities. Finally, localities lose some control over items included in the sales tax base with state administration.

Cities now issue their own licenses, collect their own deliquent accounts, establish their own field audit programs, and even decide what vendor discount to allow, if any (they range up to 5% of collections). Some municipalities tie their taxing ordinances to the state sales and use tax, thus automatically following state exemptions, but not all do. Municipalities disagree on the taxability of sales of food for at-home consumption, prescriptions and prosthetic devices, alcoholic beverages, livestock feed, farm implements, and so on. Boulder even provides a food tax refund system to reduce sales tax regressivity, a rarity patterned after the credit process used in some states (including Colorado until 1979).[5] Without constitutional revision, state administration cannot be required. It can spread further only by local option.

Illinois. In 1981, following failure of the city of Chicago and the state to agree on additional aid for the Regional Transit Authority system, Chicago

---

[5]Persons who live in Boulder for the entire fiscal year may file for the refund of $4.67 from the city. An additional refund is provided those over sixty-five years of age and the blind.

TABLE 10.3 Administration of Louisiana Local Sales Taxes

Taxing Unit	Self	Parish	Parish School Board
Parish (14)	43		29
Parish or City School Board (49)	67	8	4
City (96)	81	1	11

Source: Compiled from "Local Sales Tax Administration in Louisiana," *PAR Analysis*, no. 235, February 1979 (Baton Rouge: Public Affairs Research Council of Louisiana).

imposed a 1% sales tax under home rule powers. It also imposed a separate 1% tax on virtually all services, but this was held to be unconstitutional by the Illinois Supreme Court. The 1% sales tax, with the same base as the state levy (except that food and prescription medicines are exempt), is administered by the city, quite separate from the 1% state-collected retailers occupation (sales) tax. Chicago is the only city in the country to have both a state administered and locally administered sales tax on the same transactions. The state revenue department has encountered some difficulty with vendors sending their city returns and payments to the state.

Louisiana.   Cities, parishes (counties), and school boards (city and parish) in Louisiana have, initially by specific authorization, the right to levy locally collected sales taxes.[6] Some parish taxes are not collected in component cities that use sales taxes, but this pattern is not the rule. The maximum combined local rate is 3%, or a combined 6% state-local rate. A 1978 law repealed an earlier prohibition against levying local sales taxes on items exempt from the state sales tax, although most taxes continue to copy the state base.[7] Local taxes do, however, tax food and prescription drug purchases; the state does not. Advance collection at the wholesaler level, a feature of the state tax, is not generally permitted the localities. Most city rates are 1%; parish taxes are 1% or 2%. Municipalities often have no rigorous audit program, though New Orleans has an extensive system which duplicates the state audit force. New Orleans audit coverage has, however, declined dramatically over the past ten years. The state has shown little interest in administering the local taxes, and the localities apparently are satisfied with local administration, evidently because of a fear of state interference and a reduction in local tax collecting jobs. The state does share information (new regis-

[6]Localities originally received individual authorization, but authorization changed to class of locality. The 1974 constitution authorized local sales taxes for all major local governments.
[7]"Local Sales Tax Administration in Louisiana," *PAR Analysis*, No. 235, February 1979 Baton Rouge (Public Affairs Research Council of Louisiana, 1979), p. 2.

Administering Unit (%)			
City	*Joint City-Parish or -Parish School Board*	*Sheriff*	*Private Bookkeeper*
7	7	14	0
8	4	6	2
1	5	0	0

trations, etc.) with the localities and a number of localities administer sales taxes levied by other units, as table 10.3 shows. Of localities for which data are available, however, 73% administer their own tax.

Minnesota. Minnesota cities received authorization for local sales taxes in 1953, but no cities enacted the tax until Duluth voters approved a charter revision levying a 1% tax starting January 1, 1970. (Legislation in 1981 canceled authority for any additional adoptions.) The tax generally corresponds with the state tax, except that the city does not tax transient lodging accommodations and does provide a refund of all sales tax paid by low-income individuals sixty-five years of age and over who have lived the entire year in the city. The refund—based either on documentation from accumulated receipts or, more frequently, on amounts taken from a formula prescribed by the city—is by annual application.

The state could collect the tax, but the city has chosen local administration of both the sales tax and its compensating use tax, which applies to both interstate and intrastate purchases. The desire for continued application of a use tax was an important factor in the failure to switch to state administration. Duluth is trying to have the state secrecy statute revised to have access to state audit information. The city assumes it can accomplish tax administration of higher quality and at lower cost than the state.

Features of Administering Locally Administered Sales Taxes

Actual operation of the local taxes cannot be examined in the same detailed fashion as the states. Tables 10.4 and 10.5 give some basic information about a list of larger communities administering their own taxes (all were estimated to have 1975 populations above 10,000). Phoenix, Denver, and New Orleans are the largest cities in the group. Phoenix has more registered vendors than the five states with the fewest vendors (Idaho, Nevada, North Dakota, Rhode Island, and Vermont). Denver and New Orleans, together

TABLE 10.4 Local Administration of Local Sales Taxes: Accounts, Audits, and Delinquencies in 1979 (population greater than 10,000 in 1975)

State/Locality	Number Sales & Use Tax Accounts	Account Turnover (%)	Employees		Auditors	Accounts per Auditor
			Full Time	Part Time		
Alabama						
Birmingham	6,000		2	20	7	857
Decatur	1,500	13	5	1	0	—
Fairfield	318	8	0	4	1	318
Jasper	490	4	3	0	0	—
Mobile	4,000		12	4	7	571
Opelika	630	4	1	0	0	—
Alaska						
Kenai Peninsula	2,700	11	2	1	1	2,700
Ketchikan-Gateway	1,100	5	1	3	1	1,100
Sitka	750	7	0	1	0	—
Arizona						
Chandler	1,750	20	1	1	1	1,750
Mesa	6,000	33	7	0	4	1,500
Phoenix	33,597	22	59	0	29	1,159
Prescott	1,425	34	2	1	1.5	950
Tempe	5,462	22	6	5	4	1,366
Tucson	13,763	29	40	0	15	918
Colorado						
Arvada	2,166	9	4	0	2	1,083
Aurora	2,900	7	4	0	2	1,450
Boulder	3,136	26	3	3	1	3,136
Colorado Springs	4,500	6	12	0	3	1,500
Commerce City	1,457	6	4	0	2	729
Denver	16,000	25	28	0	19	842
Durango	1,900	11	1	1	0	—
Englewood	2,700	11	2	2	1	2,700
Fort Collins	1,562	6	1	0	0	—
Littleton	1,100	18	1	1	1	1,100
Longmont	1,350	27	2	0	1	1,350
Northglenn	699	14	2	0	1	699
Pueblo	5,000	12	9	1	5	1,000
Thornton	791	11	2	0	1	791
Illinois						
Chicago (1982)			28	0	15	
Louisiana						
Abbeville	775	4	3	0	0	—
Baton Rouge	8,500	7	17	7	4	2,125
Bogalusa	650	5	1	0	0	—
Bossier City	2,500	13	5	0	2	1,250
Eunice	1,100	3	2	0	0	—
Hammond	850	18	0	2	0	—
Lafayette Parish	5,411	8	7	0	2	2,706
Lake Charles	2,600		5	1	3	667
Natchitoches	670	15	2	0	0	—
New Orleans	14,278	21	79	4	19	751

Number of Accounts Audited	Audit Recovery (% of Total)	Accounts Typically Delinquent (%)	Vendor Compensation for Compliance (%)	Approximate Collections per Capita per 1% Sales Tax Rate ($)
430	1.3	3.0	1.5	52.86
—	—	3.0	3.0	108.48
	0	2.0	1.5	57.79
—	—	2.0	5.0	84.28
24	1.83	10.0	3.0	47.07
—	—	0.5	a	37.51
20			3.0	53.51
20	1.82	9.0	0.5	
—	—	10.0	b	61.86
24	2.5	7.0	0	69.12
200	2.5	11.0	0	95.39
463	5.35	30.0	0	93.55
29	2.5	21.0	0	78.78
115	2.0	15.0	0	72.10
590	1.8	5.0	0	63.30
186	1.0	10.0	3.0	29.58
314	less than 1	10.0	1.5	56.39
55	0.34	7.0–8.0	1.5	76.08
300	2.0	5.0–10.0	3.0	57.91
31	3.6	13.7	2.0[c]	79.34
1,042	3.0	15.0	2.0	62.64
—	—	20.0	5.0	116.82
35	less than 1	10.0–15	1.6	61.80
25	0.42	5.0	3.0	70.97
100	2.85	2.0–5.0	2.5	44.20
0	—		3.0	60.97
50	3.0	10.0	1.0	35.84
150	3.3	less than 1	3.0	39.75
10	1.1	8.0	1.5	71.69
			2.0	
0	0	1.0	2.0	54.69
86	less than 1	20.0	1.0	75.91
0	0	20.0	1.0	26.59
30	3.5	0.2	1.5	55.08
0	2.0	10.0	2.0	60.94
0	—		1.5	93.36
0	5.0	2.0	2.0	
64[d]	2.0[e]	3.0	1.0	
0	0	10.0	2.0	51.77
350	1.0–2.0	18.0	1.0[f]	34.00

TABLE 10.4 (*continued*)

State/Locality	Number Sales & Use Tax Accounts	Account Turnover (%)	Employees		Auditors	Accounts per Auditor
			Full Time	Part Time		
Rapides Parish	2,602	19	7	0	0	—
Slidell	850	28	2	0	1	850
Sulphur	805	20	2	0	0	—
Thibodaux	900	6	2	0	0	—
Minnesota						
Duluth	2,600	12	5	0	1	2,600

[a] 5% on first $100, 2% over $100.
[b] 3% if pay mo. ($100 maximum).
[c] on sales tax only.

with Tucson, have almost as many registrants as Vermont. Only fragmentary data are available for the new Chicago tax, but Chicago is the largest city of the group.

Audit Staffs. Relative to the number of accounts, audit staffs compare favorably for the larger cities in the group (outside of those in Alabama) with those employed by the states. The audit recovery figure is comparable. Most smaller towns in these states, however, do not have auditors at all, and few of them could afford to hire a full time auditor, given the number of accounts. Even some smaller ones on the list are beginning an audit program.

Delinquency Percentage. The percentage of vendors delinquent each period is likewise comparable to the state figures—but with substantial variation, from 10% or more in Birmingham, Baton Rouge, Lake Charles, Alexandria, and Tucson, to 1% in Flagstaff. Techniques similar to those of the states are used in dealing with delinquents.

Return Mailing. Localities typically mail returns to accounts on the same cycle as returns are due. A small group mails packets of returns at less frequent intervals. It includes the Alabama cities, Prescott, Bogalusa, Bossier City, Eunice, and Sulphur. Returns are typically computer addressed. Exceptions included addressographing in Durango, Abbeville, Eunice, and Natchitoches and typing in Fairfield, Jasper, and Opelika.

Intervals for Filing Returns. Monthly, except for Kenai Peninsula and Ketchikan-Gateway boroughs in Alaska. The cities generally permit less fre-

Number of Accounts Audited	Audit Recovery (% of Total)	Accounts Typically Delinquent (%)	Vendor Compensation for Compliance (%)	Approximate Collections per Capita per 1% Sales Tax Rate ($)
0	0	10.0	2.0	
0	0	16.0	2.0	66.88
1	less than 1	less than 1	1.0	57.34
0	1.0	4.0	2.0	66.37
10	0.3	5.0	0	47.66

[d] 4 field, 60 office.
[e] 6 mos.
[f] 2% wholesale.

quent filing for small accounts. Exceptions are the Alabama cities, Prescott, Tucson, Bogalusa, Eunice, New Orleans, and Thibodaux. Duluth even provides special seasonal filing status.

Return Retention.   Returns are kept for widely varying periods. Phoenix retains returns only a month (it has microfilm); some cities keep returns forever. Filing tends to be by account number, somewhat more frequently than the batch tendency of state administration. Only a small number of localities—Mesa, Phoenix, Colorado Springs, Abbeville, Baton Rouge, Bossier City, Lake Charles, New Orleans, and Duluth—microfilm returns.

Vendor Compensation.   Generally provided, except in Alaska, Arizona, and Minnesota. The discounts range from 1% to 5% of collections.

Computer Equipment.   Electronic data processing has spread to all but the smallest jurisdictions. Several larger cities even use installations comparable to those of the states. These include Chicago, Birmingham, Denver, Lafayette Parish, New Orleans, and Duluth (IBM 370) and Baton Rouge (two NCR Century 200). Prescott, Commerce City, and Northglenn report use of outside data processing on contract. Only Fairfield, Jasper, Opelika, Abbeville, Eunice, and Natchitoches, none with a population over 25,000, report no EDP equipment used for sales tax operations.

Return Forms.   Of the cities in the group examined, only Duluth uses a card return form (figure 10.1). The remainder use paper forms, often with some taxpayer information preprinted by computer (figure 10.2). This pattern coincides with prevailing state sales tax administration.

TABLE 10.5 Local Administration of Local Sales Taxes: Return Mailing, Filing, and Retention in 1979 (Population greater than 10,000 in 1975)[a]

State/Locality	Return Mailing Interval	Filing Frequency	Return Retention		
			Period (Yrs.)	Filing	Microfilm
Alabama					
Birmingham	q	m	5.0	batch	no
Decatur	q	m	10.0	account	
Fairfield	sa	m	indef.	batch	no
Jasper	sa	m	10.0	account	no
Mobile	sa	m	10.0	account	no
Opelika	q	m	10.0		
Alaska					
Kenai Peninsula	q	q	4.0	batch	no
Ketchikan-Gateway	q	q	7.0	account	no
Sitka	q, m	q, m	7.0	account	no
Arizona					
Chandler	m, q	m, q	3.0	account	no
Mesa	m, q	m, q	3.0	account	yes
Phoenix	m, q, a	m, q, a	0.5	batch	yes
Prescott	sa	m	10.0	batch	no
Tempe	m, q	m, q, a	3.0	account	no
Tucson	m	m	10.0	batch	no
Colorado					
Arvada	m, q, a	m, q, a	3.0		
Aurora	m	m, q, a	3.0	account	no
Boulder	m	m, q, sa, a	indef.	batch	soon
Colorado Springs	m, q	m, q	7.0	account	yes
Commerce City	license choice	m, q, sa, a	3.0	account	no
Denver	m, q, a	m, q, a	3.0	batch	no
Durango	m, q	m, q	4.0	month	no
Englewood	m, q, a	m, q, a	3.0	account	no
Fort Collins	m, q	m, q	4.0	account	no
Littleton	m, q	m, q	3.0	account	no
Longmont	m, q, a	m, q, a	12.0		
Northglenn	m, q, sa, a	m, q, sa, a	perm.	account	no
Pueblo	m	m, q, sa, a	3.0	account	no
Thornton	m, q	m, q, a	6.0	account	no
Illinois					
Chicago (1981)	m	w, m, q, a	perm.	batch	no
Louisiana					
Abbeville	m, q, sa, a	m, q, sa, a	6.0	batch	yes
Baton Rouge	m	m, q	7.0	batch	yes
Bogalusa	q	m	5.0	batch	no
Bossier City	sa	m, q, sa, a	4.0	account	yes
Eunice	q	m	5.0		
Hammond	m, q, sa	m, q, sa	3.0	batch	no
Lafayette Parish	m	m, q, a	3.0	account	no
Lake Charles	m, q	m, q, a	7.0	account	yes
Natchitoches	m, q	m, q	perm.	account	no
New Orleans	m	m	[a]	account	yes

TABLE 10.5 (*continued*)

State/Locality	Return Mailing Interval	Filing Frequency	Return Retention Period (Yrs.)	Filing	Microfilm
Rapides Parish	m, q	m, q	4.0	account	no
Slidell	m, q, sa, a	m, q, sa, a	6.0	account	no
Sulphur	q	m, q, sa, a		batch	
Thibodaux	m	m	3.0	account	no
Minnesota					
Duluth	m, q, a	m, q, a	perm.	account	yes

w = weekly
m = monthly
q = quarterly
sa = semiannually
a = annually

a 4 active, 3–6 inactive

Apparently, several larger cities are administering their local taxes reasonably well, but smaller cities rarely have effective audit systems. A city with fewer than 5,000 accounts (perhaps 100,000 population) is not likely to find it economical to use efficient computer systems in processing the tax or to use an audit staff effectively. A nonindustrial city with fewer than 1,500 accounts probably cannot even make full-time effective use of even one auditor.

General Experience with Local Operation

Localities are frequently reluctant to surrender their freedom to collect their own taxes once local collection has developed, even with readily available state administration. Reasons differ according to institutional situations in the states, but several are dominant. Localities are frequently reluctant to surrender the autonomy inherent in local administration: choice of base, structure, and rates; selection of administrators and enforcement personnel sometimes by patronage; and retention of revenue by the locality of collection and with no danger of redistribution. These obstacles were successfully overcome by New York and Virginia as state administration replaced local administration with the adoption of a state sales tax, but in Alabama, Arizona, and Colorado they are not yet overcome, despite state efforts.

Evils of local administration in sales tax states are obvious from experience in the previously enumerated states, as well as in California before state administration. The most troublesome effects are:
1. Tax administration is duplicated without gain. If local administration is conducted seriously (as it often is not), two sets of officials conduct the

JUL-T1 (REV. 2/79)

CITY OF DULUTH, MINNESOTA
DEPARTMENT OF FINANCE AND RECORDS

1% SALES AND USE TAX RETURN

READ INSTRUCTIONS BEFORE COMPLETING RETURN

IF NO TAXABLE TRANSACTIONS WERE MADE DURING THE PERIOD, WRITE "NONE" ON LINES 1 AND 4, SIGN AND RETURN TO DEPARTMENT OF FINANCE AND RECORDS, DULUTH, MINN. 55802

SALES & USE TAX PERMIT NUMBER

PERIOD OF RETURN

DATE DUE:

MAILING ADDRESS

LOCATION OF THE BUSINESS TO BE REPORTED ON THIS RETURN

I hereby declare under the penalties of criminal liability for willfully making a false return, that this return has been examined by me and to the best of my knowledge and belief is true and complete for the period stated.

SIGNATURE

TITLE_____ DATE_____

DD-T 17664-OR3

DO NOT WRITE IN THIS SPACE

IF YOU USE THE ACTUAL TAX METHOD (SEE INSTRUCTIONS) CHECK HERE ☐

1.	GROSS SALES ◆	
2.	DEDUCTIONS (Enter from line 23) ◆	
3.	NET SALES (Line 1 minus line 2)	
4.	PURCHASES SUBJECT TO USE TAX ◆	
5.	TOTAL TAXABLE AMOUNT (Line 3 plus line 4)	
6.	TOTAL TAX DUE (1% of line 5) ◆	
7.	A PENALTY	
	B INTEREST	
8.	TOTAL AMOUNT DUE (Line 6 plus lines 7A & 7B) ◆	

MAKE CHECKS PAYABLE TO: "CITY OF DULUTH"

MAIL TO: DEPT. OF FINANCE & RECORDS
SALES TAX DIVISION
110 CITY HALL
DULUTH, MINN. 55802

FIGURE 10.1 SALES TAX RETURN, DULUTH

collection, audit, and enforcement programs for the same set of transactions. At best, administration is duplicated; at worst, one type of tax liability approaches a free-will contribution. Further, taxpayers may be more willing to try to cheat the locality than the state. Particular vendors may be audited by a number of different local jurisdictions.

2. The tax bases are nonuniform, both between state and locality and among localities. Not only does this divergence complicate enforcement but it also is a nuisance for both vendor and consumer in the compliance with tax laws.

3. In the absence of state coordination, use of sales taxes by different local jurisdictions creates the likelihood of overlapping tax rates, resulting in higher effective rates. The higher effective rate in turn increases the danger of sales loss and retailer migration from the higher tax to lower tax areas frequently surrounding sales tax cities. Although this situation can occur with state-administered taxes, it is more likely to occur when there is less coordination.

4. Table 10.6 summarizes policies with regard to overlap. Determining which jurisdiction taxes a particular transaction can be a substantial problem in the absence of unified tax laws and a central administrative authority. Without exchange of information, intrastate business transacted across taxing jurisdictions can go untaxed or, if use taxes are not coordinated, purchases can be taxed twice.

5. Local administration reduces the possibility of redistribution of sales tax revenue. The jurisdiction possessing the taxing power is unlikely to grant funds to contiguous governments (counties to cities, cities and counties to school districts, etc.), and further grants of taxing authority to governments needing funds serve to complicate administration still more. Local administration is, hence, a generally unsatisfactory method of financing local activity when more than one local government type has substantial revenue need.

STATE ADMINISTRATION OF LOCAL SALES TAXES

The Advisory Commission on Intergovernmental Relations has observed:

> The use of the same kind of tax by two or more levels of government is not poor public policy in and of itself. It becomes poor policy only when one level of government uses a particular tax without regard for the use made of it by another and in such a way that (a) the cumulative tax take of all governments does gross violence to an acceptable pattern of tax burden distribution, and (b) the overlapping is accompanied by inefficient use of tax enforcement resources and needless taxpayer compliance burdens.[8]

[8]Advisory Commission on Intergovernmental Relations, *Tax Overlapping in the United States: 1964* (Washington, D.C., 1964), p. 3.

CITY AND COUNTY OF DENVER
DEPARTMENT OF REVENUE · 144 WEST COLFAX AVENUE
DENVER COLORADO 80202 ·

SALES, USE AND LODGERS TAX RETURN

ACCOUNT	CK	P.E.D.	S	U	L	TYPE	AUDITOR	PART	FOR PERIOD ENDING	DUE DATE	OCCUPATIONAL TAX ACCOUNT	PHONE NUMBER

BUSINESS LOCATION

LINE	ALLOWABLE DEDUCTIONS	COLUMN S SALES TAX	LINE	COLUMN L LODGERS TAX
01	SALES OF SERVICES		01	
02	SALES TO OTHER LICENSED DEALERS FOR RESALE		02	
03	SALES OF GOODS SHIPPED OR DE- LIVERED OUT OF DENVER		03	
04	SALES TO GOV'T., CHARITIES, OR RELIGIOUS INSTITUTIONS		04	
05	OTHER EXEMPT SALES (SUPPORT WITH SCHEDULE)		05	
06	RETURNED GOODS (ON WHICH TAX WAS PREVIOUSLY PAID)		06	
07	BAD DEBTS (OPEN ACCOUNT SALES ON WHICH TAX WAS PREVIOUSLY PAID)		07	
08	TRADE – INS FOR TAXABLE RESALE WITHIN COLORADO		08	
A	TOTAL DEDUCTIONS (ENTER ON LINE "C" BELOW)		A	

MAKE REMITTANCE PAYABLE TO :

MANAGER OF REVENUE
CITY AND COUNTY OF DENVER

DO NOT STAPLE CHECK TO RETURN
DO NOT SEND CASH OR STAMPS

IMPORTANT INFORMATION ON REVERSE SIDE

CONSUMER USE TAX SCHEDULE ON REVERSE SIDE

LINE		COLUMN S SALES TAX	LINE	COLUMN L LODGERS TAX	LINE	COLUMN U USE TAX
09	GROSS SALES AND SERVICES (COLUMN 'U' = PURCHASES)		09		09	
10	BAD DEBTS COLLECTED WHICH WERE PREVIOUSLY DEDUCTED		10		10	

	Description		
B	TOTAL LINES 9 & 10	B	B
C	ALLOWABLE DEDUCTIONS (ENTER AMOUNT FROM LINE 'A' ABOVE)	C	C
D	NET TAXABLE SALES (SUBTRACT LINE 'C' FROM LINE 'B'	D	D
E	AMOUNT OF TAX (COLUMN S=3% OF LINE D) (COLUMN L=4% OF LINE D) (COLUMN U=3% OF LINE 9)	E	E
11	EXCESS TAX COLLECTED OVER AMOUNT ENTERED ON LINE 'E'.	11	11
F	TOTAL TAX LINE E PLUS LINE 11	F	F
12	VENDORS FEE (2% OF LINE 'F')	12	12
G	TOTAL LINE 'F' MINUS LINE 12.	G	G
13	GOODS PURCHASED WITHOUT DENVER TAX AND USED OR CONSUMED $ ____ X 3% =	13	13
H	NET TOTAL TAXES DUE AND PAYABLE (IN COLUMNS 'S' & 'L' ENTER TOTAL OF LINE 'G' + '13') (IN COLUMN 'U' ENTER AMOUNT FROM LINE 'E')	H	H
14	LATE FILING FEE PENALTY (10% OF LINE 'H')	14	14
15	LATE FILING FEE INTEREST (1% PER MONTH OF LINE 'H')	15	15
16	CREDITS (INCLUDE EXPLANATION)	16	16
17	ADJUSTMENTS (FOR SALES TAX OFFICE USE ONLY)	17	17
18	TOTAL (LINE 'H' PLUS LINES '14' & '15', MINUS LINE '16')	18	18
I	TOTAL (ADD LINE '18' OF COLUMNS 'S', 'L' AND 'U' AND ENTER TOTAL HERE)		I
19	LICENSE RENEWAL FEE (IF REMITTED WITH THIS RETURN)		19
K	TOTAL REMITTANCE (LINE '19' PLUS LINE 'I')		K

I HEREBY CERTIFY UNDER PENALTY OF PERJURY. THAT THE STATEMENTS MADE HEREIN ARE TO THE BEST OF MY KNOWLEDGE TRUE AND CORRECT.

SIGNATURE: _____ TITLE: _____ DATE: _____

RETURN THIS COPY WITH YOUR REMITTANCE

DSD 7509 R.E. (1977)

FIGURE 10.2 SALES TAX RETURN, DENVER

TABLE 10.6 Methods of Dealing with City-County Rate Overlapping and Distribution of Local Sales Tax Revenue[a]

State	Local Taxing Jurisdictions	Method of Local Coordination	Revenue Redistribution
Alabama	cities, counties	overlap[b]	none
Alaska	cities, boroughs	cooperative administration	none
Arizona	cities	exclusive authority	none
Arkansas	cities	exclusive authority	none
California	cities, counties	local credit	none
Colorado	cities, counties	maximum local rate	sometimes: counties can agree to division according to point of collection, motor vehicle registrations, or other contractual basis.
Florida	counties	exclusive authority	none
Georgia	joint city-county	nonoverlapping jurisdictions	yes: agreement, according to other revenue
Illinois	cities, counties	nonoverlapping jurisdictions	none
Kansas	cities, counties	partial county precedence	yes: half of county tax divided between counties and cities by tangible property levies, half divided by population.
Louisiana	cities, parishes	some cooperative administration[c]	none
Minnesota	cities	exclusive authority	none
Mississippi	cities	exclusive authority	none
Missouri	cities, counties	overlap[d]	none[d]
Nebraska	cities	exclusive authority	none
Nevada	counties	exclusive authority	yes: population basis split among cities or between county and city.

State	Jurisdictions	Authority	Distribution
New Mexico	cities, counties	overlap	none
New York	cities, counties	maximum local rate	yes: on assessed valuation or other agreed on distribution basis with school districts, cities, towns, and villages.
North Carolina	counties	exclusive authority	yes: split with cities on the basis of either population or property tax levy.
Ohio	counties	exclusive authority	none
Oklahoma	cities	exclusive authority	none
South Dakota	cities	exclusive authority	none
Tennessee	cities, counties	maximum local rate, county precedence	yes: half split according to property tax for school purposes, half by collections.[e]
Utah	cities, counties	local credit	no[f]
Virginia	independent cities, counties	nonoverlapping jurisdictions	yes: county tax divided with towns on basis of school age population.
Washington	cities, counties	local credit, county precedence	no
Wisconsin	counties	exclusive authority	yes: all revenue to cities, villages, and towns; half divided by population and half divided by equalized assessed value.
Wyoming	counties	exclusive authority	yes: divided between county and its cities and towns according to population.

[a] Transit district taxes excluded—they fully overlap any other local sales taxes.

[b] Several counties do not apply their sales tax within cities with sales taxes (or at half the normal rate in police jurisdictions).

[c] Several parishes do not apply their sales tax within cities with sales taxes.

[d] Except in St. Louis County where the county tax supersedes all city taxes.

[e] The latter half may be divided according to some other contractual agreement.

[f] Cities and county may contract for distribution on a basis other than point of collection.

A review of prevailing practices shows that some states avoid these problems more successfully than do others. State administration provides no guarantee that difficulties with overlapping use of the sales tax will disappear.

State-Administered Systems by State

The use of state administrative systems for local sales taxes is a direct response to the most severe overlapping problems. The locally imposed state-collected supplement to the state sales tax base has proved an attractive option for localities and is available for use in twenty-six states.[9] Each of the state-administered systems will be examined separately.

Alabama. As noted, several Alabama localities collect their own sales taxes, but over 260 cities and 40 counties have state-administered taxes. State collection for the cities is voluntary because they have existing licensing powers; many counties tax through enabling legislation that requires state administration. Those with state collection must use the state base, but not all employ use taxes and there are differences in rates applied to farm machinery, motor vehicles, and machinery in mining and manufacturing. Liability is established by the place of delivery.

The state charges localities a cost of collection figure calculated in one of two ways. Cities and newer county adoptions are charged the lesser of an apportioned account charge (approximately $4.85 per account per month) or 5% for units with population less than 5,000 or 10% for units with population above 5,000. Older county adoptions (approximately six counties) are charged a percentage of the cost of collecting the state tax (approximately 1.6%).

State officials report that the local taxes create substantial audit trouble, sufficient to swamp all other problems with the state sales tax.

Arizona. Cities in Arizona have applied sales taxes on the basis of charter licensing powers for more than thirty years. State administration was authorized in 1972; with few exceptions, only the largest cities continue to administer their own tax. The state does not charge for the collection service. Cities can retain taxes on items such as food exempted by the state; one city (Guadalupe) taxes food at a rate lower than it applies to other purchases. Use taxes are permitted in cities with state administration, but only three (Snowflake, Page, and Holbrook) levy them. There is no vendor compensation for either state or local portions of liability.

Arkansas. Two cities—Texarkana, since 1968, and Siloam Springs, since 1979—levied 1% sales taxes as of January 1981. The latter tax is on the

---

[9]Excluding Minnesota, where the option is not taken, and Mississippi, where only a single city can use the sales tax.

basis of special legislation; the Texarkana tax is on authorization to first- and second-class cities with population of *not* more than 40,000 that qualify as model cities under the federal Demonstration Cities and Metropolitan Development Act of 1966. (There is unused authority, granted in 1977, to first-class cities with a historic district.)[10] There is no use tax in Texarkana, but one applies in Siloam Springs, even though state officials doubt that it can be effectively enforced. The local base is the same as the state sales tax base in the city; the state base in Texarkana, however, follows the Texas tax base by law. Revenue is returned monthly, less a 2% collection fee.

Legislation in 1981 added general authority to cities of first or second class and incorporated towns to levy 0.5% or 1% sales and use taxes on voter approval, with the provision that cities may rebate any tax in excess of $25 on a single transaction. Other legislation that year provided similar authority for 1% county sales and use taxes. Under those laws, four counties and twelve cities apply taxes, all at 1%. Further 1981 legislation added authority for an additional 1% tax for counties, cities, and towns, but this power has not been used. All authorizations are for state-administered taxes.

California.   All California cities and counties currently use uniform state-administered supplements to the state sales tax, as do three rapid transit districts.[11] The Bay Area Rapid Transit District, Santa Clara County Transit District, and Santa Cruz Metropolitan Transit District all levy 0.5% taxes; other transit districts have not used authorized power to levy. Initially, cities could impose and collect their own taxes on licensing authority. Chaos was the result as both retailers and consumers were caught in the flurry of various rates, rules, regulations, and administrative confusion. Attempts to establish state administration were blocked by local autonomy objections until 1956. The Bradley-Burns Uniform Local Sales and Use Tax Law of that year authorized counties to levy a 1% countywide sales and use tax (increased to 1.25% in 1972) if tax coverage matched the state tax and if the state collected the tax. Cities could adopt taxes with rates up to 1%, credited against the county tax if the tax matched the state tax and if it was state-collected. The share of collections within a city received by the county was subject to city-county negotiation. Many cities immediately entered the system, and others entered gradually until coverage was universal in mid-1962.[12] The legislation

---

[10] A 1977 law provides that a city or town divided by a state line from an incorporated city or town in an adjoining state that does not levy an income tax may, on voter approval, impose an additional sales tax in that city. Then, taxpayers in that city are not subject to Arkansas net income tax on income from that city or from business activities there or in the one across the border. Texarkana has done this. This extra sales tax is in addition to the local sales tax rate. The rate applicable in 1981 is 5% (1% local, 1% special state, 3% regular state).

[11] From October 1, 1968, to March 31, 1969, the City of Los Angeles administered an additional 1% tax. Expulsion of the city from the Bradley-Burns system would have resulted if the tax had continued beyond the termination date.

[12] Development is outlined in the paper by R.B. Welch, "Two and a Half Years of Progress in Integration," *Proceedings of the National Tax Association for 1958,* pp. 128–39.

eliminated many nuisances of local administration, made the sales tax base essentially uniform throughout the state, and made the sales tax rate the same throughout each county and throughout the state when the system was accepted by all counties. The 1969 legislature extended the local sales tax system by authorizing rapid transit districts to levy taxes at 0.5%. These taxes do not coincide in all respects with the other local sales taxes. Deliveries outside the district are exempt. Use tax applies to deliveries into the district from in-state points as well as those out-of-state.

The California plan has several attractive characteristics:

1. Until the development of the transit district legislation, the sales tax rate was uniform across the state, thus avoiding locational distortions. The previous locally administered system had produced substantial rate differentials and retailer complaint.
2. A single return is required for submission of sales tax that is due state, city, county, and transit district. Not only is retailer compliance simplified, but also state audit and enforcement readily serves for the local taxes. For the city and county taxes, all sales are presumed to occur at the location of the retailer, not the place of delivery. This provision eliminates the tax incentive for delivery demand and the necessity for retailers to determine the tax liability and tax allocation for each delivered item. The spread of local sales taxes has rendered local use taxes irrelevant for all but out-of-state purchases, as credit is allowed for local sales tax paid.
3. Localities receive advance sales tax allocations monthly based on estimates reflecting past performances and future expectations of economic activity. Hence, localities can plan their revenue availability with greater certainty and face a smaller danger of financial surprise. The localities are charged only $.82 per $100.00 collected (changed in 1972 from cost of collection).
4. Both cities and counties receive needed revenue from the Bradley-Burns system. Counties obtain all collections from unincorporated areas and receive a portion of the collections from within cities according to mutual agreement between city and county. Cities had an advantage in the beginning because they could impose taxes outside the state system, whereas counties had no choice if they were to have a sales tax. Many cities, especially in southern California, receive all revenue. Alameda County cities receive 95%; Santa Clara County cities, 91%. The lowest percentage is 85.5%, for cities in Napa County.
5. The local taxes automatically adjust to changes in state legislation, so no city or county action is needed to make local ordinances coincide for easy administration. Localities do not face formulation of different rules and regulations for tax compliance.

The uniform system has proved clearly superior to local administration from the standpoints of administration and compliance. Yet, there have been problems:

1. The task of verifying location of stores, keeping changes up to date, and

allocating revenues has involved substantial effort. It should be noted, however, that the effort required in locating stores when sales are presumed to occur at the retailer's location is less than results when site of delivery must be discovered to determine liability.

2. Itinerant merchants have been troublesome. Total collections from such retailers are allocated among the cities in accordance with allocations based on known sales made in each city.

3. Problems arise with (a) certain multiple-unit operations when their sales offices, general offices, and factories are located in different jurisdictions; (b) contractors who do work in various jurisdictions; (c) installation work, particularly fixtures; and (d) out-of-state vendors who ship to various locations in the state. When no basis for allocation exists, funds are divided in the same ratios as collections from itinerants.

4. Uniformity between state and local taxes has not been complete. Certain sales to operators of waterborne vessels and of aircraft are not locally taxed. This is a minor irritant, not a major problem. (Utilities and common carriers had been exempt from local taxes, but were made taxable in 1974.)

5. Allocation of revenue to the location where liability was incurred has created great disparity in the amount of revenue jurisdictions receive. In Los Angeles County in 1979–80, for example, annual per capita revenues ranged from $1.18 in Bradbury to $18,421.39 in Vernon. The City of Los Angeles collected $60.27 per capita.[13] To some extent, this disparity reflects revenue needs. Frequently, cities with substantial retail activity must provide many government services. But matching up revenue and expenditures is not perfect, and the local tax system does not permit redistribution. In addition, the system sets 1.25% as a ceiling for total city-county rate. Some cities desire additional revenue beyond that produced by the maximum rate.

The system has worked well on the whole, especially in comparison with the locally administered chaos. Yet the system is now undergoing substantial pressure, both with regard to the level of revenue produced and the allocation of revenue among cities. The problem derives from the widely noted nationwide urban crisis, but the pressure is directly felt by the uniform city-county tax system. Any local changes in rates would need voter approval because of Proposition 13 requirements.

Colorado.   As noted already, some Colorado cities collect their own sales taxes, whereas others employ state administration. As of April 1982, state collection occurs in approximately 130 cities, 25 counties, and the Denver Regional Transit District (RTD), in contrast to 30 cities in which the tax was collected locally (but these 30 include Denver, Boulder, Colorado Springs,

---

[13]Computed from California State Board of Equalization, *Annual Report 1979–80,* using June 30, 1979, population estimates reported in California State Controller, *1978–79 Annual Report of Financial Transactions Concerning Cities of California.*

and other large cities). All county taxes must be state-administered. Liability depends upon place of delivery. State-collected levies include use tax on interstate transactions but not on intrastate ones, and the tax is limited to motor vehicles and building materials. Not all units levy use taxes. Locally administered taxes have intrastate use tax features. No charge is made for state collection. The base for these sales taxes matched the state until 1979. Since then, cities and the RTD can tax the food, manufacturing machinery, and residential gas and electricity purchases exempted by the state.

The Denver RTD tax applies in Denver, Boulder, and Jefferson counties, the western halves of Adams and Arapahoe counties, and parts of Douglas County. These areas include better than 54% of retail sales in Colorado (fiscal year 1979), so the revenue production of the tax is substantial. In fiscal year 1979, the RTD tax produced $44 million at the 0.5% rate; state-collected city taxes at rates ranging from 1% to 4% produced $38 million; and state-collected county taxes at rates from 0.5% to 2% produced $18 million. Legislation in 1980 provided the RTD with authority from January 1, 1981, to December 31, 1997, to levy an additional 0.75% sales tax, subject to voter approval. At the same time, the RTD would lose authority to tax food, manufacturing machinery, and residential gas and electricity purchases, so that its base would match the state base. Voters rejected the proposal.

Florida. Legislation in 1976 provided charter counties in Florida authority to levy local sales taxes for development, construction, equipment, maintenance, supportive services, and related costs of fixed guideway rapid transit systems. Sales above $1,000 on a single transaction were not to be taxable, although the state-administered taxes were otherwise to be patterned after the state tax. Taxes required referendum approval. No counties have levied the tax. Legislation in 1982 added general county authority for a 1% tax for 1983, open to city adoption by voter approval, if not imposed by the county.

Georgia. The joint county-municipal sales and use taxes came from 1978 legislation. "Special districts," which are defined as conterminous with each county, legally levy the 1% taxes on voter approval. Revenues are split between qualified municipalities in the county (a qualified municipality is one that imposes a tax other than the sales tax and provides at least three of the following: water, sewerage, garbage collection, police protection, fire protection, and library) and the county.[14] A process is established to cause this revenue to be used for property tax rate reduction, and individual property tax bills are prepared to show the amount of millage reduction caused by the sales tax. One hundred eleven of 159 counties levy the tax. The local bases coincide with the state bases, except that local taxes apply to motor fuel sales.

[14]This law replaced the 1975 Local Option Sales Tax Act, which was ruled unconstitutional because it had a rollback of county property taxes in unincorporated areas but not in municipalities.

Another local sales and use tax supports the Metropolitan Atlanta Regional Transit Authority (MARTA). The state-administered 1% tax (scheduled for reduction to 0.5% on June 30, 1997) applies in Fulton and DeKalb counties (including Atlanta). Cobb, Clayton, and Gwinett counties can join the two by choosing to have a rapid transit contract with MARTA. (All five counties voted in the referendum to enact the tax, but only the two accepted it). MARTA's vendor liability basis and use tax provides it legal jurisdiction over a healthy portion of sales in the state.

Illinois. Cities in Illinois received power to impose sales taxes in 1947 but only with voter approval, which none received.[15] The ending of the referendum requirement in 1955 brought widespread adoptions. The tax has become almost universal, with the exception of some border communities that fear tax-induced sales loss. As of April 1982, all 102 counties and 1,250 municipalities impose the tax. Under the enabling legislation, local tax coverage must be identical with the state. Local use taxes (authorized in 1974) apply only to registered or titled property purchased at retail outside of Illinois and are optional, although most localities have enacted them. Liability is at the location of the retailer.

Transportation district taxes add a second level (third level in Chicago) of local sales taxation. The Chicago area Regional Transit Authority and the Metro East Mass Transit District taxes are similar to the other local taxes, except they apply in addition to any city or county tax. The rate of the former is 1% in Cook County (Chicago) and 0.25% in five surrounding counties (Du Page, Kane, Lake, McHenry, and Will). The latter levies a 0.25% rate in Madison and St. Clair counties.[16]

The system, as initially developed, created tax rate differentials between cities and their unincorporated suburbs, with encouragement to develop shopping centers outside the cities, especially in more populous areas. To reduce this problem, in 1959 counties received the power to impose sales taxes. County rates apply only outside of incorporated municipalities, regardless of whether the city applies a tax. Rate overlap is thus eliminated.

Local tax is collected simultaneously with the state tax, and payments are made monthly to the localities. The state retains 2% of local collections as a fee for administration. (No charge is made for administration of the transit district taxes.) This fee, totaling almost $10 million in fiscal year 1979, produces continuing complaint from the cities. Retailers are allowed no compensation on the local tax, though they are compensated for filing the state return.

The Illinois system has encountered few problems of administration, though the same revenue distribution difficulty exists as in California. Revenue remains with the jurisdiction of collection, creating the possibility that urban needs may be underfinanced. But little pressure for change is apparent.

[15]Counties received authorization to levy state-collected sales taxes in 1932. None used the power, which expired a year later.

[16]A 0.165% rate was imposed for a time in Monroe County.

Response to revenue pressure has been an escalation of the permissible local rate: 0.5% in 1955, 0.75% in 1967, and 1% in 1969. The last increase in local tax was matched by a reduction in the state tax rate, a reduction made possible by the enactment of a state income tax. Most localities adopted the 1% rate as soon as the option became available. However, as of April 1982, there are still approximately twenty cities with 0.5% rates and about forty cities with 0.75% rates. No counties have a basic rate below 1%, although not all apply the full rate to services, vehicles, and machinery. This differential is, of course, a nuisance and a possible influence on location. Further, cities and counties can tax or exempt machinery and equipment used in manufacturing and farm machinery and equipment. The decisions create rate differentials on those purchases.

On the basis of home rule powers, Chicago added in 1981 a supplemental 1% sales and use tax on tangible personal property purchased in Chicago or purchased at retail elsewhere for use in the city. The tax is administered by the city, as described earlier.

Kansas.   Cities and counties in Kansas received authorization to levy sales taxes (no use taxes) in 1970. Cities can use a rate of 0.5%; counties can choose either 0.5% or 1%, although only one has the 1% rate. County adoption of the higher rate terminates the sales tax of any cities in the county. The state administers the taxes at no charge, but the base is not identical with the state base (utility and industrial and farm machinery exemptions do not apply). Adoption is by voter approval; county tax elections may result from petition by cities, petition by voters, or county board action. Revenue from any county-wide tax is split among the county and cities in the county by formula: half of the collections are divided according to the tangible property tax levies of the prior year, half by population. The law specifically prohibits any sales tax revenues to be used as guarantee of bond payment. Forty-seven municipalities and seven counties levied the tax in April 1982.

Kentucky.   No units have applied sales taxes under authorization provided Kentucky transit authorities in 1976. The state-administered levies with rates up to 0.5% would require voter approval.

Mississippi.   General authorization for city sales taxes ended in 1968. Bay St. Louis received, however, special authority to levy a 0.5% tax to pay off city liability from a damage suit involving a swimming pool accident. There is no accompanying use tax, the state base is used, and there is no charge for state collection.

Missouri.   Incorporated cities, towns, or villages with a population of 500 or more received specific authorization for state-administered sales taxes, at a rate of 0.5% or 1% in 1969. Currently, there is no population limit and a rate of 0.875% is also permitted. Furthermore, counties were permitted rates of

0.25%, 0.375% or 0.5% in 1979. Transportation taxes up to 0.5% are also permitted. All require voter approval and state administration. Revenues are remitted to the localities monthly after subtraction of a 1% charge for administration. Some city officials have complained that they, rather than the state, have been forced to administer portions of the tax, and some localities claim revenues have not been allocated properly. The location of the retailer determines tax liability, except for motor vehicles, for which the place of registration determines the liability. All vendor discounts permitted under the state tax apply to the local tax. The taxes follow the state base, except cities can reimpose the tax on residential power, and about two-thirds of them have. Only four cities had the 0.5% rate in early 1982 (Kansas City is one) and about twenty levied a 0.875% rate; the remaining cities levied the full 1% rate. Sixty-three counties levied taxes under the 1979 authority, only two below the 0.5% rate. Those using the tax are required to reduce their property tax levy by 50% to 100% of sales tax revenue collected in the year. The county taxes overlap any city taxes, with the exception of St. Louis County (which does not include St. Louis). There, the county tax replaced all existing city sales taxes and county tax revenue is divided with the cities. Group A cities (thirty-three), those with taxes before the county, receive revenue collected in their limits; Group B cities (fifty-six) receive a distribution based on population, with the county receiving the unincorporated area share. In addition to the city and county taxes, transit district taxes at rates to 0.5% are permitted; Kansas City, St. Louis City, and St. Louis County levy them at the maximum rate. It should be noted that Missouri cities have and use extensively the power to levy local income taxes.

Nebraska. The Local Option Revenue Act of 1969 authorized any incorporated municipality to adopt either 0.5% or 1% city sales and use taxes (Omaha received special authorization to tax at 1.5%.) The state administers any such tax along with the state tax and retains a 3% administration fee. Retailers file a single return for both state and local liability, and proceeds are returned to cities monthly. Initially, tax liability was based on the location of the retailer, including the tax on motor vehicle purchases, even though county treasurers collect the tax at the time of registration. The city of Lincoln objected to this liability rule, and situs was ultimately determined as the location where possession of tangible personal property is taken by the purchaser. The base is identical to the state tax, except that the use tax applies only to intrastate sales. Only seven cities had levied the tax by July 1981, at rates from 1% to 1.5%. Any taxes levied after 1979 require voter approval, but that provision is not retroactive.

Nevada. Nevada counties (and Carson City, a city-county) received authorization to levy .5% sales taxes in the County-City Relief Tax Law of 1969. These taxes were in addition to mandatory taxes for school support imposed in 1967. The taxes followed the state base with state administration. All counties but Esmeralda and Eureka adopted the tax. Although there was no referendum requirement, a county could levy this tax after petition by the governing bodies of all cities within the county or by its own action. Legislation in 1981 made the county taxes mandatory, effective May 1981. The combined state and local rate became 5.75%—2% state, 1.5% school support, and 2.25% county. The local taxes have become an earmarked state tax. Counties may, on voter approval, levy a 0.25% tax for public mass transportation by 1981 legislation; none have done so.

New Mexico.   New Mexico merged an extensive system of locally administered city sales taxes with the state levy in 1969 to simplify administration, eliminate locational competition, and provide more state revenue. One percentage point of the state rate is returned to municipalities according to place of business, including location of contract work. Revenue from sales outside municipalities remains with the state. In 1975, incorporated cities, towns, and villages received new authorization to levy a state-administered 0.25% tax. The tax could be levied without a referendum, although voter approval is optional. The same units were authorized in 1979 to add up to 0.5% additional tax (in 0.25% increments) with voter approval. In early 1981, twenty-six retained 0.25%, twenty-seven had the 0.5% rate, and forty-two levied the full 0.75% rate. Santa Fe and Albuquerque had rates of 0.5% and 0.25%, respectively.

Counties have separate taxing authority to finance courthouses, provide hospital care for indigents, and provide fire protection. The county taxes can be up to 0.5% on voter approval, but they remain at 0.25%. These taxes are collected by the state through a separate line on the return form and revenue is returned monthly. Neither cities nor counties levy use taxes.

New York.   When the state of New York adopted a sales tax in 1965, thirteen localities were using local sales and use taxes on specific authorization.[17] The economies from unified administration were apparent, as was the potential disarray from continued local administration, so previous enabling legislation for local sales taxes was replaced by optional state-administered taxes. Localities (cities, counties, school districts) were authorized to levy several consumption-based taxes: sales and use, utility, restaurant meals, admissions, and hotel occupancy. The state would administer any tax levied. The locality had two options: it could adopt any of the other taxes without the sales and use tax or it could adopt the sales and use tax along with some other taxes. The maximum total local rate was 3% (in New York City and Yonkers, the local sales tax maximum is now 4%) with prior right belonging to different local units using the tax. For the sales and use tax, county and city each had prior right to half the maximum. County-wide tax revenue can be distributed to component juris-

[17]W.H. Selden, "Administration of Local Sales and Use Taxes," paper presented to annual conference of National Association of Tax Administrators, Detroit, 1970.

dictions, and twenty-one counties share some of their sales tax revenue. Distribution formulae are not rigid, so sharing can be fitted to local circumstances. The trend has been toward county use at the maximum rate, hence, the potential importance of intracounty revenue allocation.

As of 1982, the tax is levied by over seventy-five local taxing jurisdictions, at rates of 1% to 4%. Point of delivery determines the liability for local tax. Local use taxes are placed on both interstate and intrastate purchases. Separate lines are provided on the return form for the various local taxes.

The New York experience suggests several lessons in the operation of local sales taxes. Favorable characteristics include the following:

1. The transition from local to state administration was smoothly accomplished by eliminating permissive legislation for local taxes on the enactment of the state sales tax and by introducing optional state-administered taxes. These special circumstances, specific previous authorization, and the new state tax prevented the problems experienced by Colorado and Alabama in transition from local to state administration and suggest the utility of erasing existing legislation before altering administrative structures.
2. State administration has proved attractive to localities. Administration is accomplished with greater quality and at a lower cost than by the previous local administration.
3. Legislation provides for intracounty allocation of revenue. The basic focus of the local taxes has become the county, thus reducing sharp rate differentials at many city boundaries but at the same time making revenue distribution from the county to subordinate units important.

Some undesirable features of the New York system, however, have developed:

1. State tax administrators have experienced difficulties because local tax coverage has some options. Localities can use taxes on hotel room occupancy, restaurant meals, and utilities without using the general sales tax. If the sales tax is chosen, the tax on hotel room occupancy and restaurant meals must be repealed. School districts can retain the utility tax. As cities, counties, and school districts can be involved in the taxing of these transactions, the administrative complexities are obvious.
2. Administration is further complicated by the failure of state and local bases to coincide on the treatment of certain purchases. The state exempts machinery and equipment purchased for use or consumption directly and exclusively in the production of tangible personal property, gas, electricity, refrigeration, and steam for sale. Local tax in New York City does not provide this exemption.[18] In other localities, the exemption also includes parts with a useful life of less than one year, as well as tools and supplies used with exempt machinery and equipment. Localities also can eliminate, reduce, or

[18]New York City then credits this tax paid against its locally administered business income tax.

continue their sales tax on residential heating and energy sources, which the state exempted in late 1980.

3. Local taxes are destination taxes with the point of delivery or use determining the applicable rate. Vendors making deliveries must ascertain the correct rate to be charged and must allocate revenue collected to the correct jurisdiction on each sale for delivery. The state administrators must guide vendors in the collection activities (including the distribution of frequent rate and address advisory sheets and the revision of tax returns to keep up with local tax changes) and handle audit activities to ensure proper payment.

Localities have compensating use taxes that apply to both interstate and intra state purchases. The state remits revenue monthly. Collections from the previous month are distributed by the twelfth of the following month. Further, collections during the first twenty-five days of June and December are distributed before the end of those months to give localities the maximum revenue before the end of their fiscal year. The effort to prepare disbursements (and later to make revisions) is the major thrust of the processing division. The state deducts the cost of administration, around 0.75%. The charge has never exceeded 1%.

In addition to other local taxes, a 0.25% sales and use tax is applied within the Metropolitan Commuter Transportation District (New York City plus Dutchess, Nassau, Orange, Putnam, Rockland, Suffolk, and Westchester counties). The tax is administered by the state and is identical to the state tax. That brings the combined state and local tax rate in New York City to 8.25%.

North Carolina. Mecklenburg County (Charlotte) received authorization in 1967 to impose, with voter approval, a 1% sales and use tax. The state collected the tax and distributed revenue to the county and component municipalities in proportion to property tax collections. State collection was mandatory, as was the 1% rate. Two years later, all counties received similar authorization and twenty-five approved the tax, under local option sales and use tax act. The more recent legislation had two particularly interesting characteristics:

1. All counties were required to hold elections on sales taxes in November 1969. Collections in the counties approving the tax—of which there were twenty-five out of one hundred, mostly middle-size and rural—began on the same date. In counties that rejected the tax, another election could be held after one year at the request of the county commissioners or by voter petition.

2. Collections from the local taxes were divided between the county and its component municipalities. The combination of revenue distribution and county taxes eliminated city rate differentials and provided revenue to the cities.

Local taxes followed the state base, except for county use taxes, with credit for the tax paid the other county, if any. Only items subject to the state 3% tax were taxable, and tax was collected simultaneously with the state tax.

In January 1971, the North Carolina Supreme Court held the Local Sales and Use Tax Act unconstitutional; therefore, only the Mecklenburg County tax remained in operation. The 1971 legislative session, however, reenacted a new law, similar to the old except for the mandatory election requirement. The county commissioners may impose the tax without a referendum if no election has been held in the past five years. Deliveries into non-taxing counties are exempt. The counties now have the option to collect their own taxes. By April 1982, all counties but one (Burke) had enacted the tax, all state-collected. County commissioners annually choose between a per capita (sixty-one counties) or per dollar of ad valorem tax levy (thirty-eight) split of revenue with its cities.

Ohio.   In 1967, Ohio counties were given permission to levy 0.5% sales taxes collected by the state. (Legislation in 1981 increased the limit to 1%.) Initially, there was no requirement of voter approval, but in 1969, two years after the initial authorization, the legislation was amended to permit submission to the voters. The county commissioners hold hearings on the proposal and voters have thirty days to petition for an election. Alternatively, the commissioners, by unanimous vote, can impose the tax as an emergency levy without a vote. Coverage of the taxes must match the state tax. Liability is determined by vendor location, except on motor vehicles, which are subject to county use taxes according to destination. Fifty-three counties had approved by late 1981 the tax (well over half of state-wide taxable sales are subject to a local tax). They receive monthly remittances of the tax. The state makes no charge for administration of the county taxes. Until 1978, Ohio local use taxes had applied only to out-of-state purchases. The Ohio Supreme Court held in that year that this treatment represented an unconstitutional discrimination against out-of-state firms.[19] In that same year, the legislature extended the local use tax to intrastate transactions as well.

Transit authorities were authorized to levy sales taxes in their territories in 1974. These units must have a referendum to apply the tax and, contrary to the situation with county taxes, a charge of 1% is made for state administration. Three authorities—Cuyahoga County, Montgomery County, and Central Ohio Transit Authority (Franklin County and portions of three other counties)—applied the tax in early 1981; the authorities do not all coincide with county boundaries.

Oklahoma.   Cities in Oklahoma levy state-collected sales taxes on the basis of 1965 legislation that authorized, on voter approval, use of any tax the state could levy.[20] From initial adoptions in the Oklahoma City area, the taxes have spread through much of the state. As of April 1982, 424 municipalities, with

[19]*American Modulars Corp.* v. *Lindley* (1978), 54 O.S. 2d 273.
[20]Municipalities have the unused authority to levy a sales tax at a rate not to exceed 1% in case of a major catastrophe.

over 95% of all sales, had imposed the tax. Voters have rejected no more than ten of the levies. All cities use at least a 1% rate, in part because the state will not collect a lower figure. All use state collection, though not required to do so. About 250 use the 2% rate and about 10 the 3% rate. The collection arrangement between the state and the cities is contractual: the fees are 2.5% from a 1% rate, 1.5% from a 2% rate, and 1% from a 3% rate. The state collects the city taxes simultaneously with its tax.[21] The 3% vendor discount is given by cities as well as by the state, even though coverage is the same and a single return fulfills both state and city obligations. State and city bases coincide, except cities may opt to tax residential utilities exempted by the state. Liability is determined by the location of the vendor, except when an order is called in. If the vendor delivers in his own vehicle or has a store in the locality, the jurisdiction of delivery receives the tax. Cities historically levied no use tax; the state levied in 1977 an extra 2% state use tax over and above the sales tax rate with its proceeds distributed to cities according to local sales tax collections. This tax was found invalid in 1978.[22] In 1980, the legislature authorized local use taxes applicable to out-of-state purchases of tangible personal property costing more than $5,000.

South Dakota. The "Uniform Non-Advalorem Tax" Law of 1969 permits governing bodies of cities or towns to impose any nonadvalorem tax, except a motor vehicle fuel tax, at any rate. Prior voter approval is not required, but a petition may bring the issue to the voters. A 1977 law requires that new municipal taxes must match the state base and limits the rate to 1% (those above that level can continue). Some of the pre-1977 taxes do not tax food; later taxes conform to the state base. Sioux Falls, Deadwood, and Pierre levy a 1% rate; Rapid City uses a 1.5% rate. All are administered by the state, though it is not required. Remittances are made quarterly, less 1% of collections. Liability depends on place of delivery. Local use taxes are placed on intrastate sales, with credit for previous tax.

Tennessee. The 1963 Tennessee legislature provided for county and city sales taxes based on the state law, with optional administration by the state. Vote of the people is required. If a measure is defeated, it cannot be proposed again for a year. Coverage of local taxes matches state tax for the most part. Energy-producing items (electric power or energy, natural or artificial gas, coal, and fuel oil), however, are exempt from the local tax but are covered by the state tax. The maximum rate was initially one-third of the state tax but was changed to one-half of the state figure (or 1.5%) in response to rising local revenue pressures in 1968 and is now 2.25%. The maximum tax on any one

---

[21] An attorney general opinion in 1965 held that the state could collect, but not enforce, the local taxes, so cities were expected to do their own enforcement. A 1979 law permits cities to contract for enforcement as well.

[22] *Ted M. Phillips* v. *Oklahoma Tax Commission* (March 14, 1978).

item is $5.00 for rates not above 1% and $7.50 for higher rates. County use of the maximum rates precludes city use. Cities can levy a tax equal to the difference between the maximum and the county rate. Use tax applies on in-state purchases only. The total local tax burden is thus controlled, and a ceiling for rate differentials is established. Liability depends on location of the vendor, with minor exceptions.

The legislature recognized that county action could eliminate a possibly vital city revenue source with no city recourse. Hence, the act controls revenue distribution from any county tax. Half of the revenue is distributed in the same manner as the county property tax for schools, and half is distributed back to the location of collection, with the provision that city and county agreements could provide for other distribution of the second half. Cities are thus guaranteed local sales tax revenue, even though the trend has been toward the use of county-wide taxes. Frequently, cities and counties have disagreed on the distribution of the second half and many different formulae have been used. The point of sale allocation dominates. State charge to localities for collection is now 1.5% of collections. The state revenue department reports difficulty in keeping local rates up-to-date and accurate in their computer.

Ninety-four of the ninety-five counties have the tax. The other county contained cities with a sales tax in early 1982.

Texas. After approval at an election called by a city governing board or by a voter petition, Texas will administer 1% city sales and use taxes that match the state tax in coverage.[23] All state rules and regulations apply for the city taxes. As of April 1982, approximately 950 cities, including Houston and Dallas, use the tax. Sales are presumed to occur at the location of the retailer. The state charges a 2% fee for collection of the taxes. The state must transmit collections at least twice per year, but it currently remits monthly with overnight delivery of funds. Retailer discounts apply to the city taxes as well as to the state tax. Voter approval has proved no barrier to adoption.

Separate taxes levied by metropolitan transit authorities (MTAs) were authorized in 1977. Because the MTAs receive revenue from sales by vendors in the authority plus use tax on purchases brought in, the districts enjoy a sizable tax base. Transit authorities in Houston (1%) and San Antonio (0.5%) use the tax. Boundaries do not conform to city or county limits, so the state must map and define taxability by street. No units employ an additional Regional Transit Authority tax authorized in 1979.

Utah. The Uniform Local Sales and Use Tax Law of 1959 established a city-county tax system.[24] As in California, a city tax is a credit against a county tax, and sales are allocated to the location of the retailer. (Counties and cities can

---

[23] A suit by U.S. Steel forced the use tax to apply to intrastate purchases as well as interstate purchases (since June 13, 1979).

[24] Utah cannot constitutionally impose a state tax for the benefit of local governments.

agree to a distribution of revenue by means other than point of sale.) In Utah, however, cities do not have the option of operating outside the state system of administration. The city cannot act until the surrounding county has adopted a tax (the city may continue its tax if the county should repeal its tax), and the cities receive all revenue collected within their limits with no bargaining between city and county on the share. The 0.75% taxes are collected by the state at a charge no greater than 2.5% of collections. There is some pressure to switch to a state-wide tax with revenue divided half by origin and half by population. County transit districts received authorization for 0.25% sales taxes in 1974; city districts received authorization in 1977. Both require voter approval. Three counties (Salt Lake, Weber, and Davis) and one city (Park City) were using the transit tax in early 1982.

Virginia.   Local sales and use taxes are used by every county and independent city in Virginia. Rates do not overlap because counties and independent cities do not overlap. The effect is a statewide 1% tax allocated to local uses, as coverage of the state and local taxes coincides. These state-administered levies replaced the several locally administered levies at the time Virginia adopted a state sales tax. The transition from local to state administration was easily accomplished; the 1966 General Assembly eliminated authority for locally administered taxes in the same legislation that established the new system. The state charges nothing for administration of the local taxes, and liability is established at the location of the retailer. Local use taxes on interstate transactions were authorized in 1968. When use tax cannot be allocated to a locality, it goes into a pool and is distributed on the same basis as the sales tax revenues. Revenue directors of cities that formerly used locally administered sales taxes register one complaint: the lack of choice of sales tax rate.

Two characteristics of the Virginia local taxes merit additional notice. First, the 3% retailer discount for payment before the deadline is not allowed for the local tax. As the state and local taxes are essentially the same, compensation for collection of the latter makes little sense. Second, two types of revenue allocation are employed. Allocation between independent city and county is done on sales transacted within the jurisdiction. Towns within counties constituting special school districts, however, receive a share based on school-age population. Towns lack the authority to use local sales taxes if the county has imposed the tax, as all counties have.

Washington.   Legislation in 1970 authorized cities and counties to levy state administered sales and use taxes, with a base identical to that of the state tax. Both cities and counties can levy the taxes, but the city tax is a credit against any county tax due. The local tax rate is 0.5%. When both city and county adopt the tax, the full county tax applies in the unincorporated areas; the city rate is 0.4%, and the county rate is 0.5% with full credit for the city rate. Taxpayers with several sites may report all sales together (pool) and let the state apportion revenue among taxing districts. The state charges the cost of administration up to 2% of collections and remits receipts bimonthly. State collection is mandatory. Liability is determined by the location of the vendor. There is no local use tax. At least 265 cities, including Seattle, Spokane, and Tacoma, and all counties but one (Wahkiakum) levy the tax; one city in the nonadopting county levies the tax. Voter approval is not required. In addition to the city and county taxes, transit districts are permitted taxes at rates from 0.1% to 0.6%. These taxes require voter approval. Transit taxes may not be pooled.

Wisconsin. When 1969 legislation amended the Wisconsin sales tax base to include all items of tangible personal property except those specifically exempt, the law also authorized state-collected county sales taxes. The 0.5% taxes would piggyback on the state base. Taxes become effective on January 1 of the year following enactment, but there have as yet been no adoptions. Taxes can be enacted by county ordinance, and revenue is distributed to the cities, villages, and towns of the county. Half of the distribution is based on equalized assessed valuation in the localities, half on population. Counties apparently are unlikely to adopt the tax because none of the funds goes to the county.

Wyoming. Wyoming counties are permitted 0.5% or 1% sales taxes in 1973 legislation. Voter approval is required. In early 1982, fifteen of twenty-three counties, generally the ones growing most rapidly, levied the tax, all using the 1% rate. The tax applies in Cheyenne (Laramie County), but not Laramie (Albany County). According to 1980 law, all counties with the tax must also impose a use tax. Liability is on a delivery basis and state collection is required. Proceeds are distributed between the county and its cities and towns according to population shares. This revenue is in addition to the one-third portion of the state sales tax which is divided among counties according to collections and within counties on a population basis.

Experience with State Administration

State administration of optional local sales taxes has proved a practical and efficient technique for giving financial assistance to localities. Local autonomy and responsibility are maintained, the state legislature avoids blame for higher taxes, and the frequent near-chaos of local administration can be avoided. Several conclusions on features of state administration emerge from a review of experience:
1. The switch from local to state administration can most effectively be accomplished by eradicating authority under which the locally administered taxes are levied. Quality, thoroughness, and value in state administration fail to compensate completely for the pleasures of local autonomy.
2. The presumption that sales occur at the location of the vendor involves

substantially less administrative and compliance trouble than does the location of liability at the site of delivery, especially when local taxes become widespread. The delivery rule, attractive when only a few cities use the tax, presents an opportunity for residents of surrounding notax areas to avoid the tax, though still shopping in the city. As the taxes spread, the rule becomes less important as a determinant of tax liability and more important as an allocator of revenue between taxing localities. Cities that may have avoided some sales loss by use of the delivery rule in the early days of the taxes may now stand to lose sizable revenue to outlying areas as the taxes spread. The retailer location rule has much in its favor as it matches state and local bases.

3. With electronic data processing equipment at the state level, remittances of state-collected local sales taxes can be made at least quarterly, and the trend is toward monthly payment. There appears to be little justification for collection fees exceeding 1%.

4. Local use taxes on interstate purchases can be administered as easily as state use taxes. If a state use tax is applied, little is to be lost by applying a local use tax on interstate purchases. On transactions involving collection from an out-of-state vendor when the vendor cannot easily determine which local unit should receive the money, the revenue should go into a pool and be distributed by formula.

   Local use taxes on intrastate purchases are unjustified and are a major source of nuisance and possible multiple taxation. Some courts have, however, found the absence of intrastate use taxes a violation of the commerce clause.

5. When state coverage and local coverage coincide, when a single return is used for both taxes, and when liability is determined by location of the vendor, there is little justification for allowing compensation for vendor compliance on the local portion of the tax.

6. Difference between the state tax and the state-administered local tax is inexcusable as it leads to greater administrative complexity and frequently to loss of local revenue. The spread of state exemptions makes uniformity more difficult because localities dislike the loss of revenue that exemption brings.

7. Unless cities, towns, and school districts have no revenue needs, the choice of county-wide taxes necessitates some technique for revenue distribution between the county and other local jurisdictions, particularly if county action can eliminate anticipated city sales tax revenue.

THE BORDER CITY PROBLEM

Complaints of business loss to surrounding lower tax areas often accompany changes in sales tax rates. The problem appears in the border areas of states, though the spread of state sales taxes has reduced its magnitude, and in cities adopting local sales taxes. In states the debate frequently dies out with the passage of time and troublesome borders have often been eliminated with the adoption of sales taxes in adjoining states. The difficulties cities face, however, have been more long-lived since, in the absence of compensating local tax rates in surrounding areas, a rate differential remains as long as the city has the tax.

Empirical Studies

A few studies have been made of the border city problem. Maliet's study of the effects of the Illinois and Iowa sales taxes in encouraging persons to buy outside the state, based on analysis of sales and sales tax collections in border and nonborder counties, concluded that the tax resulted in some business loss in Illinois border counties but without evidence of loss in Iowa counties. Even in Illinois, the loss was of minor significance relative to total retail sales. The problem was most acute in areas where an Illinois city immediately adjoined a state with no sales tax.[25]

In 1958 McAllister exhaustively studied the border city problem in Washington. Three border cities and three nonborder "control" cities were chosen. Trade patterns in each city were compared and families in each border city were interviewed on out-of-state purchases. The study concluded that

in every case for the three cities of Vancouver, Walla Walla, and Pullman, the trade pattern is different from what would be expected if the sales tax were not a factor in buying decisions. An examination of the reasons given by buyers for purchasing in nontax areas shows that escaping the sales tax is a dominant reason in people's minds. The unusual buying patterns, coupled with the fact that people overwhelmingly feel that the tax is important, makes it difficult to escape the conclusion that a desire to gain a price advantage by not paying Washington's retail sales tax is one important reason why border residents will shop in nontax states.[26]

Two studies have examined the sales deflection resulting from the New York City sales tax. Hamovitch used regression analysis of data from 1948 to 1965 to estimate the loss of sales tax base resulting from increases in the New York City tax rate. After allowing for changes in the city disposable income, he concluded that approximately 6% of the implicit tax base was lost with a one percentage point increase of the New York City tax rate. Hamovitch also compared the effects in New York with those in Alabama, and found that in the latter, no measurable effect on sales was attributable to increases in the sales tax rate.[27]

Levin approached the same problem in New York but, rather than investigating the effects on the entire tax base, he focused on the impact on ap-

[25]L. Maliet, "Illinois Retailers Occupation Tax and Iowa Retail Sales and Use Taxes," Ph.D. dissertation, University of Illinois, 1955.
[26]H.E. McAllister, "The Border Tax Problem in Washington."
[27]W. Hamovitch, "Effect of Increases in Sales Tax Rates on Taxable Sales in New York City," and "Sales Taxation."

parel and home furnishings sales with data from Censuses of Business from 1929 to 1963. Using multiple regression techniques to account for the influence of disposable income levels and changes in prices of nontaxable goods, he showed evidence of loss of sales of taxed goods and of gains of sales at stores selling nontaxed goods in New York City.[28] The results of both studies suggest the existence of the border city problem. Each deals only with New York City, however, a possibly atypical case, and there is a variety of statistical problems with their estimates.

Mikesell estimated retail sales loss from city-suburb tax rate differentials without focusing on a single city. Analysis of data from a sample of central cities of SMSAs suggests a 95% probability that a 1% increase in the ratio of the city tax relative to the sales tax in the surrounding area will cause per capita city retail sales to be between 1.69% and 10.97% lower.[29] The result implies that much of the sales loss can be eliminated if the area in which the tax applies is widened. County-wide sales taxes produce less sales loss than does a city-wide tax. Increased transportation cost since the time of that study may well have reduced prospective sales loss.

Conclusions of the Studies

A review of both state experience and empirical studies suggests several conclusions:
1. The extent of the border city problem has been reduced by the spread of the sales tax to almost all states. To find an area in which sales tax can be entirely avoided is difficult. Any state, however, that raises its sales tax rate can still expect some influence on sales as favorable rate differentials are reduced and unfavorable rate differentials are created or widened. The magnitude of the problem depends on the border situation of the state.
2. For states, the problem is aggravated when a substantial population is near the border, and the principal shopping center for the area is across the state line in the lower tax area. If the principal shopping center is in the higher tax area, there is less difficulty.
3. For cities, strong empirical evidence shows that a rate differential causes significantly lower per capita sales. When a local tax system is established that substantially reduces differentials, as in California, Illinois, and Virginia, the loss is also substantially reduced. This evidence speaks strongly for the use of county-wide taxes when sales loss is feared.
4. The problem for states reaches its extreme form where a city straddles the border and part of its business district is in each state. Not only can sales loss be substantial, but tax administrators, retailers, and consumers face dif-

---

[28]H. Levin, "An Analysis of the Economic Effects of the New York City Sales Tax," p. 668.
[29]J.L. Mikesell, "Central Cities and Sales Tax Rate Differentials."

ficult problems in the collection and enforcement of sales taxes on either side of the border.

SUMMARY

From the experience with local sales taxes come several major conclusions:
1. Locally administered sales taxes can cause substantial and unnecessary expense for vendors and, if widely used in a state, can produce near chaos. The problem becomes particularly bad if the cities impose use taxes against purchases made elsewhere in the state, exempt sales for delivery outside of the city, and deviate from the coverage of the state taxes. In the typical situation, the results are so objectionable as to outweigh any considerations of preserving local autonomy. However, if only one or two large cities in a state require the tax, if there exists a longstanding tradition of noncooperation between state and city, or if state-city relations are restricted by constitutional provisions, local administration may be unavoidable.
2. State administration does not significantly reduce local autonomy or financial responsibility, since the taxes must still be imposed by the local governments. If local sales taxes become almost universal, as in California, Illinois, and Virginia, the result is essentially the same as if the state raised its own rate and allocated the tax back to the local governments based on location of transaction. When widespread coverage at the maximum rate is attained, it may be well to raise the maximum rate to again permit local autonomy on the rate for the sales tax.
3. Undesirable effects on location can best be minimized by a system of county-wide taxes, rather than individual city taxes. The Utah system ensures this result by preventing use by cities until their counties enact the tax. States permitting only county taxes automatically avoid location effects and states in which counties have prior right to sales taxation do so as time passes.
4. When county adoptions preclude city use of a sales tax, usually a system of revenue redistribution to component cities must be established to relieve urban fiscal pressures. Distribution is frequently per capita, though other formulae are applied.
5. Whether state administration should be mandatory, as in Virginia, or voluntary, as in California, is a question that can be answered only in a broader context of policy determination of local-state powers. If the voluntary system is accompanied by strong enough inducements to adopt the system, as in California, it will function as well as a mandatory system.
6. Regardless of the system, a uniform base for state and local tax will greatly simplify the task of the retailer. Such a base requires both uniform coverage and determination of tax status according to location of vendor rather than

place of delivery. Local use taxes applying to purchases made at other points within the state are particularly objectionable and should never be permitted.

7. Local government sales taxes produce substantial revenue for areas that have high concentrations of retail activity. This revenue distribution may not coincide with the location of fiscal need. Within metropolitan areas, the distributional pattern may become bizarre. This result is the most serious indictment against local sales taxes and the most significant argument for distributing a portion of the revenues of a state sales tax on bases other than origin of revenue.

11. Overall View

As suggested in earlier chapters, a tax can be evaluated only by accepted standards. Such standards include:

1. Minimization of adverse effects upon the functioning of the economy, including loss in efficiency in production and distribution, distortion of resource allocation (that is, shifting of consumption and production from some goods to others), distortion of location of business activity, loss of factor supplies, and unnecessary restriction of output and economic growth.
2. Attainment of equity in distribution of the costs of the governmental activity financed by the taxes.
3. Collection of the tax at cost regarded as reasonable, with minimum costs of compliance for the taxpayers and a high degree of effectiveness of collection.

Failure to attain these objectives results in loss of potential revenue, inequity among various taxpayers, waste of resources, and pressure for additional evasion.

From these criteria and the analysis of the preceding chapters, summary overall evaluation of the sales taxes can be made.

STRUCTURE OF THE TAXES

The relatively broad coverage of the state sales taxes has important merits for the objectives. Revenue is maximized at a given rate, and discrimination among consumers by relative preferences and alteration of consumption patterns are avoided. Compliance and administration are simplified. A strong case exists against introducing any exemptions into a sales tax unless justification is substantial and specific for a particular instance. Similar arguments apply to use of differential tax rates.[1] Unfortunately, in the last decade there has been a strong trend toward additional exemptions.

[1]Unless equity is ignored and a rate structure to maximize labor supply and output could be devised, as noted in chapter 2, note 1.

Exemptions

Of the exemptions provided, that for prescription drugs has perhaps the strongest justification. Expenditures on these items, necessitated by misfortune, are very unevenly distributed among families. Food exemption, though making the tax much more acceptable on equity grounds, is a second-best substitute for a credit against income tax representing sales tax paid on minimum necessary purchases. As outlined in chapter 3, an income tax credit is a far more equitable method of reducing burden on the poor, costs much less revenue, and is much easier to administer. Unfortunately, food exemption has far more political appeal than the credit system. Other exemptions of commodities have little to justify them. Clothing exemption is a source of considerable administrative difficulty and makes the tax more, not less, regressive. Exemption of commodities subject to excises is a mistake. Applying two taxes is far easier than exempting commodities from the general tax. Exemption of sales to religious, educational, charitable, and similar institutions may be defended on grounds of social policy, but it does impair administration and paves the way to abuse.

Services

The question of the taxation of services is a much more complex one. The general failure to tax services creates some discrimination against those persons who have relatively higher preferences for commodities than for services, and must cause some alteration of consumption toward greater use of services. A sales tax with no services taxed is likely to be more regressive than one with all services taxed. Unfortunately, however, an attempt to include services encounters several problems. One major group of services—medical, dental, hospital, legal—appears to many persons to be inappropriate for taxation, because the activity is necessitated by misfortune. The expenses are often high relative to overall family budgets. Education is likewise unsuitable for taxation because of its importance to society.

Another major group of services, such as foreign travel, expensive education outside of the state, and the work of personal servants, cannot be reached for administrative reasons. It is these items that make total service expenditures progressive relative to income. A third major group is rendered primarily to business firms, and taxing them not only is objectionable as a matter of principle but will encourage firms to produce the services with their own employees, thus escaping tax. Larger firms are aided at the expense of the smaller firm less able to provide the services internally. If these categories are excluded, much of the total base is lost, revenue potentialities are greatly reduced, and taxation of the remainder will probably not make the tax structure less regressive. Nevertheless, extending the tax to commodities rendered by commercial establishments similar to retail stores, such as repair, dry cleaning and laundry, beauty and barber shop service, transient lodging, admissions, and related activities is justified. The revenue potential, however, is not great, perhaps 10% additional at best.

Producers Goods

Though coverage of the sales taxes is not seriously defective for consumption goods, the taxes include within their bases a substantial volume of producers goods.[2] Taxation of such transactions is contrary to the principle of the sales tax as a levy on consumption expenditure and has several undesirable consequences. The distributional impact of this portion of the tax is obscure and haphazard, resting in part on the consumers of the goods made with the taxed items, probably in part on the owners of the firms. The tax element increases the costs of the firms in the state compared to those in states not taxing these items and lessens the ability of U.S. firms to compete in world markets with firms not subject to similar taxes. The tax may also distort the choice of production methods. It places a tax penalty on investment and may affect location decisions, especially of manufacturing plants.

Administrative considerations probably preclude exclusion of all sales for business use from tax, but exclusion of parts and materials (as is now universal), farm feed, seed, and fertilizer; industrial fuel and consumables; and farm and industrial machinery and equipment is entirely feasible, though some administrative problems are created. States that have gone beyond these categories in the farm field to exclude miscellaneous farm hand tools and supplies find that administrative complications are greatly increased by so doing. In general, an "ideal" sales tax, in the sense of one confined to consumers goods, is probably not possible, but many states could much more closely approximate one than they do. They are often reluctant to make the change, however, because of revenue considerations and the political dislike of shifting tax burden from "business" to "individuals," even though individuals likely end up paying the tax initially imposed upon business firms.

Other Structural Defects

Sales taxes of a number of states contain minor defects in structure that cause unnecessary loss of revenue, create inequities and economic distor-

---

[2]An estimate by R.F. Fryman indicates that 24% of the Illinois sales tax was collected on producers goods; see his article, "Sales Taxation of Producers Goods in Illinois." At that time, Illinois taxed food at the basic rate and did not exempt industrial machinery. An Ohio estimate supplied by the Ohio revenue department is that 14% of the tax is collected on producers goods; Ohio has a very broad exemption of such goods. A Texas estimate indicated that 58% of the tax is on purchases by business. Texas exempts food but not industrial machinery; see *Fiscal Notes*, Office of Planning and Research, Texas Comptroller of Public Accounts, May 1979, p. 1. This figure has been questioned.

tions, and in some instances complicate administration. Several examples follow:

1. Taxing motor vehicles at lower rates and allowing trade-in deductions for motor vehicles but not other items are contrary to the most elementary notions of equity, since they make the tax more regressive.

2. A few states fail to tax rentals of tangible personal property.

3. Complete escape from taxation of some goods used in interstate commerce. Apparently no state is successful in taxing commercial aircraft, which, since the service is not available, can justifiably be included in the base.

4. Some states require payment of "excess collections" or "breakage." This requirement is more trouble to the vendor and for audit than it is worth. Far better is a system allowing the retailers to keep the breakage in lieu of compensation.

5. Vendor compensation, though strongly urged by the retail groups, costs the states that provide it more than the costs of administering the tax, and the payments are unrelated to actual expenses of individual firms for handling the tax.

6. Club dues, frequently untaxed, represent a particularly good object for taxation.

7. The rules for handling of meals and take-out food, in some states, not only are illogical but create serious nuisance problems. Exemption of all meals costing more than a relatively high figure, perhaps $5.00, is more logical and equitable and minimizes the "take-out" problem, if food is exempt.

8. The nonretail elements in some taxes are not objectionable if noncascading, that is, if they apply only once, as, for example, to the sale to the retailer. But where they apply in cascade fashion to each successive sale, as in Hawaii, and in the business occupation taxes, they are highly objectionable because of the adverse effects on nonintegrated businesses, economic distortions, and inequities. The low .5% rate in Hawaii lessens the significance of the problem but does not eliminate it. Of all sales tax structures today, that of Hawaii is the least satisfactory from this standpoint. The business occupation taxes of Washington and West Virginia are almost equally bad.

9. Failure of four states to give credit for sales taxes paid other states and of several to allow trade-in deduction for use tax though allowing it for sales tax are serious discriminations against interstate commerce.

10. In Arizona and Nevada, for constitutional reasons, there are three taxes (two in Nevada plus county supplement). In Illinois there are four. This situation adds to complications on the return forms and in other respects. In Nevada the legislature cannot amend the sales tax because it was approved by popular vote.

11. North Carolina (and a few cities, with local sales taxes) set maximum

amounts of tax that can apply on an individual transaction. This rule is extremely troublesome administratively and makes the tax more regressive. It is perhaps the worst single feature ever introduced into sales tax laws.

12. Limitation of the exemption of industrial machinery to that for new and expanded industry, in several states, is very troublesome operationally and completely unwarranted.

Local Sales Taxes

In many respects the development of local sales taxes has been an unfortunate trend. The system is workable if the local taxes have the same base as the state tax, if liability depends strictly on location of vendor, if no use taxes are placed on intrastate transactions, and if the tax is state-administered. Economic distortions arising from location decisions are still possible unless the tax has become universal throughout the state. Even though these taxes are workable, however, the pattern of distribution of revenues is unrelated to fiscal needs, as the almost bizarre figures for Los Angeles County show very clearly. Locally administered sales taxes or a system of state-administered taxes that vary in coverage and rate create very serious problems for vendors and for audit and can lead to almost complete chaos in the operation of the sales tax. Alabama, with part local, part state collection, and New York State, with its diverse pattern of local taxes, are probably the most chaotic today. The ideal solution, but one not always politically practical, is to raise the rate of the state tax and distribute the money on some measure of need, by population if no other.

ADMINISTRATIVE ASPECTS

Costs of Administration

Unfortunately, figures of costs of administering sales taxes are not available for half of the states. Availability is somewhat less than it was two decades ago. A number of states do not bother to compile the necessary information. But more seriously, with the functional type of administrative structure growing in importance, a precise cost figure is increasingly difficult to ascertain for any one tax. The time of top level, enforcement, and audit personnel and computers is used jointly for sales, income, and other taxes.

Table 11.1 indicates the costs of collection expressed as a percentage of revenue for the fiscal year 1979–80 and for earlier years for which data have been compiled. For the jurisdictions for which data are available (twenty-three), the average is 0.73%. The California figure of 0.79%, one of the most accurate, is reasonably typical of costs with a highly effective audit program.

TABLE 11.1 State Sales Tax Administration Costs as a Percentage of Revenues, Selected Years

State	1940	1948	1959–60	1969–70	1979–81
Alabama	4.5	2.2	1.6	1.02	1.00
Arizona	4.0	1.3		0.50	0.30
Arkansas	3.0	2.0			
California	2.6	1.9	1.7	1.12	0.79
Colorado	5.0	1.4	1.9		0.60
Connecticut	—				0.43
Florida	—	—	1.1	0.47	0.59[a]
Georgia	—	—	1.1		
Idaho	—	—	—	1.20	1.00[b]
Illinois	2.0	2.0	0.7	1.33	
Iowa		1.1	0.9		0.90
Kansas	2.5		1.4		
Kentucky	—	—	1.3	0.67	0.75[a]
Louisiana					0.61
Maine	—	—	1.5	1.0	
Maryland	—		1.2	0.89	0.50
Massachusetts	—	—	—	1.00	
Michigan	1.7	1.0	0.8	0.50	0.36
Mississippi	3.6	1.6	1.0	1.00	0.79[a]
Missouri	2.0	1.0	1.6		
Nebraska	—	—	—		0.90
Nevada	—	—	1.4	1.40	1.68
New Mexico		1.9			
New York	—	—	—	1.00	1.20[a]
North Carolina		0.7	1.4	1.60	
North Dakota			0.6		0.45
Ohio	1.9	1.1	1.2	0.60	0.50[b]
Oklahoma	0.9		1.4	2.00	
Pennsylvania	—	—	1.8	0.82	0.98
Rhode Island	—	1.2			0.60[a]
South Carolina	—	—		1.17	
South Dakota		1.5	1.0	0.69	
Tennessee	—	1.1	0.7	1.13	
Utah	2.2	0.9	1.0		
Washington		0.7	0.8	0.79	0.70
West Virginia	—	1.0	0.8		
Wisconsin	—	—	—		0.72
Wyoming	3.1	1.5	1.0	0.80	
District of Columbia	—	—		0.90	
Average	2.8	1.3	1.1	0.98	0.73

Sources: 1959–1960, 1969–70, and 1979–81 data compiled by the authors from information provided by the states. Data for other years from J. H. Maloon and C. V. Oster, "State Sales Tax Administration Costs," National Tax Journal 10 (September 1957): 221–35.

[a] All state taxes.
[b] Estimate.

The 0.73% average compares with an average of 0.98% in 1969–70, 1.1% in 1959–60, 1.3% in 1948, and 2.8% in 1940.

Table 11.2 shows the data for the more recent periods expressed as a percentage of revenue per 1% of tax rate. These figures have declined noticeably, from 0.45% in 1959–60 to 0.29% in 1969–70 and 0.19% currently.

It is important to stress that the appropriate objective of a state is not to obtain the lowest possible percentage figure of collection costs but to strike an optimal balance between additions to revenue, both directly, through audit and collection, and indirectly, through improved voluntary compliance and additional administrative costs. Expenditures need to be extended somewhere beyond the figure at which the marginal cost, the additional out-of-pocket cost, from extending administrative activity just equals the marginal direct dollar gain because of the indirect gain through better voluntary compliance. This point is difficult to ascertain. But based on the California experience, many states are spending too little and their costs per dollar of revenue are too low. By increasing this figure, with optimal use of the funds, total revenue would increase, an optimal balance approached between revenue and administrative costs.

Compliance Costs

Real economic costs of tax administration include the costs to the vendor as well as to the state. These costs are very difficult to determine, and few systematic studies have been made. The costs take several forms: those involved in additional bookkeeping and preparation of sales tax returns and supplying information to sales tax auditors, and the costs of additional clerk time—probably the most significant element. The latter is particularly difficult to ascertain as many stores cannot keep their employees busy at all times, and thus the out-of-pocket cost is nil when the time used in handling the tax would otherwise be idle.

The only thorough study of sales tax vendor compliance costs was undertaken in 1960–61 under the auspices of the Bureau of Business Research of the Ohio State University.[3] A sample of 526 stores in eight major classes of retailing was selected scientifically. Costs arising from the tax were ascertained by (1) study of records of the firm, (2) observation of time used by employees in work created by the tax, and (3) interviews. The study concluded that the average costs of compliance for all vendors, exclusive of the stamp system then in use in Ohio, amounted to 3.93% of tax liability.

Costs were highest relatively for stores that have low per-unit transactions and a high percentage of exempt sales. (In any particular line of retailing, costs were found higher relative to tax liability in small stores than in large

[3]J.C. Yokum, *Retailers' Cost of Sales Tax Collections in Ohio.*

TABLE 11.2 State Sales Tax Administrative Costs as a Percentage of Revenue per 1% of Tax Rate, Selected Years

	1959–60		1969–70		1979–80	
State	Tax Rate	Administrative Costs as a % of Revenue, per 1% of Tax Rate	Tax Rate	Administrative Costs as a % of Revenue, per 1% of Tax Rate	Tax Rate	Administrative Costs as a % of Revenue, per 1% of Tax Rate
Alabama	3	.53	4	.25	4	.25
Arizona	2		3	.17	4	.08
California	4	.43	5	.22	4.75	.17
Colorado	2	.80	3		3	.20
Connecticut					7	.06
Florida	3	.37	4	.12	4	.15
Idaho			3	.40	3	.33
Iowa	2	.45	3		3	.30
Kentucky	3	.44	3		5	.15
Louisiana			5	.13	3	.20
Maryland	3	.38	4	.22	5	.10
Michigan	3	.27	4	.13	4	.09
Mississippi	3	.34	5	.20	5	.16
Nebraska					3	.30
Nevada	2	.70	3	.47	3	.56
New Mexico					4	.30
North Dakota	3	.31			3	.15
Ohio	3	.40	4	.15	4	.13
Pennsylvania	4	.45	6	.14	6	.16
Rhode Island					6	.10
Vermont					3	.15
Washington	4	.20	4	.20	4.6	.18
Wisconsin					4	.18
Average		.45		.29		.19

TABLE 11.3   Direct Costs of Sales Tax Collection and Compliance in Ohio, by Type of Vendor, 1960-61

Business	% of Tax Liability
Department stores	1.23
Furniture stores	2.55
Men's clothing stores	3.64
Variety stores	4.56
Hardware stores	6.03
Restaurants	6.37
Drug stores	6.80
Grocery stores	10.77

Source: J. C. Yokum, *Retailers' Costs of Sales Tax Collections in Ohio* (Columbus: Bureau of Business Research, Ohio State University, 1961), p. xxi.

stores.) Principal costs of collecting arise from preparing returns and clerk time for adding tax.

Figures in table 11.3 are substantially higher than might be anticipated, but the relative patterns by type of retail establishment are comparable to those that would be expected from *a priori* reasoning.

An estimate by J. K. Fisher of the J. C. Penney Company indicates that with a 4% tax rate, the typical cost is 2.51%, for the department store type of business.[4]

Compensation of Vendors

States are almost equally divided on the practice of giving vendors a discount (compensation) for collecting tax. Twenty states do not provide percentage compensation: Arizona, California, Connecticut, Hawaii, Idaho, Kansas, Maine, Massachusetts, Minnesota, New Jersey, New Mexico, New York, North Dakota, Rhode Island, South Dakota, Utah, Vermont, Washington, West Virginia, and Wyoming, plus the District of Columbia. Compensation systems in the other states are noted in table 11.4. Between 1970 and 1982 only Indiana, Iowa, and Michigan added compensation.

In some states, discount is given on payment of use tax by consumers as well as on tax on sales; in others (e.g., Pennsylvania and Wisconsin) it is not. Most states give the discount only if tax is paid on time; a few give it anyway.

No particular correlation appears between the provision of compensation and the basic nature of the tax. Some vendor tax states give no compensation. Other vendor tax states give compensation. On the other hand, most strictly consumer tax states give compensation.

[4]"How Much Does It Cost to Collect Sales Taxes?" *Proceedings of the National Tax Association for 1961,* pp. 619-24.

TABLE 11.4   Vendor Compensation Systems, 1980

Uniform %	
1	Indiana,[a] Ohio, Pennsylvania, Texas, Wisconsin
1.2	Maryland
1.5	Louisiana
2	Arkansas, Illinois, Missouri, Tennessee
3	Florida, Georgia, Iowa, Nebraska, North Carolina, Oklahoma, Virginia
3.33	Colorado
3.586	Nevada[b]

Diminishing with Amount of Tax	
Mississippi:	2% $50 maximum discount per month
Alabama:	5% on tax to $100, thence 2%
Kentucky:	2% to $1,000 tax, thence 1.25%
South Carolina:	3% to $100 tax, 2% to $1,000 tax, 1% above $1,000

[a] Except utilities.
[b] 2% of the basic 2% tax, 1/2% for each of the 1% state and 1/2% local taxes.

The question of the desirability of compensation is not easily answered. Retailers incur certain costs in handling the tax. Since they are real economic costs for which the tax is responsible, it can be argued that they should be made clearly apparent and borne by the state, not buried in the retailer's overhead. A second argument is that compensation will help obtain the cooperation of retailers. Third, since in most states the vendors lose their compensation if the return is not filed on time, it is argued that the system lessens the amount of delinquency. Most state tax administrators discount this third factor, partly because many delinquents owe so little tax that the amount of the compensation is negligible.

There are two principal objections to compensation. First, if the compensation of vendors is large enough to be worthwhile, the tax revenue loss will be significant. In all states that grant percentage allowances, the amount of the allowance exceeds the cost of administration. The principle that taxpayers should not be compensated for their work of compliance with taxes has long been accepted in federal, state, and local governments in the United States, with minor exceptions.

The second major argument stems from the costs to the vendors, per dollar of tax due, varying tremendously; thus a flat percentage is grossly inequitable. Costs per dollar are low for firms having high per unit sales, such as motor vehicle, industrial equipment, and building materials dealers. They are high for variety stores, and particularly high for firms having a large percentage of exempt sales (on which they receive no compensation). Thus, the systems do not actually compensate the vendors for their costs in handling the tax, since the amounts received by each firm are not related to the costs to the firm, and some retailers receive a substantial bonus. A few states have sought to improve the compensation system by graduating the rate according to the amount of tax due. However, this scheme does not solve the basic problems noted. Any other form of adjustment is difficult to make.

Difficulties with the Taxes

Interviews with the persons responsible for administration of the state sales taxes reveal stress on the following difficulties with the operation of the taxes.

Exemptions. Exemptions as a source of administrative problems were mentioned more than any one element: exemptions in general in Colorado, Maine, Michigan, Minnesota, New Jersey, New Mexico, North Dakota, and Rhode Island; food in Maryland and Vermont; farm items in Idaho, Maryland and North Dakota; industrial consumables and machinery in Illinois, Maine, Oklahoma, and Rhode Island; and short-life industrial items in Minnesota. These exemptions create interpretative questions, lessen effectiveness in compliance, and increase audit difficulties.

Multiplicity of Rates or Acts. The use of more than one rate is regarded as a source of difficulty in the District of Columbia. Separate motor vehicle taxes cause trouble in Vermont.

Problems on Contracts, Repair, and Related Questions. New Jersey and South Carolina mention contract work as a source of problems.

Interstate Aspects. Interstate sales are a source of some difficulty in all states, but particularly in Maine, Massachusetts, and New Jersey.

Municipal Taxes. Alabama, Colorado, New Mexico, New York, Tennessee, and Texas (local use tax) mention municipal taxes as problems.

Enforcement Powers. Arkansas, Oklahoma, and Pennsylvania cite a lack of adequate enforcement powers.

Personnel and Salaries. A lack of adequate personnel and salaries is noted in a number of states but particularly Missouri.

Miscellaneous. Other items mentioned by one or more states include: real estate developers (Arizona); religious and charitable organizations (Maryland and Michigan); maximum dollar tax on any one transaction (North Carolina and Tennessee); occasional sales (Maine); definitions in the law (Kansas); the corporate veil on liability (Iowa); and fractional rates (New Mexico).

Efficiency of Collection

A precise evaluation of the degrees of efficiency in collecting is impossible.[5] However, all evidence that is available, particularly the results of such work as the California audit study, suggests that the extent of escape from tax is small. In a state with a highly effective audit program, such as California, probably not in excess of 1% of potential revenue is lost. Likely no more than 5% is lost in states with the most limited programs of control and audit. The states as a whole are losing probably between $400 million and $600 million from inadequate audit. One major reason for low collection losses is that a high percentage of all sales tax revenue is paid by relatively few firms, as noted earlier. Large vendors are, of course, least likely to attempt deliberate evasion of tax, and their records are the most complete. The tendency of the firms to regard themselves as tax collectors rather than taxpayers, so far as sales taxes are concerned, lessens their desire to evade. Also, for the typical retailer, the opportunities for significant evasion are limited, since a rough estimate of its sales is easily obtained.

Virtually all states, however, are losing a substantial sum of revenue even though a small percentage of the total yield of the tax, from inadequate audit programs. The experience of California and other states reveals the productivity of a good audit program. Most states have only a small fraction of the optimal number of auditors. Much of the difficulty lies with the legislatures, in failing to provide adequate salaries and adequate numbers of positions. A few states are still plagued with political selection of personnel. Likewise, some states have unreasonably high delinquency rates. In some, this high rate of delinquency is a product of defective legislation that fails to give the revenue department adequate enforcement powers. In others, it is a result of lack of adequate staff and initiative in cracking down on delinquents.

Comparison of effectiveness in 1981 with that in 1961 and 1971 is impossible in any scientific fashion. Improvements have been great in the use of computers, which not only speed up the processing of returns and ascertainment of delinquents but also offer great possibilities for analysis of data for improved management and for selection of accounts for audit. Audit staffs and audit coverage, however, have decreased in general from a decade ago. Improvements in hardware have been much better than in audit staffs. A few states, under the initiative of new governors, have made remarkable progress—Iowa, New Mexico, and North Dakota in the sixties and South Dakota and Wyoming in the seventies being the most obvious cases. Several states—Kansas, Maine, and Minnesota—appear to have slipped somewhat.

[5]A study in the early seventies comparing figures of taxable sales with retail sales reported by the Department of Commerce concluded that there was no mass evasion, but noncomparability of the data prevented any precise evaluation of the effectiveness of administration by state; J.F. Due, "Evaluation of the Effectiveness of State Sales Tax Administration.

SALES TAX REFORM

Most states do very little in the way of serious and systematic study of tax structures and the need for tax reform or of tax administration. Administrators become aware of difficulties and often seek to have changes made in the law to eliminate them, and various outside groups bring pressure on the legislature to make changes. Systematic continuing study, however, is largely absent. Less than half the states currently have significant research staffs in the revenue department or the broader agency of which revenue is a part—Arizona, California, Florida, Hawaii, Iowa, Kentucky, Minnesota, Nebraska, New Mexico, New York, Ohio, Pennsylvania, Tennessee, Texas, Virginia, and Washington, plus the District of Columbia. In all of these states, much of the research time is devoted to routine matters, such as revenue estimation for the new budget. In some states—for example, Illinois and Hawaii, and New York, plus the District of Columbia—special tax study commissions have made extensive studies of the sales tax in the past.[6]

Statistics

Statistics prepared by the revenue departments, which serve in part for reform, are primarily data of yields by type of vendor and by county. Policies vary substantially. For example, Louisiana, Missouri, Rhode Island, and Wisconsin are currently publishing nothing at all, though some data are cumulated for internal use. On the other hand, detailed data of collections by S.I.C. code, by county, and S.I.C. code by county are published monthly or quarterly by California, Idaho, Illinois, Iowa, Nevada, and other states. Those publishing at least by county and S.I.C. code statewide include Arizona, Arkansas, Colorado, Florida, Kansas, Maryland, Minnesota, Nebraska, New Mexico, New York, North Dakota, Pennsylvania, Texas, Virginia, Washington, and West Virginia. South Dakota provides the information to the University of South Dakota to publish, Wyoming to other state agencies.

Most state administrators regard this information as relatively useless, publishing it or making it available only because of pressure from local community groups that desire information on trends. Information is also used by universities and other research organizations in preparing figures of trends in business activity in the state.

Few states have made any systematic analysis of what may be called management data: for example, of revenue tax payments by size class (though more in the area has been done as the states have turned to use of several intervals for tax returns), delinquency by type of vendor and by size of store.

---

[6]Note, for example, State of New York, *Preliminary Report of the Governor's Temporary Commission to Review the Sales and Use Tax Laws,* Albany, 1974.

Modern computers have made this task relatively simple, but few states have the personnel to make use of it.

Few revenue departments prepare detailed analysis of operation of tax. Texas undertook a major study of sales tax audit when it revised its audit system in the mid-seventies. California publishes an annual *Program Analysis* of the work of the State Board of Equalization. Outside agencies have made a recent study on Florida and are preparing one on New York.

ACIR

The Advisory Commission on Intergovernmental Relations (ACIR) has given substantial attention to the question of state sales taxes and has prepared a model act,[7] based on the Virginia law. The proposal calls for a very broad-based tax, without exemption of consumers goods such as food or drugs, and with the taxation of a considerable range of services: transient accommodations, admissions, repair of tangible personal property, laundry and dry cleaning, barber and beauty parlor service, parking and docking space charges, and related items, but not professional services. Excluded from tax are sales for resale, including items becoming physical ingredients; consumables; machinery and equipment used directly in manufacturing; and farm feed, seed, and fertilizer. ACIR also favors the use of the income tax credit in lieu of food exemption to reduce the burden on the lowest income groups.

SUMMARY OF PROPOSED CHANGES

Major improvements in state sales tax structure and operation require, in summary, the following changes, some of which are virtually impossible politically:
1. Ideally, consumption goods exemptions, except possibly of drugs and medicine, should by eliminated, replaced by a credit against income tax (with refund if the credit exceeds the income tax liability). This change is politically very difficult to make; about the only hope is to remove some miscellaneous exemptions and check further increases in exemptions.
2. Removal of various anomalies in the laws that are responsible for difficulties and inequities, such as the application of separate taxes and lower rates to motor vehicles and failure to tax rental of tangible personal property.
3. Extension of the taxes to a selected list of services rendered primarily to individual consumers by commercial, as distinguished from professional,

---

[7]Advisory Commission on Intergovernmental Relations, "Broad-Based Sales Tax," in *New Proposals for 1969,* Washington, D.C., 1968.

establishments. This change will not produce substantial additional revenue, nor will it greatly improve the equity of the taxes, but the broader coverage has merit.

4. Standardization of the exclusion of producers goods to cover sales for resale, including materials and parts, industrial consumables, industrial machinery and equipment used directly in production, feed, seed, fertilizer, livestock, and insecticides sold for farm use, and farm machinery, but not a large number of minor items.

5. Elimination of local sales taxes, at least in most states, raising the state rate and distributing the revenue to the localities on some standard measure or, at least requiring a uniform base of state and local taxes, placing of liability on location of vendor, and ensuring state administration.

6. Substantial increases in audit staffs, through increased numbers of positions and better salaries, to bring audit coverage to a level at least approximating that of California's.

7. In a number of states, improved delinquency control, by changes in legislation to provide better enforcement powers, more satisfactory penalty systems, and more vigorous action.

8. Greater emphasis on analysis of administration from a management standpoint to improve operations.

Selected Bibliography

BOOKS, MONOGRAPHS, AND STATE STUDIES

Prior to 1945

Buehler, Alfred G. *General Sales Taxation: Its History and Development.* New York: Business Bourse, 1932.

Haig, Robert M. and Shoup, Carl. *The Sales Tax in the American States.* New York: Columbia University Press, 1934.

Jacoby, Neil H. *Retail Sales Taxation: Relation to Business and Consumers, and Administrative Problems.* New York: Commerce Clearing House, 1933.

"Consumption Taxes." *Law and Contemporary Problems* 8 (Summer 1941): entire issue.

"State Sales Taxes: Summary of Principal Provisions and Practices." In *Considerations Respecting a Federal Retail Sales Tax,* pp. 1205-30. Reprinted from U.S. Congress. House. Committee on Ways and Means. *Hearings on Revenue Revision of 1943.* 78th Cong., 1st sess. 4-20, October 1943.

1945-1971

Hawaii's General Excise Tax. Report by Arthur D. Little, Honolulu: 1968.

Maliet, L. "Illinois Retailers Occupation Tax and Iowa Retail Sales and Use Taxes." Ph.D. dissertation, University of Illinois, 1955.

Moak, L.L. and Cowan, Frank, Jr. *Manual of Suggested Practice for Administration of Local Sales and Use Taxes.* Chicago: Municipal Finance Officers Association, 1961.

Morgan, D.C. *Retail Sales Tax: An Appraisal of New Issues.* Madison: University of Wisconsin Press, 1964.

Oster, C.V. *State Retail Sales Taxation.* Columbus: Ohio State University Press, 1957.

Sidhu, Nancy D. "The Effects of Changes in Sales Tax Rates on Retail Prices," Ph.D. dissertation, University of Illinois, 1971.

Singer, J.T. and Due, J.F. *The North Dakota Sales and Use Tax.* Bismark: North Dakota Legislative Research Committee, 1963.

Somers, H.M. and Launie, J.J. *The Sales Tax.* Assembly Interim Committee on Revenue and Taxation, Assembly, California Legislature, 1964.

"A Symposium on Sales Taxation." *Vanderbilt Law Review* 9 (February 1956): 121-371.

Wheeless, V.B. *The Sales and Use Tax: Its Origin and Background in Mississippi.* Jackson: Mississippi State Tax Commission, 1966.

Yokum, J.C. *Retailers' Costs of Sales Tax Collections in Ohio.* Columbus: Ohio State University, Bureau of Business Research, 1961.

U.S. Congress. House. Committee on Judiciary. *State Taxation of Interstate Commerce: Report of the Special Subcommittee on State Taxation of Interstate Commerce, H.R. 565.* 89th Cong., 1st sess., 1965, Vol. 3.

Since 1971

Conn, R.L.; Williams, P.F.; and Young, W.E. *Analysis of the (Florida) Department of Revenue's Procedural and Selection Processes Regarding Sales Tax Accounts Audit.* Tallahassee Committee on Finance and Taxation, Florida House of Representatives, 1982.

Daicoff, D.W., and Glass, R.H. *Who Pays Kansas Taxes?* Lawrence: Institute for Economic and Business Research, University of Kansas, 1978.

New York. Governor's Temporary Commission to Review the Sales and Use Tax Laws. *Report.* Albany: State of New York, 1979.

Penniman, C. *State Income Taxation.* Baltimore: Johns Hopkins University Press, 1980.

Phares, D. *Who Pays State and Local Taxes?* Cambridge, Mass.: Oelgeschlager, Gunn and Hain, 1980.

Rhode Island. House Fiscal Advisory Staff. *Sales Tax on Services.* Providence, 1978.

U.S. Congress. House. Committee on the District of Columbia. *Technical Aspects of District's Tax System.* Papers Prepared for the District of Columbia Tax Revision Committee. 95th Cong., 2d sess., 1978, Serial S-11, pp. 37-66.

ARTICLES

Prior to 1970

Asch, P. "Some Implications of Sales Tax Reciprocity." *National Tax Journal* 21 (June 1968): 176-82.

Davies, D.G. "An Empirical Test of Sales Tax Regressivity." *Journal of Political Economy* 67 (February 1959): 59-71.

_____. "Commodity Taxation and Equity." *Journal of Finance* 16 (December 1961): 581-90.

_____. "Progressiveness of Sales Taxes in Relation to Various Income Bases." *American Economic Review* 50 (December 1960): 987-95.

_____. "A Further Reappraisal of Sales Taxation," *National Tax Journal* 16 (December 1963): 410-15.

_____. "The Sensitivity of Consumption Taxes to Fluctuations in Income." *National Tax Journal* 15 (September 1962): 281-90.

Due, J.F. "Application of Sales Taxes to Producers Goods." *Canadian Tax Journal* 17 (September-October 1969): 354-60.

_____. "Liability of Out-of-State Mail Order Vendors for Collection of Use Tax." *National Tax Journal* 20 (December 1967): 463-68.

————. "The New State Sales Taxes, 1961–68." *National Tax Journal* 21 (September 1968): 266–87.

————. "Sales Taxation and the Consumer." *American Economic Review* 53 (December 1963): 1078–84.

————. "State Taxation of Interstate Commerce." *Canadian Tax Journal* 13 (November-December 1965): 519–25.

————. "Trends in State Sales Taxation in the United States." *Canadian Tax Journal* 16 (July-August 1968): 307–15.

————. "The Unique Illinois Use Tax." *National Tax Journal* 12 (September 1959): 260–64.

Fryman, R.F. "Sales Taxation of Producers Goods in Illinois." *National Tax Journal* 22 (June 1969): 273–81.

Hamovitch, W. "Effect of Increases in Sales Tax Rates on Taxable Sales in New York City." In *Financing Government in New York City.* New York: New York University, Graduate School of Public Administration, 1966.

————. "Sales Taxation: An Analysis of the Effects of Rate Increases in Two Contrasting Cases." *National Tax Journal* 19 (December 1966): 411–20.

Hansen, R.R. "An Empirical Analysis of the Retail Sales Tax with Policy Recommendations." *National Tax Journal* 15 (March 1962): 1–13.

Hellerstein, Jerome R. "The Scope of the Taxable Sale under Sales and Use Tax Acts." *Tax Law Review* 2 (March 1956): 261–301.

Kendrick, M.S. "Improving the Use Tax." *National Tax Journal* 20 (March 1967): 93–102.

Legler, J.B. and Shapiro, P. "The Responsiveness of State Tax Revenue to Economic Growth." *National Tax Journal* 21 (March 1968): 46–56.

Levin, H. "An Analysis of the Economic Effects of the New York City Sales Tax." In *Financing Government in New York City.* New York: New York University, Graduate School of Public Administration, 1966.

Leong, Y.S. and Kamins, R.M. "Hawaii's General Excise Tax after a Quarter of a Century," *National Tax Journal* 16 (December 1963): 365–88.

Leong, Y.S. and Rhyne, Iola. "Hawaii's Inversely Graduated Tax Credits." *National Tax Journal* 22 (December 1969): 446–65.

Maloon, J.H. and Oster, C.V. "State Sales Tax Administration Costs." *National Tax Journal* 10 (September 1957): 221–35.

McAllister, H.E. "The Border Tax Problem in Washington." *National Tax Journal* 14 (December 1961): 362–74.

Morgan, D.C. "Reappraisal of Sales Taxation." *National Tax Journal* 16 (March 1963): 89–101.

Schaefer, J.M. "Sales Tax Regressivity under Alternative Tax Bases and Income Concepts." *National Tax Journal* 22 (December 1969): 516–27.

"Municipal Sales Taxes in the United States and Canada." *Municipal Finance* 28 (February 1956): entire issue.

Since 1970

Adams, R.D., and Walker, D.J. "The Lifetime Incidence of Consumption Sales Taxes." *National Tax Journal* 30 (December 1977): 463–66.

Browning, E.K. "The Burden of Taxation." *Journal of Political Economy* 86 (August 1978): 649–71.

Davies, D.G. and Black, D.E. "Equity Effects of Including Housing Services in a Sales Tax Base." *National Tax Journal* 28 (March 1975): 15–38.

Due, J.F. "Changes in State, Provincial and Local Sales Taxation in the Last Decade." *Canadian Tax Journal* 27 (January-February 1979): 36–45.

_____. "Evaluation of the Effectiveness of State Sales Tax Administration." *National Tax Journal* 27 (June 1974): 197–219.

_____. "Nexus for Use Taxes and National Geographic." *National Tax Journal* 39 (June 1977): 213–18.

Due, J.F. and Mikesell, J.L. "State Sales Tax Structure and Operation in the Last Decade—A Sample Study." *National Tax Journal* 33 (March 1980): 21–44.

Friedlaender, A.F.; Swanson, G.J.; and Due, J.F. "Estimating Sales Tax Revenue Changes in Response to Changes in Personal Income and Sales Tax Rates." *National Tax Journal* 26 (March 1973): 103–10.

Ghazanfar, S.M. "Equity Effects and Revenue Potential of Sales Taxation of Services." *Public Finance Quarterly* 3 (April 1975): 163–90.

Hellerstein, J.R. "State Tax Discrimination against Out of Staters." *National Tax Journal* 30 (June 1977): 113–24.

Mikesell, J.L. "Central Cities and Sales Tax Differentials." *National Tax Journal* 23 (June 1970): 206–13.

_____. "Income Elasticities of State Sales Tax Base Components." *Quarterly Review of Economics and Business* 17 (Spring 1977): 83–94.

_____. "The Structure of State Revenue Administration." *National Tax Journal* 34 (June 1981): 217–34.

_____. "Local Sales Taxes in North America." *Municipal Finance* 43 (February 1971): 133–40.

Nelson, O.E. "Progressivity of the Ontario Retail Sales Tax." *Canadian Tax Journal* 18 (September-October 1970): 411–15.

Papke, J.A. and Shahen, T.G. "Optimal Consumption Base Taxes." *National Tax Journal* 25 (September 1972): 479–87.

Smeeding, T.M. "Are Sales Taxes Progressive?" University of Wisconsin Institute for Research on Poverty Discussion Paper 545, June 1979.

Vaillancourt, F. and Berthiaume, J. "A Comparative Analysis of the Incidence of Retail Sales Tax in Ontario and Quebec, 1970." *Canadian Tax Journal* 26 (September-October 1978): 596–604.

PROCEEDINGS OF ANNUAL CONFERENCES[1]

Proceedings of the National Tax Association:

1968: Sales taxes

Cantor, A. "Impact of Sales Taxes," 8–18.

Drabkin, M. "Sales Taxation in an Urban-Metropolitan Setting," 19–26.

Brown, R.C. "Observations on the Distribution of Local Sales Taxes in California," 27–39.

---

[1]Papers from proceedings for years prior to 1968 are listed in J.F. Due, *State and Local Sales Taxation* (Chicago: Public Administration Service, 1970), pp. 325–27.

1969:   Sale of services under state sales taxes

Davies, D. "Significance of Taxation of Services for the Pattern of Distribution by Income Class," 138–46.
Bennion, F.W. "Broad Coverage of Services—Hawaii's Experience under the General Excise Tax Law," 147–60.
Forst, W. "Limited Coverage of Services—the Iowa Experience," 161–66.
Schoeplein, R. "Some Perspectives in Sales Taxation of Services," 167–76.

1971
Sidhu, N.D. "The Effects of Changes in Sales Tax Rates on Retail Prices," 720–33.

1973
Due, J.F. "State Sales Taxation and Interstate Transactions," 424–33.
Johnson, J.A. "The Treatment of Interprovincial Transactions Under the Sales Tax," 434–46.

1974
Holland, F. P. "Taxation of Computer Services, Data Processing and Time Sharing," 13–17.
Wright, S.H. "The Taxation of Leased Equipment Used in Interstate Commerce," 18–33.
Connock, S.W. "Tax Exemptions for Production and for Materials Consumed in Production," 34–37.
Leib, H. "Taxation of Services," 44–50.

1975
Connock, S.W. "The Past, Present, and Future Work of the Production Exemption Subcommittee," 7–8.
Paine, L.S. "Sales and Use Tax Exemptions for Machinery Used in the Recycling of Tangible Personal Property," 9–11.
Deasy, J.A., Jr. "Key Words in the Production Exemption—A Suggested Definitional Approach to Uniformity," 12–16.
Dudley, E.M. "Sales and Use Tax Application to Computer Services and Data Processing—Statutory Provisions and Regulations," 20–22.
Darter, O.L., Jr. "Sales and Use Taxation of Computer Services and Data Processing—Recent Cases," 23–28.

1977
Reese, C.E. "Local Sales Taxation—Current Practices and Future Prospects," 20–36.
Rosenblum, M. "Sales Tax Administrative Problems from the Business Viewpoint," 37–38.
Glaser, S. "Problems in Sales Tax Administration: The Tax Administrator's Views," 39–40.

1978

Deasy, J.A., Jr. "Sales Tax Exemption for Equipment and Materials Used in Production—The Taxpayer's View," 16-17.

Trasente, N.G. "Sales Tax Exemption for Equipment and Materials Used in Production—The Administrator's View," 18-20.

Glaser, S. "New Jersey's Experience—Exemption of Machinery and Equipment Used in Manufacturing," 21-29.

1979

Ritter, R.J. "Committee Report on National Survey of Production Exemptions under Sales and Use Tax Laws," 169-89.

Heintz, J.A. "Applying Statistical Sampling in Use Tax Audits," 190-93.

1980

Cornia, Gary C. "Local Sales Tax: A Case Review," pp. 193-96.

Reese, Craig E. et al. "The Impact of a Federal Value Added Tax on Sales and Use Taxation," pp. 198-203.

Revenue Administration, Proceedings of the Annual Conferences,
National Association of Tax Administrators:

1968

Kinnear, G. "The Multistate Tax Commission," 28-30.

Jaillet, C.F. "Experience with Per Capita Credit in Lieu of Sales Tax Exemptions," 50-53.

1969

Forst, W.H. "Extension of Sales Tax to Services—Productivity and Administrative Problems," 18-20.

Piontek, T.J. "The Use of EDP in the Administration of the Sales Tax," 98-102.

Hanselman, C. "Administration of Sales Tax Under a Functional Organization," 103-5.

Booker, R. E. "Auditing of Industrial Accounts for Use Taxes—Industry Comment," 106-11.

O'Riley, H. "Reciprocal Interstate Use Tax Collection Agreements," 112-15.

Corrigan, E.F. "Multistate Tax Commission—Jurisdictional Standards for Sales and Use Tax," 116-17.

Malone, T.R. "A Quick Look at the Multistate Tax Compact," 118-119.

1970

Freeman, H.F. "Selective Auditing—Sales and Use Taxes," 96-101.

Holderied, B.C. "Sales Tax Audit Selection in Michigan," 102-3.

Haney, H.D. "Application of Sales and Use Taxes to Property Used by Interstate Carriers," 104-8.

Herrell, K.R. "Taxation of Materials Brought into a State by an Out-of-State Contractor," 109-11.

Backe, G.T. "Administration of Local Sales and Use Tax—Nebraska," 112-14.

Selden, W.H. "Administration of Local Sales and Use Tax—New York," 115-18.

Cunningham, D.E. "Review of Important Legal Decisions in the Sales and Use Tax Field," 119-23.

Lambert, W.N. "A New Approach to Interstate Sales and Use Taxation," 124-27.

Craven, W.A. "Problems in State-Local Financing—Local Sales Tax Enabling Legislation," 131-34.

Hampton, S.W. "Application of Video Terminal and Computer System to Sales Tax Data Record System," 146-47.

Hogan, J.E., Jr. "Problems in Complying with Local Sales and Use Taxes Both Independently and State-Administered," 148-49.

Lynch, J.W. "State Collection of Local Sales Taxes—Some Recent Developments," 150-52.

1971

Nemeth, S.C., Jr. "An Evaluation of the Sales and Use Tax Interstate Taxation Problems and the Position of Business and Industry," 119-22.

Jones, F. "Application of Gross Receipts Taxes to Interstate Commerce and the Imposition of Taxes on Users of Services in Interstate Commerce," 123-26.

Perry, C.A. "Interprovincial Cooperation in the Administration of Sales Taxes," 138-49.

Keating, D.S. "Compliance Problems of Retailers," 150-54.

1972

Miller, G.H. "A State Value Added Tax," 44-45.

Garland, S. "Sales and Use Tax Problems in Realty Construction Activities," 73-77.

Heidmann, J. "Retailer Compliance Problems," 78-79.

Fitzpatrick, J. "Computer Industry Compliance Problems," 80-83.

Brady, D.F. "Out of State Auditing," 84-86.

1974

Smith, D.G. "Computer Programs for Control of Delinquency," 33-35.

Clark, D.H. "Use Tax and Intangible Tax Blocks on Income Tax Returns," 36.

Dotson, J.D. "Taxation of Computer Software Under the California Sales and Use Tax Law," 119-21.

Herrell, K.R. "Recent Sales and Use Tax Cases," 122-31.

1975

Trasente, N.G. "Impact of Energy Programs on Sales and Use Tax Programs," 116-17.

Russ, F.H. "Bonding Texas Retailers for Sales and Use Tax," 118.

Buehler, F.F. "Federal Legislation on State Taxation of Interstate Commerce," 119-21.

Krol, R.J. "Review of Significant Sales/Use and Gross Receipts Tax Cases," 122-26.

Mitchel, P. "The Use of Felony Prosecutions for Sales Tax Evaders," 127-28.

Wilber, W.E., "Sales and Use Tax Implications of the Sale of Precious Metals," 129-32.

1976

Glaser, S. "New Jersey's One-Stop Audit," 53.

Forst, W.H. "Accelerated Collection of Sales and Withholding Taxes," 54.

Whitler, R.M. "Accelerated Tax Collection in Illinois," 55.

Snead, A.B. "Progress of the Low Income Comprehensive Tax Credit: New Mexico's Broad-Based Tax Relief Program," 58–59.

Wickes, R.P. "Two Perspectives on the Interstate Collection of Sales Taxes," 63–64.

Friedman, D.H. "The State Tax Liability of Federal Contractors," 65–76.

Clark, D.H. "State Exchange-of-Information Agreements," 84.

Loyd, R.S. "Fractional Local Taxes Administered by the State," 156–57.

Walsh, B. "Sales Tax Audit Selection in Texas," 158–59.

Bradley, R.C., Jr. "Louisiana's Advance Sales Tax Collection System," 160.

Maloney, F.X. "The Casual Sale of Motor Vehicles," 161–63.

Putnam, T.P. "Recent Judicial Rulings Affecting Sales and Use Tax Administration," 164–67.

Beckwith, F.L. "Sales Taxation of Interstate Carriers," 63–65.

de Looze, T.W. "Developments in State Taxation of Multistate and Multinational Corporations," 66–77.

Oleson, C.A. "Sampling in Sales and Use Tax Auditing," 193–95.

Puffer, F.S. "Techniques and Methods of Collecting Delinquent Sales and Use Taxes," 196–98.

Maloney, F.X. "New York State and Local Sales Tax: Processing Returns," 199–202.

Nunes, R. "Sales Tax Audit Selection in California," 203–6.

Wendorff, J. "Audit Selection System in the Illinois Department of Revenue," 207.

Landerkin, E.W. "Audit Selection in New Jersey," 208–11.

1978

Golomb, W. "Functional Organization and Combined Auditing in Illionis," 27–29.

Peters, W.E. "Nebraska Functional Organization and Combined Auditing," 30.

Hogan, T.F. "Functional Organization and Combined Auditing in the New York State Department of Taxation and Finance," 31–34.

Krol, R.J. "Nexus and Jurisdictional Problems of Sales and Use Taxes," 201–3.

Phillips, J.M. "Processing of State and Local Sales Taxes," 204–5.

Cordi, S.M. "Sales and Use Taxation of Interstate Transactions," 206–9.

Coe, R. "Sales Tax Problems Confronting Industry," 210–12.

Castelda, C.A. "Sales and Use Taxation of Services: Some Special Considerations," 213–14.

Barnes, J.R. "Methods of Improving Delinquency Control of Sales Tax Accounts," 215–217.

Person, F. "Taxation of Computers, Software, and Related Services," 218–19.

Dietrich, W.L. "Sales Taxation of Construction Contractors," 220–21.

Lewis, F.W. "Sales and Use Tax Compliance Programs Implemented by States and Their Evaluation," 222–24.

1979

Kaplan, M.A. "An Analysis of the States' Administrative Tax Appeal Process," 67–71.

Griger, H.M. "The Taxable Moment Use Tax Doctrine Revisited," 92–96.

Bowman, J.H. "Changes in Sales Tax Regressivity over Time," 228–36.
Dotson, J.D. "Taxation of Software Under the California Sales and Use Tax Law," 256-58.
Turpen, C.D. "Sales Tax Simplification Through the Use of Income Tax Credits," 259-63.
Castelda, C. "Reciprocal Interstate Use Tax Audit and Information Agreements," 264–65.
Matson, R. "Sales and Use Tax Laws: View by Heavy Industry," 266–67.
Mundahl, D.S. "Sales Tax System Overview," 268–71.
Jankofsky, D.P. "Sales Tax Audit Selection," 272–74.
Smith, J.S. "Sales Tax Delinquency Follow-Up Program," 275–76.

1980
Henderson, K.D. "Organization of a Revenue Department by Function," 79–81.
Decker, J.L. "Functional Organization in State Revenue Departments," 82–86.
Anderson, W. "Sales Taxation of Computer Software in Texas," 159–61.
Hagan, H.J. "Taxation of Real Property Used in Manufacturing," 162–66.
DeYoung, J.E. "Sampling Techniques in Sales and Use Tax Auditing," 167–72.
Schuler, F.A. "Mobile Home Taxation," 173–76.
Tarman, M. "Vending Machines: A Colorado Sales Tax Puzzle," 177–79.
Granner, R.H. "Taxable Transactions Involving Services," 180–85.
Price, L.J. "Recent Sales Tax Cases," 186–89.

1981
Due, J.F. "The Past Decade in Sales Tax Administration," 30–33.
Bystron, G. "Taxation of Computer Software," 143–47.
Gillaspie, T. "Taxation of Advertising Agencies," 147–51.
MacPherson, I. "Sales Taxation of Contractors Doing Business with U.S. Government," 151–54.

SELECTED PUBLICATIONS ON FOREIGN SALES TAXES

Due, J.F. *Indirect Taxation in Developing Countries.* Baltimore: Johns Hopkins Press, 1970.
———. *Provincial Sales Taxes.* Rev. ed. Toronto: Canadian Tax Foundation, 1964.
———. "The Evolution of Sales Taxation," in *Fiscal Issues: Essays in Honor of Carl Shoup,* edited by R. Bird and J. Head. Toronto: University of Toronto Press, 1972. Pp. 318–44.
Cnossen, S. "Sales and Excise Systems of the World," *Finanzarchiv,* no. 2 (1975) Pp. 177–236.
Federal Sales Tax: Proposals for Reform. Toronto: Canadian Tax Foundation, 1975 Conference Report. Pp. 188–227.
Organization for European Economic Cooperation. *The Influence of Sales Taxes on Productivity.* Paris: OEEC, 1958.

The literature on value-added taxation is not very extensive.

Index